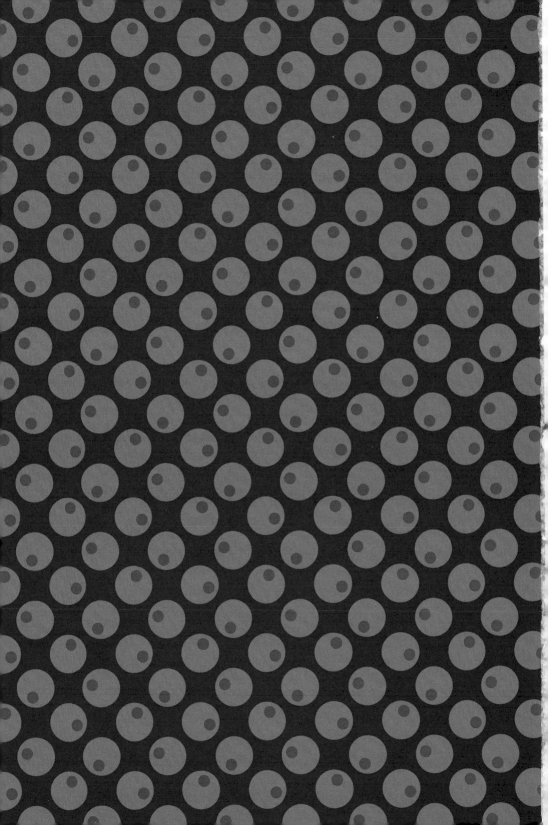

# THE ESSENTIAL
# New York Times
# BOOK OF COCKTAILS

Edited by Steve Reddicliffe

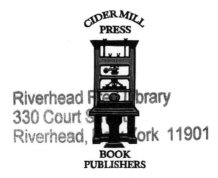

CIDER MILL PRESS
BOOK PUBLISHERS
KENNEBUNKPORT, MAINE

# CONTENTS

# FOREWORD

## by CHRISTOPHER BUCKLEY

What's the happiest word in the English language? "Cocktails," surely.

Happiest sound: a cocktail being shaken, in the hands of an expert bartender.

Happiest icon: a Martini glass.

I stipulate that the unhappiest word in the language is "hangover," although some years ago Hollywood managed to turn that sad state into an occasion of screen hilarity. Come to think, hangovers provided Kingsley Amis and Tom Wolfe with imperishably comic scenes in their respective masterpieces, "Lucky Jim" and "The Bonfire of the Vanities." But enough. My theme is not The Morning After, but The Night Before.

Why do cocktails and booze in general make for such wonderful reading? You'll find in this—indeed—"essential" compendium writing so entertaining, amusing and informative that even non-participants at the table of Dionysus would keep it on their night-stand as Platonic reading matter. The dedicated quaffer, in whose happy company I number myself, will find in these pages wisdom, philosophy, science—science of the most rigorous, empirical kind!—and the very best company.

One can get a bit carried away singing hymns to mixology. Or can one? For many years, a New Yorker cartoon was Scotch-taped (no pun intended) to my refrigerator. It showed heaven, consisting of a vast panorama of cumulonimbus clouds, on which perched hundreds of winged angels, all of them holding in their hands the iconic glass. The caption, spoken by one angel to another in the foreground: "Superb Martinis!"

The heavenly distillate of the juniper berry was not discovered until the middle of the 17th century, too late to be known to the noble scriveners of the King James Bible. A pity, for surely they'd have been tempted to render Genesis, chapter 2, verse 2 thus:

And on the seventh day, God took twelve parts Gin, unto which He added two parts Vermouth, and shaking them together, poured them thereof into a Glass, which He garnished with an Olive. And God said, "Ahh."

This isn't the first time I've been asked to contribute a paean on the subject. I wonder: is it a good sign when one is continually asked to compose hosannas about booze? One suspects one editor telling another: Ran into Buckley the other day. Drunk, as usual. We might ask him. Assuming he's sobered up. In vino veritas. But happily do I belly up to this bar, at which such splendid writers as those represented here in these pages have sat.

Composing my thoughts for this foreword, I made a list of my cocktail memories. It was uh, embarrassingly long. Thankfully, my word allotment prevents me from revealing myself at tedious length for the ethylated sot that I am. And yet as I jotted these memories, it was with a smile, even if the aftermath of some were episodes of excruciating, self-loathing clarity.

In his marvelous memoir "Hitch-22," my late friend Christopher Hitchens wrote that he skipped the baby talk phase of very young childhood and went directly to complete sentences, one of which, according to family legend, was, "Let's all go and have a drink at the club." No one familiar with Christopher or his prodigious oeuvre will doubt for a second that this was his first recorded utterance. He and I once had a lunch that began at one o'clock in the afternoon and ended at eleven-thirty that night. My memory is somewhat vague, but I do absolutely remember that Christopher's speech, even after ten and a half hours of incessant libation, was unslurred, gnomic and eloquent. Mine surely consisted of Cro-Magnon-like grunts.

I certainly can't top Christopher's precocity, but cocktails were a concept that came to me early in life. I can't have been much older than seven when my mother instructed me how to prepare her bourbon-and-soda, which I would bring to her while she sat at the mirror getting ready for the evening. I loved those hours with her. To this day I hear her say, "Bourbon and soda. Lots of ice and not too much soda."

I remember, too, the cocktail book my parents kept in the drinks pantry. It's long since lost, and I can't remember its title, but I do recall that it was illustrated with fetching and coy Vargas Girl-like ladies, and gentlemen wearing white tie, and looking like younger, sleeker versions of the Monopoly Man with his white moustache and top hat and monocle. I remember poring (again, no pun intended) through its pages, a sorcerer's apprentice examining a forbidden text, memorizing the recipes for the concoctions with exotic, alluring names: Stinger, Sidecar, Manhattan, Moscow Mule, Fog Cutter, Mai Tai, White Russian.

My initiation in actual mixology came at the rather-too-tender age of sixteen when, after dismal experimentation, I discovered that if you put the harsh-tasting vodka in Fresca, you couldn't taste the vodka. How sophisticated I felt! Until the next day.

The daughter of a friend worked her way through university tending bar. To qualify, she had to memorize how to mix some—I think it was— 300 different drinks, without referring to the guide.

"Three hundred?" I said incredulously. "Yup," she said, including something called "The Slippery Nipple," a revolting thing consisting of Bailey's Irish Cream and—uch—Sambuca.

After graduation, she applied to the C.I.A. and put me down as a reference. In due course a man showed up on my doorstep pretending to be with "the Defense Department." We conversed pleasantly. I mentioned her training as a bartender and, laughing, "The Slippery Nipple." He looked up from his notepad and said, trying to sound casual, "Is that something she invented?" I said, "No. It's in the manual." He smiled, satisfied that his aspirant Jane Bond was neither deviant nor nymphomaniacal. She went on to serve her country with valor in Iraq and ... elsewhere. Perhaps as I type she's expertly mixing a Slippery Nipple for a Russian FSB agent in hopes of luring him over to our side. Or inflicting a grievous hangover.

I have other cocktail stories, but the editor of this excellent volume has called closing time. I leave you in the best of hands. Have one on me. Or two.

A dependable cocktail book is as indispensable to the well-equipped bar as the tide tables are to a sea-going vessel.

HAPPY HOUR AT THE CLUB HOUSE BAR, NEW YORK CITY, 1992

# INTRODUCTION
## by STEVE REDDICLIFFE

The Times was early into juleps. Very early. Late 1800's early.

A story in September 1886 described its preparation: "With her sleeves rolled up, the rosy granddaughter stirs sugar in a couple of tablespoonfuls of sparkling water, packs crushed ice to the top of the heavy cut-glass goblet, pours in the mellow whisky until an overthrow threatens and then daintily thrusts the mint sprays into the crevices."

You have to admit, 129 years later, that sounds pretty great.

Over the next two decades, the paper would continue to report on the "refresher" (its origins, its seductiveness), but even a century ago it wasn't just about the julep. There were punches, highballs, and cocktails made by what The Times referred to in 1910 as "thirst scientists" at hotels like the Knickerbocker, St. Regis, and the Waldorf Astoria; the article assured readers that "any novice can acquit himself most creditably with the proper ingredients, a shaker, a strainer, plenty of chipped ice, and fruit."

(As it happens, my maternal grandfather was a New York newspaper man at the time, one who frequented places like the St. Regis. He wrote in his diary in 1911: "Saw Fanny and became intoxicated. Spent the night in riotous spree, of which I remember little.")

Post-Prohibition, Jane Cobb surveyed the variety of planter's punches served at New York hotels in 1939 and concluded, "The chances are ten to one that most people who drink the punches like them very much, no matter which version is served. Anyway, the sensible thing to do is to drink slowly and stop fussing."

And then Jane Nickerson and Craig Claiborne joined in, setting a tone for cocktail coverage that has endured for more than 60 years—enthusiastic, inquisitive, witty and free of fussing, to use Ms. Cobb's word.

An archive that runs from juleps to the Kumquat and Clove Gin and Tonic constitutes an entertaining and genuinely useful chronicle of American drinking—a good amount of history, plenty of humor, and hundreds of appealing recipes. That makes for a multitude of fine drinks and lots of enjoyable reading.

"Tequila has an odd, almost ineffable taste," Mr. Claiborne observed in 1960. "It is vaguely sweet, a trifle musty, and whatever else may be said of its flavor, it is certainly pronounced." Celebrating the sidecar in 2002, William L. Hamilton wrote, "Here's a drink that has it all. You would date this drink. And not wait a day to call it."

In 2013, Julia Moskin asked, "Don't you just love amari, those bittersweet Italian liqueurs like Cynar and Aperol that are so popular now? Me neither." Nevertheless, she gamely tried a number of sharply flavored cocktails, demonstrating that when it comes to drinks, Times writers are intrepid.

R.W. Apple Jr. reported from Brazil on the caipirinha; Colin Campbell from the Raffles Hotel in Singapore on its famed Sling; Jeremy W. Peters on gin martinis from a string of hotels on the campaign trail; and Steven Kurutz from a Lebowski Fest held in a bowling alley on the wonders of the White Russian.

Cocktails are almost always fun, a good time in a glass. But that's not all they are.

Sometimes they are about family: "In 14 years of tending bar, I've lent my personal spin to every drink I've come across," Toby Cecchini wrote in 2002, "but I've never been able to better my father's rendition of the gin and tonic." And sometimes they are about memory. In a lovely column in 2012, Rosie Schaap wrote about her late husband's favorite cocktail: "I first drank Manhattans in Frank's company, and now I drink them in his honor."

It is a cocktail worth some thoughtful exploration, she wrote, "because different versions suit different moods."

One of the phrases that has appeared frequently in Times recipes over the years is "if desired"; it is usually used in reference to a garnish, or the substitution of one spirit for another, but it also could be said to be the operating principle behind the reports, essays, and meditations on cocktails that have appeared in its pages, and now this book.

Want to learn about the Boulevardier and the best way to make one? Mr. Cecchini knows. Sound advice on nightcaps? That would be Ms. Schaap. Curious about the Tom and Jerry? Robert Simonson can explain.

They're all here, in the company of Jonathan Miles (Old-Fashioneds and Manhattans), Melissa Clark (a hot rum punch), Amanda Hesser (a coconut daiquiri), Eric Asimov (the Sazerac), William Grimes (the Bronx, and all kinds of fizzes), Pete Wells (irresistible blender drinks) and Mark Bittman (a Moscow Mule, a Champagne Cocktail).

That's a nice invite list for an animated cocktail party (and a nice menu, too), and the timing is right to throw one. This is an era of good drinking, as evidenced by the volume and variety of cocktails that have appeared in the pages of The Times over the past decade, and at bars, boîtes, lounges, and taverns everywhere.

Over the last couple of years, I have spent a fair number of evenings on the bar beat for a Times feature called "A Quiet Drink," savoring rye Manhattans at the "21" Club in New York City and barrel-aged Negronis at the bar at Del Posto. Amor y Amargo in the East Village is a bitters banquet, and every time I am in Chicago I make a point to stop by Billy Sunday in Logan Square for a Victorian, a perfect orchestration of sweet and sharp.

I dropped by Peacock Alley at the Waldorf Astoria in New York City not long ago to talk with Frank Caiafa, the bar's longtime beverage director (his recipe for the Robert Burns appears on page 179), who said he thought "the lost art" of the cocktail "is only coming back now," a century after bartenders at hotels like his were creating many of the drinks still being enjoyed today. The earlier incarnation of the Waldorf lays claim to the Bronx and the Rob Roy.

Mr. Caiafa said he found himself drawn to cocktails when he made gin martinis and Rob Roys ("Mostly dry!") for guests at his parents' parties.

The path to this book, I like to think, also started with a party, one my wife, Connie, and I had soon after moving to the New York suburb of Larchmont, at which we served a cocktail of that name.

I had no idea at the time that the drink was the creation of David A. Embury, who  lived for many years just a block from my house, and who was a valued contributor to Mr.  Claiborne's articles (in his engaging book, "The Fine Art of Mixing Drinks." Mr. Embury described the cocktail as "one of my favorites which I have named after my favorite community.").

The Larchmont really is an excellent rum drink (the recipe is on page 132), and if you have a couple, who knows where it will lead. A blackberry bourbon julep? A horseradish pomegranate margarita? Or maybe another by Embury?

Who, after all, can resist the call of a cocktail called the Appendicitis de Luxe?

SHAINA LIPMAN AT THE VELVET TANGO ROOM, CLEVELAND, 2009

## CHAPTER 1

# STARTS AND SMARTS

# THROUGH A COCKTAIL GLASS, DARKLY

## By WILLIAM GRIMES

If you think it's tough to get a decent dry martini, try tracking down the origin of the word. Or for that matter, getting the real story behind any cocktail—not only long-forgotten rip-snorters like the fog-cutter, the snap-neck and the leg tangle but also bona fide classics.

At every turn, the student of bacchanology faces the bewildering blend of misinformation, lore and legend that constitutes barroom etymology—a pseudoscience bearing the same relation to real etymology that barroom philosophy bears to the thought of Hegel.

Take the sidecar, a fine old drink of brandy, Cointreau and lemon juice. According to David A. Embury, author of the invaluable "Fine Art of Mixing Drinks" (1948), it was invented "by a friend of mine at a bar in Paris during World War I and was named after the motorcycle sidecar in which the good captain customarily was driven to and from the little bistro where the drink was born and christened."

Note the distinguishing barroom-etymology features. The inventor of the drink, of course, is a good friend. The time and place are supplied, but hazily. Embury specifies his good friend's rank but fails to give his name. And then there's the wild leap that somehow gets a motorcycle sidecar into a cocktail glass. Why not the Three Wheeler or the Bald Front Tire?

The spurious-origin story has walked hand in hand with the cocktail for nearly two centuries. The word cocktail has inspired perhaps the most notorious fraud of all—the Flanagan Fallacy. Virtually every account of the cocktail's origins drags in Betsy Flanagan, an innkeeper during the Revolutionary War who stirred a drink with a rooster tail and dubbed it a cocktail. Some versions place the inn at Four Corners, in Westchester County, N.Y.; others locate the sacred ground a few miles away in Elmsford. For the real location, turn to Chapter 16 of James Fenimore Cooper's "Spy," published in 1821 but set in the 1780's. There, Flanagan and feather first appear, as real as fiction.

Even eyewitness testimony tends to arrive through the distorting lens of a shot glass. The Bronx cocktail, rather quaint today but once a major player in saloons across the country, would appear to be well documented. "Johnny Solon is the inventor of the original Bronx cocktail!," wrote Albert Stevens Crockett in his history of the old Waldorf Astoria's bar. And how did Crockett know? He talked to Solon himself, the Waldorf's bartender, who recalled the day early in the century when he mixed up a variation on the duplex (equal parts French and Italian vermouth, with a twist of orange peel). Solon decided to add gin and orange juice. And the name?

"I had been at the Bronx Zoo a day or two before," Crockett quotes Solon as saying, "and I saw, of course, a lot of beasts I had never known. Customers used to tell me of the strange animals they saw after a lot of mixed drinks." And so the Bronx—not the borough but the home of pink elephants. The story is about as convincing as a heffalump.

The most elusive, legend-encrusted cocktail of them all is, of course, the mighty martini, that beguiling blend of gin and vermouth. The Oxford English Dictionary gives the earliest use of the word as 1894, citing an advertisement for Heublein's Club Cocktails—a line of premixed bottled drinks. But the drink is older than that. William F. Mulhall, bartender at the swank Hoffmann House hotel in New York, recalled mixing martinis back in the 1880's. And in his splendid treatise on the subject, "The Silver Bullet," Lowell Edmunds, chairman of the classics department at Rutgers University, turned up a martini recipe in the 1888 edition of Harry Johnson's "Bartender's Manual."

The O.E.D. also asserts that martini comes from Martini & Rossi vermouth—even though the Italian vermouth was not exported to the United States at the time. (John Simpson, co-editor of the O.E.D., concedes that the etymology may be more complicated than previously thought and that the next edition of the dictionary will acknowledge the fact.)

There are other claimants to the martini title. One is the Martini-Henry rifle, used by the British army between 1871 and 1891. No shred of evidence has ever been offered linking the drink and the gun, other than the fact that both have a strong kick. Slightly more tantalizing is the shadowy figure of Martini di Arma di Taggia, bartender at the Knickerbocker Hotel in New York early in the century. In his "World of Drinks and Drinking," the British writer John Doxat claimed to possess the tape-recorded testimony of an Italian bartender who recalled arriving at the Knickerbocker in 1912 and encountering a new cocktail of dry gin, dry vermouth and orange bitters invented by Martini. The late date torpedoes that theory.

A third candidate is something called the Martinez cocktail. Perhaps named after the Northern California town of the same name, it pops up in the 1887 edition of Jerry Thomas's "Bon Vivant's Companion," the most famous of the early American books on drinks. The only problem is the recipe: one dash bitters, two dashes maraschino, one ounce Old Tom (i.e., sweet) gin, one wine-glass sweet vermouth, with optional dashes of sugar syrup. This is no martini; it's a molten gumdrop.

Nevertheless, the drink has set off a ferocious dispute between the cities of Martinez and San Francisco. In the San Francisco version of the martini's invention, a thirsty traveler on his way to Martinez stopped at the El Dorado saloon, where Jerry Thomas tended bar, and asked for "something new." Presto! The Martinez. In the Martinez version of the story, a prospector returning from the gold fields stopped in a Martinez saloon and, after asking for two bottles of whisky, threw down a nugget on the bar. Instead of change, he got a new drink.

The bogus origin story continues to haunt the troubled discipline that H. L. Mencken once called "alcohololology." In the early 1970's, the makers of Galliano liqueur decided to promote their product by suggesting it be mixed with vodka and orange juice to make a new drink: the Harvey Wallbanger. As part of its advertising campaign, the company created a fictional surfer by the same name. Inevitably, the cartoon character has taken on a life of his own. Today, reputable cocktail books duly note that the drink was named after a Californian named Harvey who tended to bang into walls after having had a few too many. Now that I think about it, I seem to remember the guy. That's right—he was a good friend of mine.

*August 25, 1991*

# STOCKING THE BAR
## By TOBY CECCHINI

Bear with me if this post seems a bit elementary, but so many customers have asked me over the years what they should buy to make drinks at home that I thought a brief rundown on some very basic tools every bartender, home and pro, should be using might be worthwhile. Some of these things may be puzzling at first, but after using them a couple of times you will see the obvious superiority of them over the poorly functioning, overdesigned stuff in most "home bar kits" for sale. All the items can be had from a combination of BarProducts. com, which has the best prices and the worst Web site in all the land, and Amazon.com.

There are currently—in New York anyway—two schools of thought on the two-cup or Boston shaker. The traditional one is a 28-ounce stainless steel cup with a 16-ounce mixing glass

fitted into it to form the top. You can build the drink in either half and cap it up to shake, always pointing the heavier, glass part toward you. For stirred drinks, you can build them in either half, with some people claiming the steel gets them colder, but most preferring the glass to view the process. The second, and more recent school, the 28/18, uses two steel mixing cups, the 28-ounce and an 18-ounce cup, that fit more snugly and are much lighter, allowing you to shake with one hand if you like, or shake two at once. Which should you try? It's the bar equivalent of surfing's long board versus the short board. Some bartenders swear by each, but either is superior to the kinds of three-piece home shakers you get with the little caps on them. That's because their "throw"—the amount of space inside for the ingredients to be mixed and the ice to break up—is much greater. They're quite inexpensive, so you might try one of each and see what suits you.

You'll need separate **strainers** to clap on these mixing cups before you pour. The metal cups take the hawthorn strainer, which has a large coil on it to hold back the ice. (I've had good luck with Oxo's hawthorn strainer, a cleverly abbreviated version with no long handle to get in your way, plus a rubber cleat to hold it down where your index finger goes.) The glass mixing cup requires a julep strainer, which is a concave disc with holes in it.

Bartenders can get wiggy about **spoons**. I have a ton of them, but I honestly only use three: a regulation twisted bar spoon; a thin stirring spoon, which I love for its ability to slip in and out of the cup without pulling ice with it; and a big, heavy spoon for cracking ice and grabbing cherries and olives.

**Bar knives** can get as fancy as the handmade Japanese Damascus steel dreams at Korin. But in my kit I carry a $5 serrated paring knife from Victorinox that is superb for twists and other tight garnish work, and a 6-inch, scallop-edged Sani-Safe professional kitchen knife from Dexter-Russell to pare down larger game like grapefruit and pineapples. A small, light cutting board that is reserved only for your bar is a must (no onions or garlic allowed).

Because citrus juice is ubiquitous in cocktails, and because it oxidizes so quickly, squeezing your own fruit fresh is the single biggest leap toward making better cocktails. At home, a hand-held "clamshell" **juicer** can churn out plenty of juice for even decent-size gatherings. My favorite is a Mexican aluminum model labeled Victoria that reduces side spray, available at Win Restaurant Supply at 318 Lafayette Street.

Pros can count or eyeball a perfect pour, but super-pros still measure to make certain each drink is consistent. At work, I use two **jiggers**, a 1/2-ounce and a 3/4–1/2-ounce, and a dedicated teaspoon. At home, I supplement with a small, easy-to-read Oxo measuring cup.

A heavy **muddler** is important to have for crushing fresh fruit, herbs and spices. I prefer wooden ones for their grip, both in the hand and on the receiving end. Mr. Mojito makes a good line of solid, hand-turned muddlers in various woods.

For drinks that involve seeds, pulp or other loose sediment, a small tea strainer is required for "double-straining" above the drink to present a clean cocktail. Look for a simple wire-handled one that is easily cleaned.

The elegant fulcrum that is the folding **waiter's corkscrew** is still the best and cheapest way to open a bottle of wine. If you're paying stiff money for a huge apparatus with rabbit ears or pneumatic handles to get a cork out of a bottle, you may suffer from an excess of both cash and gullibility.

Rounding out my kit is a pair of **bamboo tongs**, a small **Microplane grater** for cinnamon and nutmeg, a **channel knife** for doing long strips of zest and my desert-island tool, the **clam knife**: a dull, short, pointed blade I employ for everything from opening blister packs to prying off stuck bottle caps—in short, all the tasks you don't want to dull your good knives with.

This entire collection should run you roughly $100, leaving you more money to throw at better spirits and glassware—the subject for an entirely different rant.

*January 12, 2010*

**EDITOR'S NOTE:** Many cocktail recipes call for the use of simple syrup to add smoothness and sweetness, and as Michael Dietsch has written at Serious Eats, "it's a basic, indispensable part of the cocktailian's arsenal."

There are are a number of recipes for simple syrup, but the most common by far is made with good old granulated sugar and water. That go-to recipe follows the one made with Demerara sugar described by Melissa Clark below. The Demerara syrup uses a brown sugar to add, in her words, "a toffee-like taste" to drinks. All simple syrups keep, in the refrigerator, for a good month, so feel free to make a double batch.

# SIMPLE SYRUP CAN ADD MORE THAN SWEETNESS TO THE MIX

## By MELISSA CLARK

I had always considered simple syrup to be nothing more than the liquid sugar often responsible for making my cocktail too darn sweet. Yes, a restrained drizzle was often necessary to offset the lemon or lime in the shaker. But beyond that, I thought its usefulness was moot.

What I never realized was that in the hands of a great mixologist, simple syrup can add a lot more than just sweetness to the mix.

For example, when the syrup is concentrated and thick, it also adds body and viscosity, making your daiquiri feel like velvet on the tongue. Most simple-syrup recipes call for equal parts sugar to water. But to make a more concentrated syrup,

some bartenders prefer two parts sugar to one part water.

Then there's the variety of sugar used. While white granulated may taste purely sweet, different types of brown sugar can lend all kinds of interesting flavor notes ranging from caramel to butterscotch to faint hints of burnt sugar. In general, the darker the sugar, the stronger and more intense the molasses component will be.

I learned all this from Joaquín Simó of Pouring Ribbons, an East Village bar. After one small sip, I knew his sidecar was different from (and better than) any other sidecar I had tried before. The rather simple secret was the simple syrup. He used a concentrated concoction made from two parts Demerara sugar to one part water, which added a compelling toffee-like taste and silky texture to the amber booze.

Brown-sugar simple syrups are also wonderful in nonalcoholic drinks, particularly lemonade and ice tea, and they will last for months in the fridge. Or try this Demerara syrup poured over cubed pineapple or yogurt. It turns out, not all simple syrups are as simple as you'd think.

## DEMERARA SIMPLE SYRUP
YIELD: ABOUT ½ CUP

½ cup (125 grams) Demerara sugar

**1.** In a small pot over low heat, simmer the Demerara sugar with ¼ cup cold water.

**2.** Stir until sugar has melted, about 5 minutes, and let cool.

*October 15, 2013*

## CLASSIC SIMPLE SYRUP
By Robert Willey
YIELD: 1 CUP

1 cup sugar

**1.** Put the sugar into a saucepan with 1 cup water and bring to a boil. Reduce heat to a simmer and stir a minute or two, until the sugar dissolves.

**2.** Take off heat and cool to room temperature.

**3.** Store in a very clean jar; any solid particles may cause crystals to form. Refrigerate, tightly covered, up to a month.

**Simple syrup may be made in larger or smaller quantities with the same ratio of water and sugar.**

*June 21, 2011*

# BE YOUR OWN MIXOLOGIST: ADD A SPLASH OF AD LIB

## By MARK BITTMAN

Here's how I learned to make cocktails. Some years ago, I discovered mojitos, which I liked a lot, at least when they were made well. But they varied wildly when I ordered them in bars and restaurants. So I began tinkering at home and found my way: dark rum, a little simple syrup (half water, half sugar, heated until the sugar melts; see classic recipe on page 27), loads of lime, not much mint. No club soda (a weakening aberration, even if it's "correct"). No muddling (too much work, too showy, and I don't even like the sound of the word). No white rum (unconventional, but I like rum with flavor).

After a while, I would go to bars and ask for "a mojito made with Barbancourt (or whatever) rum, a little syrup, a lot of lime and a little mint."

When I got sick of mint, I switched to margaritas. In general, you can't find a good one in a bar, not in Mexico and not in New York. So I took the same approach. I figured out how I liked my margarita and ordered it that way: good tequila, a teaspoon or so of triple sec, and lots of lime. (Some bartenders acted like that was a novel drink. Others said I wanted a traditional margarita. I suppose.)

Then I did some thinking and reading about cocktails. It turns out that if you use vodka instead of tequila, the margarita becomes the kamikaze. Swap cognac for the vodka and

lemon for the lime and you have a sidecar.

Look at the pattern—you might call it the basic recipe—of these drinks, many of which might be grouped as "sours": they combine liquor with water (usually in the form of ice), a sour flavoring (usually citrus juice) and a sweetener (simple syrup, or something more expensive and flavorful, like Cointreau). You might add a splash of soda or, if you like, fruit juice, which gets you into beachcomber or cosmo territory.

Master this pattern and you can mix hundreds of cocktails at home without a book or recipe. For me, most cocktails look like this: A stiff pour of alcohol, say a quarter cup, over ice; very little sweetener, a teaspoon or at the most two; a tablespoon or more of lime juice (which I find more refreshing than lemon juice); and, if suitable, a garnish like mint (which I chop), or an orange slice. Not only can the proportions change to your taste, they should.

The parallels with cooking are clear. You can start with good ingredients, or not. You can start with someone else's recipe (on which there are usually a score or more variations) or make the cocktail your own. The point—and this clearly comes from the perspective of cook, not bartender—is this: Why not make cocktails from scratch, ignoring the names and acknowledging your preferences? Why not treat the margarita like a dish of pasta with tomatoes, assuming a few given ingredients but varying them according to your taste?

You learn your preferences by mixing the drink at home, not according to someone else's recipe, but according to your will. Then you can duplicate your drink anywhere, and precisely. It's very empowering.

Here are some drinks that follow this pattern:

**GIMLET** Gin (traditionally) or vodka (more recently), with sugar and lime (or Rose's Lime Juice).

**TOM COLLINS** Gin with lemon instead of lime, sugar and club soda. There are also bourbon, rum, or vodka collinses.

**SLOE GIN FIZZ** Tom Collins with sloe gin.

**DAIQUIRI** Gimlet with rum, more or less.

**MARGARITA** Gimlet with tequila, with triple sec instead of sugar.

**KAMIKAZE** Margarita with vodka.

**COSMO** Kamikaze with a splash of cranberry juice.

**SIDECAR** Margarita with cognac and lemon instead of lime.

By now you get it. This pattern does not cover all cocktails, of which there are thousands. Those made with bitters, egg white (a nice addition to anything you're shaking or blending), combinations of different liquors, rose water or flaming orange zest mist get a bit more complicated.

But if you consider this an approach for creating classic, simple, personalized cocktails, using pure ingredients; if you put aside the recipe book and think about this as you would cooking—combining flavors you like with imagination guided by experience—you're well on your way.

As for the silly names, make them up, or forget about them. If one of your guests asks for an old-fashioned (bourbon, bitters, sugar, maraschino cherry and orange), you can always look it up.

*June 25, 2008*

# TOASTING THE JOYS OF IMBIBING PROPERLY

## A Review by DWIGHT GARNER

**Everyday Drinking**
**The Distilled Kingsley Amis**
By Kingsley Amis
302 pages, Bloomsbury

Got a hangover? Search Google, and you'll find a thousand home remedies, from mild palliatives (buttermilk, honey, bananas) to shock therapy (pickle juice, kudzu extract, raw cabbage). If you can drag yourself into Walgreens or Rite Aid, there's usually a potion or two that promises relief.

The problem with these cures, the British novelist Kingsley Amis (1922-95) wrote in his now-classic 1972 book "On Drink," is that they deal only with the physical manifestations of a hangover. What also urgently needs to be treated, he observed, is the metaphysical hangover—"that ineffable compound of depression, sadness (these two are not the same), anxiety, self-hatred, sense of failure and fear for the future" that looms on the grizzled morning after.

Amis's ideas for curing a physical hangover were fairly routine, though a few of the crazier ones will make you laugh. ("Go up for half an hour in an open aeroplane, needless to say with a non-hungover person at the controls.")

His notions about fixing a metaphysical hangover are where things got interesting. Amis recommended, among other things, a course of "hangover reading," one that "rests on the principle that you must feel worse emotionally before you start to feel better. A good cry is the initial aim."

Thus he suggested beginning with Milton—"My own choice would tend to include the final scene of 'Paradise Lost,' " he wrote, "with what is probably the most poignant moment in all our literature coming at lines 624-6"—before running through Aleksandr Solzhenitsyn, Eric Ambler and, finally, a poulticelike application of light comedies by P. G. Wodehouse and Peter De Vries.

It was a witty, bravura performance, this essay on the hangover, and rereading it now is a reminder of how good all of Amis's writing was about being what he called a "drink-man": smart, no-nonsense and, above all else, charming.

Before he was knighted in 1990, Amis published three books about the judicious but enthusiastic consumption of alcohol: "On Drink," "Everyday Drinking" in 1983 and "How's Your Glass?" in 1984. Long out of print, these volumes have finally been gathered together and reissued under a single cover, topped off with a fizzy introduction by Christopher Hitchens. These books are so delicious they impart a kind of contact high; they make you feel as if you've just had the first sip of the planet's coldest, driest martini.

Amis was an unorthodox guide to the drinking arts. "Not much of a wine man," he nonetheless drank it and wrote about it often and well. He preferred spirits and beer, and complained about wine snobs and the "pro-wine pressure on everybody." Among his essays is one titled "The Wine-Resenter's Short Handy Guide."

Amis mostly wrote about preparing cocktails at home, for one's self and for guests. He stressed, again and again, the importance of making a genuine effort. "Serving good drinks," he wrote, "like producing anything worth while, from a poem to a motor-car, is troublesome and expensive."

While he looked for ways to trim costs, Amis loathed all forms of social stinginess. ("With alcoholic ritual," Mr. Hitchens writes in his introduction, "the whole point is generosity.") One essay collected here—it deserves to be rediscovered and widely anthologized—is "Mean Sod's Guide," a tongue-in-cheek tutorial about how to "stint your guests on quality and quantity" while seeming to have done them very well. Among his tips for a host determined not to pour too many drinks: "Sit in a specially deep easy-chair, and practice getting out of it with a mild effort and, later in the evening, a just-audible groan."

Throughout his life Amis was absurdly quotable on almost every topic, but on imbibing especially. On diets: "The first, indeed the only, requirement of a diet is that it should lose you weight without reducing your alcoholic intake by the smallest degree." On why serious drinkers should own a separate refrigerator for their implements: "Wives and such are constantly filling up any refrigerator they have a claim on, even its ice-compartment, with irrelevant rubbish like food." On the benefits of sangria: "You can drink a lot of it without falling down."

As anyone who has read Zachary Leader's 2007 biography of Amis knows, alcohol did unspool his mind a bit at the end. But you finish this book, and Mr. Leader's, believing that it added more to his life than it took away.

Amis wrote with feeling about alcohol's place in society. "The human race," he noted, "has not devised any way of dissolving barriers, getting to know the other chap fast, breaking the ice, that is one-tenth as handy and efficient as letting you and the other chap, or chaps, cease to be totally sober at about the same rate in agreeable surroundings." And he could not help observing the way that "hilarity and drink are connected in a profoundly human, peculiarly intimate way."

Did I mention that "Everyday Drinking" has recipes? Amis described the effects of his tequila-based version of a Bloody Mary (you'll want to try it) this way: "a splendid pick-me-up, and throw-me-down, and jump-on-me. Strongly disrecommended for mornings after."

*June 4, 2008*

BELVEDERE BLOODY MARY

## CHAPTER 2

# THE BLOODY MARY

# A STUDY IN SCARLET

## By WILLIAM L. HAMILTON

I'm not stupid. It's the end of a three-day weekend, and the only cocktail you're going to be willing to read about, or mix, is a bloody mary.

The bloody mary would be an American classic—perfect as the last firework of a Fourth of July celebration—if it had been invented here. But it was invented at Harry's New York Bar in Paris in the 1920's, and arrived in New York with its inventor, Fernand Petiot, who was hired by Vincent Astor to work at his Fifth Avenue hotel, the St. Regis.

Petiot was also asked to rename the drink to appease delicate sensibilities. He called it the Red Snapper, which is how the hotel's King Cole Bar still presents it. The original Mary, depending on which wild goose you chase, was 1.) Mary, Queen of Scots, who died in a bucket of blood; 2.) Mary Tudor, who thirsted for Protestant blood; 3.) a patron at the Bucket of Blood Club in Chicago; or 4.) a woman who was repeatedly stood up at Mr. Petiot's bar in Paris, which is, as the English would say, pretty bloody.

The Red Snapper is a gin, not a vodka drink. An astute bartender will know that, though the St. Regis now serves its version with vodka.

But it is as the bloody mary, with vodka, that the cocktail became the country's house drink in the 1960s—a real workhorse, ready to start the day as a popular hangover remedy, show up at picnics and tailgating parties, and the first to hit the patio as the sun dropped and the charcoal began to glow.

And there's the name, too, like a Nichols and May routine. Not just adult, but funny.

Vaguely nutritious because of the vegetable content, bloody marys were like multivitamins for WASPs. I had a college acquaintance at the University of Virginia in the 1970s, Bob Edens, the kind of frat boy who wore sunglasses indoors and played Monopoly with cash, who looked strangely unnatural without a bloody mary in his hand. Bob, wherever you are, cheers.

The bloody mary today is synonymous with the idea of brunch, and at brunch, everyone's a bartender with a secret—pickling seeds, wasabi powder, jalapeño peppers. Restaurants have introduced make-your-own bloody mary carts, more salad bar than bar. As a virgin mary or a bloody shame, the drink is apparently good without vodka. I wouldn't know.

I like the Red Snapper. It's a Type B bloody mary: basic, relaxed, assured. The St. Regis uses Sacramento tomato juice, which Gavin Fitzgibbon, tending bar on Tuesday, believes is the best.

Try one tonight. Or, wait until tomorrow.

## RED SNAPPER (BLOODY MARY)
Adapted from the KING COLE BAR at the St. Regis Hotel, New York City

2 dashes salt
2 dashes black pepper
2 dashes cayenne pepper
3 dashes Worcestershire sauce

1 dash lemon juice
1 ounce vodka
2 ounces tomato juice

**1.** Add the salt, peppers, Worcestershire sauce and lemon juice to a shaker glass. Add ice, vodka and tomato juice and shake.

**2.** Pour into a highball glass, garnish if you wish, and serve.

*July 6, 2003*

# DON'T GET TOO CUTE WITH YOUR BLOODY MARYS
## By ROSIE SCHAAP

I didn't always like bloody marys. I blame an early childhood incident in which we coated our collie with tomato juice after a run-in with a skunk. (The juice was supposed to make the stench go away.) But my mother, who considered the viscous vermilion swill a tonic for nearly any affliction, loved them. So I was more than happy to make them for her now and then: All it took was a good slug of Smirnoff (the only vodka we had in the house, and one I still like), a can of tomato juice (or, as my mother sometimes preferred, Clamato), a shake of Lea & Perrins Worcestershire sauce, a heaping teaspoon of grated horseradish, a few shakes of black pepper, a good stir with ice, a lemon wedge for garnish, and that was that.

The bloody mary's origins remain shrouded in a black-pepper-and-celery-salt cloud. Some say it was born at the hands of a barman in Paris around 1921. Another theory—with a pleasurable dash of irony—is that it is an adaptation of an alcohol-free, Prohibition-era drink promoted by the tomato-juice industry. All that's certain is that ever since, it has been subjected to oodles of sadistic ministrations. (Perhaps you've seen the photo of the bloody mary garnished with a small cheeseburger?) Some bartenders and civilians apply lip-numbing spice mixes to the rim of the glass. Thick strips of bacon stand at attention where a modest celery stick once casually leaned. Anything that can be pickled and impaled with a toothpick has had its moment.

But like many classic cocktails, a bloody mary depends most heavily on a harmonious balance of flavors. And I think this is a special case in which freshest does not necessarily mean best. Does fresh tomato juice make a bloody mary taste fresher? Sure, but juice from a can could spare you from drinking down what tastes like a glass of spiked salsa. (Where horseradish is concerned, though, only the freshly grated stuff will do.)

Lately, many bars have been offering a make-your-own version: They mix the basic drink; you choose the garnishes. This may be gimmicky, sure, but most of us, given the choice, wouldn't mind having some say in how we top off our bloodys. The key is to keep the drink itself straightforward—an overabundance of hot sauce or Worcestershire or celery salt ruins it—so that the garnishes can shine a little. Decades after making bloody marys for my mother, I found that the garnishes helped me come around to how bracing and fortifying the drink can be. I'll take a poached shrimp, a celery stick, a wedge of lemon and a big, frilly fennel frond. You can have the slider. While this recipe is adapted from my years as a lady who brunched, the bloody mary should not be confined to the early afternoon. I honor the quietly rebellious sort who bellies up to a bar, alone, well after the sun has set and orders a bloody mary. Because why not have one at midnight too?

## LU'S BLOODY MARY
### Adapted from LU RATUNIL

*My friend Lu Ratunil was the man behind the bar on Sundays at Good World, my favorite brunch spot when I was still the sort of person who went out to brunch. He considers himself a bit of a purist when it comes to bloody marys, explaining that "since the drink has so many ingredients, the key is to balance them."*

Lemon wedge

Lime wedge

4 ounces tomato juice

2 dashes Tabasco

2 dashes Worcestershire sauce

Pinch of sea salt

Pinch of celery salt

Pinch of coarsely ground pepper (pepper too finely ground will bring more heat and less flavor)

¼ teaspoon peeled and freshly shredded horseradish (avoid using prepared horseradish from a jar)

2 ounces vodka (not flavored)

**GARNISH**

Slice of seedless cucumber

Pitted green olive

Lemon wedge

Black pepper

**1.** Squeeze lemon and lime wedges into a shaker. Add all other ingredients except the vodka and garnishes and stir. Taste the mix, and adjust the seasoning if needed. Put the mix in the fridge, and let it sit overnight.

**2.** Pour vodka into the shaker. Add ice cubes, and shake.

**3.** Fill an 8-ounce glass about halfway with ice, and strain the shaker contents over it.

**4.** For garnish, I prefer a slice of seedless cucumber, also known as a hothouse or English cucumber, rather than celery. (This isn't a deal breaker, though.) Cut a ½-inch-thick slice of cucumber on the bias. Cut a slit in the slice, and place on the rim of the glass. Spear the pitted green olive with a toothpick, and stick it through the rind of the lemon wedge. Place the wedge on the rim of the glass. Crack a little freshly ground pepper on top.

*April 18, 2014*

**FRANK'S BAR IN HARLEM, 1968**

## MARIA'S BLOODY MARY

Adapted from MARIA CENNAME, Black Horse Pub, Brooklyn, by Rosie Schaap

| | |
|---|---|
| 1 ½ ounces Stolichnaya orange | 4 dashes hot sauce |
| 3 ounces Clamato juice | Pinch of pepper |
| ½ teaspoon soy sauce | Pinch of salt |
| juice of 1 lemon wedge | **GARNISH** |
| ½ tablespoon horseradish | Carrot sticks |
| 4 dashes powdered ginger | Slice of cucumber |

**1.** Shake all ingredients except garnish with ice.

**2.** Pour into a glass and garnish with carrot sticks and a slice of cucumber.

*October 14, 2012*

# A BRUNCH STANDARD THAT CAN STAY UP LATE
## By JONATHAN MILES

Some years ago, in New Orleans, I witnessed the following: Man walked into a bar. Middle-aged guy, wearing pleated khakis and a plaid shirt; had the look of a Midwestern convention-eer. Let's call him Bob.

It was early in the evening, and the bar was mostly empty. Happy hour had yet to get happy. Bob ordered a bloody mary. The bartender winced but went to work. An older local near the end of the bar, peering over his newspaper, said to Bob, "You know it's after 5."

Bob looked confused. "So?" he said. "Shouldn't drink bloody marys after 5," came the reply. "It's bad form." Plaintively, Bob stared down at the soupy crimson drink, with its protruding tuft of celery, as the bartender set it before him. "But I like bloody marys," he protested.

Bob, wherever you are, I'd like you to meet Claire Smith. She is a former bartender with a résumé that includes stints at highbrow London cocktail bars like Lonsdale and the Rockwell Bar. She now represents Belvedere, the Polish vodka. She likes bloody marys, too.

"That great sense of savory and sweetness," she said, "and that lovely saltiness."

Yet she also knows where that old New Orleanian was coming from. "It's a bit of a meal, isn't it?" she said. "It's seen as a drink for curing a hangover, or for drinking with Sunday brunch or at a breakfast meeting."

Too hearty a drink, that is, for the evening. It doesn't so much whet one's appetite, the way a proper cocktail should, as demolish it.

Ms. Smith wondered if there was a way to reconfigure the bloody mary into a lighter, more refined drink—to re-dress it, so to speak, in evening attire. "It seemed such a shame," she said, "to relegate that great combination of flavors to when you're feeling worse for the wear, or to brunch."

Her creation, the Belvedere bloody mary, breaks down the classic cocktail into its flavor components, then reassembles them.

She muddles cherry tomatoes with watercress and lemon juice, then adds citrus-infused vodka and dashes of the bloody mary's traditional elements, Tabasco and Worcestershire, plus simple syrup to round the edges. Double-strained and served in a martini glass, it's airy but savory, as if the bloody mary's soul has been extracted from its too-hefty body.

"It's cleaner and more streamlined," Ms. Smith said, and fresher, since it eschews canned tomato juice.

And Bob, if you're listening, this drink is good form. Any time.

## BELVEDERE BLOODY MARY
Adapted from CLAIRE SMITH

| | |
|---|---|
| 6 cherry tomatoes, plus 1 (optional) for garnish | 2 ounces Belvedere Cytrus or other citrus vodka |
| 1 sprig watercress, plus 1 (optional) for garnish | 1 dash simple syrup (page 27) |
| ½ ounce freshly squeezed lemon juice | 1 dash Tabasco |
| | 1 dash Worcestershire sauce |

**1.** Muddle the tomatoes with the watercress and lemon juice in the bottom of a cocktail shaker. Add remaining ingredients with ice, and shake well to combine.

**2.** Using the cocktail strainer and a fine strainer or sieve, double-strain into a chilled martini glass. Garnish with an additional cherry tomato speared with a watercress sprig, if desired, and serve.

*February 10, 2008*

# BLOODY MARTINI, ANYONE?

## By AMANDA HESSER

Perhaps no other drink has been humiliated by interpretation the way the martini and the Bloody Mary have. For the serious drinker these days, even a straight one invites suspicion.

The Peppar Tomato at Wallse in the West Village, however, could be the first (and only) exception, for it manages to be an interpretation that plays it straight. It is part martini and part Bloody Mary, with the best qualities of both.

There is the crispness and chill of the vodka—quickly converted to a flash of alcoholic warmth on the tongue. It is joined by the familiar tomato and salt, and finally a pinch of heat at the back of your throat. It is as startling as it is delightful. It is clean yet meaty. Savory yet sweet. A martini yet a Bloody Mary.

After a few sips—which you will surely take in quick succession—a sweetness sinks in. Not a cloying sweetness but a round, fresh sweet-ness like that of a ripe plum.

The drink uses two kinds of vodka, but its foundation is tomato water, made with ripe beefsteak tomatoes, from the Greenmarket. Kurt Gutenbrunner, the chef at Wallse, purées them with salt and strains the mixture overnight in cheesecloth. What is left is a pale yellow juice, as thin as water, as concentrated and saline as oyster liquor.

The bartender mixes the tomato water with Absolut vodka and Absolut Peppar vodka and lets in a drop of Tabasco and a dash of celery salt. Then he shakes it and shakes it, straining it into a chilled martini glass.

The first sip, if you get it quickly enough, will be frothy, as a well-made drink should be.

Then the salt will come. Then the sweetness.

Soon it will be gone, and all that will be left is a question: Why on earth did he call something so lovely such a peculiar name?

## PEPPAR TOMATO
### Adapted from WALLSE, New York City
YIELD: 4 DRINKS

2 pounds very ripe, fragrant tomatoes, cored and cut into chunks

½ teaspoon sea salt

1 tablespoon chopped lemon thyme or lemon grass

4 ounces pepper vodka

4 ounces vodka

¼ teaspoon celery salt

4 drops Tabasco

Yellow, red and green cherry tomatoes, for garnish

**1.** In bowl of a food processor, combine tomatoes, sea salt and lemon thyme. Purée tomatoes for about 1 minute. Line a colander with cheesecloth, allowing cloth to overhang by several inches. Set colander over a bowl, and pour in tomato mixture. Tie ends of cheesecloth together, and set aside to drip for 2 hours.

**2.** If necessary, twist cheesecloth to extract any remaining juice. Set bowl of tomato water aside.

**3.** In a shaker filled with ice, combine pepper vodka, vodka, celery salt, Tabasco and 2 cups tomato water and shake well.

**4.** Strain into four martini glasses with cherry tomatoes.

*August 30, 2000*

## CHAPTER 3

# CHAMPAGNE

# CHAMPAGNE'S FANCY TRICKS
## By ROBERT SIMONSON

How to toast the new year? Perhaps some Champagne. Or maybe a cocktail. Then again, why choose when you can have them both in one glass?

Most people think nothing of popping a bottle of Champagne on New Year's Eve. Yet after that first celebratory glass, few consider taking an extra step and using the wine as the foundation for a cocktail or two.

There are those who consider mixing fine Champagne with anything else a desecration. Why would you add anything to an elixir so pure, so perfect?

But that's a shame. Champagne-based cocktails are some of the oldest mixed drinks on the books. Pick up any bartenders' manual from the 19th century and you'll find a variety. Champagne cobbler, Champagne julep, Champagne sour, Champagne cup—they all sound fairly exotic today, but were once widely popular drinks, enjoyed by those brocade-vested swells who dedicated themselves to the high life.

The Champagne cobbler, a luxe refreshment if there ever was one, is a best seller at the Raines Law Room in the Flatiron district. Also on the Raines menu are original concoctions: the Andean Dusk, which pairs rosé Champagne with pisco, and the Taylor Precedent, a more complex integration of apple brandy, green Chartreuse, sweet vermouth and cinnamon syrup.

Meaghan Dorman, the head bartender, is an affirmed fan of Champagne cocktails.

"They're bright and crisp and delicious," she said. And ideal for New Year's Eve. "They are usually low in spirit, so if I'm out having a few drinks, I would have French 75s. It's wine and spirit, so I'd feel I wasn't overdoing it on superstrong spirit drinks."

She and her fellow bartender Lauren Davis call this judicious drinking tactic the Champagne Maintain. "It's our theory on lasting all night and still staying a lady," Ms. Dorman said.

Her first step in getting patrons to order fizzy drinks is to alert them to their existence. "That's one of the questions we ask people" when they order, she said. "Do you want bubbles or without?" The option often comes as a surprise. "They go, 'Oh! Champagne!'"

Menus that dedicate an entire section to sparkling cocktails are more common in London.

"I would not dream of putting together a cocktail menu without a Champagne cocktail," said Charlotte Voisey, portfolio ambassador for the liquor company William Grant & Sons USA, who got her bartending start in London.

At the elite Connaught Bar in the Mayfair section, the "Bubbles" page includes a Champagne julep and something called Mayfair's Delight, featuring Cognac, cucumber, fresh ginger, lemon juice and agave nectar.

"I like the light and fruity aroma you can get from the wine," said Agostino Perrone, the bar's director of mixology. "Also, Champagne cocktails tend to have a glamorous personality."

In choosing a Champagne to make your own drinks, tread a middle path in quality and price—$40 to $50. A quality wine will certainly improve the flavor of the drink, but one need not go overboard. As most Champagne drinks involve a sweetener, you'll want to stick with a brut style. And Ms. Dorman finds that the more buttery notes of blanc de blancs and blends that are heavy with chardonnay do not work well in cocktails.

For the home bartender, another argument for making Champagne cocktails is that the most famous are also among the most easily assembled creations in the mixed-drink canon. Classic examples rarely contain more than three or four ingredients. The kir royale's only other ingredient is crème de cassis. The French 75 requires just sugar, lemon juice and either gin or Cognac.

None are quite as beautifully 1-2-3, however, as the undisputed king of this effervescent family: the simply titled Champagne cocktail. Soak a sugar cube in Angostura bitters, toss it into the bottom of a flute, fill with icy Champagne, garnish with a lemon twist and congratulate yourself on a job well done. You not only get a peerless refreshment—one whose flavor evolves as the sugar slowly dissolves—but also a drink that furnishes visual stimulation, fine bubbles flowing up from the fast-disappearing cube.

Oh, and for those who were wondering: no, the mimosa is not the king of Champagne cocktails. Now go back and finish your brunch.

## CHAMPAGNE COBBLER
Adapted from MEAGHAN DORMAN, Raines Law Room, New York City

½ ounce simple syrup (page 27)
1 lemon wheel
2 strawberries, halved

Crushed ice
5 ounces Champagne

**1.** Pour syrup into wine glass, then gently muddle lemon wheel and one strawberry in bottom.

**2.** Fill glass halfway with crushed ice and add Champagne. Top off with more crushed ice and garnish with strawberry half.

## ANDEAN DUSK
Adapted from MEAGHAN DORMAN, Raines Law Room, New York City

3 red grapes
½ ounce lemon juice
½ ounce simple syrup (page 27)

1 ounce blended pisco (preferably La Diablada)
3 ounces rosé Champagne

**1.** In a mixing glass, muddle grapes. Add lemon juice, syrup and pisco, then shake with ice in a cocktail shaker.

**2.** Strain into chilled flute. Top with Champagne.

## FRENCH 75
Adapted from MEAGHAN DORMAN, Raines Law Room, New York City

1 ounce gin or Cognac
½ ounce fresh lemon juice
½ ounce simple syrup (page 27)

2 ounces Champagne
Lemon twist, for garnish

**1.** In a cocktail shaker filled with ice, shake gin or Cognac, lemon juice and syrup.

**2.** Strain into chilled flute or cocktail coupe. Top with Champagne. Garnish with lemon twist.

*December 21, 2012*

## AMERICAN 25
By ROBERT SIMONSON

*This drink, intended as a holiday-season quaff, is a simple riff on the French 75, a Prohibition-era Champagne cocktail that includes lemon juice, simple syrup and–depending on which scholar or bartender you consult–gin or Cognac. (Both versions taste good.) Substituting for the traditional spirit is flavorful, fruity apple brandy (make certain you get the bonded version) and peaty Scotch (either single malt or blended will do, as long as there's plenty of smoke on it). The two are natural liquid partners. The aromatic, effervescent result is as pleasing to the nose as it is to the tongue. The name is a nod to the provenance of the primary spirit (apple brandy is as old as the republic) and the day of year it's meant for, Christmas.*

1 ounce bonded apple brandy (preferably Laird's)
¼ ounce smoky Scotch (preferably Peat Monster or Laphroaig 10-year-old)

½ ounce fresh lemon juice
½ ounce simple syrup (page 27)
3-4 ounces Champagne
Lemon twist

**1.** In a cocktail shaker filled three-quarters with ice, combine the apple brandy, Scotch, lemon Juice and simple syrup. Shake until chilled, about 30 seconds.

**2.** Strain into a flute and top with chilled Champagne. Squeeze the lemon twist over the glass, rub it across the rim, then drop it into the drink.

*December 24, 2014*

## CHAMPAGNE COCKTAIL
By MARK BITTMAN

¾ teaspoon bitters
½ ounce lemon juice
¼ ounce maple syrup

6 ounces Champagne
Twist of lemon

**1.** Stir the bitters, juice and syrup in a flute.

**2.** When combined, add the Champagne. Squeeze the lemon twist over the top, wipe the rim with it and discard.

*January 25, 2011*

# THE GERMAN 71 COCKTAIL
## By DAVID LEONHARDT

Few people are more worthy of a toast this week than members of the German national soccer team. They defied the modest expectations of their fans and produced one of the most incredible displays in World Cup history by thrashing Brazil—the favorite and host—7-1. So in honor of the Nationalmannschaft, as they're known, we bring you this Upshot cocktail: the German 71.

It's a riff on the French 75, the classic cocktail from the early 20th century. The cocktail is so good that we're not going to mess with its essential ingredients. We'll instead use it as a chance to focus on German sparkling wines, which are far less known than Champagne or cava but have a rich history as well.

Phil Bernstein, known as the "German wine nut" at Addy Bassin's MacArthur Beverages in Washington, recommends the Dr. L Sparking Riesling, from Loosen Bros., which is dry, crisp and affordable (usually $12 to $15). There's no point in getting too fancy when you're going to add citrus, sugar and liquor to a wine.

As for the gin, you can go with anything convenient. To stay German, look for Monkey 47, a relatively new German gin that has just become available in the United States. Supporters of Argentina have a tougher shopping task, at least outside South America, but there is now a high-end Argentine gin: Príncipe de los Apóstoles.

The important thing to remember about the German 71—as with the French 75 or the Nationalmannschaft—is that it's stronger than first impressions may suggest. If the Germans are on their game again Sunday, you may not want to pour a new drink with every goal.

---

## THE GERMAN 71

| | |
|---|---|
| 1 ounce Monkey 47 gin | 2 ounces Dr. L Sparkling Riesling |
| ½ ounce fresh lemon juice | Lemon twist |
| ½ ounce simple syrup (page 27) | |

**1.** Fill a cocktail shaker with ice, gin, lemon juice and syrup.

**2.** Pour into flute or cocktail glass, chilled if you like. Top with sparkling wine. Add lemon twist.

*July 11, 2014*

# COCKTAIL COUTURE

## By KIMBERLY STEVENS

It's a busy Thursday night at Isla, and Eric Sanchez, a bartender at this hot Cuban restaurant in downtown Manhattan, is mixing some of the best-dressed cocktails in town: a frothy piña colada, adorned with feathery shards of coconut and a pineapple leaf; a tall rum cocktail sporting a paper-thin deep-fried plantain with burned sugar around the edges; a cool mojito sprouting bouquets of fresh green mint; a María Sangrosa with a skewer of pickled okra, a bright red cherry tomato and a cocktail onion.

Welcome to the world of cocktail couture. Like the stiletto heel or miniskirt, the garnish has come and gone—and come again. At upscale restaurants, hotels and bars from California to New York, cocktails are dressed to kill.

For a while, a simple lime wedge was perfectly acceptable, and a maraschino cherry wrapped in an orange slice was a walk on the wild side. Not anymore. Today, all kinds of garnishes, edible and not, hang and droop out of glasses in all shapes and sizes. Tiny electric-blue popsicles swim in the Azure, a signature vodka martini at the Royalton Hotel; sunglasses stick out of That Bar and Restaurant's gin martini; and jalapeño peppers give a hot jolt to the Chili Margarita at Suba.

Often it is the garnish that creates a cocktail's popularity. A candy fish in the namesake drink at the Times Square restaurant Blue Fin has made such a splash that a few thousand people a month are intoxicated by it.

But be careful for what you wish: not just anyone, dressed in any old thing, can handle such a drink. Like the mojito that comes with a huge bouquet of fresh mint at the popular refurbished Viceroy hotel in Santa Monica, California. "It's the girls in the little black dresses that can pull off a cocktail with a really amazing garnish," says Heather Simon, a bartender at the Viceroy. "The garnishes can be intimidating—I've seen customers come in with jeans and a T-shirt, take one look around, order a beer and head for the back of the bar."

For many adventurous souls, the garnish is an expectation.

"Drinks have become more complicated, more interesting to look at," says Ruby Fay, the bar manager at the Hudson Hotel in Midtown Manhattan. "Having an elaborate garnish is all part of this concept." When the Hudson runs out of some toppings, like the pansies for the Hudson Cosmopolitan (the hotel goes through 10 cases a week), customers immediately ask, Hey, where are they?

The garnish has a colorful history. David Wondrich, the author of "Esquire Drinks: An Opinionated and Irreverent Guide to Drinking" (Hearst), says that descriptions for punches adorned with fruit and berries began to appear in English cookbooks in the 18th century. The first book on bar culture and cocktails, "The Bon

Vivant's Companion," published in 1862 in New York, also mentioned garnishes, he says.

But the real garnish explosion happened in America in the 30s and 40s, at bars like Trader Vic's and Don the Beachcomber. "These drinks were all part of the Tiki-bar phenomenon," he says. They included gardenias, cultured pearls—even an ice igloo over a glass, with a straw sticking through.

During the counterculture movement of the 60s and 70s, cocktails became less popular. But with the return of lounge culture—and the whole craze for signature cocktails—the more outlandish the topping, the better.

But Wondrich cautions: "People should watch out—garnishes can be dangerous. Sherwood Anderson died after swallowing a martini olive on a toothpick." Ouch.

Even traditional drinks have new looks. At Prune, a downtown Manhattan restaurant, the Chicago Matchbook Bloody Mary has a garnish to make a celery stalk weep: a skewer of onions, green beans and caper berries (all pickled) and a fresh radish.

At Town, the chic watering hole in the Chambers Hotel, Albert Trummer, who calls himself a bar chef, uses pomegranate and fig slices for a rum-based Pomegranate Punch. And for a twist on the Champagne-and-bitters cocktail, which "can look a bit naked" on its own, he adds Grand Marnier, rose water—and a sprinkling of shimmery gold leaf. "It's a drink out of a fairy tale," exclaims a Prada-clad woman perched on a stool next to her boyfriend.

To fashion!

## TOWN GOLD CHAMPAGNE COCKTAIL
Adapted from TOWN, at the Chambers Hotel, New York City

5 ounces Moët & Chandon
   Champagne
1 dash bitters
1 dash Grand Marnier

1 dash rose water
1 tablespoon edible gold leaf flakes
   (see note)

**1.** Pour Champagne into glass.

**2.** Add bitters, Grand Marnier and rose water and stir with swizzle stick or long spoon.

**3.** Sprinkle gold leaf on top.

**Edible gold leaf is available at bake-supply shops in flakes or sheets, which can be easily crumbled.**

*November 10, 2002*

# DANCES WITH TASTEBUDS

## By WILLIAM L. HAMILTON

Trying to come up with a drink that holds the holidays in a glass is a tall order.

I've never been sold on eggnog, to me a nauseating idea from its name on down to the nutmeg. The fact that you can buy it in supermarkets, in dairy cases, like a quart of brunch omelets, doesn't help.

But Champagne—what's not to like a lot? It pops; it bubbles; it knows how to work a glass. It acts like a party guest. And Champagne cocktails can be an improvement on the drink, which is strangely banal after a flute or two, like beauty without any social backup.

A midpriced bottle of Champagne or a similar sparkling wine, $18 or so, is a useful economy too, served as kir royales, with the addition of a fruit liqueur like crème de cassis or crème de framboise. You can look for less likely, more exotic flavors, like crème de pêche, which is peach, or crème de mûre, blackberry. It's a nice touch to have a bar stocked with an interesting variety. With white wine, they make a good rotation of aperitifs year-round.

The standard Champagne cocktail is Champagne poured over a sugar cube soaked in Angostura bitters. The drink dates back to the 19th century and had a heyday in the 1930s. A variant with Cognac was called the Gloria Swanson in the late 1940s, shortly before she played Norma Desmond in "Sunset Boulevard." The

drink, besides being Ms. Swanson's calling card, was also known in other circles as the king's ruin, named for the society cafe and hotel bar habits of deposed European royalty. You feel lightheaded without the crown anyway—why not drink all day?

The diamond fizz is Champagne with the juice of a lemon and a teaspoon of sugar. The black velvet adds Guinness stout. My favorite, the stratosphere (who wouldn't try it to find out?), calls for crème Yvette, which is produced from Parma violets and turns out a purple cocktail. You garnish it with cloves.

At Craft, Tom Colicchio's ingredient-fanatical restaurant in New York, the house drink is a Champagne cocktail that is seasonal like the food.

During the fall and winter, Matthew MacCartney, the beverage director, mixes Champagne with cubes of Bartlett pear, bathed briefly in a pear liqueur. The taste, as simple as something perfectly ripe, is fresher than the sum of its parts.

"You don't want to overcomplicate it," Mr. MacCartney said. "You don't want to cover up its taste. Adding pear gives the drink an extra subtlety, more aroma, and it's pleasing to the eye."

Craft claims that if you make the cocktail correctly, the pear will "dance" in the glass.

For a holiday drink, how much happier can you get?

## CHAMPAGNE COCKTAIL
Adapted from CRAFT, New York City

| | |
|---|---|
| 1 fresh Bartlett pear | 5 ounces Champagne |
| Pear liqueur (preferably Belle de Brillet) | |

**1.** Peel, seed and dice the pear into equal ¼-inch cubes. Place the cubes in a plastic container, and pour in enough pear liqueur to cover. Let the pear macerate in the refrigerator for 2 hours (not more, or the cubes will become oversaturated). If the pear is properly macerated, the cubes will dance in the glass.

**2.** When ready to serve, spoon about 1 teaspoon of macerated pear into the bottom of a Champagne flute. Pour Champagne slowly into the flute (preferably a Riedel Restaurant Series glass, with more of a wineglass shape), because it tends to bubble up in reaction to the pears.

*December 22, 2002*

# TRYING TO CLEAR ABSINTHE'S REPUTATION
## By HAROLD McGEE

Readers of Ernest Hemingway know "Death in the Afternoon" as a book about bullfighting. But to drinkers with a taste for obscure booze, it is also a cocktail that Hemingway contributed to a 1935 collection of celebrity recipes. His directions: "Pour one jigger absinthe into a Champagne glass. Add iced Champagne until it attains the proper opalescent milkiness. Drink three to five of these slowly."

When I heard about this concoction last week and wondered how Champagne bubbles would fare in the milkiness, I couldn't just go to my local liquor store and buy absinthe. I had to substitute one of the anise-flavored alcohols that took absinthe's place when it was banned in France and in the United States about a century ago.

Today absinthe is legal again throughout Europe, and while it is still banned in this country, it is easy to buy over the Internet. Its reputation, however, remains as cloudy as the cocktails that are made with it. Some welcome clarification has now arrived in the form of a new study by a team of German chemists and physicians.

Absinthe is a distilled spirit flavored with a variety of herbs and spices, primarily wormwood, an aromatic, bitter shrub. The key constituent of wormwood is a chemical called thujone, which gives it—and absinthe—a penetrating evergreen aroma. (Thujone is also a major component of the herb sage.) Thujone and the other aromatic compounds are what cause absinthe to become milky when it's diluted. The aromatics are more soluble in alcohol than in water, so when the concentrated spirit is cut with wine or water, they cluster together in tiny droplets that reflect light from their surfaces. Instantly, what was a clear liquid clouds over.

Absinthe became tremendously popular throughout Europe in the 19th century. It was blamed for causing hallucinations, mental instability and criminal behavior, which medical authorities attributed to thujone. This belief helped get absinthe banned. But according to the new study, by Dirk W. Lachenmeier and colleagues, the modern medical consensus is that absinthism was either simple alcohol poisoning—some absinthes were 70 percent alcohol, nearly double the strength of most distilled drinks—or caused by methanol and other toxic adulterants found in some cheap absinthes.

Thujone is true to its reputation in one respect: it does turn out to have unusual pharmacological properties. It interacts with several neurotransmitter systems in the brain, including one that is also activated by the cannabinoids in marijuana. But while absinthe will get you drunk, it won't make you stoned. In one experiment, a dose of thujone equivalent to a pint of absinthe lowered the subjects' performance on attention tests and made them more anxious. Very large doses are toxic, but moderate consumption appears to be safe.

But buyer beware: Europe currently has no regulations on how absinthe is made or what it can be made from. The German chemists think some rules are a good idea: some Czech brands they sampled were tinted turquoise, were flavored with mint instead of wormwood, tasted sweet instead of bitter and were so dilute that they didn't grow cloudy when mixed with water.

Which brings me back to my Death in the Afternoon cocktail. When I poured the Champagne into my absinthe substitute, Pernod, a good milkiness developed, but after the initial whoosh there were only a couple of lonely bubble clusters on the surface, slowly and invisibly replenished from the murky depths. I felt only a slight prickle on the tongue. It seemed a waste of effervescence, especially after what I've been learning from the world expert on the subject.

Gérard Liger-Belair is a physicist at the University of Reims, where he trains a high-speed digital camera through a microscope onto glasses of wine from local cellars. His 2004 book, "Uncorked: The Science of Champagne," revealed that most Champagne bubbles arise from something you might be tempted to scour from your flutes: dust.

Kitchen towels and the ambient air deposit tiny hollow cellulose fibers from cotton, paper and other plant products on the surface of a clean glass. The air pockets in those hollow fibers allow dissolved carbon dioxide molecules in the wine to collect and pop off in a bubble, which leaves a remnant behind to start the process all over again. As they rise in the glass, the bubbles gather more carbon dioxide, so they expand and accelerate. When they burst at the surface, they shoot tiny jets of liquid as much as an inch into the air, tickling the nose and delivering aroma.

In more recent work Professor Liger-Belair has shown just how lucky we are in the quality of our plant dust. It turns out that the cellulose fiber hollows are of just the right size—about a tenth the diameter of a human hair—to produce small, regularly spaced bubbles that keep coming for a long time. If they were much narrower, then the bubbles would be released faster and closer together, and the gas would be exhausted from the glass much sooner. If the fiber interior were as wide as a hair, then the bubbles would be more coarse, and we wouldn't get as many of them.

Because the fibers and the gas pockets are scattered across the glass surface, each bubble train rises in undisturbed isolation. The result is a clockwork release of bubbles, evenly spaced and pleasing to the eye.

Champagne flutes are sometimes scratched or engraved to encourage more predictable bubbling, but the research shows that this produces a microscopic trench in which gas pockets grow into one another and coalesce, so the bubble size and release are irregular and chaotic. Help may be on the way, though. "We are working hard with glassmakers to produce artificial nucleation sites with the same properties as cellulose fibers," Professor Liger-Belair wrote in an e-mail message. "This is a nice little challenge for nanotechnology!"

Another challenge: With all Professor Liger-Belair has discovered about the birth and life of Champagne bubbles, is there a way to make "Death in the Afternoon" a bit more lively?

*January 3, 2007*

# LAST COME THE BUBBLES
## By WILLIAM L. HAMILTON

Dushan Zaric has, to my mind, a unique and concise view of life.

"You like sweet? You like sour?" he asked me last week. "You like bitter? You like dirty? Straight?"

I thought about all that, maybe a little too deeply.

Mr. Zaric is a bartender, and we were talking about cocktails. He is also, with Jason Kosmas, a fellow bartender, a partner in Cocktail Conceptions, a consulting service in Astoria, Queens, in the apartment the two men share and where they develop cocktails for restaurants, bars and liquor companies.

One of Cocktail Conceptions' latest assignments was the cocktail menu at Schiller's Liquor Bar. It is Keith McNally's newest venture, at the corner of Rivington and Norfolk Streets. The white neon sign makes it look, cleverly, like an all-night pharmacy in a bad neighborhood.

There was a point when it might have been brilliant to put Mr. McNally on the City Planning Commission. He invaded and occupied frontier territories like TriBeCa with the restaurant Odeon in 1980 and eastern SoHo with Pravda in 1996 and Balthazar in 1997. Mr. McNally's recent posts are more like cleanup missions in well-publicized locales: Pastis in the meatpacking district in 1999 and Schiller's, opened last month, on the Lower East Side.

Mr. McNally asked Mr. Zaric, who also works at the bar, for frozen margaritas and then cut him loose to invent the house drinks. "I didn't want us to appear too fancy, but to bring it down a little—not just cocktails," Mr. McNally said. "And I like them. But I've got quite bad taste."

In Astoria, the request sent a freezing chill down the spines of Mr. Zaric and Mr. Kosmas like the time Mr. Kosmas saw a maraschino cherry in a cosmopolitan.

"I threw away a lot of it," Mr. Zaric said of their research, conducted at a dining table beneath a portrait of Tito, the president of the former Yugoslavia. Mr. Zaric is from Belgrade.

At Schiller's on Wednesday, it was business as usual—Mr. McNally's standard bistro background and, in the crowd, Europeans in track suits, artists with children and couples who probably weren't of age when Mr. McNally opened his last restaurant. There were also older men in short-sleeved polyester shirts—the aging aristocracy of the East Village and the Lower East Side.

If Schiller's frozen margaritas are an honorable escape, the Sparkling Mango is a triumph. There are nights when you think you'll never drink again, and then you come upon a drink like it, a piece of exoticism whose simplicity is its surprise.

"You get this sweet-and-sour kind of thing, but then, you get the bubbles," Mr. Zaric said proudly.

Consider it the newest of life's choices.

## SPARKLING MANGO
Adapted from SCHILLER'S LIQUOR BAR, New York City

| | |
|---|---|
| ¾ ounce 80 proof vodka | Chilled Champagne or sparkling water |
| ¾ ounce Hiram Walker Fruja Mango | Thin slice of fresh mango, for garnish |
| ½ ounce fresh lemon juice | |

**1.** Pour all ingredients except the Champagne and mango slice into a mixing glass. Add ice and shake well for several seconds.

**2.** Strain into a chilled 5-ounce martini glass, and top to the brim with Champagne. Garnish with a mango slice.

*September 28, 2003*

## KIR ROYALE 38
Adapted from LA CARAVELLE, New York City, by William Grimes

1 teaspoon cognac
1 teaspoon Grand Marnier

6 to 8 ounces Champagne
½ orange slice, for garnish

**1.** Pour the cognac and Grand Marnier into the bottom of a champagne flute.

**2.** Fill glass with champagne and garnish with the orange slice.

*January 20, 1999*

## THE GRAPE ROYALE
Adapted from CAFÉ GREY, New York City, by William L. Hamilton

¼ ounce dark purple grape juice
¼ ounce grappa (Nonino Merlot
  grappa)
4 ½ ounces Vouvray Foreau, sparkling

white wine or Champagne
For garnish:
Small bunch Champagne grapes
1 tablespoon superfine sugar

**1.** Stir purple grape juice and grappa in a Champagne flute and top off with chilled sparkling wine.

**2.** Garnish with grapes dusted in sugar, hung on the side of the glass.

*October 10, 2004*

APEROL SPRITZ

## CHAPTER 4

# WINE

# IT'S TIME TO UPDATE THE WINE SPRITZER

## By ROSIE SCHAAP

I was lucky enough to spend a few summers on Fire Island in the late '70s, and—with no cars, no school, no schedule, no shoes—it was a pretty happy place to be a kid. Most days, after a swim in the bay, I'd walk the narrow, sunny lanes and fill buckets with fat blueberries. Once a week, a club in one of the villages opened its doors early for the elementary-school set: for an hour or so, we got hopped up on soda and boogied to the Bee Gees and Donna Summer.

For us, the living was easy, but this was not equally true for our mothers, many of whom were recently divorced or separated. They'd cluster together, our newly single moms, on one or another's deck and commiserate over white-wine spritzers, Dubonnet spritzers, Lillet spritzers. Melissa Manchester's rendition of "Don't Cry Out Loud" was a big hit back then, and to my considerable annoyance, my mother and her friends listened to it over and over, as if it gave voice to their collective grief.

So it's no wonder that I came to think of the spritzer not only as a ladies' drink but more specifically as a drink for women in crisis. And one that was tightly timebound to the Carter administration. In later years, it surprised me whenever someone ordered one, as if it were a willfully retro gesture. Inevitably, I'd have a flashback.

Maybe it's a marker of age that I've come around. As much as I love gin and whiskey, my go-to drink at the end of most days is wine. More often than not, it's just decent, honest, even slightly plonky red, drunk from a highball (stemmed glasses can be a bit of a bother, so I reserve those for when I'm having the really good stuff). But sometimes, particularly as the weather warms up, I want my wine transformed into something a little more festive. Beyond the familiar spritzer (and the Bellini, and the mimosa, and sangria), wine can be a surprising, refreshing component in a mixed drink, and not just the fizzy kind.

Creative bartenders in New York and elsewhere recognize what a versatile player wine—red, white, rosé, flat, sparkling—is. It's easy enough to mix it with soda and add a squeeze of citrus, but there are innumerable other, more delicious possibilities. And galvanized by stronger spirits (even richly flavorful ones like cognac and rum), a wine-based drink packs a far more powerful punch. I can't help thinking that these cocktails might have cheered up those ladies in the summer of '79 a little faster than their spritzers.

## SOUS LE SOLEIL

*A homage to my mom, who loved the song of a similar name by Godard's muse, Anna Karina.*

| | |
|---|---|
| 1 grapefruit segment | 2 ounces Lillet Blanc |
| 3 dashes Fee Brothers Grapefruit Bitters | 1 ounce cognac |
| ½ ounce Morris Kitchen Preserved Lemon Syrup | Grapefruit twist, for garnish |

**1.** In a mixing glass, muddle the grapefruit with the bitters. Fill with ice, add all the other ingredients except grapefruit twist and shake vigorously.

**2.** Strain into a chilled coupe. Garnish with a grapefruit twist.


## THE BATTLE OF IVREA
**Adapted from TYLER DRINKWATER, Dell'anima, New York City**

*Tyler Drinkwater of the West Village restaurant Dell'anima has proved how well wine, rum and bitters can work together. This drink is named after the Italian city where residents re-enact the Battle of the Oranges and pelt each other with the fruit.*

| | |
|---|---|
| 1 slice each, lime, lemon and orange | ½ ounce Campari |
| 3 dashes Hella Bitter citrus bitters | Enough sparkling Moscato to "float" |
| 2 ounces light rum | Lemon twist, for garnish |

**1.** In a mixing glass, muddle the fruits. Fill with ice, add the other ingredients except lemon twist and shake.

**2.** Strain into a highball over ice. Float the Moscato on top. Garnish with a lemon twist.

*May 17, 2012*

# THE SPRITZ, A VENETIAN STAPLE, IS WELCOMED ABROAD

## By ELISABETTA POVOLEDO

In its glory days, Venice sent out its fearsome fleet to conquer international trade. Today, a gentler envoy is conquering international cocktail menus: the spritz.

This fizzy aperitif, a longtime staple of local bars in which Aperol, Campari, Cynar or Select liqueurs are mixed with white wine and sparkling mineral water, has been popping up in a variety of guises: from the Venetian Spritz in New York's Union Square Cafe to Berlin's Veneto Sprizz.

"Goodbye beer, it's spritz time," read one Italian newspaper headline this summer, gushing over the newfound popularity of the drink in Germany. (Though the article, in the Milan daily Corriere della Sera, noted that Italian expatriates were aghast at one Teutonic variation served with frozen berries "like minuscule fleets of colored icebergs.")

When Gruppo Campari began distributing the fluorescent orange herb and root liqueur Aperol in the United States in 2004, after buying it the year before, it promoted the spritz as its signature cocktail. Campari has aggressively marketed the Aperol spritz to a young crowd, including a 30-second commercial this year that could pass as a mini "Baywatch" episode.

But a decade ago, the wine consultant Giovanni Lai said, the spritz was mostly "an older person's drink" in the Veneto region around Venice, where the aperitif took root.

It found fertile ground, said Massimiliano Lo Duca, owner of the El Réfolo bar, a popular spritz spot near the gardens that house the national pavilions for Venice's Biennale art exhibition. "There's a saying in Venice," Mr. Lo Duca said, "that bars and churches never go out of business here."

Venice, Padua and Trieste all claim paternity rights to the spritz, but its origins probably lie in the Austrian Empire, which took over Veneto in the early 19th century. Hapsburg soldiers, local legend has it, would water down the strong local wine with a squirt (spritzen) of sparkling water.

The spritz has many local versions that vary from town to town, even bar to bar. The ratio of white wine to carbonated water is flexible and, of course, a lot depends on which spirit is added. A spritz with Aperol is lighter than the more bitter Campari version (which also packs a stronger alcohol punch), and differs from a spritz with Cynar (the artichoke-based liqueur also owned by Gruppo Campari), which has its own, smaller, flock of followers.

Select, a bright red liqueur with notes of orange, whose label boasts that it was "born in Venice in 1920," is also a popular ingredient in spritzes here, but is little known outside Veneto.

"If there's a magic combination, it's in the hands of the bartender mixing the drink," said Enzo Di Ciccio, owner of Al Campanile, a cozy bar known for its spritzes and just an ice cube's throw from Piazza San Marco. (Though some purists might frown on Mr. Di Ciccio's garnishing the drinks with olives, which he said "add a touch of class.")

It's hard to know what purists would think of the cocktail inspired by the spritz at 'Inoteca Vino, Cucina e Liquori Bar in the Kips Bay section of Manhattan, where Aperol is blended with fresh-squeezed lemon juice, egg white, honey and prosecco.

"It's very balanced, very clean," said Matt Piacentini, the bar manager and head mixologist.

Then there's the concoction at the Clover Club in Brooklyn, where the bar manager, Brad Farran, mixes rhubarb purée, when in season, with prosecco, Aperol and a splash of strawberry. "It's a very complete flavor," Mr. Farran said of the balance of sweet and bitter notes. And it's "not going to knock you out."

In fact, the relatively low alcohol content of the spritz is repeatedly cited as key to its success. In Venice, locals say, one spritz easily leads to another. "Here you're constantly bumping into people you know, and it's natural to drink a spritz while you chat," explained Giuseppe Zanon, one of the owners of the Al Mercà bar just off the Rialto Bridge. (As they move from bar to bar, Mr. Zanon said, very popular people can opt for the "pallino," which is a spritz in a smaller glass, though in Venice drinking and driving "is usually not an issue.")

The spritz is also an affordable drink here, averaging between 2.50 to 4 euros (about $3.40 to $5.50 at current rates). (Spritzes are around $12 in New York, where they are also served at the Cipriani restaurants, offshoots of Harry's Bar in Venice, where spritzes are not on the menu.)

While many bartenders take pride in their spritzes, some see them as a way to use up low-quality wine, which can lead to the dreaded spritz headache, said Mr. Lo Duca of El Réfolo.

Veneto bars used to pride themselves in their "noble draft wines," but that culture has been waning, and many bartenders have been mixing spritzes with prosecco.

Some experts lament that the fad for spritzes inhibits young people from developing an appreciation for wine.

"If you don't know wine and don't know what to drink, you get a spritz," said Michela Scibilia, who has written guidebooks and an iPhone app to Venice's restaurants and bars. "It's a fine drink for places where you only have modest wines, but in fact in wine bars where they serve great wines they probably don't serve spritzes at all."

## VENETIAN SPRITZ
**Adapted from AL CAMPANILE, Venice**

3 ounces prosecco
1 ½ ounces Aperol or other bitter aperitif

1 ½ ounces soda water
Green olive, for garnish

**1.** Gently stir all ingredients except olive over ice in a tumbler.

**2.** Add olive.

*October 5, 2010*

## BOHEMIAN SPRITZ
**Adapted from KATIE STIPE by Steven Stern**

*While Americans content themselves with Rudolph and Frosty, rural Austrians revere a more outré member of the holiday pantheon: Krampus, the malevolent goat-horned demon. A pre-Christian holdover, he wields birch branches and rusty chains, enacting a sort of good cop, bad cop routine with Old St. Nick.*

*Krampus is probably the most dramatic example of the age-old winter solstice symbols and rituals—the pine tree and the Yule log among them—that still poke up through Christmas traditions.*

*For those slightly weary of the familiar fa-la-la, or for those who are opposed to even the slightest whisper of organized religion, a solstice party provides a refreshing diversion. While actual hard-core pagans are probably drinking something murky and ancient, a more streamlined beverage might be better for dabblers. The Bohemian Spritz (another creation of Vandaag's Katie Stipe) is a light, fizzy wine drink with compellingly arboreal undercurrents, provided by pine and elderflower cordials. It is ideal for welcoming the long nights, for putting the Krampus back in Christmas.*

3 ounces dry white wine
½ ounce dry vermouth
½ ounce elderflower liqueur
¼ ounce pine liqueur

1 ounce club soda
1 ounce dry sparkling wine
1 slice of grapefruit peel, for garnish

**1.** Combine wine, vermouth and liqueurs in a large wineglass filled with ice.

**2.** Stir to chill, then top with club soda and sparkling wine. Twist grapefruit peel over it and drop into glass.

*November 10, 2010*

THE BAR AL MERCA, VENICE

# A COCKTAIL MIXED WITH A PUNCH LINE

## By JONATHAN MILES

A Manischewitz and bourbon cocktail? Now there's some chutzpah.

Meet the Drunken Pharaoh, a drink that sounds like a Sammy Davis Jr. routine served over ice. (And I haven't even mentioned yet the rim of crushed matzo on the glass.) Along with a liver-and-bacon-on-challah dish entitled "The Conflicted Jew," it's on the menu at JoeDoe, a 27-seat bistro at 45 East First Street, and it was the liquid starter to the "Progressive Passover" seder that the restaurant held Tuesday. After all, as the comedian Jackie Mason once said, "a seder without sweet Manischewitz would be like horseradish without tears, like a cantor without a voice, like a shul without a complaint, like a yenta without a big mouth, like Passover without Jews."

Jill Schulster, who co-owns the restaurant with its nickname-sake, chef Joe Dobias, and is a professional ballet dancer on the side, would agree with Mr. Mason. "I love Manischewitz, and grew up drinking it," she said. "But I wanted to make it more..." Here Ms. Schulster paused. "More palatable," she said. "I wanted a funky way to enjoy it."

To add some funk to Manischewitz, the notoriously sweet kosher wine that's used as often for a punchline as, say, a punch ingredient, Ms. Schulster mixed it with Old Pogue bourbon along with a splash of lemon juice and some mellowing fizz from club soda. "To remind you that it's Passover," she said, she added a chunky and slightly chewy rim of crushed matzo, tempered with confectioner's sugar, to the glass the drink is served in. While the Manischewitz's cloying sweetness comes through (one suspects it would take a full gallon of bourbon to subdue that candied Concord grapiness), the drink is determinedly balanced, and rather festive to boot. The matzo rim is an odd gimmick, but then so is the drink itself: a modern-day cocktail that traces its roots back to Moses.

Eh, sort of. The Manischewitz is kosher, as is the matzo. But after that, the drink's theological status gets dicey. "Unfortunately, it's not kosher for Passover," said Ms. Schulster, who identified herself as a Reform Jew, then added, with a laugh, "a Long Island Jew!"

Her and Mr. Dobias's goal, she said, was to incorporate an "untraditional element" into their secularized seder. "Bourbon is made from corn, so it could work for Sephardic Jews," she said. "The rules get twisted all the time. Though it's fair to say Orthodox Jews probably won't be drinking this cocktail."

## DRUNKEN PHARAOH
Adapted from JOEDOE, New York City

Simple syrup (page 27)
Sugared matzo, for rimming glass (see note below)
1 ½ ounce bourbon

2 ounces Manischewitz wine
½ ounce lemon juice
Club soda, to top

**1.** Coat rim of a glass with simple syrup, then dip it into the matzo mix so that the matzo adheres to the edge.

**2.** In a cocktail shaker, combine the bourbon, Manischewitz and lemon juice, with ice, and shake.

**3.** Strain into the glass, over ice, and top with the club soda.

**For the matzo rim, crush a piece of matzo with the back of a spoon until coarse. Add about 1 tablespoon confectioner's sugar to the matzo, and mix.**

*April 10, 2009*

# ODE TO A COCKTAIL
## By ROBERT SIMONSON

What would Keats drink?

On Thursday, at a celebration in Chicago honoring the centenary of "Poetry" magazine, guests will raise a cocktail created especially for the occasion. Named the Hippocrene—the mythological source of poetic inspiration—it is the work of Brian West, a web developer at Columbia College Chicago and cocktail enthusiast, and is primarily inspired by John Keats's "Ode to a Nightingale."

Mr. West became interested in mixology during the three and a half years he worked as Web producer for the Poetry Foundation, which publishes the magazine. When he was asked to create the drink, he said in an e-mail, he looked at the myth around the Hippocrene spring and the Pegasus, but also at a few lines from "Ode to a Nightingale." As the tale goes,

Pegasus—the winged horse that has long been the symbol of Poetry magazine—struck the mythical Mount Helicon, a peak sacred to the muses, and out gushed the Hippocrene.

The fountain is invoked in many poems, including "Ode to a Nightingale." The lines Mr. West focused on came from the second stanza:

*O, for a draught of vintage! that hath been*
*Cool'd a long age in the deep-delved earth,*
*Tasting of Flora and the country green,*
*Dance, and Provençal song, and sunburnt mirth!*
*O for a beaker full of the warm South,*
*Full of the true, the blushful Hippocrene,*
*With beaded bubbles winking at the brim,*
*And purple-stained mouth;*

*That I might drink, and leave the world unseen,*

*And with thee fade away into the forest dim:*

"It was obvious that we needed a sparkling wine," said Mr. West, pointing to those "beaded bubbles winking" in the stanza's seventh line. "I was also inspired by the line, 'Tasting of Flora and the country green,' to add some herbal notes with gin, mint, ginger and basil," he said.

He found both Prosecco and Korbel Extra Dry performed nicely as the sparkling wine in his concoction, and for the gin—given Keats's British heritage, what other base spirit would have been appropriate?—Mr. West thinks Ransom Old Tom Gin, Farmer's Gin and Small's Gin work best. The ginger in the drink comes in the form of ginger liqueur, and the mint arrives as mint tea. The drink also includes lemon juice, grapefruit juice and grapefruit bitters. (With so many glories of the garden in this concoction, surely Wordsworth would have joined Keats in a glassful.)...

## THE HIPPOCRENE
### Adapted from BRIAN WEST
YIELD: 1 DRINK OR COMBINE IN GREATER QUANTITIES AS A PUNCH

1¼ ounces gin

¾ ounce ginger liqueur (domaine de canton)

½ ounce fresh grapefruit juice

¼ ounce fresh lemon juice

1 tablespoon mint tea (brewed at double strength) and chilled

2 ounces dry, sparkling wine

Fresh basil, for garnish

Dash or two grapefruit bitters

### SINGLE-GLASS PREPARATION

**1.** Combine all ingredients except sparkling wine, basil, and bitters (if using) in a mixing glass over ice. Stir and strain into a glass and top with remaining ingredients.

### PUNCH PREPARATION

**2.** Combine all ingredients (in greater quantities) except sparkling wine, basil and bitters in an adequately sized serving bowl, along with some large blocks of ice.

It's best to let this mixture chill and dilute a little while before adding everything else, but if time is short, it could be refrigerated beforehand and water (sparkling or still) can be added along with the rest of the ingredients at service time. The basil should still be added directly to the glass, as it is the aroma and not necessarily the flavor that you're after. It would also be nice to garnish the mixing bowl with some citrus slices, for color and a generally vigorous appearance.

*October 4, 2012*

## PROSECCO AND LOVAGE COCKTAIL
**Adapted from FRANNY'S, by Melissa Clark**
YIELD: 8 DRINKS

1 cup sugar
½ cup lovage leaves

1 bottle (750 milliliters) prosecco or other sparkling wine, chilled
8 lime wedges, for garnish (optional)

**1.** Combine sugar and a cup of water in a small saucepan, and bring to a boil. Stir until sugar dissolves, then turn off heat. Add lovage leaves and let syrup infuse for 3 hours. Strain, discarding lovage.

**2.** Measure 2 teaspoons syrup (or more to taste) into each of 8 Champagne flutes or other glasses. Top with prosecco and garnish with lime wedges.

**Leftover syrup is nice tossed with plums.**

*November 3, 2004*

## BICYCLETTE
**Adapted from FERGUS HENDERSON, London**

2 ounces Campari

1 ½ ounces dry white wine

**1.** Add Campari to a wine glass, fill glass two-thirds full with ice and add wine.

**2.** Stir, taste and adjust as desired.

*November 4, 2007*

## ENCHANTRESS
**By JIM MEEHAN**

2 ounces port
1 ounce cognac
½ ounce orange Curaçao

½ ounce lemon juice
Orange twist, for garnish

**1.** Shake all ingredients except orange twist with ice.

**2.** Strain into a rocks glass filled with ice and garnish with an orange twist.

*June 12, 2012*

THE OLD-FASHIONED AT PASSERBY, BROOKLYN

## CHAPTER 5

# THE OLD-FASHIONED

# ARE YOU FRIENDS, AFTER AN OLD-FASHIONED?

## By PAUL CLARKE

In certain quarters, when discussing drinks, it's probably best not to mention the old-fashioned.

In the years before I started goofing around with spirits and cocktails, I was a lackluster home bartender. My martinis were all bad gin and too little vermouth; my caipirinhas were rendered lumpy and opaque by my confusing superfine sugar with powdered confectioner's sugar, which typically includes chunk-inducing cornstarch; and my margaritas—constructed using a newspaper recipe I later realized was incredibly lame—had a sweetness and viscosity akin to that of a glass of Mrs. Butterworth's.

I did have something, however, that I felt I made well: an old-fashioned. Back then I didn't know, or particularly care, that the old-fashioned is one of the most venerable drinks in cocktaildom. It's a combination that drinks historian David Wondrich has proclaimed one of the four pillars of mixological wisdom. I simply knew that it was delicious, an appealing way to utilize the bottle of Knob Creek I received for Christmas, and the bibulous answer to the question that had nagged at me for years: what are you supposed to do with those little paper-wrapped bottles of Angostura bitters?

Still apprehensive about my understanding of the drink, however, I eyeballed what local bartenders did when I ordered one, and saw that I appeared to be skipping several steps— some mashed maraschino cherries and orange slices in the glass, resulting in a sugary fruit salad that appealed to my inner five-year-old; others took the half-full glass of whiskey and ice and topped it off with club soda, making too much of a no-longer good thing. Still others employed both approaches, so that the whiskey was a watery afterthought and the fruit streaked the glass like smears of old lipstick; the resulting drink was so saggy and tired that it begged to be garnished with a lit Pall Mall.

What gives? I thought—it's an old recipe, right? Isn't there some agreement on how it's supposed to be made?

This is perhaps the ultimate question today for many bartenders, bloggers and home cocktail enthusiasts (a much nicer term than "geek", I'm reminded), and the mystery that has pushed so many into cocktail aficionado-dom in recent years.

I soon realized that the old-fashioned is merely one battle line, albeit a significant one, in a much larger discussion among cocktail fans online that sometimes flared with passion (for regardless of the topic, the Internet has become no place for even-tempered debate). And while the subject of how to mix drinks is typically a pleasant one, the debates over proper recipes, spirits, tools and techniques that are conducted in person—typically over cocktails that have been exactingly described to an increasingly exasperated bartender—or on blogs or online forums such as eGullet and the soon-to-be-defunct Drinkboy forums, can sometimes veer into serious, clinically dry and even belligerent arenas.

Coming from the blogosphere and prone to geekish tendencies in every manner of my life, I of course initially followed and engaged in discussions on all types of spirituous arcana: can a gimlet be properly made without Rose's Lime Juice? (The general consensus is no.) What is the true genesis of the Sidecar cocktail? (Short answer: who knows?) Can a style of cocktail shaker made by fitting two metal mixing tins together achieve greater mixological nirvana than a shaker made with a tin and a mixing glass? (Quite possibly.) And exactly how many drops of vermouth can dance on the head of a pin? (Jury's still out.) Over the years I've formed friendships, and strained them, in heated discussions over the serving sizes of cocktails in London in the 1930s, and the styles and flavor profiles of the vermouth that was sold in New York at the turn of the last century.

I can already see the "get a life" comments this confession will incite (though really, is fantasy baseball that much cooler?), and indeed, there are times when ardent cocktail fans gather—whether in person at an event like the annual Tales of the Cocktail in New Orleans, or online in the Mixoloseum, a blogger-oriented chat room with an atmosphere and maturity level not unlike that found in a yellow school bus on the way to junior-high band camp—that, in certain circles, the geek-ness hangs so heavy in the air that there's real danger a game of Dungeons & Dragons might break out at any moment.

But I've grown weary of what Internet arguments have become, and I've largely put my days of cocktailian combat behind me (aside from a few sensitive topic areas that you really don't want to press me on). Now, even though I usually spend my days talking, reading and writing about cocktails, I tend to approach them as Freud did his cigars: sometimes a drink is just a drink, nothing more and nothing less than a welcome distraction from the bristling cacophony of the world for a few minutes out of the day.

That's when I come back to the old-fashioned. As prone to becoming the subject of polemic, revisionism and endlessly repetitive arguments as any other cocktail—barring perhaps the cult-like madness that often accompanies the martini—when the computer is turned off and I place the whiskey and bitters on the kitchen counter, ultimately it's just a drink. Not that I don't recall the nagging questions as I mix, nor the ways I'm sure the drink would annoy partisans at polar ends of the mixological range: first a dab of sugar syrup in the bottom of a glass followed by a couple of dashes of bitters (hardcore old-fashionedistas mandate the physical crushing of a sugar cube, possibly with a swath of orange or lemon peel); then a measured dose of bourbon or rye whiskey, depending on the mood; a quick stir for everyone to get acquainted in the glass, followed by large chunks of ice and, for that inner five-year-old with maturing tastes, a single bottled Italian wild cherry for color, rinsed of any cloying syrup. No muddling, no soda, no laborious frippery or careless sploshing of ingredients. For something that inspires such debate, it's about as Zen a cocktail as you can get.

*January 11, 2009*

## THE OLD-FASHIONED
### Adapted from Toby Cecchini

1 teaspoon superfine sugar or 2 tablespoons simple syrup (page 27)
4 dashes Angostura bitters
1 slice from half an orange

2–3 ounces bourbon or rye whiskey
1 lemon twist, for garnish
1 maraschino cherry, for garnish

**1.** Combine sugar and bitters in a double-rocks (old-fashioned) glass. Add a couple of teaspoons of hot water, and stir together until sugar is dissolved. Add orange slice and mull until well mixed.

**2.** Fill glass with ice, top with bourbon, and stir well. Garnish with lemon peel, twisted to release oil, and cherry

*November 3, 2002*

# THE GREAT OLD-FASHIONED DEBATE
## By ROSIE SCHAAP

There's a terrific mini-monologue in the 1942 film "You Were Never Lovelier" in which Fred Astaire's fast-talking would-be roué tells Rita Hayworth's ingénue: "As they'd say in Brooklyn, I can't bat in your league. I'm a plain, ordinary guy from Omaha, Nebraska. Just an old-fashioned, everyday Middle Westerner. . . . But you're streamlined. You're today. Sister, I was raised amongst the grasshoppers, I am strictly from corn." And then the duo breaks into song and dance, which is where Jerome Kern and Johnny Mercer's sublime ballad, "I'm Old Fashioned," debuted.

For me, the song and the drink (which predates it by a very long time; the name dates to around the 1880s, but the recipe's essentials go back to at least 1806) go together perfectly. And even Astaire's brief speech seems to telegraph the big question among old-fashioned drinkers: Which way are you going to have it—streamlined or strictly from corn?

No cocktail (and this includes the martini) gets people as worked up about methodology as the old-fashioned. And that's probably because the two major approaches really are quite different. One is starkly minimalist, prescribing nothing more than sugar, whiskey and bitters—maybe a few teardrops' worth of water, maybe a twist of orange or lemon to finish it off. Like Hayworth, it's streamlined, it's today (even if it is one of the oldest cocktails on record). It's certainly not the old-fashioned I was taught to make at a bar in small-town Vermont in the early 1990s. There, the first time a customer ordered the drink from me, I skulked over to the manager to ask what to do. She plonked a sugar cube, a slice of orange and a cherry in a glass, dug what looked like a small nightstick out of a drawer, handed it to me as if I had any idea what to do with it and told me to add whiskey, Angostura bitters and ice. I did figure out what to do with the muddler, and that drink—the sweet and fruity, eager-to-please, raised among the grasshoppers, strictly from corn, boisterous version—instantly became my old-fashioned.

I wouldn't encounter its austere twin for more than a decade, at an East Village bar, where at the time I assumed they had just run out of fruit. But as more years piled on, I noticed that this version had ascended. It had become to many the one, the true, the correct way to drink it. I get it. It's a lovely, restrained drink, so pared-down as to feel elemental. But I like the other, more gregarious kind too. And ultimately, what I've discovered I like best of all is essentially a hybrid—like the version from Kenneth McCoy, a bartender and owner at Ward III in TriBeCa. At his dad's bar in Manhattan, they were made much as I was taught to in Vermont, and affection for that fruit-forward flavor abides, with a little adjusting.

After all, this year's fancies, the song tells us, are passing fancies.

## KENNETH MCCOY'S OLD-FASHIONED

*McCoy's old-fashioned strikes a balance between the muddled fruit and minimalist models.*

| | |
|---|---|
| Dash of Regans' orange bitters | 1 teaspoon of brandied cherry juice |
| Dash of Angostura bitters | 2 ounces of your favorite whiskey |
| Dash of simple syrup (page 27) | Orange peel, for garnish |

**1.** Stir together all ingredients, except orange peel, with ice in a mixing glass.

**2.** Strain into an old-fashioned glass over a large chunk of ice. Garnish with a thick twist of orange peel.

## JOSEY PACKARD'S AUTUMNAL OLD-FASHIONED

*Packard, a bartender at the Boston cocktail bar Drink, offers this applejack-based old-fashioned.*

½ teaspoon cinnamon simple syrup
2¼ ounces Laird's bonded applejack
Scant ½ ounce Demerara simple syrup
(page 27)

Dash of Fee Brothers Whiskey
Barrel-aged bitters
Orange peel

**1.** Build all ingredients, except orange peel, in old-fashioned glass.

**2.** Add ice, swirl and garnish with orange peel.

## OLD-FASHIONED WHISKEY COCKTAIL
### By ROSIE SCHAAP

1 sugar cube
2 dashes Angostura bitters

Dash of water
2 ounces bourbon (preferably Elijah
Craig 12-year-old)

**1.** Lightly muddle sugar cube with bitters ad water in an old-fashioned glass.

**2.** Add whiskey and ice.

*November 7, 2013*

# A GOOD DECADE TO HAVE A DRINK
## By JONATHAN MILES

By now, most of the reviews of the decade-that-just-was have been filed, and a consensus has emerged: If not "the worst decade ever," as "Time" magazine put it, the '00s were awful.

Unless, that is, you spent the decade drinking. That sounds like a joke but isn't, because among all the things that didn't improve in the last 10 years—macro stuff like the global economy, geopolitical stability, the environment, etc.—one thing, admittedly micro, did improve: the drinks we drank, for pleasure or, considering the above, analgesia.

If you observed the '00s from a barstool, and limited your reading to cocktail menus (as I did, as author of this column for almost four years), you'd be forgiven for deeming the decade a bona fide golden age. For my final column, then, a toast: to 10 years of fizzes, slings, juleps, sours, cobblers and rickeys, to a time when the avant-garde seemed to shift almost nightly, to the best decade in generations.

We greeted the decade with sugary, vodka-based "-tinis"—which, despite their suffixed claim to noble descent, were in some ways extensions of the neon drinks of the '80s:

alcoholic candy.

Yet a quiet revolution was already under way. Building upon the work of Dale DeGroff, the former Rainbow Room bartender, young bartenders, casting aside process mixers, were gleaning inspiration from their counterparts in restaurant kitchens and perusing antique cocktail books like scholars combing the Dead Sea scrolls. The first half of the decade saw a wave of creativity and experimentation come crashing through barrooms in cities like New York and San Francisco and Portland, Oregon, followed, in the decade's second half, by a counterblast of earnest classicism.

The cocktail was no longer a fashion accessory, as it was in the '90s. It was fashion itself. What had once merely lubricated conversations became the subject of conversations, in much the same way that dinner parties, with the rise of foodie-ism in the '90s, became more about the dinner and less about the party.

Bar patrons broadcast their selections over Twitter. Home bartenders blogged about their latest experiments. Surrendering your drink choice to the bartender, the way diners at sushi restaurants request whatever is freshest, became the '00s hippest drink order.

By the end of the decade, bottle service, once a mark of downtown sophistication, had come to be viewed as the province of rubes. The cocktail—especially the classic, painstakingly made variety, served with hand-cracked ice or in recherché glassware—had triumphed.

And not just here. You can get an expertly made bourbon daisy in Cleveland, an impeccable sazerac in rural Mississippi. Not long ago, in an excruciatingly remote village in the Australian Outback, I was startled to see a bartender in a cowboy hat measuring out a classically proportioned French 75—something he'd picked up on the Internet, he told me.

Call this a fad at your own peril. Some peripheral aspects of the cocktail renaissance are doomed to pass, and in some places already have: speak-easy chic, bartenders in affected period costumes, an overwrought reverence that smacks of wine snobbery. But we do not go backward from here. Pardon the pun, but the bar has been raised.

Of course, not everyone drank well this past decade. Twenty years from now, when bars are promoting nostalgic '00s theme nights, the dominant drink special will almost certainly be vodka and Red Bull. Or maybe the mojito, which introduced many Americans to fresh produce in their drink, as well as to longer wait times—owing to the bartender's need to muddle the fresh mint leaves—associated with the craft cocktail movement.

But Red Bull and vodka was a club land novelty, caffeine disguised as a highball, and the mojito was that weird exception in a decade of booming cocktail progress: a good drink that suffered from its popularity, with a flood of processed mixers corrupting the bracing integrity of the original.

No, the real story was in rediscovered drinks like the aviation cocktail, a sublimely floral combination of gin and maraschino liqueur (and later, as cocktail historians dug deeper into its origins, the violet-flavored crème de violette) that was a Web sensation before bars like Milk & Honey started featuring it on cocktail lists.

Or the old-fashioned, once dowdy but reinvigorated by bartenders like Don Lee, who recast it as the celery and nori old-fashioned at Momofuku Ssam Bar, and Phil Ward of Death & Company, whose Oaxaca old-fashioned—with tequila standing in for whiskey—proved how versatile a spare, 200-year-old formula could be.

These were artisanal drinks with history and gravitas and a contrapuntal range of flavors—sweet, sour, savory, bitter—that hadn't been balanced in generations. They're representative of a lost American art—the art of the cocktail, as practiced by pre-Prohibition bartenders—that, after the '00s, can no longer be called lost.

## OLD-FASHIONED
### Adapted from the QUARTER BAR, Brooklyn

¼ teaspoon Demerara sugar
1 orange slice
3 dashes Angostura bitters
2 ounces bourbon or rye

Dash of club soda (optional)
1 Luxardo Marasca cherry or other high-quality macerated cocktail cherry, for garnish

**1.** Place sugar, orange slice and bitters in an old-fashioned glass and gently muddle until sugar has absorbed some liquid and resembles a fine paste.

**2.** Add the bourbon or rye, along with a large ice cube or two, and stir well, about 20 times. Top with just slightest dash of club soda, if desired, and garnish with cherry.

*January 15, 2010*

# AT BAR '21,' RUBBING ELBOWS WITH HISTORY
## By STEVE REDDICLIFFE

One of the most prominent accounts of goings-on at the "21" Club bar in H. Peter Kriendler's book about that storied restaurant involves the novelist John O'Hara, who, he writes, "was bad at handling his liquor."

Mr. Kriendler was an eyewitness, having spent more than 50 years at what was then the family business.

(The title of his book is "'21': Every Day Was New Year's Eve.") He describes O'Hara picking fights with any number of customers—the New Yorker writer Brendan Gill, the actor Paul Douglas, a "distinguished neurologist"— and, on one occasion, O'Hara was seen "sprawled in a chair in the lounge, drunk and mumbling."

Based on my recent visits, there doesn't appear to be an O'Hara type in the Bar "21" these days, although there may still be a neurologist in the house.

It's a different era: boneless chicken wings, pizza and sliders are on the menu, accompaniments to first-rate cocktails that have long been a "21" hallmark.

The history of "21" can seem both intriguing and intimidating. Humphrey Bogart and Ernest Hemingway drank there; Robert Benchley quipped there.

The Frederic Remington paintings are still on the walls, but in 2013 there's nothing staid or stuffy about the place. Business casual is the rule in the bar (no jeans, no sneakers), and the room offers a grown-up brand of well-modulated liveliness.

In an age when so many of New York's best cocktail places can be found downtown, Bar "21" is the rare Midtown Manhattan drinking establishment that feels energized.

(A note: Bar "21" is not the Bar Room at "21." Bar "21" is the first space you come to when you walk in. Continuing on, you'll arrive at the Bar Room, the more famous, more formal of the two, with toys hanging from the ceiling and jackets required for men.)

The bartenders at Bar "21," who are friendly but not overly familiar, turn out excellent versions of the standards as well as cocktails of their own creation. The Perfect Manhattan on the "Classics" list is expertly balanced, made with WhistlePig rye from Vermont, bitters, and sweet and dry vermouth. The Southside, a "21" invention, is made with Tanqueray gin, lemon juice, muddled mint

leaves, a little sugar, a little soda. It's easy drinking, effervescent and just tart enough. Tara Wright, a bartender, keeps the Tanqueray and lemon theme going, following up with a really nice rendition of a Tom Collins.

The Iron Gate Old-Fashioned— substantial, worth savoring— includes Woodford bourbon and cherries soaked in brandy, and a vinegar-based gastrique that has orange, cherries and sugar in the mix.

The Beautiful Fool is a recent addition, a nod to the new movie version of "The Great Gatsby." It's a superb summer cocktail, composed of complementary ingredients: Greenhook gin made with juniper, cinnamon, camomile and elderflower; camomile syrup; St.-Germain elderflower liqueur; and grapefruit and lemon juices.

New drinks are "done as a team," the bartender Eddie Kennelly said. "It's kind of like a lot of head-bashing. You'll see something in the media like 'The Great Gatsby,' so you'll come up with a cocktail like the Beautiful Fool."

Mr. Kennelly is good with the bartender humor. After spelling his last name, he throws in: "Same as the esteemed senator from Connecticut."

This is a place, he said, where patrons tend to hang out.

"I've had people stay all day because they were having that much fun," Mr. Kennelly said.

Understandable. The martinis are as inviting as a lake at the end of a windless summer day.

How did this one, straight up with Ketel One and olives, get so smooth?

"Because I made it," Ms. Wright said.

We can go with that.

## IRON GATE OLD- FASHIONED
Adapted from BAR '21', New York City

1 maraschino cherry

1 orange slice

2 dashes Angostura Bitters

¼ ounce Old-Fashioned Gastrique (recipe follows)

2 ounces premium bourbon (preferably Woodford Reserve)

Splash of club soda

1 bourbon-soaked maraschino cherry (see Gastrique recipe below)

**1.** Add cherry, orange, bitters, and Old-Fashioned Gastrique to a rocks glass and muddle.

**2.** Fill glass with ice, add bourbon and club soda and stir gently to mix. Garnish with a bourbon-soaked maraschino cherry.

## OLD-FASHIONED GASTRIQUE
YIELD: 1 CUP (8 OUNCES)

1 cup sugar

1 cup apple cider vinegar

1 cup premium bourbon (like Woodford Reserve), plus additional for final cherry soaking

1 orange, sliced

15 maraschino cherries

1 tablespoon Angostura Bitters

**1.** In a saucepan over medium heat, add sugar and just enough water for it to dissolve. Let it sit until the sugar begins to caramelize and turns a light brown. At that moment, add vinegar to deglaze the caramelized sugar and stir until it mixes well. Remove from heat.

**2.** Add 1 cup bourbon, orange slices, cherries and bitters. Return to medium heat and let the mixture reduce to half the original volume.

**3.** Remove cherries from saucepan. Submerge in additional bourbon and let soak for use as drink garnish.

*June 20, 2013*

# TEQUILA'S NEW TAKE ON THE OLD-FASHIONED

## By JONATHAN MILES

Is tequila, as someone recently declared to me, the new cognac? Or is it rather, as another someone said, the new vodka?

"In a way, they're both true," said Marc N. Scheinman, a marketing professor at the Pace University Lubin School of Business and the author of "The Global Tequila Market," a comprehensive study of tequila's fortunes that was published last year. Mr. Scheinman sees no end in sight for the boom in tequila sales, which rose 12.5 percent last year, according to Nielsen Scantrack and Liquor Track reports.

"The aged, superpremium tequilas that we're increasingly seeing in the market have the refined air and taste of fine cognacs," Mr. Scheinman said. "And you're seeing tequila following the vodka pattern, too, with flavored tequilas entering the market and tequila having a growing presence in the cocktail culture."

Death & Co., a Lower East Side cocktailery that opened in January, serves the Oaxaca Old-Fashioned, in which tequila and its more rough-and-tumble cousin, mezcal, steal the starring role that bourbon plays in a traditional old-fashioned, with agave nectar standing in for simple syrup in the sweetener role.

"I really, really love working with tequila," said Philip Ward, the head bartender at Death & Co., where the imposing entrance, with its heavy scorched-wood doors and the windowless dark-on-dark interior put a Gothic spin on drinking. (The bar's somber facade and its name, which the owners cribbed from a Prohibition-era anti-booze poster, has sparked complaints from spooked neighbors.)

"Tequila entered the mainstream in this country at a time, in the '60s and '70s, that cocktail culture was dead," said Mr. Ward, whose revamped cocktail menu, which was to be unveiled this weekend, features an expanded roster of tequila-based cocktails. "It's not like rye whiskey, which is the base for so many classic cocktails. It's a really cool spirit to work with because there are still original things you can do with it."

As its name suggests, Mr. Ward's old-fashioned doesn't scream originality—until you taste it. This is tequila at its most nuanced, a baritone-voice cocktail with a rich, deep smokiness and dark, elusive sweetness, and it swiftly banishes questions of whether tequila is the new something else. Rather, it is the new tequila: still growing, but decidedly mature.

## OAXACA OLD-FASHIONED
Adapted from DEATH & CO., New York City

| | |
|---|---|
| 1 ½ ounces El Tesoro Reposado tequila | Dash of Angostura bitters |
| ½ ounce Los Amantes Joven mezcal | Orange twist, for garnish (see note) |
| 1 teaspoon amber agave nectar | |

**1.** Combine all ingredients, except orange twist, in a cocktail shaker filled with ice and stir.

**2.** Strain into a rocks glass filled with ice cubes. Garnish with the orange twist.

**At Death & Co., the peel is flamed. To do this, hold a section of peel—skin side down, gently grasped between thumb and forefinger—a few inches above the drink and just above a lighted match. Squeeze the peel quickly, expelling the peel's oil into the flame, where it will momentarily burst, and onto the surface of the drink. It may take practice.**

*April 15, 2007*

# TAKE A SIP OF HISTORY
## By ROBERT SIMONSON

The old-fashioned may finally be earning its name.

One of the most venerable of whiskey-based cocktails, it has a history that stretches back farther than the martini's. For decades it has suffered under the reputation of something your grandmother drank—overly sweet, fruit-laden and spritzed-up. But grandma wouldn't recognize what's happened to it lately.

The old-fashioned is one of the most requested mixed drinks at some of New York's newest and most self-consciously artisanal drinking dens, including Prime Meats in Carroll Gardens, Brooklyn; Elsa in the East Village; Rye in Williamsburg, Brooklyn; Jack the Horse in Brooklyn Heights; and the White Slab Palace on the Lower East Side.

Cocktail aficionados say it couldn't have happened to a nicer drink.

"The old-fashioned is one of the original cocktails, in the true sense of the word," said Damon Boelte, bar director at Prime Meats. "It's kind of like having a Model T on your menu."

It's so old that it was called a "whiskey cocktail" until late-19th-century parvenus like the martini and manhattan forced purists to order an "old fashioned" whiskey cocktail. But while the martini and the manhattan came through the cocktail dark ages of the 1970s and '80s with much of their dignity, the old-fashioned developed a personality disorder.

Its majestically austere profile (basically a slug of rye with minuscule touches of water, bitters and sugar) was tarted up with a muddled orange slice and maraschino cherry, and a diluting dose of soda water. This rendition has its advocates, and remains popular in supper clubs across America. But it sends shudders down the spines of the new breed of cocktail classicists.

"A bastardization of the original drink," said Kevin Jaszek, a bartender at Smith & Mills in TriBeCa who designed the cocktail list at Elsa.

Disciples of the cocktail renaissance, like Mr. Boelte and Mr. Jaszek, have restored the old-fashioned to what they feel is its rightful form—"back to integrity," as Julie Reiner put it. The Clover Club, her Boerum Hill bar, opened last June with an entire menu section devoted to the old-fashioned and its variants.

Yes, variants. Devotees are not completely doctrinaire in their recipes, varying the type of bitters or sweeteners used.

And old-fashioneds built on bourbon (PDT in the East Village), rum (the Oak Bar) and tequila (Death & Co. in the East Village) are not unheard-of. Just keep that maraschino cherry well away.

## RYE OLD-FASHIONED
Adapted from RYE, Brooklyn

1 teaspoon Demerara sugar
2 ounces rye whiskey
1 or 2 dashes Angostura bitters
1 or 2 dashes orange bitters
1 strip lemon peel

**1.** Spoon sugar into a shaker and add about a teaspoon of very hot water for a simple syrup. Stir until dissolved, adding a little more water if needed.

**2.** Add whiskey and bitters, and stir again. Add several ice cubes and stir well to chill.

**3.** Strain into an old-fashioned glass, add 2 or 3 big ice cubes, twist lemon peel over the top and drop it in.

*June 3, 2009*

## GABRIELLA MLYNARCZYK'S SMOKY BROWN-BUTTER OLD-FASHIONED
By ROSIE SCHAAP

¾ ounce simple syrup (page 27)
2 dashes Scrappy's cardamom bitters
2 dashes Angostura bitters
2 dashes liquid smoke
2 ounces brown-butter bourbon (page 82)
1 thick orange twist

**1.** Add the simple syrup, bitters and liquid smoke to a chilled old-fashioned glass, and muddle with a bar spoon.

**2.** Add brown-butter bourbon and stir 15 to 20 seconds to chill. Spritz the orange oils from the twist over the drink, then rub twist on rim of glass and drop it in.

**3.** For intense orange flavor, you can flame the twist (see note on page 80).

## BROWN-BUTTER BOURBON
YIELD: ENOUGH FOR 8 OLD-FASHIONEDS

| | |
|---|---|
| 16 ounces of bourbon (such as Buffalo Trace) | 1 stick unsalted butter |

**1.** Pour the bourbon into a screw-top jar. Put the butter in a heavy-bottomed pan, and set over a medium flame to caramelize the milk solids. Once the butter melts, it will start to foam and brown and give off a nutty aroma; there should be some caramelization at the bottom of the pan. The process is quick, so keep an eye on it.

**2.** Remove from heat, and pour into the jar of bourbon. Screw the lid on tight, and give a good shake. Let it sit for 30 minutes to an hour, then refrigerate it for at least an hour. The butter fat will solidify and rise to the top of the jar.

**3.** Scoop off the hardened fat, and strain the bourbon through a coffee filter. Store in a refrigerated airtight container, to use for old-fashioneds.

*March 30, 2014*

## SOUR-CHERRY OLD-FASHIONED
By MARK BITTMAN

*Sour cherries are too tart to eat raw, but go down amazingly easy when you muddle them with sugar and douse them with whiskey in this spin on a classic old fashioned.*

| | |
|---|---|
| 2 sour cherries, stemmed and pitted | 2 or 3 dashes bitters |
| 1 (2-inch) strip orange peel | 2 ounces rye or bourbon |
| 1 sugar cube (or ½ teaspoon sugar) | |

**1.** Put the cherries, orange peel, sugar and bitters in an old-fashioned glass; crush the sugar and cherries with a muddler, spoon or anything else that will get the job done.

**2.** Fill the glass with ice, add the whiskey and stir until the drink is cold, about a dozen times.

*June 18, 2014*

## DATE OLD-FASHIONED
Adapted from JAY BEAVERS AND CHRIS CONATSER of Justus Drugstore, Smith-ville, Mo, by CHRISTINE MUHLKE

1 orange

2 brandied or maraschino cherries (optional; recipe below)

3 dashes Angostura bitters

2½ ounces (5 tablespoons) date-infused bourbon (recipe below)

**1.** Leaving the peel on, cut the orange in half lengthwise, then cut a ¼-inch-thick slice. Cut the slice in half horizontally. Combine the orange slice half, one cherry and the bitters in a tumbler and crush with a muddler or the back of a wooden spoon.

**2.** Add a few cubes of ice and the bourbon and stir. Top with the remaining cherry.

## BRANDIED CHERRIES
YIELD: 1 POUND CHERRIES, ENOUGH FOR MANY DRINKS

1 pound dark, sweet cherries (prefera-bly fresh, but frozen is okay)

2 tablespoons sugar

2 teaspoons lemon juice

1 small cinnamon stick

3½ tablespoons brandy

**1.** Wash and pit the cherries. Combine the sugar, 2½ tablespoons water, lemon juice and cinnamon stick in a medium saucepan. Bring to a boil, then reduce the heat to low, add the cherries and simmer for 3 minutes. Remove from heat.

**2.** Discard the cinnamon stick and stir in the brandy. Cool. Store in a sealed jar and refrigerate until ready to use.

## DATE-INFUSED BOURBON
YIELD: MORE THAN 4 CUPS, ENOUGH FOR MANY DRINKS

15 dates

750-ml bottle bourbon

**1.** In a jar fitted with a lid, combine the dates and bourbon. Cover tightly and store in a dark place for 2 to 4 weeks. (The longer it sits, the sweeter it becomes.)

**2.** Strain, then pour through a coffee filter for clarity. Store in a sealed bottle or jar until ready to use.

*March 1, 2009*

LENELL SMOTHERS' PERFECT MANHATTAN

## CHAPTER 6

# THE MANHATTAN

# THE REAL MANHATTAN

## By JONATHAN MILES

The Manhattan is back.

Not back in fashion, I mean. That story is at least a decade old, and even then it wasn't much of a story. Unlike many other cocktails that have recently been roused from long hibernation, the Manhattan never really slumbered, having been kept drowsily awake through the lean years of cocktaildom by French-cuffed businessmen and other habitués of old-guard hotel bars and private clubs. But even those Manhattans—typically mixtures of bourbon or Canadian whiskey, bitters and vermouth finished off with the crimson syrup-grenade we call maraschino—aren't what I'm talking about.

No, I'm talking about the original Manhattan. The daring, woodsier Manhattan of the 1800s—when New York City was only Manhattan and its eponymous cocktail was the boss of all drinks. Back then, bartenders left out the gloppy maraschino cherries—those didn't arrive at our shores until 1900 or so—and made the drink exclusively with rye whiskey, bourbon's sharper-tongued cousin. (For an analogy, think of the difference between rye bread and corn bread). In all likelihood, that rye whiskey came from upstate New York, because, as Ralph Erenzo points out, "There were 1,200 distilleries operating in New York before Prohibition."

Mr. Erenzo should know. Along with his partner, Brian Lee, Mr. Erenzo is the proprietor of Tuthilltown Spirits, based out of a converted granary and 18th-century gristmill in Gardiner, N.Y., near New Paltz, that has yielded artisanal batches of bourbon, vodka and the sort of unaged corn whiskey sometimes referred to as moonshine.

The recipe that Tuthilltown's owners cleave to comes from LeNell Smothers, who owns LeNell's, a wine and spirits boutique in Red Hook, Brooklyn. Ms. Smothers is fond of what's called a "perfect Manhattan," so called for its balanced proportions of sweet and dry vermouth rather than any claim to immaculateness. Ms. Smothers has been a staunch proponent of Tuthilltown's products, which she admires for their Hudson Valley provenance and the pride and devotion Mr. Erenzo and Mr. Lee are pouring into them. "It's really exciting to see someone local doing this," she said. "They're shaking things up a bit."

In a sense, that is. The original Manhattan was always stirred.

PEN AND PENCIL BAR, NEW YORK CITY, 1964

## PERFECT MANHATTAN
Adapted from LeNELL SMOTHERS, LeNell's, Brooklyn

2 ounces Tuthilltown Hudson Manhattan
   rye whiskey
½ ounce sweet vermouth (preferably
   Vya or Carpano Antica)

½ ounce dry vermouth
2 dashes orange bitters
Lemon twist, for garnish

**1.** Stir together all ingredients except lemon twist in a glass shaker with ice.

**2.** Strain into a chilled cocktail glass. Garnish with the twist.

*April 29, 2007*

# ABC KITCHEN RYE WHISKEY MANHATTAN

## By ERIC ASIMOV

I'm sad to confess that any discussions I've had regarding one of my favorite cocktails, the Manhattan, generally center on the choice of whiskey. I love Manhattans in their original form, made with rye rather than with bourbon or blended whiskey. As for the other components, bitters and vermouth, well, they tend to fade from the picture.

Poor vermouth, so forgotten. It reminds me of one of my favorite lines in "Casablanca."

Ugarte: You despise me, don't you Rick? Rick: If I gave you any thought I probably would.

It took an absolutely delicious Manhattan that I had before dinner recently at the excellent new restaurant ABC Kitchen to bring vermouth into the discussion.

Clearly, I am not alone in taking vermouth for granted. But, sipping the ABC Kitchen Manhattan, I tasted firsthand how a good vermouth can give a cocktail a beautiful lift, while all the ingredients can contribute to a sense of delicious purity.

Of course, what makes this particular Manhattan so good is not merely the vermouth, but the combination of superb ingredients in it. In all aspects, ABC Kitchen emphasizes ingredients that are either local, organic, or raised or created with great care. Such an ethos is one thing for choosing foods and wine, but it's another

matter for cocktails. Bernard Sun, the beverage manager for Jean-Georges Management, who devised the cocktail selection, had his work cut out for him.

For the whiskey, I'm happy to say that Mr. Sun took the rye route rather than bourbon. Nothing against bourbon Manhattans, but I love the spicy, dancing-in-the-mouth sensation that comes from a good rye whiskey. Mr. Sun chose a relatively local product, McKenzie rye whiskey, from Finger Lakes Distilling in upstate New York. While he was not able to find a local vermouth, he did choose a great Italian one, Carpano Antica.

Vermouth is a lightly fortified wine that has been infused with a range of herbs and botanicals. Many of the more common industrial vermouths take on an indistinct medicinal quality, but with Carpano Antica, the herbal basis is clear and pure, with a light anise, almost licorice accent. This vermouth is delicious as an aperitif, served over ice, and superb in a Manhattan, as long as the other ingredients are up to snuff.

For Manhattans, that would leave two more items to consider. Most recipes call for Angostura bitters, which are decent enough, but Mr. Sun was looking for something a bit smoother and found that the signature spiciness of Fee Brothers Old Fashion bitters harmonized better with the rye and vermouth than did the Angostura with its more pronounced bitterness.

Finally, there was the issue of the typical Manhattan garnish, the loathsome maraschino cherry. Not wanting to adulterate his Manhattan with red dye, Mr. Sun chose instead to use brandied cherries, with a teaspoon of the juice for good measure. Mr. Sun calls for three cherries for a garnish, but I personally prefer fewer things floating in my cocktail, so I'd use just one.

The resulting cocktail is sleek, pure, breezy and scented with anise. In the mouth, it does a little Fred Astaire, courtesy of the rye, and it slides down easy.

To make this cocktail at home, feel free to substitute any of the ingredients, except the vermouth. In other words, the rye doesn't have to be from Finger Lakes, and if you can't find Fee Brothers bitters (they are really good), Angostura will do. But I highly recommend seeking out the Carpano Antica vermouth, to see how much of a difference a really good vermouth can make. Any that you don't use for Manhattans, drink as aperitifs over the following week.

## ABC KITCHEN RYE WHISKEY MANHATTAN

1½ ounces McKenzie rye whiskey
¾ ounce Carpano Antica vermouth
2 dashes Fee Brothers Old Fashion bitters

1 teaspoon brandied cherry juice
3 brandied cherries, for garnish

**1.** Combine all ingredients except cherries in a glass shaker with ice.

**2.** Stir for 30 seconds and strain into a martini glass. Garnish with cherries.

*July 16, 2010*

A MANHATTAN STRAIGHT UP, IN MEMORY OF FRANK

# MAKE MINE MANHATTAN

## By ROSIE SCHAAP

If the martini is the undisputed king of gin drinks, the Manhattan rules the whiskey ones. And though I'm utterly intransigent about how a good martini ought to be made, I'm flexible when it comes to the Manhattan. Even in its innumerable variations, the deep and dark character stays intact. With brown-liquor season upon us, it's the drink for right now.

That said, it's a cocktail that requires a whole host of decisions. Rye or bourbon? Perfect (composed with equal measures of sweet and dry vermouth), or just sweet vermouth? Bitters? Garnish? Rocks? My advice is to try the Manhattan every which way (just not all at once), because different versions suit different moods.

According to legend, the Manhattan was created some 140 years ago, at New York City's Manhattan Club, for a banquet held by Jennie Jerome, Winston Churchill's Brooklyn-born mother. This tale has been debunked, but I still like to think it's true, for the strong sense of time and place it suggests. I was born and raised in Manhattan, but it took a man from California to indoctrinate me into the cocktail's cult. In my 20s, I was an unabashed Irish whiskey partisan. Frank, whom I met in graduate school and later married, was, at 27, already a Manhattan man. I thought it was wonderfully dashing that he had a signature cocktail, and that he was always ready, at any bar, to place a confident order. Frank tended toward bourbon more than rye, but he was game to change it up.

He might have found his favorite at Quarter Bar, which opened in our neighborhood five years ago. David Moo, Quarter's proprietor, distinguishes his Manhattan largely by a painstaking preparation of the glass, whose interior he "paints" with Angostura bitters, using citrus peel as his brush, elevating the fruit and the bitters to the foreground. When Frank found out he had cancer, he asked his oncologist very earnestly if he might still enjoy a Manhattan every now and then. His doctor told him that was just fine. I first drank Manhattans in Frank's company, and now I drink them in his honor, just as I did at Quarter Bar soon after he passed away in 2010.

For me the Manhattan will always—more than any place, or any time—summon memories of a person. They're overwhelmingly happy memories, always accompanied by a toast, with love and remembrance.

## THE SOUTHERN SLOPE
By JULIE REINER, Clover Club, Brooklyn

*This recipe is a bourbon Manhattan, sweetened up with apricot and smoothed out with vermouth. It's a strong one, and it goes down easily.*

2 ounces Basil Hayden's bourbon
¾ ounce Punt e Mes Italian vermouth
½ ounce apricot liqueur

2 dashes Angostura bitters
1 Luxardo cherry

1. Stir together all ingredients except cherry over ice.

2. Strain into a rocks glass over fresh ice and garnish with a Luxardo cherry.

*October 7, 2012*


## MOO'S MANHATTAN
By DAVID MOO, Quarter Bar, New York City

2½ ounces Old Overholt rye whiskey
½ ounce Martini & Rossi sweet vermouth
½ ounce Carpano Antica Formula

3 dashes Angostura bitters
1 (1-by-3-inch) slice lemon peel
1 (1-by-3-inch) slice orange peel
1 brandied cherry

1. Pour all ingredients except peels and cherry into a mixing glass. Add ice and stir for 30 seconds.

2. Prepare the glass: Add another dash of Angostura to a chilled coupe. Twist the lemon and orange peels directly over the coupe. Vigorously rub the peels inside the coupe, then discard them. Add 1 brandied cherry.

3. Strain the liquid into the prepared glass.

*October 7, 2012*


## BILL SAMUELS JR.'S HOUSE MANHATTAN
By Bill Samuels Jr., Maker's Mark

1½ ounces Maker's Mark
¾ ounce Dolin Rouge (sweet vermouth)

2 shakes Fee Bros. Cherry Bitters
1 bar spoon "juice" from a
    jar of maraschino cherries

1. Stir together all ingredients with ice in a mixing glass.

2. Strain into a cocktail glass.

## SHARKEY'S PERFECT MANHATTAN
By MICHAEL SHARKEY

YIELD: 2 DRINKS

4 ounces Bulleit rye

1 bottlecapfull each: dry & sweet
vermouth (Dolin in both cases)

2 or 3 dashes Angostura bitters

**1.** Shake all ingredients with ice until good and frothy.

**2.** Strain into two cocktail glasses.

Michael garnishes with a twist of lemon in the summer, but in cooler months he likes to include a couple of brandied cherries, in which case he adds a drop of the liqueur from the jar.

*October 5, 2012*

# I'LL TAKE MANHATTAN (BROOKLYN, TOO)
## By THOMAS VINCIGUERRA

Now that New York is seeing renovation left and right, with a freshly minted Grand Central Terminal and the once-derelict Times Square so crowded no one goes there anymore (as Yogi Berra may or may not have said about Toots Shor's), how about the island's signature cocktail? What happened to the Manhattan? How come it has taken so long to get a face lift?

A bar standard in the 1940s and 1950s, the drink languished for years, along with most other whisky-based concoctions in a health-and-hangover-conscious America that favored the gentler touch of light beer, wine and vodka. But a more alcoholically robust generation has recently rejected such tentativeness and is imbibing so-called classic cocktails anew, updated versions of the Manhattan among them.

"I'm seeing people in their 20s drink Manhattans," said Paul Pacult, a co-host of "The Happy Hour," a weekly radio show on WEVD-AM that is the "Car Talk" of the drinks world. "When I'm in a restaurant and I hear a bar call for a Manhattan specifying what they want in it, it kind of pricks up your ears."

A traditional Manhattan consists of rye whisky, sweet vermouth, bitters and a maraschino cherry. Sometimes called the whisky martini, it has benefited from the retro chic that has brought martini bars and their attendant veneer of smartness back into vogue.

Certainly a Manhattan is its own experience. Whereas a martini is celebratory and chrome-plated, a Manhattan is nostalgic, like a black-and-white movie. It is a cocktail noir: sip one long enough and its rich, dark retrospection will evoke double-breasted suits and Bakelite telephones with Butterfield 8 exchanges (the Lady in Red is optional).

One reason for the revival is that the current taste for single-malt Scotches has spun off into interest in premium bourbons. And bourbon, being sweeter than Scotch, complements sweet vermouth.

When Andrea Immer, beverage director of Windows on the World, created her Greater Manhattan drink for the reopening of the restaurant, she used bourbon for rye and substituted Harvey's Bristol Cream sherry for vermouth.

For those few who prefer their Manhattans dry, or "perfect" (a traditional designation meaning that the vermouth portion should be half sweet and half dry), Lori Montfort, a manager at Alva on East 22d Street, chose merlot instead of vermouth. The result—with one part merlot and three parts Maker's Mark bourbon plus a dash of bitters—is both dry and dark, so for a bit of brightness, Ms. Montfort uses a lemon peel instead of a cherry.

The linchpin of the Manhattan is the bitters, said Gary Regan, the other host of "The Happy Hour." "They bring together the herbal aspects of the vermouth and the forthrightness of the whisky and point up the best aspects of both."

David Marsden, the bar manager at City Hall, a new restaurant on Duane Street in TriBeCa, calls a good Manhattan the test of a good bartender. "It should taste like rainwater," Mr. Marsden said, "a silky, soft, very mel-low flavor from beginning to end."

Now, fair is fair. At least two other boroughs have namesake drinks: the Brooklyn, an obscure combination of rye, dry vermouth, maraschino and Amer Picon (a kind of bitters) and the somewhat better-known Bronx, composed of gin, sweet and dry vermouth and orange juice. But those are frankly also-rans.

For people in many parts of the country for whom New York is a distant fantasy rather than daily reality, a drink called Manhattan becomes a kind of totem. Rex Roberts, who now lives in Brooklyn, grew up in John O'Hara country, Schuylkill County, Pennsylvania. For him, back in the early '70s, partaking of a Manhattan at age 18 was a worldly rite of passage. "It was the first mixed drink I ever had," he recalled. "When I bellied up to the bar, I ordered a Manhattan because I loved the name, and I had always been in love with the idea of moving to New York. I was awed by the aura of the city. I drank them for quite some time without knowing what was in them."

Legend has it that the Manhattan was first concocted at the Manhattan Club in 1874. The drink is very much a product of the Gilded Age, favored by the likes of J. P. Morgan. In those days, bartenders made liberal use of vermouth, which had only recently been imported to America. The sweet or "Italian" variety, especially, reflected the tastes of the late 19th century, when sugar syrup was common in cocktails. And in the Northeast, at any rate, whisky usually meant rye.

But straight rye was a casualty of

Prohibition, when it was overtaken by Canadian spirits smuggled across the border. (Using Scotch, of course, yields a Rob Roy.)

In postwar America, the Manhattan was known as a women's drink. "A Manhattan was more palatable than a martini," Dale DeGroff, the beverage director of the Rainbow Room, said. "It had a sweetness and a roundness to it—and a cherry. It was seemly and proper."

Back in the Manhattan's first heyday, it was usually served on the rocks and in an old-fashioned glass. The drink now often finds itself strained into a martini glass to highlight its complex color. "If somebody wants ice," Mr. Marsden of City Hall said, "I can tell you it's somebody's mother or grandmother."

Karen King, wine director of the Union Square Cafe, says she is "very attached" to the Manhattan straight up.

"It's almost a piece of art to me," she said. "It's an accessory, like a nice pair of earrings—it looks lovely with the cherry bouncing around in there and the light shining down on the glass."

The secret to fully appreciating a traditional Manhattan, or today's variations on the theme, is that it should, if possible, be consumed on the island itself.

What makes the difference? Could it be that rumbling of the subway underfoot—or is it those taxi fumes in the air?

## THE GREATER MANHATTAN
**By ANDREA IMMER, Windows on the World, New York City**
YIELD: 2 DRINKS

| | |
|---|---|
| 5½ ounces Maker's Mark bourbon | 5 dashes Angostura bitters |
| 1½ ounces Harvey's Bristol Cream | 1 maraschino cherry, for garnish |

**1.** Stir all ingredients except cherry with ice, and strain into a martini glass.

**2.** Garnish with a maraschino cherry.

## THE "PERFECT" DUBONNET MANHATTAN
**By BOB ALBRIGHT, Le Cirque, New York City**
YIELD: 2 DRINKS

| | |
|---|---|
| 6 ounces Knob Creek bourbon | Dash bitters, optional |
| 1 ounce red Dubonnet | Twist of lemon, for garnish |
| 1 ounce white Dubonnet | |

**1.** Shake all ingredients except twist of lemon with ice.

**2.** Strain into a martini glass and garnish with a twist of lemon.

## THE EASTERN MANHATTAN
By DALE DeGROFF, Inagiku at the Waldorf Astoria, New York City
YIELD: 2 DRINKS

| | |
|---|---|
| 4 ounces Suntory Royale whisky | 1 ounce sweet vermouth |
| ½ ounce Ricard or Pernod | Maraschino cherry, for garnish |

**1.** Stir all ingredients except cherry with ice, and strain into a cocktail glass.

**2.** Garnish with a maraschino cherry.

*October 21, 1998*

# A CLASSIC COCKTAIL WITH A THAI TWIST
## By JEFF GORDINIER

Maybe you're not the kind of drinker who leaps to the assumption that a spirit—rye, for instance—can be made even better if the bartender just keeps dumping in more ingredients.

A wrist-flick of bitters and a slug of Italian vermouth, as in a manhattan? Absolutely. A "flavor profile" so byzantine that it would perplex Marco Polo? Eh, you wonder. Is that really necessary?

But I went against that inclination the other night, and I'm glad I did. My friend Geraint and I were getting dinner at Kin Shop, and because I've been drawn to a variety of manhattans lately (the cold weather, etc.), and because I'm a fan of massaman curry (which at least a few eaters out there consider the best dish a human being can consume—even better than Peking duck or chocolate), I ordered a drink called the Massa[man]hattan.

A curried manhattan, you think. Can that work? In this case, it does.

It was delicious enough that I wanted another. Created by Julia Travis, the beverage director at Kin Shop, the Massa[man]hattan struck me as a small, sweet triumph of balance.

In fact it was only later, after the restaurant had sent along the recipe, that I realized the syrup that's swirled in with the rye, bitters and sweet vermouth is a rather complex concoction involving cloves, nutmeg, coriander, cinnamon and cardamom pods. It hadn't tasted especially (or annoyingly) complex when I was sipping it. It had just tasted right—like a manhattan that had come back from a barely remembered bender in Bangkok.

Yes, there's effort involved, and a slightly higher degree of difficulty than I'm used to, but I'm tempted to make a Massa[man]hattan on New Year's Eve. It's not impossible that a few of our readers will be drinking that night, too, so if you want to give it a try, here's the recipe.

## MASSA[MAN]HATTAN
By JULIA TRAVIS

2 ounces Old Overholt Rye
¾ ounces Vya Sweet Vermouth
¾ ounces Massaman Syrup
(recipe follows)

Angostura bitters
Piece of orange rind

**1.** Combine rye, vermouth and syrup over ice. Stir for 30 seconds, or until very well chilled.

**2.** Strain into a lowball glass. Top with four dashes of bitters. Garnish with a nickel-sized coin of orange rind.


## MASSAMAN SYRUP
YIELD: 1 QUART

1 tablespoon ground mace
5 sticks cinnamon
2 tablespoons coriander
6 whole cardamom pods

15 cloves
2 nutmegs
2 cups dark brown sugar
2 cups water

**1.** Combine all spices in a saucepan over low heat. Toast lightly for a few minutes.

**2.** Add sugar and water and bring contents to a boil. Once boiling, turn the heat off and allow the mixture to steep for at least two hours.

**3.** Strain the contents through a sieve to remove solids, and pour into an airtight container. Syrup will keep for up to two weeks in the refrigerator.

*December 30, 2011*


## THE BITTER DARLING
By ROSIE SCHAPP

2 ounces Bulleit Rye
1 ounce freshly-squeezed clementine juice
½ ounce ginger syrup

Angostura bitters, to taste (I like several dashes)
Twist of clementine peel, for garnish

**1.** Shake all ingredients except clementine peel vigorously with ice.

**2.** Strain into a small chilled coupe. Garnish with twists of clementine peel.

*December 21, 2011*

## RUM MANHATTAN
### Adapted from RONERIA CARACAS, Brooklyn, by Jonathan Miles

2 ounces aged rum (such as Diplomático Reserva)

1 ounce Carpano Antica Formula vermouth

½ ounce bay leaf reduction (recipe follows)

Dash of Angostura bitters

Bay leaf, for garnish

Marinated blueberries, for garnish (see note)

Flamed orange peel (optional)

**1.** Combine the rum, vermouth, bay leaf reduction and bitters in a mixing glass with ice, and stir thoroughly.

**2.** Strain into a chilled cocktail glass, then add the bay leaf and several blueberries.

**3.** To flame the orange peel into the drink, cut a thumb-size wedge of peel from an orange. Holding a lighted match or lighter in one hand, squeeze the orange peel with the other hand over the flame so that the oils ignite as they pass through the flame. (This can require practice; an unflamed twist of orange will also suffice.)

**At Roneria Caracas, the blueberries are marinated in a mixture of rum and Marsala wine, refrigerated, for about five days.**

## BAY LEAF REDUCTION

**1.** Combine several bay leaves with boiling water (about 4 leaves per ¼ cup water) and let steep overnight or preferably longer, up to two days. Strain and cool before using.

*December 13, 2009*

# MAKE MINE A SULLY: A COCKTAIL TRIBUTE
## By MICHAEL WILSON

Sure, he has been called a hero. And his act of cool-headed bravery one year ago was nothing short of a miracle. But one honor may have passed Capt. Chesley B. Sullenberger III like a jet floating down the river: a cocktail in his name.

Until now.

There was the joke last year that made the rounds—twp shots of Grey Goose and a splash of water. But we here at City Room—fans of Sully and cocktails both—sought to create a definitive Sully drink to ring in the first anniversary of the river landing of US Airways Flight 1549 in the Hudson River. The only requirement was that the finished product do honor to its name.

We consulted Dale DeGroff, the so-called King of Cocktails. He thought about it and concocted a drink that has it all—heft, strength and clarity, served chilled—and leaves the imbiber with perhaps a warm sliver of the euphoria of finding oneself standing, unharmed, on the wing of a jet.

We hustled the recipe straight to Keens Steakhouse on West 36th Street, where Tim McBride, 35, the spirits buyer, smiled with admiration at Mr. DeGroff's choice of ingredients.

"It's a Manhattan—with a splash," Mr. McBride said.

Mr. DeGroff described the drink in an e-mail message: "A sweet Manhattan with a float of Champagne on top...the Manhattan for obvious reasons, but on the sweet side! And the float of Champagne to rejoice that the thing floated and didn't sink!"

Mr. McBride created the Sully and poured it into a martini glass. The sparkle and sweetness of the wine played brilliantly off the bitters and the one-to-one ratio of the liquors. It was delicious.

Here's to you, Sully.

Happy anniversary.

## THE SULLY
### By Dale DeGroff

*"A cocktail celebrating the combination of skill, luck and physics."*

- 1½ ounces rye whiskey (Keens used Sazerac)
- 1½ ounces Martini & Rossi sweet vermouth
- 1 dash Angostura bitters, "because life is bittersweet . . . luckily in this case more sweet than bitter"
- 1 float of the best Champagne you can afford
- 1 Manhattan cherry

**1.** Stir the rye, vermouth and bitters with ice to chill, and strain into a chilled cocktail glass. Top carefully with the Champagne, ensuring that it floats on top of the cocktail.

**2.** Drink the Champagne off the top of the drink first, and then slide a cherry to the bottom of the glass. Down she goes.

*January 15, 2010*

A VODKA MARTINI WITH A TWIST, 1975

CHAPTER 7

# THE
# MARTINI

# CAMPAIGN SOLVES AT LEAST ONE ISSUE

## By JEREMY W. PETERS

I wasn't prepared to find martini perfection in a Cedar Rapids, Iowa, strip mall.

Maybe my excitement had something to do with low expectations. Or maybe it was the long workday, which closed with a two-hour "Faith, Family and Freedom" town hall hosted by Rick Santorum. He is not known for brevity.

But with that first sip from the bar at Vino's Ristorante, it didn't matter where I was. This was an exceptional gin martini. It was cold, clean and crisp, shaken just enough so there was a small island of ice shavings floating at the top. The pour was generous but not too much so, stopping just short of the lip of the glass so none would spill over.

The gin, Boodles, was an unexpected find in a restaurant sharing a parking lot with a Play It Again Sports and Godfather's Pizza. I rarely come across Boodles, an airy 90.4-proof British spirit with a hint of coriander, at bars in Manhattan. So when the waitress listed it as one of the options among the more conventional brands like Tanqueray and Bombay Sapphire, I couldn't say no.

At $9, the price was right. I'd easily paid $10 more than that for a martini in some hotel bars.

I had my Vino's martini two days into a bold reportorial experiment. As a political correspondent for this newspaper, I decided as part of my campaign-trail duty to sample as many martinis across the country as I could, mostly after working hours.

The Republican primary calendar took me from Iowa to New Hampshire, then to South Carolina, Florida and on to Michigan. That's where I had my final martini in this self-assigned project, an expertly poured Beefeater one. It was a simple and satisfying number from the Motor Bar in the handsomely restored Westin Book Cadillac in downtown Detroit.

What I would come to discover over the course of this two-month assignment is that the martini is a blessedly stateless entity, created equally well in the shakers of bartenders from Manchester, N.H., to Miami. Maybe it spoke to my utter lack of sophistication, but as long as the proportions were right, as long the bartender understood the word "dry," I was happy.

For the sake of sample consistency, my order was always the same: one gin martini, very dry, shaken, with a twist. I wasn't partial to any particular gin, though I found myself mostly ordering Hendrick's, a cucumber- and rose-infused Scottish brand that has become to gin what Grey Goose is to vodka in most bars: the ubiquitous top-shelf brand. When I was in the mood for something with a more unadorned taste, I would go for Beefeater or Plymouth, if it was available.

Not that there weren't the occasional mixological mishaps. At the bar at the downtown Des Moines Marriott, my martini arrived with a lemon twist and olives. A restaurant in New Hampshire served an editor friend of mine his martini in a wineglass. It did not stop him from gulping it down.

Then there was the time in a Sioux City, Iowa, hotel bar when a columnist from another publication ordered a martini and the bartender looked at him utterly stumped. She had been on the job just a few weeks, she said, lowering her head. Luckily, she was both patient and gracious enough to follow his meticulous instructions: fill a shaker with ice, put in half a capful of vermouth and top it off with Beefeater. We made out just fine.

Many purists insist that the vodka concoctions popular with martini drinkers today are an affront to the drink's heritage. The one true way to drink a martini, they say, is with gin and dry vermouth.

I always opt for shaken over stirred, not out of any homage to James Bond, but because as a practical matter shaking makes the drink colder. And some bartenders will tell you the bruising that occurs when the ice smashes around helps release more flavor. Of course some will tell you the opposite, that bruising is a bad idea.

Over the course of my travels, some bartenders got a little carried away with the shaking. They shattered so much ice that you ended up with a drink more resembling a 7-Eleven Slurpee than something fit for Winston Churchill. His signature beverage, as lore has it, was gin, no vermouth, served icy cold. Instead of vermouth, which became scarce during World War II, he would bow in the direction of France.

I found my request for very dry martinis mostly heeded. At Soby's, a modern Southern-cuisine restaurant in downtown Greenville, S.C., the bartender said to me: "Very dry. So do you even want me to look at the bottle of vermouth?" Excellent question.

And to make my sample as broad as possible, I ordered in as many different kinds of establishments as I could, aiming for the ideal mix of high and low. In South Carolina, I headed for the Thoroughbred Club at the famed Charleston Place hotel, a monument to old world Southern decadence, where I bumped into Newt and Callista Gingrich late on the Friday night before he pulled off a 12-point victory in the South Carolina primary.

He insisted the conversation he gamely struck up with me and my partner, Brendan, be off the record. But I feel no betrayal of journalistic ethics by reporting that his drink of choice appeared to be Scotch on the rocks, while Ms. Gingrich gingerly sipped a hearty pour of white wine.

It was a different setting entirely from the bar in the north concourse at the Omaha airport, where I was given Bombay in a nine-ounce plastic cup. While I might have been able to quibble with the presentation, I couldn't complain about the liquid contents.

The bartender who poured me a

Plymouth martini at the Loews Don CeSar in St. Pete Beach, Fla., came closest to summing up the drink wisdom revealed in my two-month investigation.

I complimented her on a job well done. There was no violent jostling of the shaker, just a gentle rattling for 20 seconds or so that left my drink cold enough to the last sip. To ensure it was dry, she poured a little vermouth into an empty, chilled glass and then shook it out, leaving just the traces.

"It's so simple," she said. "But then again people mess up simple all the time."

*February 28, 2012*

# THE MARTINI PRINCIPLES
## By WILLIAM L. HAMILTON

The martini doesn't need me. It is the world's most famous cocktail, and likely to remain so. But it's lucky to have people like Dale DeGroff and John Conti.

Mr. DeGroff is a celebrity bartender and an authority on mixology, the self-styled "King of Cocktails," Lord of the Ring-a-ding-ding. He looks a little like George Clooney, and calls his wife "baby."

Mr. DeGroff is teaching a "cocktail college" at the Marriott Marquis on Broadway, one class a month on categories of drinks. Last month's class, the first, was on the martini. I called Mr. DeGroff and asked him if he had had a star pupil and he said "yes" without hesitation.

It was John Conti. Mr. Conti sat front and center and took notes.

I drove to Pawling, N.Y., where Mr. Conti lives with his wife, Ann, and two teenage children. I was eager to meet him and to have him make me a martini. Mr. Conti, a postal worker, was set up in his kitchen at the counter, where he pours. His wife and children were at church.

Mr. Conti embodies the interest in cocktails. I was reminded of Ray Bradbury's novel "Fahrenheit 451," set in a future in which books are banned and burned. People memorize books, word for word, to save them. If there is ever another Prohibition, Mr. Conti will be walking around with a perfect martini inside him. The oral tradition, nicely iced.

"You got it," Mr. Conti said, taking position, when I asked him to make me a drink.

The two questions to answer about the martini are the ratio of gin to vermouth, and how to mix it—to shake or stir. Mr. Conti uses a 6 to 1 measure and stirs.

"If you like it drier, you need it drier," he said, as if it were an adjustment to medication. Mr. Conti put ice and water into a martini glass to chill it, then put ice into a bartender's glass and poured his measures over it. He stirred with a long-necked spoon, bent slightly so that it would follow the sides of the glass, a trick he learned from Mr. DeGroff.

"You slide the spoon down and twirl, as opposed to agitating," he said. "The whole idea of a martini is a smooth drink. Agitation introduces air."

Mr. Conti emptied the martini glass, and strained his cocktail into it in a circular motion, so that the liquid wouldn't splash, then dropped a pitted green olive into it.

The martini was excellent. Mr. Conti, who appeared to get as much pleasure from making it as I got from tasting it, reached across the drink and shook my hand, beaming.

"When you're at the bar, you're connecting," he said. "The guy says, 'How would you like it?' And you watch, and he's making yours for you, to really enjoy. People are happy—and it's good to be a part of some happiness."

I agree. Cheers.

---

## THE MARTINI
### Adapted from JOHN CONTI

| | |
|---|---|
| 3 ounces gin | Green olive, for garnish |
| ½ ounce dry vermouth | |

**1.** Chill a 7-ounce martini glass by filling with ice and water. Fill a professional bartender's glass, or a tall 16-ounce glass, two-thirds full with ice.

**2.** Add gin and vermouth to the bartender's glass, and stir with a long-necked spoon, keeping the spoon close to the side of the glass as you swirl the ice.

**3.** Stir until the glass frosts, about 20 seconds. Empty the martini glass, and strain the contents of the bartender's glass into it. Garnish with olive.

*October 26, 2003*

# THE MARTINI: STIRRED, SHAKEN OR EATEN

## By FLORENCE FABRICANT

This is the age of the mutant martini. Drinks called martinis now have sake and cucumber in them. Or cranberry juice. Or creme de cacao and a chocolate kiss. Whatever happened to your basic gin with vermouth?

People who would not dream of indulging in a three-martini lunch now thrill at the sight of a multiple-martini menu. Mercury, a Miami Beach restaurant, has a list of 29 martinis. Some of them, like the South Beach (Campari, amaretto and orange juice), have nothing to do with a martini except for the glass. The Lenox Room, Pravda, the Four Seasons Hotel and, of course, Martini's, all in Manhattan, are just a few of the places that have introduced inventive martini lists.

But there is a catch. "What they think are martinis are not really martinis," Dale DeGroff, the beverage manager of the Rainbow Room complex, said of modern-day martini drinkers.

The Art Deco sophistication of the Rainbow Room, along with other high-living trappings of the '30s, '40s and '50s (thick steaks, Guerlain's Shalimar perfume and cigar smoking, to name three), have helped to fuel the martini renaissance. "They're drinking martinis and smoking cigars, even though the two don't go together," Mr. DeGroff said. "The martini is definitely a cigarette drink."

Or maybe a cigarette-holder drink.

"You look so much more glamorous holding a martini glass than a glass of white wine," said Patricia Barroll, a vice president of Carillon, importers of vodka and gin.

Does it matter what is in the glass? Hard-core purists, the same people who shudder at the thought of hazelnut-raspberry coffee or who would not be caught sipping a frozen banana margarita, insist on what is considered the classic formula: gin and dry vermouth (proportions according to taste), straight up, with a pitted olive or perhaps a twist.

Stirred or shaken? Oh, please. The stir-shaken issue, popularized by the James Bond films of the 1960s, is a red herring (at the rate things are going, somebody is bound to experiment with a red herring martini). For Bond himself might even be culpable for what has happened to the martini. He preferred vodka, not gin.

Once the cocktail crowd wanted their martinis with vodka, a neutral spirit that lacks the distinctive–some say medicinal–juniper flavor of gin, there was no turning back.

"You can do more with vodka than with gin," said Monika Caha, the chef and owner of Candy Bar and Grill, a new restaurant in Chelsea, where a dozen creative martinis account for about 70 percent of the cocktails sold. "Inventing a new drink is as much fun as inventing a new sauce. But gin is too strongly flavored and would fight other ingredients. Besides, most Americans do not like the taste of gin. They prefer vodka. We sell 10 times more vodka than gin."

Unlike many traditional cocktails whose recipes are more or less fixed, the martini, a drink with poorly documented origins that suggest it may have been invented before the turn of the century, has long been a moving target. It took decades for the martini to achieve its distinctive dryness, no more than 1 part vermouth to 5 parts gin, and often 1 to 15, or merely a wave of the open vermouth bottle over the glass of gin. Long before bartenders started in with creme de cacao, the vermouth that was used was sweet, not dry.

The martini has also grown. Ken Aretsky, an owner of Patroon, a clubby new restaurant in midtown Manhattan, said, "Not only are martinis big, they are also big." Old-timers who remember a four-ounce drink in a five-ounce glass would not recognize the modern martini. Like caffe lattes, bagels and portions of pasta, martinis have become oversize.

"There was a time, maybe six years ago, when we couldn't even sell a seven-and-a-half-ounce glass because the restaurants said it was too large," said Susan Friend, an owner of Friend & Company, which is the United States representative for the German glassware maker Schott Zwiesel. "Now they want 10- and 12-ounce glasses."

## SAKETINI
Adapted from MIREZI, New York City

> 1 to 2 ounces Chung Ha Korean sake (other types of clear sake can be substituted)
>
> 4 to 5 ounces Tanqueray vodka
> 1 slice cucumber, unpeeled, for garnish

**1.** Combine sake and vodka in cocktail shaker partly filled with ice. Shake briefly. Or stir briefly in a pitcher containing ice. Proportions of sake and vodka can be adjusted.

**2.** Strain into a chilled martini glass, and garnish with cucumber.

## JAMES BOND MARTINI
Adapted from MERCHANTS, New York City

> 1½ ounces Smirnoff vodka
> 1½ ounces Tanqueray gin
> ½ ounce Lillet blanc
>
> ½ ounce Martini & Rossi extra-dry vermouth
> Twist of lemon peel, for garnish

**1.** Combine vodka, gin, vermouth and Lillet in a cocktail shaker partly filled with ice. Shake briefly. Or stir briefly in a pitcher containing ice.

**2.** Strain into a chilled martini glass, and garnish with lemon peel.

*December 4, 1996*

# CONTINENTAL DRIFT AND THE MARTINI

## By JONATHAN MILES

For that vocal slice of Americans fearing that the country is moving toward some kind of European model, here's one more smidgen of evidence: A variety of American martini, distinguished for decades from its European counterpart by a different formula of Noilly Prat vermouth, is no more.

From the early 1960s until now, Noilly Prat, which is based in Marseillan, France, produced a dry vermouth tailored to the American palate—drier, more masculine, and so pale that it all but disappeared into the diamond hue of a martini. This American version was just that: a variation exported exclusively to the United States and Canada.

Beginning last year, however, Noilly Prat started phasing out the American blend and replacing it, "New Coke" style, with the original European formula. And here you thought your martini, at the very least, was safe from globalization's steady creep.

"The flavor has become more earthy than it used to be," said Ben Ward, the head bartender at Libation, a Lower East Side restaurant and nightclub.

But Mr. Ward was unaware, until very recently, that the change had even occurred, which speaks to dry vermouth's tenuous standing in the stateside drinking world. It's used so sparingly that for many, the change is all but imperceptible. "It's kind of the forgotten liquor," Mr. Ward said.

"The trend, after Prohibition, was to put less and less vermouth in a martini," said Ludovic Miazga of Noilly Prat on a recent visit to New York City.

The original martini was a vermouth-heavy blend, ranging from a one-to-one to one-to-three ratio of vermouth to gin. When the "dry" martini became fashionable, in the 1940s, vermouth took a beating.

Winston Churchill's martini recipe set the tone: Pour some gin into a mixing glass, and take a quick glance at an unopened bottle of vermouth.

In the United States, where the dry martini came to define an era, Noilly Prat tried to beat back the trend by reformulating its product in the '60s—lightening the color, for one thing, to disguise its presence in the glass.

To slight avail, however. "It slowly vanished from the cocktail," Mr. Miazga said.

But that's changing. Dry vermouth may still be, as Mr. Miazga admits, a "declining category," but the cocktail renaissance has caused its fortunes to rise, or at the very least stabilize. Bartenders, lionizing authenticity, are returning to wetter martinis.

Mr. Ward, for instance, last week introduced, on Libation's cocktail list, a martini that's about as wet as it gets—the Upside-Down Martini, which, in a nice bit of pop-culture dovetailing, happened to be Julia Child's favorite cocktail. It's one part gin to five parts vermouth.

"It's a great, crisp summer drink," Mr. Ward said. It's also much closer in spirit to the way dry vermouth is consumed in Europe—as a solo aperitif, rather than a meek cocktail modifier.

As to those drinkers miffed that their uniquely American martini has now, however subtly, been sucked into the cocktail category of the One World Order, Mr. Miazga was sanguine: "You will always have disappointed, nostalgic customers."

## UPSIDE-DOWN MARTINI
### Adapted from LIBATION, New York City

¾ ounce gin
3¾ ounces Noilly Prat vermouth

Lemon twist, for garnish

**1.** Combine the gin and vermouth in a mixing glass with ice and stir.

**2.** Strain into a chilled cocktail glass and garnish with the lemon twist. (Alternatively, you can serve it on the rocks; combine the ingredients in a rocks glass with ice, garnish and serve.)

*August 16, 2009*

# ROMANCE IN A GLASS

## By WILLIAM L. HAMILTON

I stopped into the rustic little bar at Fleur de Sel the other night to celebrate the Liberation—the news last week, published in a study in The New England Journal of Medicine, that drinking often is good for you. Dr. Kenneth Mukamal of the Harvard Medical School, who directed the study, speculated that regular, moderate drinking thins the blood, which reduces the risk of heart attack by about a third.

Thank you, Dr. Mukamal, from the bottom of my glass.

I chose a French martini to greet my freedom from worry, guilt and doubt—a drink with the pink of health. A French martini is typically a vodka martini, with the addition of Chambord Liqueur Royale de France, a black raspberry Cognac liqueur that also includes citrus, cinnamon, vanilla and French acacia honey.

It is bottled in a spherical decanter with a crown for a cap, which looks like a cross between the pope's private stock and a Haitian church altar ornament. Recalling the French Riviera more than the Sun King, Chambord is also a feature of Sex on the Beach.

Because of a soft, not a spirited, edge, the French martini has a double appeal as a cocktail and as an aperitif. Variations incorporate Lillet, and a variety of fruit juices like pineapple. I have it on some authority, from a rearrived ex-pat, that the drink was popular a few years ago in Paris, on the bar row of the Rue de Lappe.

The French martini can also be served as a "shooter" called an Adrenaline. A shooter is a shot-glass-based cocktail, meant to do business quickly. Au revoir and out.

At Fleur de Sel, a restaurant on East 20th Street, the French martini has a fan of mandolin-thin green apple slices lining the glass, as in a tart pan.

What Ratha Chau, the general manager, called a cappuccino of frothed French cider graces the drink at the surface, poured as a flourish from a second shaker.

The cocktail has a classic, if quiet, taste, with a too-many-cooks quality to the presentation. I would lose the pie and the pond scum. The appearance of a drink's liquid is the sum total of its elegance in a glass, and you want to see it. The French martini is Chanel pink—don't squander opportunities like that.

I swung by a liquor store, picked up a mini-orb of Chambord, headed home and tried making my own. I ramped up the vodka, to stiffen the pastel in the palate, and topped the cocktail with a splash of sparkling cider, to give it effervescence without a cloud. I left its jewel-like color to speak for itself.

It talked tough like a martini. But it was in the language of love.

## FRENCH MARTINI
Adapted from FLEUR DE SEL, New York City

Thinly sliced green apples
Pinch of fleur de sel
1 ounce vodka

¼ ounce Chambord Liqueur Royale de France
Splash of pineapple juice
Splash of apple cider

**1.** Line martini glass with green apples, with the skins coated with fleur de sel.

**2.** Mix vodka, Chambord and juice in a shaker with ice and chill.

**3.** Strain into glass. Shake cider till it foams and pour on top.

*January 19, 2003*

## APPLE MARTINI
Adapted from H.K., New York City

5 ounces vodka
2 ounces Berentzen apple liqueur

1 ounce Midori melon liqueur
slice of green apple, for garnish

**1.** Combine all ingredients except apple in a shaker with ice and shake until chilled.

**2.** Strain into an 8-ounce martini glass, and garnish with apple.

*January 4, 2004*

## THE DIRTY JANE
By GLENN HARRIS, Jane, New York City

2 ounces Ketel One vodka
1 ounce liquid from pickled green tomatoes

Thin wedge of a pickled green tomato, for garnishing the rim

**1.** Combine vodka and pickling liquid in a shaker filled with ice and shake.

**2.** Strain into a chilled martini glass and garnish with tomato wedge.

*October 27, 2002*

# MAKE MINE ORGANIC

## By JONATHAN MILES

Really, an organic martini? The point of the organic movement is to rid produce and other ingestibles of potentially harmful chemicals, but isn't the theory behind liquor to turn produce into, well, a potentially harmful chemical?

Still, it's hard to imagine a more congenial way of saving the world than sipping an eco-friendly cocktail, which may be why organic spirits—those distilled from grains, fruit or sugarcane that's been certified organic—are inching their way behind the bars of a few of the city's more crunchy establishments. Mas, in the West Village, offers an array of organic drinks, including a Champagne cocktail, made with Champagne, lump sugar soaked with house-made orange bitters, and pomegranate (all organic), while those having brunch at Josie's Restaurant and Bar in Murray Hill can cleanly kick-start the day with an organic Bloody Mary or spike some squeezed juice with a shot of organic vodka.

The epicenter of organic cocktails, however, is the bar at Counter, an East Village vegetarian-slash-vegan bistro that's been slinging all-organic drinks—and nothing but—since adding hard liquor to its menu a few months back. Deborah Gavito, an owner, explained: "Everything on my menu is organic. If I served meat, it would be organic. So why shouldn't our martinis be organic?"

The bartender, Joe McCanta, who helped concoct the restaurant's signature drinks, brings an earthy classicism to these creations, updating old lounge standards like the French Martini and Bloodhound with herbal-infused Rain vodka and organic fruit nectars. "The hardest part is finding organic mixers," he said. "We're looking for an organic Triple Sec now." Mr. McCanta's swoop of spiky hair belies his second career as keyboardist for garage glam rockers Semi-Precious-Weapons. Counter's Married in a Fever, a red wine-poached pear nectar mixed with smoked pear-infused vodka, packs a sweetly charred flavor, which Mr. McCanta admits was the point. "We couldn't find a scotch that was organic," he said. "But I like that smoky taste, and wanted to find a way to recreate that." The alcoholic equivalent of a tofu burger? Maybe. But an awfully good tofu burger.

The ascetic vibe of most vegetarian restaurants doesn't lend itself to vivacious cocktailing, which is why Counter, and its un-self-righteous drinks list, feels so refreshing. One's antenna doesn't pick up the low rumble of incipient activism, nor must one navigate through clouds of patchouli en route to the rest room. All of which is to say that, as Counter evidences, an organic cocktail needn't come with a sidecar of wheatgrass. After the second drink it's easy to forget you're saving the world.

It's pleasant nonetheless to be reminded, which is maybe why I took such a shine to Counter's Dirtiest Martini, made with basil-infused vodka (organic basil plus organic vodka, natch) and greased with just enough olive juice to warm your tongue rather than singe it. A basil leaf, floating faceup in the glass, seemed to wink at me, providing a constant but gentle reminder of my martini's clean dirtiness—or dirty cleanliness, take your pick. I almost felt guilty stepping outside to light up a Camel. Don't they make organic cigarettes? I could get used to this.

## THE DIRTIEST MARTINI
Adapted from COUNTER, New York City

4 ounces basil-infused organic vodka (see note below)
1¼ ounces olive juice
Splash of vermouth

3 pitted Spanish green queen olives, skewered
1 organic basil leaf, for garnish

**1.** Shake vodka, olive juice and vermouth with ice in a shaker.

**2.** Strain into a chilled martini glass, and garnish with the olive skewer and basil leaf.

To infuse the vodka, place 10 basil leaves in a 750-ml bottle of organic vodka (Rain vodka, distilled in Kentucky from organic corn, is a good choice) for two hours. Be careful not to overinfuse. You want a mild flavor and fragrance, not basil cologne.

*April 2, 2006*

THE DIRTIEST MARTINI

## THE IMPROVED DIRTY MARTINI
**Adapted from NAREN YOUNG, Empellón restaurants, New York City**

*Naren Young's "better" version of the dirty martini is called Olives 7 Ways, with several bespoke ingredients. That cocktail, served at Saxon & Parole, is fairly complicated to make, so Mr. Young came up with yet another, easier variation for the home bartender.*

375 milliliters dry vermouth, preferably Noilly Prat
½ cup chopped Cerignola olives
1½ ounces navy-strength gin, preferably Perry's Tot

A few drops of extra-virgin olive oil
Mixed olives, for serving

**1.** Combine vermouth and chopped olives in a sealed glass container and let sit for 3 days. Shake periodically.

**2.** Chill a cocktail glass by filling it with ice or putting it in the freezer for about 5 minutes.

**3.** Pour the gin and 1 ½ ounces of the infused vermouth in a mixing glass filled three-quarters full with ice. Stir until chilled, about 30 seconds, and strain into the chilled glass. Carefully drip a few drops of olive oil (with an eye-dropper, if possible) onto the drink's surface. Serve with a small dish of mixed olives.

*February 11, 2014*

## LOPSIDEDLY PERFECT MARTINI
**Adapted from TOBY MALONEY, The Violet Hour, Chicago**

2 ounces gin, preferably Tanqueray
¾ ounce dry vermouth, preferably Noilly Prat
¼ ounce sweet vermouth,

2 dashes Regan's orange bitters preferably Dolin
1 dash Angostura bitters
1 strip lemon zest, about 1 inch wide

**1.** Fill a shaker or mixing glass with ice and add gin, the vermouths and the bitters. Stir well for at least a minute, until the drink is very cold.

**2.** Strain into a chilled cocktail glass and drop in the lemon zest.

*December 3, 2008*

## BLACKBERRY MARTINIS
**Adapted from Janie Hibler's "The Berry Bible," by JONATHAN REYNOLDS**

*One of the most exquisite exploitations of the blackberry is accomplished by teaming it with a little booze and presenting it in a sugar-rimmed martini glass, making what might be called a blacktini. The original recipe, from "The Berry Bible," suggests vodka, but I find the complexity of the drink enhanced by the gin's juniper-berry accent. I think vodka is dull, actually, but if you like it (most of America seems to), go with God.*

YIELD: 4 DRINKS

| | |
|---|---|
| 2 cups blackberries | Superfine sugar |
| ¼ cup berry brandy or crème de cassis | 1 cup gin (or vodka) |
| 1 tablespoon sugar | 2 tablespoons Triple Sec |
| 4 lemon wedges | 2 tablespoons fresh lemon juice |
| | Simple syrup (page 27) |

**1.** Purée the berries, brandy and sugar in a food processor until smooth.

**2.** Prepare four martini glasses: rub the rims with lemons, then pour a layer of superfine sugar on a plate and twirl the glasses in it. Place them in the freezer.

**3.** Fill a martini shaker with ice, then add the gin (or vodka), Triple Sec and lemon juice. Add 2 tablespoons of the sugar syrup and ¼ cup of the berry purée. Shake robustly for 10 seconds and strain into the glasses. Serve immediately but sip slowly.

*August 22, 2004*


## GINGER MARTINI
**By ABDUL TABINI, The Odeon, New York City**

| | |
|---|---|
| 2 to 3 pieces fresh ginger, peeled | ½ ounce simple syrup (page 27) |
| 2 ounces Ketel One Citroen vodka | ¾ ounce Cointreau |
| ½ ounce lemon juice | 1 dash orange juice |

**1.** Muddle ginger in a mixing glass.

**2.** Add ice and the remaining ingredients and shake.

**3.** Strain into a chilled cocktail glass.

*October 18, 2013*


## MARTINI ON THE ROCKS
**By ROSIE SCHAAP**

*A martini straight up will wilt on a hot day, but on the rocks it's just right.*

| | |
|---|---|
| 3 ounces London Dry-style gin | 1 small strip of lemon peel |
| ¾ ounce dry vermouth | |

**1.** Fill a mixing glass with ice. Pour in gin and vermouth and stir for 30 seconds.

**2.** Strain into an old-fashioned glass over fresh ice. Twist the lemon peel over the drink, then drop it in.

*May 21, 2014*

# THE OTHER VERMOUTH

## By WILLIAM L. HAMILTON

While ultrapremium gins and vodkas make splashy entrances in martinis all over town, segregating drinkers into two camps like a turf war at a club, no one is paying much attention to what goes with them.

It's vermouth, of course, and generally it is not encouraged to speak up.

The dry martini, with a minimum of dry vermouth, is the little black dress of drinks, and that's what the young martini moguls want a hot handhold on. You order it dirty if you're freaky.

But some of the more stylish players on the cocktail scene are hitting on a different flavor: sweet vermouth.

Sweet vermouth is, like dry vermouth, a brandy-fortified wine mixed with botanicals like herbs, flowers and roots. Sweet vermouth is closer in taste to what people associate with a standard aperitif base, like Lillet or Dubonnet.

Sweet vermouth is a component in two popular aperitiflike cocktails, the Negroni and the Americano, each of which includes Campari. And the Manhattan, one of the 19th-century drinks that began to reduce the fanciful art of the cocktail to a science by the 20th century, prefers sweet vermouth, though it can include dry, too. BLT Steak, a new bistro on East 57th Street, is serving a bourbon Manhattan, with a reserve bourbon, as a house specialty. Sweet vermouth handles it like a pro, letting it brag and softening the bluster.

At La Bottega, in the Maritime Hotel, on Ninth Avenue between 16th and 17th Streets, the bar serves a Martini Rossi Rosso, which is a vodka martini with sweet rather than dry vermouth.

The switch is a clever one. Though the taste is new, the idea is old. Among the major branches of the martini's genealogical tree is the Martinez, a gin and sweet vermouth cocktail, mixed in a reverse proportion to the modern martini, that presses a paternity claim called into question by the fact that no one can agree on who fathered the original Martinez, or where or with what.

With its varnished wood ceiling, La Bottega, scarred and mirrored and yellow-lighted, is like drinking inside an antiquated jukebox, one in Havana that no one has the money to replace.

(Last Sunday, three drunken men with three sober women were at the bar celebrating the University of Connecticut's supremacy on the basketball courts—what a sports watcher called "Coed Huskie Mania." Both the men's and women's teams went on to win National Collegiate Athletic Association championship titles on Monday and Tuesday nights.)

My Martini Rossi Rosso was tinted ruby, a novel touch, and not sweet as you might expect. It is a martini with a mind of its own. Slightly bitter, with traces of orange blossom and spice, the cocktail has what film and fashion agents call "unconventional beauty."

You decide if you can be comfortable with that.

## MARTINI ROSSI ROSSO
Adapted from LA BOTTEGA at the Maritime Hotel, New York City

| 4½ ounces vodka | ⅛ ounce orange bitters |
| 1½ ounces sweet vermouth | Orange twist, for garnish |

**1.** In a shaker filled with ice, shake vodka and sweet vermouth.

**2.** Strain into chilled martini glass. Add a healthy dash of orange bitters. Garnish with orange twist.

*April 11, 2004*

# FOR THE PERFECT MARTINI, WETTER IS BETTER
## By ROSIE SCHAAP

The most memorable martini I've ever had was made at the bar in the Merchant Hotel in Belfast, by a charming young man named Luke. I requested it with Beefeater, straight up with a twist, and asked him not to be shy with the vermouth. As I watched Luke stir the drink patiently and rhythmically, then produce a diminutive coupe glass from the freezer, I sensed that the martini would be sublime. Expert execution is one thing, but an elegant setting and a genial bartender made my martini add up to more than the sum of its parts. A flawless cocktail fashioned by an imperious "mixologist" in a bar where people don't talk to one another is no fun at all.

I've spent more of my life in bars—on both sides—than I ought to admit. An ice-cold bottle of pilsner or a whiskey on the rocks can make me just as happy as a great cocktail, but my first column is an occasion to honor a classic. I take a pretty hard line on the martini. I prefer gin because, unlike vodka, which is valued for its neutrality, it's packed with flavor. The taste we most strongly associate with gin is the juniper berry, which is reminiscent of pine and faintly citrusy. Beefeater, my favorite for a classic martini, also includes Seville orange peel, coriander seed and almond, among other ingredients. It's assertive but beautifully balanced.

Still, drinking should be a pleasure, not a chore. If gin isn't your poison, go with vodka. If you can't imagine a martini without an olive, have an olive (I find the saltiness too much). But if you've never had a martini any way but bone dry, I implore you to give a wetter version a chance: vermouth—fortified wine flavored with botanicals—adds depth and imparts a spicy, subtly fruity quality. It's what makes a martini a cocktail rather than just a chilled spirit.

Making your own martini should be a pleasure, making the act of drinking it more enjoyable. The most important thing you can do, however, is serve it in a glass with a capacity of no more than four and a half ounces. In the mid-1990s, the conical cocktail glass was supersized, resulting in massive martinis that quickly concede their vital, bracing chill. There's also no need to fill it to the rim. It looks cool, but it's harder to drink—and who needs the trouble?

## THE CLASSIC MARTINI

4 parts Beefeater gin
1 part Noilly Prat dry vermouth

1 small strip of lemon peel

**1.** Fill a mixing glass with ice. Pour in the gin and vermouth and stir for 30 seconds.

**2.** Strain into a chilled coupe. Twist the lemon peel over the drink, then place it on the coupe's edge. The mildly adventurous can garnish with a fresh sage leaf instead.

## THE VESPER

*Gin or vodka? The Vesper—which first appeared in Ian Fleming's novel "Casino Royale"—lets you have it both ways. Lillet stands in for its close cousin, dry vermouth. I normally stir rather than shake, but, in this case, I defer to James Bond.*

3 parts Gordon's gin (007's preference)
1 part vodka (any Russian will do)

½ part Lillet Blanc
1 generous strip of lemon peel

**1.** Pour the gin, vodka and Lillet into an ice-filled mixing glass and shake.

**2.** Strain into a chilled coupe. Twist the outsize peel over the drink, then drop it in.

*October 20, 2011*

MINT JULEP FROM THE RITZ CARLTON HOTEL, NEW ORLEANS

CHAPTER 8

# THE JULEP

# HERITAGE AND PRIDE, WITH A KICK

## By SUZANNE HAMLIN

Tomorrow, Derby Day, I'll be watching the 129th Run for the Roses—not on home turf in the grandstand or mashed in with thousands in the infield at Churchill Downs. Instead, I'll be in Brooklyn, watching it on television along with millions of other Derby devotees. But in spirit, in an annual sentimental meltdown, with mint julep in hand, I will be there, just as I have been for the 30-odd years since I left my childhood old Kentucky home—"LOO-a-vul," as it is still and rightfully pronounced.

And it won't be just any old mint julep I'll be making, drinking and serving. It will be a real julep, the now classic julep first served to Derby guests in 1875 by Col. Meriwether Lewis Clark Jr., the founder of Churchill Downs. Now, as then, it is made with just four ingredients: finely crushed ice, a little sugar water, fresh spearmint and fine, aged, 90-proof straight Kentucky bourbon.

There is a fifth element, too, the essential silver julep cup. The idea of drinking a julep from a plastic glass, a foam cup or a tall Collins glass is about as abhorrent as adulterating the basic elements of the drink with some foreign substance like citrus juice. (Those thousands of people in the infield drinking "mint juleps" from commemorative Derby glasses? They are actually drinking bourbon highballs.)

The classic nine-ounce julep cup, originally made of coin silver, is a specific size and shape: three and a half to four inches tall, with a top diameter of about three inches, a flat bottom and straight sides that flare slightly. Often there are thin, grooved bands running around the bottom and top, but otherwise a julep cup is severely, elegantly and purposely plain. Ornate decoration would disturb the beautiful visuals of a mint julep—the iconic coating of frost that icy cold silver produces.

Perhaps even more crucial, the slightly metallic taste of the silver is the perfect balance to the warm, rich, smoky, sweet bourbon and the spicy scent of the mandatory spearmint sprig. All together, wrote a besotted tippler in the 1800s, "one of the most delightful and insinuating potations that was ever invented."

In spite of the fact that I wasn't allowed to drink mint juleps in public until I was 16, by the time I was 13 I was well on my way to owning a baker's dozen of sterling-silver julep cups. In that once-upon-a-time Louisville, girls were often given the cups on birthdays and graduations, a kind of Derby dowry. I received each one dutifully—with an excitement slightly above getting a savings bond, despite my mother's assurances: "You'll be very happy some day to have them, Boo. You'll use them all the time, you'll see."

Well if not all the time, at least every Derby.

# KENTUCKY DERBY MINT JULEPS

YIELD: UP TO 20 DRINKS

Metal julep cups, about 9 ounces, preferably silver

1 cup spring or bottled water

1 cup granulated sugar

½ cup small spearmint leaves, no stems

Finely crushed or shaved ice, enough to fill the cups completely

High-quality Kentucky bourbon like Maker's Mark or Woodford Reserve

Sprigs of spearmint, for garnish

**1.** The day before serving, or even earlier, put the julep cups in the freezer. Put the water and sugar in a small saucepan, bring to a boil without stirring, and boil for 2 minutes, or until sugar is completely dissolved.

**2.** Put the mint leaves in a glass jar or cup, pour the slightly cooled syrup over them, let cool, then cover and refrigerate for 12 hours or longer. When ready to use, strain out the mint leaves.

**3.** Half an hour before serving, pack the julep cups tightly up to the rim with crushed ice and return them to the freezer.

**4.** For each julep pour 3 ounces of bourbon over the ice, followed by two teaspoons of mint syrup. Do not stir or agitate. Use a cloth to hold each cup by the rim so as not to disturb the frost. Use a short straw or a chopstick to make a hole in the ice on the side of the cup and insert a sprig of mint. Serve immediately, preferably on a silver tray.

*May 2, 2003*

# HENRY CLAY'S SOUTHERN MINT JULEP

Adapted from JIM HEWES, the Willard Hotel, Washington, D.C.

12 fresh red-stemmed mint leaves

1 teaspoon sugar

2 ounces bourbon

Cracked ice

Fresh water

Carbonated water

**GARNISHES**

Mint sprigs

Lemon zest

Powdered sugar

**1.** Gently bruise 12 mint leaves in a tall crystal tumbler, and muddle with sugar and a dash of bourbon.

**2.** Fill the glass halfway with cracked ice, and agitate with a spoon.

**3.** Pack the rest of the glass with ice and fill with the rest of the bourbon and equal parts fresh water and carbonated water.

**4.** Garnish with mint sprig. Twist a lemon zest over the leaves, and dust with powdered sugar. Serve with two short straws.

## CITRUS JULEP
**Adapted from RONNI LUNDY**
YIELD: 6 DRINKS

| | |
|---|---|
| 1 lime | 1 cup water |
| 1 orange | 1 cup mint leaves |
| 1 lemon | Finely crushed ice |
| 1 cup sugar | Bourbon |
| | Mint, for garnish |

**1.** Scrub the fruit, and use a zester or sharp knife to scrape slivers of rind from each. Set the fruit aside.

**2.** Combine sugar and water in a saucepan, and bring to a quick boil.

**3.** Add zests, turn heat to low and simmer for 2 minutes. Turn off heat, and allow to cool.

**4.** Put mint leaves in a quart jar or crock, and use the back of a wooden spoon to bruise them slightly, releasing the fragrance.

**5.** Pour syrup, including the zest, over the leaves, and steep for 1 hour.

**6.** Juice the lime, orange and lemon, and strain into a pitcher. Pour the mint syrup through the strainer as well, using the back of the spoon to press the captured mint leaves and zest to extract remaining juices.

**7.** For each person, fill an 8-ounce glass or julep cup with ice. Pour 3 ounces of bourbon into each, then top off with the mint syrup.

**8.** Serve with short straws and a garnish of mint.

## RAINBOW JULEP
**Adapted from DALE DeGROFF, the Rainbow Room, New York City**

| | |
|---|---|
| 1 ounce Apry liqueur | Crushed ice |
| Sprigs of young mint | 3 or 4 mint sprigs, for garnish |
| 2 ounces bourbon | |

**1.** Pour the Apry into a highball glass, add 3 or 4 small mint leaves and muddle.

**2.** Add the bourbon and fill glass with crushed ice.

**3.** Stir until frost forms on outside of glass, and garnish with 3 or 4 mint sprigs. Serve with two straws.

*April 30, 1997*

# AND NOW, A SIP OF HISTORY: THE MINT JULEP, PERSONIFIED

## By PABLEAUX JOHNSON

Then comes the zenith of man's pleasure. Then comes the julep ... the mint julep."

Chris McMillian's gravelly baritone—which calls to mind Tom Waits moonlighting at the Metropolitan Opera—echoed through the dark-paneled Library Lounge at the Ritz-Carlton hotel here as he gently plucked leaves from a bouquet of mint and pushed them into a sterling silver julep cup.

"Who has not tasted one has lived in vain," he continued. "It is the very dream of drinks, the vision of sweet quaffings."

Many thousands of juleps will be poured at Churchill Downs during the Kentucky Derby this weekend. Yet those made by Mr. McMillian at this bar a block from Bourbon Street are by many accounts among the most skillfully mixed in the country. Without doubt, they are the most lavishly presented. Each order is served up with Mr. McMillian's recitation of an ode to the julep written in the 1890s by J. Soule Smith, a Kentucky newspaperman.

Dressed in his everyday work uniform—white dress shirt, black vest, bow tie and elbow garters—Mr. McMillian could easily pass for a 19th-century saloon-keeper. Simultaneously brash and genteel, he considers himself less a new-wave mixologist than an ardent student of cocktail culture past and present.

"Chris is a rare living link to this amazing old-world profession," said Dave Wondrich, drinks correspondent for Esquire and the author of the forthcoming book "Imbibe!" (Perigee Books). "There are plenty of creative younger bartenders who know how to mix, but very few who have mastered the lore and demeanor of the old days."

Mr. McMillian delights in holding court with quasi-educational bar patter. A dedicated amateur historian, a born storyteller and a co-founder of the Museum of the American Cocktail here, Mr. McMillian stockpiles esoteric tidbits of cocktail history. Every round opens up fresh possibilities for a short lecture on the lasting impact of Prohibition, Hammurabi's Code or the public drinking spaces of ancient Pompeii.

Mr. McMillian has chosen his tools of the trade carefully. A broad porcelain-headed muddler for pulverizing the sugar cubes in an old-fashioned, a straight wooden one for bruising the mint in a mojito. A flared Pyrex cylinder and stirring rod, more common in chemistry labs than bars, are used for martinis and other clear drinks in which a gentle mingling is preferred to a vigorous shake.

While most bartenders thrive on quick pours and matching tips, Mr. McMillian plies his trade at a leisurely pace, without modern shortcuts. He muddles sugar and bitters for every Sazerac instead of pouring simple syrup. He cuts and squeezes every drop of citrus juice seconds before it goes in the glass. He carves individual slivers of orange and lemon zest for garnishes on sidecars and martinis.

"At this bar, I concentrate on the classics and make them the old way," he said. "The way made them classics to begin with."

Mr. McMillian's way with a julep starts when he crushes ice cubes with a Flintstonian wooden mallet and mounds the powdered ice into a silver cup. It continues as he muddles the mint, pours the bourbon, sweetens it with peach syrup (rather than sugar) and places the cup, encrusted with a thick layer of frost, on a pressed linen napkin.

"Sip it and dream—it is a dream itself," he said, reaching Smith's last stanza. "Sip it and say there is no solace for the soul, no tonic for the body like old Bourbon whiskey."

Mr. McMillian pushed the mounded dome of bourbon-soaked snow across the bar as he added his own coda:

"Cheers."

## MINT JULEP
### Adapted from CHRIS McMILLIAN, Library Lounge, Ritz-Carlton Hotel, New Orleans

| | |
|---|---|
| 12 to 15 fresh mint leaves | 2½ ounces bourbon |
| 1 ounce peach syrup, like Monin | 1 sprig mint, for garnish |
| Crushed ice | Superfine sugar, for garnish |

**1.** Place mint leaves and ¼ ounce peach syrup in julep cup or 8- to 10-ounce old-fashioned glass and gently crush leaves with a wooden muddler, working them up sides of glass.

**2.** Loosely pack glass with finely crushed ice, then add bourbon. Drizzle remaining peach syrup on top and garnish with mint sprig lightly dusted with sugar.

*May 2, 2007*

## MINT JULEP
### By MARK BITTMAN

| | |
|---|---|
| Mint leaves, plus additional for garnish | ¼ cup whiskey |
| 1 tablespoon simple syrup (page 27) | |

**1.** Muddle mint leaves and simple syrup in a glass, then add ice and whiskey.

**2.** Garnish with lots of fresh mint.

**Be sure to have lots and lots of mint. If it seems to be too much, it's probably just right.**

*May 13, 2012*

# GET THE PARTY STARTED WITH BLACKBERRY-BOURBON

Our friend Bobby Flay, an award-winning chef and our guest picker for the Derby, sent us this mint julep recipe. Flay is a longtime racehorse owner and fan of the sport. He is Churchill Downs's official host and spokesperson of the Kentucky Derby Party program and its Web site.

## BLACKBERRY-BOURBON JULEPS
### By BOBBY FLAY
YIELD: 4 DRINKS

1 pint fresh blackberries, rinsed and dried
½ cup simple syrup (page 27)

1 big bunch of mint leaves
Crushed ice
1½ cup bourbon

**1.** Divide the berries among 4 mint julep glasses or rocks glasses. Add 2 tablespoons of the simple syrup and 8 mint leaves to each glass and using a muddler, mash the berries and mint together. Add 1 shot of bourbon to the mixture and stir.

**2.** Fill each glass with lots of crushed ice and pour ¼ cup of bourbon over the ice in each glass. Garnish with lots of mint sprigs and serve immediately.

*May 1, 2009*

## GIN JULEP
### Adapted from DAVID WONDRICH by Pete Wells

6 mint leaves, plus a sprig for garnish
¾ ounce simple syrup (page 27)

Finely cracked ice (see note)
2½ ounces genever gin

**1.** Place mint leaves and simple syrup in a tall glass and lightly press mint into syrup with a muddler or long-handled spoon. Fill glass with cracked ice.

**2.** Add gin and stir energetically with a swizzle stick or long-handled spoon until frost forms on outside of glass.

**3.** Top off with more cracked ice, plant a mint sprig on top, and serve with a straw.

**For finely cracked ice, wrap a dozen ice cubes in a linen towel or a canvas bag (a cotton dish towel will do in a pinch, but some ice will cling to cloth). Pulverize ice with a mallet, muddler or rolling pin.**

*June 24, 2009*

RUM JULEP

## RUM JULEP
By ROSIE SCHAAP

10 mint leaves, plus a few sprigs for garnish
2 teaspoons simple syrup (page 27)

Crushed ice
2 ounces light rum

**1.** Muddle mint with simple syrup in a julep glass or old-fashioned glass. Fill glass with crushed ice.

**2.** Add light rum and stir well, until glass frosts. Garnish with mint sprigs.

*May 20, 2014*

## FORT JULEP
By ROSIE SCHAAP

2 or 3 mint leaves, plus more for garnish
2 ounces Lillet Rosé

½ ounce green Chartreuse
Crushed ice

**1.** Rub 2 or 3 mint leaves inside a julep cup or old-fashioned glass.

**2.** Add Lillet Rosé and Chartreuse, fill halfway with crushed ice and swizzle or stir.

**3.** Add more crushed ice until mounded over the glass. Garnish with a small bouquet of fresh mint sprigs, spanked (see sidebar) against the back of your hand just before being inserted in the cup.

**About this business of spanking the mint:** The drink's creator, Joaquín Simó of Pouring Ribbons in Manhattan, realizes that it might sound funny ("Bad mint! Naughty, naughty mint!") but explains why it's important: "The small capillaries visible in mint leaves contain all the essential oils that create that unmistakable mintiness. There's no need to muddle the mint, as that causes near-instantaneous oxidation, which turns mint bitter. A light slapping of mint leaves against the back of your hand opens up those capillaries and releases all the aroma that one could hope for with a minimum of effort."

*August 7, 2014*

EL PARADOR, NEW YORK CITY, 1966

## CHAPTER 9

# COCKTAILS BY CLAIBORNE

# TEN DRINKS (BESIDES MARTINIS)

## By CRAIG CLAIBORNE

David A. Embury, aged 72, is the man who wrote the book which has been referred to, with apologies to Bach, as the well-tempered bartender's jigger journal and constant companion. This very special volume, titled "The Fine Art of Mixing Drinks" (Doubleday), first appeared in 1948. It was recently issued in a revised an enlarged edition and it contains a wealth of information about "glassware, gimmicks and gadgets," the origin of drinks and their various names, philosophic notes on the use and abuse of liquor and 700 recipes.

Mr. Embury is an extraordinary man. As he notes in his preface to the book he has "never been engaged in any of the manifold branches of the liquor business." He is not a distiller, importer, bottler or merchant of liquors. He is not even a retired bartender. His practical experience has been solely as a host, sometime sampler and enthusiastic researcher. A Manhattan lawyer, he apparently has a knowledge of every mixed drink under the sun. Thus, Mr. Embury seemed a logical choice as a man to nominate ten drinks particularly suited to summer entertaining. The choice of a Black Velvet for summer entertaining strikes this department as somewhat bizarre, but Mr. Embury happens to like Black Velvet.

And what does the author consider the all-time king of drinks? An ice-cold Martini, properly made.

## BLACK VELVET

| 1 part Guinness' stout | 1 part dry champagne |

**1.** Chill stout and champagne.

**2.** Pour stout into a glass, then champagne. Or pour simultaneously.

## LARCHMONT
YIELD: 3 DRINKS

| Crushed or cracked ice | 2 ounces Grand Marnier |
| ½ ounce simple syrup (page 27) | 6 ounces white Cuban rum |
| 2 ounces lime juice | Twist of orange peel, for garnish |

**1.** Fill a cocktail shaker half full with crushed or cracked ice. Add all ingredients except orange twist and shake vigorously.

**2.** Strain mixture into chilled, frosted cocktail glasses and garnish with twist.

## MINT JULEP

1 tablespoon simple syrup (page 27)

12 fresh tender mint leaves, freshly washed

2 or three dashes Angostura bitters (optional)

2 ounces best quality bonded bourbon

Crushed ice

Sprigs of mint, for garnish

Powdered sugar, for garnish

**1.** Chill a sixteen-ounce mug by leaving it close to freezing compartment for half an hour (Editor's note: these days the refrigerator or freezer will do just fine; adjust your chill time accordingly). Put syrup, mint leaves and bitters in a bar glass. Using a muddler, bruise leaves gently but do not crush. Add bourbon and stir thoroughly.

**2.** Remove the mug from the freezer or refrigerator and pack with crushed ice. Strain contents of bar glass over it. Using a long bar spoon, churn the contents a few minutes. Add more ice and fill glass to within a half inch with bourbon. Churn until glass frosts.

**3.** Insert long straw; garnish with springs of mint dipped into powdered sugar while moist. Serve at once.

## DAIQUIRI DE LUXE

YIELD: 2 DRINKS

Finely crushed ice

½ ounce Orgeat or Crème d'Ananas

1 ounce citrus juice (lemon and lime combined)

4½ ounces white Cuban rum

**1.** Fill a cocktail shaker half full with finely crushed ice. Add remaining ingredients and shake well.

**2.** Strain into chilled, frosted cocktail glasses.

## SINGAPORE GIN SLING

Crushed ice

1 teaspoon simple syrup (page 27)

Juice of ¼ large lemon or ½ of a large lime

1 ounce kirsch

1⅓ jiggers gin

1 dash Angostura bitters

Splash of charged water (club soda or seltzer water)

Twist of lemon peel, for garnish

**1.** Fill a cocktail shaker half full with crushed ice. Add all ingredients except charged water and twist of lemon and shake well.

**2.** Strain into a highball glass. Add one large ice cube and a splash of charged water. Garnish with a twist of lemon peel.

## GIN RICKEY

Juice of one small or half a large lime
2 ounces gin

1 teaspoon simple syrup (page 27)
Charged water [club soda or seltzer water]

**1.** Combine all ingredients except charged water in an eight ounce glass.

**2.** Add two large ice cubes and fill the glass with charged water.

**3.** Stir again and serve with a stirring rod or small bar spoon.


## APPENDICITIS DE LUXE

YIELD: 2 DRINKS

Cracked ice
½ ounce Grand Marnier
1 ounce lime juice

1 egg white
4 ounces gin

**1.** Fill a cocktail shaker full with cracked ice.

**2.** Add all ingredients except gin and shake vigorously until blended and creamy. Add one-quarter of the gin at a time, shaking after each addition.

**3.** Strain into chilled cocktail glasses.


## PLANTER'S PUNCH

Crushed ice
1 ounce simple syrup (page 27)
2 ounces lemon juice
3 ounces dark Jamaica rum

2 or 3 dashes Angostura bitters
Charged water [club soda or seltzer water]
Fruits, for garnish

**1.** Fill a cocktail shaker half full with crushed ice. Add all ingredients except charged water and fruit garnish and shake vigorously.

**2.** Pour without straining into Collins glass. Pack glass with crushed ice and fill to within half an inch of the top with charged water. Turn with a bar spoon until glass starts to frost. Garnish with fruits and serve immediately.


## ABACAXI RICACO

1 small pineapple
Juice or one large lime
2 teaspoons simple syrup (page 27)

3 to 4 ounces Cuban gold label or Barbados rum
Crushed ice

**1.** Cut top off pineapple; scoop out center, leaving half-inch shell. Chill shell.

**2.** Trim core from flesh and discard. Blend remaining flesh in electric blender. Add remaining ingredients except crushed ice and blend for 2 minutes. Add small tumblerful of crushed ice and blend for 1 minute more.

**3.** Pour, without straining, into chilled pineapple shell. Serve with long straws.

## TOM COLLINS

| | |
|---|---|
| 1 teaspoon simple syrup (page 27) | 2 jiggers gin |
| Juice of one lemon | Charged water (club soda or seltzer water) |

**1.** Stir all ingredients except charged water in a Collins glass, add four large ice cubes and fill with charged water.

**2.** Stir quickly and serve.

*June 15, 1958*

# MARGARITA IS NOW COMPETING WITH BLOODY MARY AT COCKTAIL HOUR IN NEW YORK
## By CRAIG CLAIBORNE

The mixologists of Manhattan, the barmen, state that New Yorkers are not for the most part adventurous in their drinking habits. They are slow to change their established habits of Scotch on the rocks, martinis extra dry and, particularly before noon, bloody Marys.

There is one spirit, however, that is sold increasingly hereabouts, no doubt in part to Mexican tourism and in part to the increasing numbers of Mexican restaurants that have opened in New York in recent years. The drink is tequila, an altogether delightful liquid that can be sipped straight or converted into several commendable cocktails.

Tequila has an odd, almost ineffable taste. It is vaguely sweet, a tri-

fle musty and, whatever else may be said of its flavor, it is certainly pronounced.

Tequila is called the national drink of Mexico and a favored method of drinking is straight followed by a pinch of salt and a bite into a wedge of lime. The most likable use for it, however, is in a cocktail called Margarita, a blend of tequila, lime or lemon juice and an orange liqueur such as Cointreau or Triple Sec, shaken and served in a salt-rimmed glass.

Tequila has a natural affinity to lime and salt. Although tequila is potent enough, a Margarita is not nearly so lethal as an extra dry martini.

Almost equal in popularity with the Margarita in Mexico City is something called a sangrita, a drink vaguely related to the bloody Mary with its tomato juices and spices, but different.

The sangrita is taken two ways: with the tequila and the juice mixture served separately, or as a cocktail with the tequila and the tomato juice shaken together and strained. Most Americans seem to prefer the mixed drink.

Tequila is thought to be the first spirit distilled in the Americas. The Aztecs were distilling it when the Spaniards conquered Mexico, and it is made today as it was then from the fermented juice of a desert cactus plant.

Some of the restaurants where tequila drinks are much in evidence include the well-known (and crowded) El Parador, 561 Second Avenue (near 31st Street); La Fonda del Sol, 123 West 50th Street; Fonda la Paloma, 156 East 49th Street (which should be better than it is), and El Charro, 4 Charles Street.

Here are three recipes using tequila, which is available in most wine and spirit shops hereabouts.

## MARGARITA

1½ ounces tequila
1 ounce Cointreau or Triple Sec
1 ounce lime or lemon juice
Salt

**1.** Combine the tequila, Cointreau and lime or lemon juice in a cocktail shaker.

**2.** Use the squeezed lime or lemon to rub the rim of a cocktail glass. Immediately dip the rim of the glass into a container of salt. Shake the glass slightly to remove excess salt.

**3.** Add ice to the tequila mixture and shake well. Strain into the salt-rimmed glass and serve.

## SANGRITA
YIELD: 2 OR MORE DRINKS

⅓ cup orange juice
⅓ cup tomato juice
Juice of half a lemon
½ teaspoon Worcestershire sauce
1 tablespoon Grenadine syrup
Tabasco sauce to taste
Salt and freshly ground black pepper to taste
3 (one-ounce) jiggers tequila (see note)

**1.** Combine all ingredients in a cocktail shaker and add ice cubes and shake well.

**2.** Strain into cocktail glasses.

The tequila in the Sangrita is frequently served on the side. To serve it this way, shake all ingredients except tequila with ice. Strain into two glasses and serve tequila in very small glasses on the side.

## TEQUILA PUNCH

YIELD: 4 TO 6 SMALL DRINKS

2 juice oranges
1 large, sweet grapefruit
2 tangerines (optional)

Grand Marnier or Cointreau
3 tablespoons tequila

**1.** Squeeze the oranges, grapefruit and tangerines. Mix juices and stir. The quantities will depend on the size and juiciness of the fruit. Blend the fruit juices with Cointreau.

**2.** To serve, measure out two parts of the fruit mixture to one part tequila. Add ice and stir until well chilled.

*February 9, 1966*

## VODKA AND CITRUS SHRUB

YIELD: 6 DRINKS

1 (6-ounce) can undiluted frozen fruit concentrate (orange or grapefruit or blended grapefruit and orange)

6 ounces vodka
Shaved ice
Fresh mint, for garnish

**1.** Combine the fruit juice concentrate with the vodka.

**2.** Pour over shaved ice in cocktail glasses and stir briskly.

**3.** Garnish with fresh mint.

*July 30, 1960*

## JACK ROSE COCKTAIL
YIELD: 6 DRINKS

1 jigger grenadine
2 jiggers lemon juice

8 jiggers applejack
Cracked or crushed ice

**1.** Combine grenadine, lemon juice and applejack in a cocktail shaker. Add plenty of cracked or crushed ice and shake vigorously.

**2.** Strain into chilled cocktail glasses.

*November 25, 1957*

## TRADITIONAL GLOGG
YIELD: 12 TO 20 DRINKS (10 CUPS)

1 (12-ounce) bottle beer
½ cup dried raisins
12 pitted prunes
6 dried figs
4 whole cardamom pods
1 (2-inch) cinnamon stick

4 whole cloves
5 tablespoons honey
2 bottles dry red wine
½ cup blanched, slivered almonds
3 cups brandy

**1.** Pour the beer into a kettle and add the raisins, prunes, figs, cardamom, cinnamon stick and cloves. Cook down until the liquid is reduced to about one-half cup.

**2.** Add the honey and wine and remove immediately from the heat. Let stand until cool. Refrigerate until ready to serve.

**3.** Combine the almonds and brandy with the wine mixture. Bring the liquid almost but not quite to the boiling point and serve.

*December 28, 1983*

# EASTER BRUNCH
## By CRAIG CLAIBORNE

Although the word "brunch" may still strike certain ears as a profanation of the English language, the meal which bears that name can be counted among the pleasanter aspects of Sunday and holiday eating. Because the hour at which brunch is served—generally between 11 A.M and 1 P.M.—it can be the most unhurried of meals. The menu is seldom elaborate, consisting for the most part of a single course and beverage.

## BLOODY MARY

½ cup tomato juice
2 ounces vodka
1 teaspoon Worcestershire sauce
Juice of half a lemon
Tabasco sauce
Salt and freshly ground black pepper
Shaved ice or three cubes of ice

**1.** Combine tomato juice, vodka, Worcestershire sauce, lemon juice and a few drops of Tabasco in a shaker.

**2.** Add salt and pepper and shaved or cubed ice and shake vigorously.

**3.** Pour into a chilled glass and serve.

## BULLDOZER

1 jigger vodka
¾ cup canned bouillon
Lemon juice (optional)
Salt and freshly ground black pepper, to taste

**1.** Pour vodka and bouillon over ice cubes in an old-fashioned glass.

**2.** If desired, add a few drops of lemon juice. Season with salt and pepper.

## WHISKY SOUR

2 ounces rye or bourbon whisky
1 or 2 teaspoons sugar
1 tablespoon lemon juice
Cracked or shaved ice
Maraschino cherry, for garnish
Thin slice of orange, for garnish

**1.** Combine rye or bourbon, sugar and lemon juice in a cocktail shaker. Add a scoop of cracked or shaved ice and shake vigorously.

**2.** Strain into a whisky sour glass and garnish with a maraschino cherry and thin slice of orange.

**If desired, this drink may be made with gin, rum, brandy, applejack or Scotch whisky.**

*March 30, 1958*

JOHN BONING, FAR RIGHT, PUTS STUDENTS THROUGH THEIR
PACES AT THE BARTENDER'S SCHOOL, NEW YORK CITY, 1949.

CHAPTER 10

# THE CLASSICS

# STIRRING UP THE PAST

## BY WILLIAM GRIMES

Logically, there shouldn't be any such thing as a classic cocktail. Mixed drinks tend to be invented on a whim, named as an afterthought, consumed on the spot and forgotten in an instant. Like other products of American popular culture—from movies and cartoons to television commercials and funny T-shirts—most cocktails earn their oblivion. Who will mourn the Fluffy Ruffles, a Prohibition favorite? Or the Locomotive, a rebarbative mixture of claret, curacao, honey and egg yolk that oozed its way into cocktail glasses just before the turn of the century?

But the democratic process has dealt some injustices along the way. Genuinely distinguished drinks have suffered the same fate as their emetic colleagues, tossed down the drain of history along with the Ants in the Pants, the Maiden's Blush and the Pacemaker. These forgotten classics deserve to be rescued, not for antiquarian reasons but because they are fine drinks.

Perhaps the most puzzling case of neglect is the Bronx—a tasty shake-up of gin, orange juice, and sweet and dry vermouth. Created in the early 1900s, reputedly at the old Waldorf Astoria bar, it instantly caught the public fancy. And therein lay the problem. "The Bronx was fashionable," wrote Bernard De Voto, the "Easy Chair" editor for "Harper's Magazine" in the 1930s and 1940s. "The gay dogs of the Murray Hill Age drank it, the boulevardiers who wore boaters with a string to the left lapel and winked at Gibson Girls as far up Fifth Avenue as 59th Street. It had the kind of cachet that Maxim's had, or Delmonico's."

It was, in short, the white-wine spritzer of its day, the height of fashion for a time, but before long, a pathetic cliche. In F. Scott Fitzgerald's "This Side of Paradise," Amory Blaine and his Princeton chums order up a round circa 1915, so the Bronx enjoyed a decent enough run. Even today, the standard bar guides include a recipe. But unless a customer wanders in wearing a raccoon coat and waving an Ivy League pennant, few bartenders will ever hear the word. It's a shame. Snappy, refreshing and light on its feet, the Bronx is everything a cocktail should be.

The Jack Rose, too, has slipped down fame's greasy pole through no fault of its own. A beguiling combination of applejack, lemon juice and grenadine, the drink achieves an elegant synthesis of sweet and sour, lemon and apple. And with its cool, translucent coral glow, it scores high in eye-appeal.

So what happened? Applejack went out with spats and took the Jack Rose with it. Once upon a time, hundreds of little distilleries in New Jersey were busy turning apples into the liquid refreshment known as Jersey lightning. Today only one, Laird's, remains—lone survivor of the Johnny Appleseed era of American drink, which reaches well back into the colonial period.

The origins of the name "Jack Rose" are obscure. Popular legend has it that the drink commemorates a famous New York gangland murder. In 1912, a gambling-house operator named Herman Rosenthal was gunned down near Times Square. A rival gangster by the name of Jack Rose eventually turned state's evidence in the case, and he and the drink have marched through history together ever since. The story is colorful but dubious. Common sense suggests a more likely derivation: a contraction of "applejack," plus the rosy hue of the drink.

The Sazerac presents no such etymological difficulties. A New Orleans specialty, it began life as a simple brandy-and-bitters cocktail at the Sazerac House, which opened in 1859, and was named after the house brandy, made by the Sazerac-de-Forge company of Limoges, France. With time, the ingredients mutated. Brandy gave way to rye whiskey and eventually bourbon. Somewhere along the way a dash of absinthe was added for interest. When the law decided that absinthe was a little too interesting, Pernod (or Herbsaint, a New Orleans specialty), was substituted.

The drink survives only as a kind of artifact, like the embalmed Dixieland music at the aptly named Preservation Hall. It deserves better. The subtle licorice zing that comes from the Peychaud's bitters and Pernod teases extra sweetness and fruit out of a good bourbon while keeping the drink nice and dry. The Sazerac, by the way, is one of the very few cocktails that tastes better cool than ice-cold.

All three cocktails should immediately be reinstated in the canon. Mixed drinks constantly undergo the same sort of cultural sifting and reevaluation that T.S. Eliot analyzed so keenly with respect to great literary works. The garish fad drinks disappear forever, throwing the genuine classics into sharp relief. The author of "The Cocktail Party" might have turned his attention to the subject with gratifying results, perhaps even have generated a recipe or two. The "Burnt Norton" could have given the Jack Rose a run for its money.

## THE BRONX

1½ ounces gin
½ ounce sweet vermouth
½ ounce dry vermouth
¼ orange

**1.** Combine gin, sweet vermouth, dry vermouth and the juice of one-quarter of an orange in a cocktail shaker and shake with ice.

**2.** Strain into a cocktail glass.

## JACK ROSE

1½ ounces applejack or Calvados      1 ounce lemon or lime juice
½ ounce grenadine syrup

**1.** Combine applejack or Calvados with grenadine syrup and lemon or lime juice in a cocktail shaker and shake with ice.

**2.** Strain into a cocktail glass.

*November 3, 1991*

# IN THE BIG EASY, 2 COCKTAILS REIGN
## By ERIC ASIMOV

I've been leafing through a bunch of cocktail manuals recently. Aside from the vicarious pleasure, I've been trying to figure out the logic of the Louisiana legislature, which, apparently having finished its work with the Hurricane Katrina cleanup, has moved on to the pressing business of selecting an official cocktail for the city of New Orleans. It has chosen the sazerac.

Now, if any American city deserves its own cocktail, it is New Orleans. It certainly has earned the right to unwind with its beverage of choice after the hurricane, not to mention years of failures by the Saints, as well as the presence of hordes on Bourbon Street toting drinks that are decidedly not sazeracs in vessels the size of jerrycans. What's more, the grand opening of the new Museum of the American Cocktail takes place next week in New Orleans, in recognition of the city's long association with joyous imbibing.

But why the sazerac? Oh, cocktail authorities can make an eloquent defense of its historic place in New Orleans. It was not the original cocktail, as some have claimed, but it is one of the oldest, and its history extends back 150 years in New Orleans. It is manly in its simplicity, essentially rye whiskey mixed with a little sugar, a few dashes of Peychaud's bitters and a rinse of absinthe. Peychaud's is a New Orleans product and absinthe—well, even when it was illegal, one could still count on tracking it down in New Orleans.

"It's a simple drink that is one of the original whiskey cocktails, and it kind of got fossilized in New Orleans, where it's still made today even as everybody else forgot about it," said David Wondrich, author of "Imbibe!" (Perigee, 2007), a history of classic cocktails.

I grant all these points, yet I have one problem with sazeracs: I really don't like them. Not that I would presume to be the arbiter of New Orleans cocktails, but the anise flavor of the absinthe, along with the herbal-anise flavor of the bitters, renders the sazerac overpoweringly medicinal, and I say that as a licorice lover. May I suggest that instead of being the official cocktail of New Orleans, the sazerac ought to be its official digestif?

In place of the sazerac, I would nominate the Ramos gin fizz. The fizz is a wonderful cocktail. It's refreshing and it's complex, but it's hardly simple. In fact, the authentic Ramos gin fizz is one of the most labor-intensive cocktails around.

Legend has it that Henry Charles Ramos, the New Orleans bartender who invented the drink in the late 19th century, employed young men whose job was to shake the cocktail for longer than could possibly be good for human arms. The problem was to combine two essential ingredients, cream and an egg white, that resist each other with polar opposition. You blend those with gin, naturally, lemon and lime juice, sugar, seltzer and—the pièce de résistance—orange flower water. Then, as Ramos once told The New Orleans Item-Tribune, you "shake and shake and shake until there is not a bubble left but the drink is smooth and snowy white and of the consistency of good rich milk."

Now that's a delicious cocktail. Lolis Eric Elie, a columnist with "The Times-Picayune," agrees with me. "I don't want to sound unpatriotic, but I don't especially like sazeracs," Mr. Elie said. "The New Orleans drink that I think is far and away more tasty is the Ramos gin fizz."

For years the sazerac was made with absinthe substitutes, like Pernod or Herbsaint. And even though absinthe was cleared for sale in the United States last year for the first time since 1912, the cocktail still carries the shiver of forbidden fruit. "They have resurrected a drink that has long been illegal," Mr. Elie said. "I think that's part of the thrill—not only to celebrate it but to officialize it."

One could argue that the gin fizz also has a sense of the illicit about it: those raw egg whites will not win the nod of approval from the food police.

Mr. Wondrich, for one, seemed Solomon-like when I asked him which cocktail he preferred. "I love a sazerac," he said. "It's poetry in a glass, though so's a gin fizz. I can't have too many of those because of all the cream and the eggs. Of course, I can't have too many sazeracs either, because I'll fall down."

To decide for yourself, here are recipes for each cocktail. Both are adapted from historic New Orleans recipes recounted in "Imbibe!" (A Ramos Gin Fizz recipe appears on page 154.)

## SAZERAC
**Adapted from "Imbibe!" by DAVID WONDRICH**

1 sugar cube
2 to 4 dashes Peychaud's bitters (do not
  substitute Angostura bitters)

2 ounces rye whiskey
Splash of absinthe
Lemon peel, for garnish

**1.** Fill an old-fashioned glass with ice. Take a mixing glass and muddle the cube of sugar in two to four dashes of bitters. Add rye whiskey and some ice. Stir until chilled.

**2.** Remove ice from old-fashioned glass and add a splash of absinthe. Rinse well with the absinthe and pour out remainder. Strain cocktail into glass and garnish with twisted lemon peel.

*July 16, 2008*

PAUL GUSTINGS AT BROUSSARD'S, NEW ORLEANS

## SAZERAC
**Adapted from PAUL GUSTINGS, Broussard's, New Orleans By Robert Simonson**

Paul Gustings, the bartender at Broussard's in New Orleans, is nothing if not exacting when it comes to his Sazerac. "It has to be Old Overholt," he said of his choice of rye. And not the standard two ounces, but an ounce and three-quarters. The glass must be rinsed with the anise-flavored liqueur Herbsaint, not absinthe. And, he said, "I use much more Peychaud's that others do: 11 dashes." That's only, however, if you're halfway through the bottle of bitters. If you've just opened it, it's 13, according to Mr. Gustings, who says the dashes are smaller at that point; if you're near the end, make it 10 dashes. The extra dose of bitters gives the drink a rosier glow than most Sazeracs, and a very dry finish.

1 ¾ ounces Old Overholt rye
½ ounce simple syrup (page 27)
11 dashes Peychaud's bitters

3 dashes Herbsaint liqueur
Lemon twist

**1.** Chill a rocks glass. Meanwhile, in a mixing glass three-quarters filled with ice, mix the rye, simple syrup and bitters and stir until chilled, about 30 seconds.

**2.** Pour the Herbsaint into the chilled rocks glass and rotate until the liqueur coats the inside of the glass. Strain the contents of the mixing glass into the rocks glass. Rub the lemon twist along the rim of the rocks glass, twist over the drink and discard.

*August 6, 2014*

## VIEUX CARRÉ
**By JIM MEEHAN**

1 ounce rye whiskey
1 ounce cognac
1 ounce sweet vermouth

¼ ounce Benedictine
Dash of Angostura bitters
Dash of Peychaud's bitters

**1.** Stir all ingredients in a cocktail shaker with ice.

**2.** Strain into a chilled rocks glass over ice.

*June 12, 2012*

# THE BOULEVARDIER

## By TOBY CECCHINI

I'm puzzled that the Boulevardier cocktail hasn't found wider fame in the current fast-moving mixology environment, where old and storied is as revered as bitter and brown. Ask most mustached bar wags what their favorite cocktail is and a strong percentage would cite either the Negroni or the Manhattan. No surprise there; these are bedrock classics that, even done haphazardly, are tastier than most everything else going. Ask those same self-anointed experts to make you a Boulevardier and a strong percentage might be left scratching their heads. I can't fathom why; the Boulevardier is a marvel of a cocktail with an enviably colorful peerage, and it's effectively the bastard child of those two other cocktails I mentioned. In these colder months, it's a magnificent drink to have as a fallback when you want something richer and more complex than just a whiskey but can never seem to think of what else to order.

Considering this drink in the abstract is like looking at one of those M.C. Escher prints: it's a flock of snowy geese migrating or, depending on how you squint, a phalanx of black crows. It's composed of two parts American whiskey (rye or bourbon work equally well), with one part each of sweet vermouth and Campari, the famed bright red Italian bitter that smacks so forcefully of grapefruit peel. Taken one way, it's a Manhattan with a portion of Campari swapped in for the regular few drops of Angostura or other aromatic bitters. Seen the other way, it's a Negroni with whiskey in place of the gin.

The drink is credited to Harry McElhone, the founder and proprietor of Harry's New York Bar in Paris, and dated to 1927. It is mentioned only glancingly in his book "Barflies and Cocktails," not in the 300-odd cocktail recipes that make up the bulk of that volume, but rather in a tongue-in-cheek epilogue that follows, recounting the antics of his regular customers. In a brief paragraph, he cites: "Now is the time for all good barflies to come to the aid of the party, since Erskinne Gwynne crashed in with his Boulevardier Cocktail: 1/3 Campari, 1/3 Italian vermouth, 1/3 Bourbon whisky." McElhone's earlier volume, "Harry's ABC of Mixing Cocktails," has the cocktail listed using Canadian Club as the whisky. Two things of interest in this exhumation: the original recipe had the ingredients at equal parts, as with the Negroni; and McElhone seems to defer to Gwynne as the actual inventor of the drink.

The origin of the name now becomes magically obvious to students of 1920s Paris. Erskine Gwynne was a wealthy young American lad who flitted off to Paris to start a literary magazine in 1927, something along the lines of The Dial, The Transatlantic Review and other English language pamphlets that reaped a bountiful harvest by giving an early forum to writers like Hemingway, Joyce, Dos Passos, Sinclair Lewis, Noël Coward, Thomas Wolfe and others. His magazine, for which there was also a full-page ad at the back of "Barflies and Cocktails," was called The Boulevardier.

As a bartender, I find this drink so useful because, with just the slightest tweaks, it's transformed. It's a great in its de facto form, but I often find Campari a bit of a bully to softer whiskies, even at the modern recipe's half up ratio of 2 parts whiskey to 1 of Campari. By cutting the 1 part of Campari in half, or even thirds, one can swap in dozens of other amari, or what are known as potable bitters, and create new versions of the drink ad infinitum. Try half an ounce of Campari with a quarter-ounce each of Amaro Ramazzotti and Zwack Hungarian bitter, with a swath of orange zest instead of the lemon. Or try thirds each of Campari, Cynar, the artichoke-based amaro and Braulio, a wonderful old Alpine bitter with a stark, piney grab that is brand new to the American market. Playtime is limited only by your patience and your budget. Add to those factors the variance in different whiskies and vermouths and you have a simple drink that can present you with new facets forever. Nitpickers will suggest these variations are all technically different drinks, and should have their own names and sub-phyla; that's why they're called nitpickers. I just call it putting a little English on a Boulevardier, with a tip of the hat to Mr. Gwynne. The exception to that is if you use dry vermouth in place of the sweet, whereby it becomes an Old Pal Cocktail, pegged to the same source book and year (a very worthy, slightly drier alternative).

Some bartenders wander even farther from the original recipe. Richard Knapp, a co-owner of Mother's Ruin in Manhattan, cuts the Campari to ¾ of an ounce, adds a barspoonful of house-made pecan orgeat syrup and a dash of orange bitters, and still has the audacity to call it a Boulevardier. All to the good; whether donning plumage or cleaving to the conservative course, that the drink is at last turning up on lists here and there is heartening. Damon Boelte, the head bartender at Prime Meats in Carroll Gardens, Brooklyn, is winging a nouvelle tilt on the Old Pal, called the New Buddy, employing bourbon, Aperol, sweet white vermouth and grapefruit bitters, while at the new American bistro Battersby on Smith Street in Brooklyn, Rachel Kim has concocted a tight menu of classic cocktails in which a by-the-book Boulevardier finds a perfect nest. Still, the drink remains a rare enough find that you'd do well to add it to your quiver. Consider the recipe below a starter map, and find your bliss by adjusting the volumes and testing out other bitters.

EDDIE EAKIN AT BOULEVARDIER, DALLAS

## THE BOULEVARDIER

2 ounces rye or bourbon

1 ounce Campari

1 ounce sweet vermouth (I love a half and half mixture of Cinzano Rosso and Carpano Antica Formula)

Twist of lemon peel

**1.** Stir together all ingredients except twist of lemon in a mixing glass filled with ice.

**2.** Strain into either a stemmed cocktail glass or a rocks glass with ice and garnish with a twist of lemon zest.

*February 2, 2012*

## OLD PAL
By JIM MEEHAN

2 ounces rye whiskey

¾ ounce dry vermouth

¾ ounce Campari

**1.** Stir all ingredients with ice.

**2.** Strain into a chilled coupe glass.

*June 12, 2012*

# A DRINK AS COMPLICATED AS MOTHERHOOD

## By CLAIRE CAIN MILLER

On Sunday, mothers will be celebrated with flowers, or with breakfast in bed. On Monday, most will return to jobs where they are likely to be paid less than their male colleagues—precisely because they are mothers. Studies have repeatedly shown that women lose career opportunities and earnings after they have babies (even though fatherhood increases men's earnings.)

American motherhood is bittersweet, and in honor of Mother's Day, so is this week's Upshot cocktail.

We turned to Dear Mom, a beer and whiskey bar in San Francisco, to create a cocktail that would capture the duality of a working mother's role.

Brendan Heath, a bartender at Dear Mom, was inspired by a Boulevardier, a Parisian 1920s cocktail making a comeback. It combines bourbon, sweet vermouth and Campari. The Upshot twist: He replaced the vermouth with a lavender shrub involving kumquats, dried lavender and pink peppercorns. Shrubs, or drinking vinegars, are "labor-intensive and expensive" yet rewarding, he said—just like motherhood. He used an assertive rye and the bitter Campari to offset the shrub's sweetness.

The result is a blood-red cocktail that is sweet at first, stiff in the middle and bitter at the end. Happy Mother's Day.

## THE NOSTALGIA (A MOTHER'S DAY BOULEVARDIER)
By BRENDAN HEATH, Dear Mom, San Francisco

1 ounce strong rye whiskey (preferably Rittenhouse 100)

1 ounce Campari

1 ounce lavender shrub (recipe on page 152)

Orange peel

Kumquat, for garnish

**1.** Stir all ingredients except orange peel and kumquat 50 times quickly on ice in a mixing glass.

**2.** Strain into a coupe glass. Express orange peel over the drink and discard. Garnish with half a kumquat on a toothpick.

## LAVENDER SHRUB

| | |
|---|---|
| 1 cup brown sugar | 2 tablespoons lemongrass |
| 1½ cups halved kumquats | ⅔ cup blood orange balsamic vinegar |
| 4 tablespoons dried lavender | ⅓ cup apple cider vinegar |
| 2 tablespoons pink peppercorns | |

**1.** Mix together all ingredients except vinegars in a bowl and gently knead with hands. Cover and refrigerate for 24 hours.

**2.** Strain the resulting liquid through cheesecloth, then add vinegars.

*May 9, 2014*

# RECIPE REDUX;
# 1935: RAMOS GIN FIZZ

## By AMANDA HESSER

Nowadays, when a politician wants to make a point to the "folks," he goes to the diner to meet and greet and empathize while scarfing a grilled cheese. For all of its hokeyness, it's a safe strategy because, according to health experts, fried foods are what most Americans subsist on, and for some irrational reason, people trust a politician who appears to eat the same foods they do.

So I had to laugh—and feel a little sad too—when I came across an article in The Times from 1935 in which Huey Long, the colorful Louisiana senator known as the Kingfish, chose not a diner in Peoria but the Hotel New Yorker in New York City as his venue for attacking President Roosevelt's New Deal. In the photo op, Long stood surrounded by journalists and friends, waving a cocktail shaker.

The senator had arranged for the head bartender from the Hotel Roosevelt in New Orleans to fly to New York to make the drink—a good use of taxpayers' money—while Long talked shop. "Now this here chap knows how to mix a Ramos gin fizz," Long explained. And mix he did, while to a growing crowd Long expounded on the fine points of the fizz and the dull points of Roosevelt's plan, calling the president "no good" and a "faker." "Why don't they hold the Democratic convention and the Communist convention together and save money?" Long asked his audience. The contemporary photo-op equivalent—Hillary Clinton dutifully slugging back beer and a shot of whiskey in Crown Point, Ind.—makes for a rather depressing contrast.

Gin fizzes, which the cocktail historian Dale DeGroff defines as "just a sparkling version of a sour," had been around since the mid-19th century. Back then, before seltzer and club soda were widely available, bartenders created the fizz with baking soda. The

Ramos gin fizz, which was invented in 1888 by Henrico C. Ramos at the Imperial Cabinet Saloon in New Orleans, is embellished with cream, milk and orange-flower water.

Long's crowd-pleasing recipe called for a "noggin" of gin, egg white, orange-flower water, vanilla, milk, cream, powdered sugar, seltzer and ice, and was to be shaken for 10 minutes (although I find that implausibly, or anyway exhaustingly, long). His fizzes were passed around to the journalists, and The Times observed, "After some more posing for photographers and the talkies—the whole performance consumed fully an hour—the Kingfish left the bar with a broad grin, leading a crowd of reporters to his apartment on the 22nd floor of the hotel, where he spent two hours discoursing on the political situation."

The following week, however, Long's recipe was politely questioned by W. D. Rose, a reader from Schenectady. "While the writer does not feel equal to enter into a controversy with the versatile and able senator on any subject, much less on that of Ramos fizzes," Rose wrote, "and while not denying that the formula announced by Senator Long may be that of a perfect fizz, still the writer feels obliged to submit to the readers of The Times the only authentic and original formula for that famous and delectable decoction."

Now that is national discourse! Rose's Ramos gin fizz does not contain egg white, vanilla or seltzer, and is shaken for just one minute before being strained into a glass. Long's version is similar to those found in any cocktail book, so I chose to feature Rose's instead.

Rose promised that the drink would "conjure up visions . . . of wistaria [sic] blooming in old patios, of sights and smells associated only with the Vieux Carre. Those were not the first images that came to mind when I made the Rose version, but I was certainly bewitched by this cocktail, which doesn't so much impress you as consume you. Beneath a dense cap of froth and a misty overlay of orange-flower water is an oddly sweet yet tart, cool and creamy drink.

I loved Rose's Ramos gin fizz, but not every modern drinker will. Duggan McDonnell, of Cantina in San Francisco, whom I asked to reinvent the drink for this column, referred to the vintage recipe as a "Krispy Kreme cocktail." (It is much richer and floral than the lean Long version.)

"The orange-flower water in there is this component of dissonance," McDonnell said. "It gives it this unique perfumey quality."

And yet McDonnell didn't stray far from the original. After a little playing around, he came up with what he calls a "Californiafied Ramos gin fizz," made with low-fat milk, orange marmalade instead of orange-flower water and agave nectar rather than sugar. "I was not intending to reverse that and make it a kind of diet Ramos gin fizz," he said, "but that's sort of what it is." Don't let the "diet" idea scare you off: it contains plenty of flavor—and plenty of gin—and the Kingfish would have lapped it up.

## 1935: RAMOS GIN FIZZ

*This recipe appeared in a letter to "The Times," written by W. D. Rose. The original recipe called for "rich milk," which I took to mean old-style milk with a layer of cream. So I replicated the milk with a mixture of whole milk and a dash of heavy cream.*

| | |
|---|---|
| 1 tablespoon simple syrup (page 27) | ¼ teaspoon orange-flower water |
| 1 teaspoon lemon juice | 5 ounces milk |
| 1½ ounces gin | 1 tablespoon heavy cream |

**1.** Combine ingredients with 5 ice cubes in a cocktail shaker and shake for 2 minutes.

**2.** Strain into a tumbler.

## 2008: CALIFORNIAFIED RAMOS GIN FIZZ

By DUGAN McDONNELL, of Cantina, San Francisco

| | |
|---|---|
| 2 ounces low-proof gin (preferably Plymouth) | 1 teaspoon very bitter orange marmalade |
| 3 ounces 2-percent milk | ¾ ounce agave nectar syrup (1 part agave nectar to 1 part water) |
| 1 small egg white | |
| ½ ounce lemon juice | Seltzer water, for serving |

**1.** Combine all the ingredients except the seltzer water in a cocktail shaker. Remove the spring from your four-pronged Hawthorne strainer (the classic stainless-steel bar strainer with the horseshoe-shaped spring) and drop it into the shaker. Cover the strainer with the shaker top and "dry shake" (without ice) to emulsify and aerate the cocktail for what will seem like way too long (or, say, a commercial break).

**2.** Uncover the shaker, remove the spring, add ice, recap and shake vigorously once again. Strain into a Champagne flute and top with a spritz of seltzer. Serve.

*June 15, 2008*

# A 1920s PARISIENNE, REVIVED WITH PANACHE

## By WILLIAM L. HAMILTON

Here's a drink that has it all. You would date this drink. And not wait a day to call it. The sidecar has three ingredients—perfect ingredients. When you make it right, you get a 10. A 12. Cognac, Cointreau, freshly squeezed lemon juice. Tasted, the sidecar's sweet-to-sour sway, and back again, has the smart, sublime balance of a Zen riddle, served in a sleek glass.

With its suede rose color and serious spirit content, men can drink it and feel like men, women can drink it and feel like women. Couples can equate.

For cocktail-culture devotees, there's a neatly cuffed scuffle about who invented the sidecar. The Ritz's Little Bar and Harry's New York Bar both claim it, in Paris, in the 1920's. Harry's owner, Harry MacElhone, concocted it, says John J. Poister, author of "The New American Bartender's Guide" (New American Library, 2002). Mr. MacElhone served hot dogs with martinis, too.

Whoever or wherever, the sidecar watched the martini, popularized in the 1930's, grow up.

Now resurgent, the sidecar is a subtle spokesman for a second wave of interest in classic cocktails, a Prohibition-era relic being recreated for recent New Yorkers in East Village bars like Angel's Share, on Stuyvesant Street, a speakeasy behind an unmarked door in a second-floor Japanese noodle house. And it has been preserved for those who remember it in uptown hotel bars like the Cafe Pierre at the Pierre.

"Most people these days ordering sidecars have been turned on to them," said Connor Coffey, the beverage director at the Red Cat, a bar and restaurant in Chelsea in New York. "It's not a drink they've seen on 'Sex and the City.'"

The key to the sidecar is fresh lemon juice, which keeps it bright. Asked if he could make a sidecar and asked if he used fresh lemon juice, Eben Freeman, the happy-dog bartender on duty at the Red Cat last Sunday, said "of course," twice. Use lemonade or sours mix, and the drink's a cookie.

"Would you like a sugar rim, sir?" asked Richard Weyant, the bartender at the Cafe Pierre that same night.

For purists and/or fetishists, the sidecar has, as every great drink should, a point of honor, to be decided on a personal basis by those who drink it. Does the glass have a sugar rim, swiped with a lemon wedge and dusted with sugar (connoisseurs use confectioners' sugar), or is it presented plain?

The real issue is in being asked. Like any classic cocktail, the sidecar, in this day and age, is at its greatest use as a Global Positioning System. If you find yourself in a place where they don't know the question—"sugar rim, sir?"—then they can't make the answer.

You're not in a place that will support life.

·

SIDECAR FROM THE CAFE PIERRE, NEW YORK CITY

## SIDECAR
**Adapted from RICHARD WEYANT of the Café Pierre, New York City**

1 ½ ounces Courvoisier
¾ ounce Cointreau
½ ounce of fresh-squeezed lemon juice

Lemon wedge, for glass
Sugar, for glass

**1.** Shake Courvoisier, Cointreau, and lemon juice with ice.

**2.** Strain into a glass. For a sugar rim, swipe the rim with a lemon wedge; dab with sugar.

*April 28, 2002*

## POURING RIBBONS SIDECAR
**By MELISSA CLARK**

*In the hands of a great mixologist, simple syrup can add a lot more than just sweetness to the mix, and it is the secret to this delicious sidecar. Joaquín Simó of Pouring Ribbons, an East Village bar, uses a concentrated concoction made from two parts Demerara sugar to one part water, which add a compelling toffee-like taste and silky texture to the amber booze. Brown-sugar simple syrups are also wonderful in nonalcoholic drinks, particularly lemonade and ice tea, and they will last for months in the fridge.*

Orange slice, for garnish
Granulated sugar, for rim
½ teaspoon Demerara simple syrup (page 27)
2 ounces Cognac, Preferably Pierre Ferrand 1840

¾ ounce dry Curaçao, preferably Pierre Ferrand
¾ ounce fresh lemon juice
1 dash orange bitters
Orange twist, for garnish

**1.** Rub orange slice around half the outer rim of a coupe glass. Place sugar in a small dish. Holding glass parallel to dish, coat with sugar only the half you've rubbed with the orange. Set aside.

**2.** Combine simple syrup, the cognac, Curacao, lemon juice and bitters in a mixing glass. Add ice, then cover, shake and strain into the sugared glass. Garnish with an orange twist and serve.

*October 15, 2013*

# WHITE RUSSIANS ARISE, THIS TIME AT A BOWLING ALLEY

## By STEVEN KURUTZ

Among the significant dates in the history of Kahlúa, the Mexican coffee liqueur, surely March 6, 1998, rates a mention.

That was the release date of "The Big Lebowski," the Coen Brothers movie about an aging slacker who calls himself the Dude, and who, after a thug urinates on his prized rug, becomes caught up in a Chandleresque mystery.

Played with slouchy brio by Jeff Bridges, the Dude's chief pursuits involve bowling, avoiding work and drinking White Russians, the sweet cocktail made with vodka, Kahlúa and cream or milk.

The movie was a flop when it was released, but in the decade since, "The Big Lebowski" has attracted a cult following, and as the film's renown has grown, so has the renown of the White Russian, or, as the Dude calls them, "Caucasians." The drink is the subject of experimentation at cutting-edge bars like Tailor, in SoHo, which serves a crunchy dehydrated version—a sort of White Russian cereal. The British electro-pop band Hot Chip, meanwhile, recently invented a variation named the Black Tarantula. Not long ago, the cocktail was considered passé and often likened, in its original formula, to an alcoholic milkshake.

"When I first encountered it in the 1970s, the White Russian was something real alcoholics drank, or

beginners," said David Wondrich, the drinks correspondent for Esquire. Now, ordering the drink is "the mark of the hipster," he said.

Americans' renewed appreciation for coffee, spurred by Starbucks, which now markets its own coffee liqueur, may have also contributed to the White Russian's comeback.

To see the White Russian renaissance in full bloom, it is instructive to attend a Lebowski Fest, the semi-annual gatherings where fans of the movie revel in the Dude's deeply casual approach to life. There, the White Russian is consumed in oil-tanker quantities.

This was much in evidence at a fest held last month in New York, where 1,000 or so "achievers," as the movie's buffs call themselves, took over Lucky Strike Lanes, a bowling alley in Manhattan. The White Russian demand was such that, in addition to two bars, a White Russian satellite station had been set up and bartenders were in back mixing vats of reinforcements.

It turned out that management was following a directive from the event's organizers. "When we line up a venue, we always have the White Russian talk," said Will Russell, a founder of the Lebowski Fest.

Mr. Russell has learned from experience to lay in provisions. He recalled an incident at an early festival in his hometown of Louisville, Ky.

"Milk sold out within a one-mile radius of the bowling alley" where the event was held, he said. "We had to go to every local mini-market and gas station to satisfy the requirements of the achievers."

At Lucky Strike Lanes, the line at the White Russian station was often 10 deep, and it wasn't uncommon for someone to sidle up to the counter and say, "I'll take four." The bartender would lift a 12-quart plastic tub, straining to hold it steady as the mud-colored liquid sloshed.

Several people were dressed in character, including four men who showed up as white Russians: white painter pants, white T-shirts, brown fuzzy hats. Each drank their namesake, except one guy, who nursed a bottle of Miller Lite. "I'm lactose intolerant," he said.

The White Russian is not for the faint of stomach. "The cream is going to build up," said Ted Haigh, the author of "Vintage Spirits & Forgotten Cocktails." "If you're drinking these all night, the sugar will build, too, and you'll have a hell of a hangover."

If not an expanded waistline. A popular deviation is the Slim Russian, made with either soy or low-fat milk.

Still, some prefer the drink precisely because it is so rich. "I'm one of those fat guys that guzzle milk by the gallon," said Steve Barber, 28, an antique motorcycle restorer from Saugerties, N.Y., who was attending his first Lebowski Fest and came dressed in a flak vest like the Dude's Vietnam veteran buddy, Walter. Unlike a lot of Lebowski fans, Mr. Barber has a taste for the drink that predates his viewing of the movie. Several years ago, he said, he used to mix himself a White Russian every day for breakfast: "I called it the 'Big Boy Milkshake.' "

Lebowski viewers often develop a taste for White Russians that carries beyond the film or the festivals.

"I'd had them before, but not regularly," said Don Plehn, 39, a district court clerk from Baltimore. "I drink a lot more of them now." Mr. Plehn took a sip of his third White Russian of the night and said, "It's a slow-sippin' drink."

Lebowski adherents may have vaulted the White Russian to icon status, but serious cocktail enthusiasts still deride it for being simplistic and overly sweet—a confection designed to appeal to unserious drinkers.

"It's hard to think of a more boring drink, except, perhaps, when it's spraying from the Dude's mouth," said Martin Doudoroff, a historian for CocktailDB.com.

Skeptics like Mr. Doudoroff would probably blanch at a variation called the White Trash Russian. "You take a bottle of Yoo-hoo," Mr. Russell said, "drink half, then fill it with vodka and enjoy."

Believed to date to the 1950s or early 1960s, the White Russian has no great origin story; its culinary precursor is the Alexander. Having been popular in the disco '70s, the cocktail is, in the words of Mr. Doudoroff, "a relic of an era that was the absolute nadir of the American bar."

As it happens, this was the period when Jeff Dowd was living in Seattle, driving a taxi and doing a lot of "heavy hanging," as he put it. Mr.

Dowd, 59, an independent film producer and producers representative, is the inspiration for the Dude—a character Joel and Ethan Coen created by taking what Mr. Dowd was like back then and exaggerating a bit, although the White Russians preference is spot on.

"There was a woman I lived with named Connie," Mr. Dowd said, by phone from his office in Santa Monica, Calif., beginning a rambling oration that was highly Dude-like. "She and her boyfriend, Jamie, were mixologists. We were hanging out and drinking at that time. We went from White Russians to Dirty Mothers, a darker version of a White Russian. It was a very hedonistic period."

Mr. Dowd moved on from White Russians years ago, but has started drinking them again, mainly so as not to disappoint fans. "When I first met Cheech at the Sundance Film Festival," he said, referring to Cheech Marin of the comedy duo Cheech and Chong, "the first thing we all wanted to do is smoke a joint with him so we could tell our grandchildren, 'Hey, I smoked a joint with Cheech.' Well,

people want to say they had a White Russian with the Dude. I don't want to turn them down, which has added a little extra tonnage to me."

It has become customary for achievers to scrutinize "The Big Lebowski," parsing the film's most trivial details for deep meaning. Which begs the question: Why is the White Russian the Dude's chosen beverage, beyond the fact that Mr. Dowd briefly drank the cocktail years ago? Theories abound.

"The Dude is very laid-back and the White Russian has a laid-back element," Mr. Russell said. "You can't just grab it and go. There's a ritual to it."

Mr. Barber said: "The Dude almost holds himself to a higher class than he's in, which could explain the White Russian. It requires more thought than just popping a top."

Then again, the reason could be even simpler.

"When I do drink a White Russian, it does go down easy," Mr. Dowd said. "It actually is a good drink. It's essentially a liquefied ice cream cone that you can buy in a bar."

## WHITE RUSSIAN
Adapted from DALE DeGROFF

1 ounce coffee liqueur                    1½ ounces heavy cream
1 ounce vodka

**1.** Scoop a big handful of ice into a shaker, add all ingredients and shake well.

**2.** Strain and serve in an old-fashioned glass.

Variations: Substitute brandy for the vodka and the drink is called a Dirty White Mother. Substituting brandy for the vodka and milk for the cream results in a Separator.

*December 3, 2008*

## CORPSE REVIVER #2

¾ ounce gin                              Scant bar-spoon-ful quality absinthe
¾ ounce lemon juice                         (see note)
¾ ounce Cointreau                        Lemon twist, for garnish (optional)
¾ ounce Cocchi Aperitivo Americano       Maraschino cherry, for garnish (optional)

**1.** Combine all ingredients except twist and cherry over ice in a cocktail shaker and shake vigorously.

**2.** Strain into cocktail coupe or pony glass. A garnish is unnecessary, but different recipes call for either a twist of lemon or a real maraschino cherry.

When absinthe was unobtainable, the drink was routinely made with pastis, and a dash or even a rinse in the glass was the call. Good absinthe, though much stronger in alcohol, is far more nuanced, so I prefer a scant bar-spoonful in the shaker itself.

*April 21, 2010*

## CORPSE REVIVER VARIATION
By ROSIE SCHAAP

1½ ounce gin                             ½ ounce simple syrup (page 27)
½ ounce Cointreau                        1 dash absinthe
½ ounce Lillet Blanc                     Twist of lemon, for garnish
¾ ounce fresh lemon juice

**1.** Shake all ingredients except lemon twist with ice in a cocktail shaker.

**2.** Strain into a coupe and garnish with a twist.

*October 11, 2012*

# A REAL DRINKING BAR

## By WILLIAM L. HAMILTON

Bobby Flay, the celebrity chef, is a bourbon drinker, so it would make sense that there would be a bourbon drink, the Whiskey Smash, on the cocktail list at his restaurant, Bar Americain, at 152 West 52nd Street.

"My wife is from Texas, so we drink a lot of bourbon at home," Mr. Flay said on Tuesday, sitting at the 28-foot zinc bar that is the centerpiece of Bar Americain with his business partner, Laurence Kretchmer, who devised the drinks list. "In the warm weather I'm a total sucker for mint juleps." (In the winter it's Manhattans.) Mr. Flay added that when he attends the Kentucky Derby, which is frequently, "I'm bathed in bourbon and mint."

Mr. Flay and Mr. Kretchmer's other restaurants, Mesa Grill and Bolo, have themes: the American Southwest and Spain, respectively. They've done Las Vegas too, with a Mesa Grill at Caesar's Palace. Bar Americain also has a theme, which is brasserie-style dining, but the not very hidden subtext is cocktail drinking.

The two-story bar and its huge, ornate mirror greet those entering the dining room like Prometheus rising above the fountains at Rockefeller Center: a mythological place to take the waters. The restaurant was designed by David Rockwell, an architect and set designer who is the Walt Disney of the New York theme dining world.

In Paris a brasserie with a "bar américain" is classically a place where you can order a mixed drink, as well as wine and beer. So Mr. Kretchmer's cocktail list, appropriately, is classics, including a Hemingway daiquiri (Papa's purist version, with rum and fresh citrus) and the Bronx cocktail, invented at the Brass Rail bar in the Waldorf Astoria Hotel in honor of the opening of the Bronx Zoo in 1899, when the Waldorf was on 34th Street. The Whiskey Smash, a mint-infested julep, has a sunburst of lemon juice.

"We don't want to serve the next kumquat mojito," Mr. Flay said of the era of cocktail innovation now upon us. "I'm a native Manhattanite, at least that I know of, fifth generation, from the Lower East Side. My grandfather was this really Damon Runyon character. He knew everyone: good guys, bad guys. That's the way New York was. The judges and gangsters all hung out in the same bars."

That's very elaborate cocktail nostalgia, and one can only wish the same sort of success for Bar Americain, updated but with the kind of notorious elbow rub at the bar that makes hoisting a drink in unfamiliar company so enjoyable an enterprise.

No, the pleasure's mine. What did you say you did again?

BOBBY FLAY'S WHISKEY SMASH

## WHISKEY SMASH

2 lemon wedges
Several sprigs of fresh mint
¾ ounce simple syrup (page 27)

1½ ounces Maker's Mark bourbon
Splash of club soda
I mint sprig, for garnish

**1.** Muddle lemon, mint leaves and syrup in the bottom of an Old-Fashioned glass.

**2.** Add bourbon and club soda with ice and stir. Garnish with a mint sprig.

*April 24, 2005*


## BROOKLYN
### By JIM MEEHAN

2 ounces rye whiskey
¾ ounce dry vermouth

¼ ounce maraschino liqueur
¼ ounce amaro

**1.** Stir all ingredients with ice.

**2.** Strain into a chilled coupe glass.

*June 12, 2012*


## AVIATION
### By JIM MEEHAN

2 ounces gin
¾ ounce lemon juice

¾ ounce maraschino liqueur

**1.** Shake all ingredients with ice.

**2.** Strain into chilled coupe glass.

*June 12, 2012*


## CAPRICE
### By JIM MEEHAN

1½ ounce gin
1½ ounce dry vermouth
½ ounce Bénédictine

Dash of orange bitters
Orange twist, for garnish

**1.** Stir all ingredients except twist with ice.

**2.** Strain into a chilled coupe glass and garnish with an orange twist.

*June 12, 2012*

## EL PRESIDENTE
By JIM MEEHAN

2 ounces rum
1 ounce blanc vermouth
¼ ounce orange Curacao

1 bar spoon of grenadine (about 1 teaspoon)
Orange twist, for garnish

**1.** Stir all ingredients except twist with ice.

**2.** Strain into a chilled coupe glass and garnish with an orange twist.

*June 12, 2012*

## FANCY FREE
By JIM MEEHAN

2 ounces rye whiskey
½ ounce maraschino liqueur
Dash of Angostura bitters

Dash of orange bitters
Orange twist, for garnish

**1.** Stir all ingredients except twist with ice.

**2.** Strain into a rocks glass filled with ice and garnish with an orange twist.

*June 12, 2012*

## HARVEST SLING
Adapted from JOHN DERAGON, PDT, New York City, by Jim Meehan

1½ ounces apple brandy
½ ounce sweet vermouth
½ ounce Bénédictine
½ ounce Cherry Heering

½ ounce lemon juice
Splash of ginger ale
Orange wheel, for garnish

**1.** Shake all ingredients except the ginger ale and orange wheel with ice.

**2.** Strain into a Collins glass filled with ice. Top with a splash of ginger ale and garnish with half an orange wheel.

*June 12, 2012*

## JASMINE
**Adapted from PAUL HARRINGTON, Clover, Spokane, Wash., by Jim Meehan**

2 ounces gin
1 ounce Cointreau
¾ ounce lemon juice

½ ounce Campari
Lemon wheel, for garnish

**1.** Shake all ingredients except lemon wheel with ice.

**2.** Strain into a chilled coupe glass and garnish with a lemon wheel.

*June 12, 2012*

## JOURNALIST
**By JIM MEEHAN**

¾ ounce gin
¼ ounce dry vermouth
¼ ounce sweet vermouth

¼ ounce orange Curaçao
¼ ounce lemon juice
Dash of Angostura bitters

**1.** Shake all ingredients with ice.

**2.** Strain into a chilled coupe glass.

*June 12, 2012*

## JUNIOR
**By JIM MEEHAN**

2 ounces rye whiskey
¾ ounce lime juice

½ ounce Bénédictine
2 dashes of Angostura bitters

**1.** Shake all ingredients with ice and strain into a chilled coupe glass.

## LAST WORD
**By JIM MEEHAN**

¾ ounce gin
¾ ounce maraschino liqueur

¾ ounce green Chartreuse
¾ ounces lime juice

**1.** Shake all ingredients with ice and strain into a chilled coupe. No garnish.

*June 12, 2012*

## WIDOW'S KISS
**By JIM MEEHAN**

2 ounces apple brandy
¼ ounce yellow Chartreuse

¼ ounce Bénédictine
2 dashes of Angostura bitters

**1.** Stir all ingredients with ice and strain into a chilled coupe glass.

*June 12, 2012*

## MARY PICKFORD
By JIM MEEHAN

2 ounce white rum
¾ ounce pineapple juice

½ ounce maraschino liqueur
¼ ounce grenadine

**1.** Shake all ingredients with ice and strain into a chilled coupe glass.

*June 12, 2012*

## PEGU CLUB
By JIM MEEHAN

2 ounces gin
¾ ounce orange Curaçao
¾ ounce lime juice

Dash of Angostura bitters
Dash of orange bitters
Lime wheel, for garnish

**1.** Shake all ingredients except lime wheel in a cocktail shaker with ice.

**2.** Strain into a chilled coupe glass and garnish with a lime wheel.
June 12, 2012

## ROSITA
By JIM MEEHAN

1½ ounces tequila
½ ounce Campari
½ ounce sweet vermouth

½ ounce dry vermouth
Dash of Angostura Bitters
Orange twist, for garnish

**1.** Stir all ingredients except orange twist with ice in a cocktail shaker.

**2.** Strain into a chilled coupe glass and garnish with an orange twist.

*June 12, 2012*

## SIESTA
Adapted from KATIE STIPE, Flatiron Lounge, New York City, by Jim Meehan

2 ounces tequila
¾ ounce Campari
½ ounce lime juice

½ ounce grapefruit juice
Grapefruit twist, for garnish

**1.** Shake all ingredients except grapefruit twist with ice.

**2.** Strain into a chilled coupe glass and garnish with a grapefruit twist.

*June 12, 2012*

# SINGAPORE SLING IS SPOKEN HERE

## By COLIN CAMPBELL

It would be satisfying if you could slide down sweatily into one of the bamboo chairs at the Long Bar of Singapore's old Raffles Hotel, where the first Singapore sling is supposed to have been mixed in 1915, and know for a certainty that the cold, pink, frothy mixture in front of you was the only authentic Singapore sling in the world.

It may be. Your dour bartender is likely to be a member of the same family, the Ngiams, whose forebear, Ngiam Tong Boon, is still honored as the drink's inventor. And if you're leisured or dissolute enough to find yourself under the spacious bar's ceiling fans at an unfrequented time of day—late in the morning, say, before busloads of tourists have hit the place, downed their gallons of slings at about $2.50 a glass and hurtled off alarmingly into the equatorial technopolis—you're likely to discover on looking around that the three or four other people in the room are almost impossible to place. Stir these mysteries with the "delicious, slow-acting, insidious thing" that is the Singapore sling, as a prewar epicure named Charles H. Baker Jr. once described it, and the whole scene is apt to wobble off into gorgeously seedy tropical fantasies.

Not everyone loves the Raffles. Some find it dowdy. But it's the place, after all, that was not only named after a relative genius among British imperialists—Sir Stamford Raffles ~ but that also housed and soothed (or was the sort of place that might have housed and soothed) Kipling and Conrad, Maugham and Coward, and constellations of other moody travelers, pleasure-seeking adventurers, romantics, lords, salesmen, fops.

The hotel, moreover, is expected soon to get its most thorough refurbishment and re-authentication ever. A new high-rise hotel tower is to be built next door, to take advantage of the Raffles name and to house more guests, while most of the clumsy architectural accretions of the decades are to be stripped away from the fine old 1887 French Renaissance building.

According to the hotel's energetic manager, Roberto Pregarz, the ballroom, for instance, and the present Long Bar, which were stuck on in the 1920s, cluttering the grand entrance, are to vanish. And for all Mr. Pregarz knows, the original Long Bar where Mr. Ngiam worked, which twisted among the lobby's columns, may be restored. The air-conditioned Writers Bar—known until recently as the Tudor Bar and still indistinguishable from Tudor Bars at motels across America—may also disappear. The Raffles today is said to be in much better shape, and it handles a lot more guests, than a decade or so ago, but to take full advantage of its wide marble floors, porticoed verandas and still-magical Palm Court it needs a ruthless architectural and decorative sweep.

The best spot, in any case, to have a drink at the Raffles is the Palm Court, where at lunch under the awning, or out on the lawn, you can hear the twitter and crawk of tropical birds in the palms, and where at night you can listen to a pretty good piano player. The wicker screens on the sidelines are white, the chairs are white, the stucco's white, the piano's white. Unabashedly colonial, it's still a nice place to sit.

(The grilled white pomfret—a flat silvery fish of the Indian and Pacific Oceans that is known here as ikan bawal—is one of the best things a human being can eat. No offense to the "maitre d'hotel butter" the Raffles serves it with, but it's even better simply grilled, with plenty of fresh limes to squeeze over it, and forget the butter. The chef was happy to oblige.)

At a table beside the piano a young American dressed in a blood-orange tropical shirt was telling a young woman with her chin on her hand and an orchid behind her ear, "I was looking at this black yawn of death, dangling over the side." He had recently been to sea.

Drinks called "slings" have been mixed for a century and a half (the word is apparently American) and it's possible that even Kipling and Conrad tried some sort of gin sling at the Raffles. Of course, it's easier to imagine Conrad drinking stengas, from the Malay for "half," the measure of whiskey tossed into the glass with water or soda. A bit later, the British rubber-planters who frequented the Raffles drank innumerable such halves.

The hotels that catered to Europeans around the Orient all had their own special slings after a while, but the "Singapore Raffles gin sling," as Baker called it, was already famous in the 1920s—or after the local good life's Goanese orchestras had given way to White Russian cellists and jazz bands from England and America.

The Raffles version, at least by Baker's account, was topped off with club soda and a spiral of lime peel, whereas the modern and allegedly original version contains no club soda and is garnished with pineapple. This discrepancy is only one reason it may be doubted that the modern version re-enacts the moment in 1915 when Mr. Ngiam poured the model of gin slings from his shaker. Today's Singapore sling at the Long Bar, for instance, is sweeter than at the Writers Bar—and there are at least three radically different recipes floating around the Raffles that all purport to be authentic.

Soda and lime peel sound cool, no doubt—but then the Singapore sling is something more than a coolant. It's a tour de force, a specimen of wit.

If you're simply hot there's always beer, and the bars and tables of the Raffles are haunted by the memory of at least one terrifying beer-swiller. He was a Dutch archeologist, a gigantic man named Pieter van Stein Callenfels, and during the '20s and '30s he liked to pad around the Raffles in curry-stained pajamas. "When five of Callenfels' friends failed to show up for their curry tiffin," Ilsa Sharp, a recent historian of the Raffles, has written, "he ate for six," and always washed down such light midday meals (which is what a tiffin is in Anglo-Indian) with a dozen quarts of beer.

During the Raffles' quietest time of day, when everybody seems to be taking an afternoon nap, the Palm Court is a good place for reading, and I'm sorry I never found Victor Purcell's "Memoirs of a Malayan Official," from which the Callenfels stuff is said to come. Purcell, later a lecturer at Cambridge, is best known for his erudite "The Chinese in Southeast Asia," and I'd love to know what he and Callenfels talked about.

Maugham found the Raffles good for writing as well—though how he could sit out in the Palm Court, in the sun, morning after sweltering morning, and knock off even a Malayan short story about the usual desperate planters and secretly impassioned wives, much less "Of Human Bondage," is hard to imagine.

One sultry afternoon, I was sitting in the court reading Patrick Anderson's "Snake Wine: A Singapore Episode," a memoir by a young Englishman who came here to teach in the early 1950's, when the energetic Mr. Pregarz zoomed up and suggested that Derrick Lee, head barman of both the court and the Writers Bar, would now show me how to make a perfect Singapore sling.

After a couple of samples, and a delightful lesson in why you must use pineapples from Sarawak, I padded off down the veranda to the hotel's cavernous barber shop. There, under a slow fan, an old Singaporean had the miraculous good sense, having snipped away gently for what seemed like hours, to clap his hand down smartly on the crown of my head.

Mystifyingly, he did it several times, with a loud clapping sound. It felt as bracing as the rainstorm just breaking outside the window, and seemed somehow very Raffles.

## SINGAPORE SLING
### By DERRICK LEE

*Derrick Lee has been at the Raffles for only 12 years, but he's a splendid teacher, and this is how he makes a single Singapore sling...*

| | |
|---|---|
| 1 ounce, or jigger, of gin | 2 ounces fresh pineapple juice |
| ¾ ounce cherry brandy | 1 to two drops of bitters |
| "a few drops" of Cointreau | 1 dash of grenadine, for color. |
| Truly a few drops of Benedictine | Wedge of pineapple, for garnish |
| Juice of half a medium-size lemon | Maraschino cherry, for garnish |

**1.** Add all ingredients except wedge of pineapple and maraschino cherry to a cocktail shaker containing four ice cubes. Cover the shaker and shake it hard for about 10 seconds.

**2.** Pour the result, which should foam, into a 10-ounce glass with two ice cubes. Garnish with a wedge of pineapple and a maraschino cherry.

*December 12, 1982*

# THE GIBSON
## By WILLIAM L. HAMILTON

Looks are everything, as any cocktail drinker will tell you.

The right shaker, the right glass, the right garnish—you don't want anything less than perfect approaching your lips as you close your eyes for that first shy sip. Drink dirty well water with a ladle if you disagree.

Despite New Year's resolutions to be less superficial, I can't get past thin shakers, thick glasses or dumb garnishes. A cocktail should look as sharply executed as it tastes. Ounce for ounce, it is a precise measure of intention. You can relax when the drink's in your hand.

The simplest cocktails have the finest points. A gibson is a martini with an onion instead of an olive. So

what? I can hear someone say.

Jacques Sorci, the executive chef for the Ritz-Carlton New York, Battery Park, buys small, sweet onions from an organic farm in Quakertown, Pa., and cooks and pickles them à la grecque in chicken stock, white wine vinegar, bay leaves and fresh thyme, to serve as a garnish for gibsons at Rise, the hotel's bar.

That's so what. The Rise gibson has an aesthetic singularity that commodifies its value as an experience like the pearl in an oyster.

A black olive would make the gibson a buckeye. A niçoise olive would make it excellent, as my experience has shown.

## THE GIBSON
Adapted from the RISE BAR at the Ritz-Carlton New York, Battery Park, New York City

| | |
|---|---|
| 3 ounces of Hendrick's gin | Cocktail onions |
| A touch of dry vermouth | |

**1.** Chill martini glass. Fill shaker with ice. Pour in gin. Add vermouth. Cover and shake.

**2.** Put several cocktail onions on a stick and place in chilled glass. Pour cocktail over onions and serve.

*January 5, 2003*

## JUNIPERO GIBSON WITH PICKLED RED ONION
By GABRIELLE HAMILTON, Prune, New York City

*The cocktails I like best have the same kind of directness. In our gibson, for example, I use a gin called Junipero. It has a powerful juniper flavor, which I like. My bartender fills a spritz bottle with vermouth and mists the interior of the chilled glass. Rather than using white cocktail onions, we pickle our own—the same ones used in the Garrotxa snack. I'm partial to drinks that are salty, clean-tasting and just this side of savory. With little ceremony they get right to the point: they revive and satisfy that basic thirst.*
YIELD: 4 COCKTAILS

| | |
|---|---|
| ½ red onion, very thinly sliced into ribbons | ¼ cup red wine vinegar |
| Kosher salt | Dry vermouth |
| | 16 ounces Junipero gin |

**1.** Place onion in a bowl, and season with salt. Let sit for 10 minutes. Sprinkle vinegar on top, and let sit 10 minutes more.

**2.** Chill 4 martini glasses in freezer. Fill a spray bottle with ¼-inch vermouth, and spray the inside of each glass. Or pour a little vermouth in each glass, swirl it, then pour it out, so glass is just lightly coated.

**3.** Fill a large cocktail shaker with ice, and pour gin over it. Shake vigorously. Strain into glasses. Serve.

*May 16, 2001*

## THE BIJOU
By ROBERT SIMONSON

*The Bijou is a gin-based minor classic from the 1890s that is a favorite among mixologists. An ounce of sweet vermouth satisfies the sweet tooth, while an equal portion of herbal Chartreuse lends some complexity. Tell your more worldly guests that this drink is found in the "Bartenders' Manual" of the 19th-century bar legend Harry Johnson, and you'll win their approval. (Some choose to increase the gin content to create a more dry, less herbal drink. You may want to test drive the recipe before serving.)*

| | |
|---|---|
| 1 ounce London dry gin | 1 ounce Chartreuse |
| 1 ounce sweet vermouth | Dash orange bitter |

**1.** Still ingredients over ice and strain into a chilled cocktail glass.

*November 24, 2011*

## IRISH WHISKEY SOUR
By ROSIE SCHAAP

2 ounces Redbreast 12-year-old whiskey
1 ounce fresh-squeezed lemon juice
1 scant teaspoon simple syrup (page 27)
A dash of Angostura orange bitters

1 teaspoon egg white (optional, for extra froth).
1 half-wheel of orange, for garnish
1 cherry, for garnish

**1.** Fill a shaker with ice, and add all ingredients except half orange wheel and cherry. Shake vigorously.

**2.** Strain into a 4-ounce sour glass or Champagne flute (for straight up) or into a highball over ice. Garnish with a half-wheel of orange and a cherry.

*March 8, 2012*

## STONE FENCE
By ROSIE SCHAAP

1 shot Old Overholt (or whatever rye you like)
3 dashes Angostura bitters

8 to 10 ounces cider
Apple slice, for garnish

**1.** Pour rye into a pint glass, then add ice and bitters.

**2.** Top up with cider and garnish with apple.

*January 31, 2014*

# PAYING HOMAGE, A BIT BELATEDLY, TO A MIX MASTER OF RENOWN
By DAVID WONDRICH

Last Sunday, the many-armed God of Bartenders was smiling on Woodlawn Cemetery in the Bronx. Perhaps it was because the gods like to see their prophets honored. In any case, the sun was shining, the breeze was gentle, the ice stayed cold, and Jerry Thomas's grave was right where it was supposed to be.

I'd been a little worried on that score. In death, Jeremiah P. Thomas, to give his full name (or as much of it as anyone has ever been able to ferret out) was a slippery character. In life, he was solid enough: as this newspaper noted upon his death in 1885, he was "at one time better known to club men and men about town than any other bartender in the city."

The various saloons he ran were showplaces of the mixologist's art and drew a crowd heavy with the sporting and theatrical celebrities of the day. In 1862, "the Professor," as he was known, achieved immortality when he published "How to Mix Drinks, or the Bon-Vivant's Companion," the world's first bartender's guide. It sold widely and went into many editions.

As famous as Jerry Thomas was to his contemporaries, he trod very lightly in the historical record. In the course of researching an annotated edition of his book, time and again I've dug up some contemporary source that should mention him—census records, city directories, memoirs of sporting characters—only to find that he has slipped away. So when I finally tracked down his death certificate at the Municipal Archives and saw "Woodlawn" entered as his place of burial, I knew I had to go there, but I also knew he might not be around to meet me. Even after calling the cemetery and securing a plot number, I still had my doubts.

If I was to go on a wild goose chase, I wasn't going to do it alone. But since Jerry Thomas is to modern cocktail culture roughly what Louis Armstrong is to jazz, even the mere possibility of finding his grave was enough to lure a distinguished group of bartenders and cocktail enthusiasts to Grand Central Terminal at the ungodly hour of 1 on a Sunday afternoon. Among others, the faithful consisted of Audrey Saunders of the Bemelmans Bar, Julie Reiner of the Flatiron Lounge, Toby Cecchini of

Passerby, Del Pedro of L'Acajou, Martin Doudoroff of CocktailDB.com, Allen Katz of the Slow Food organization and the writer John Hodgman.

The No. 4 train carried us to the Bronx, and a pleasant stroll through Woodlawn's old trees and patrician mausoleums brought us to Section 55 of the "Poplar" plot, where the grave was supposed to be. At first, it seemed as if the old Thomas jinx was asserting itself: the plot was large, and so thickly strewn with headstones that it would be easy to miss one. Then a cry came from Mr. Pedro, searching near the northeast corner of the plot. He had found it—a plain hunk of granite marked simply "J P. Thomas" (note the mysterious punctuation).

An enormous cocktail shaker was produced, and most of a bottle of straight rye whiskey was poured into it (rye being the traditional mixing whiskey of New York), followed by a much smaller quantity of thick sugar syrup and a couple dozen dashes of Angostura bitters. In went the ice, which had miraculously survived the long journey from Brooklyn, and everyone gave the thing a couple of ceremonial shakes.

Lemon twists and cocktail glasses were issued (the Professor would not have approved of plastic cups) and Ms. Reiner poured the drinks, including one for the man we had come to see. For Jerry Thomas, it had been a long time between drinks.
*October 10, 2004*

FROM LEFT, MARTIN DOUDOROFF, AUDREY SAUNDERS, DEL PEDRO,
TOBY CECCHINI (PARTIALLY HIDDEN), KAREN RUSH AND
JULIE REINER TOAST JERRY THOMAS

## BLUE BLAZER
### Adapted from DAVID WONDRICH

*Jerry Thomas's signature drink is essentially a hot toddy for pyromaniacs.*
YIELD: 2 DRINKS, AND, WITH LUCK, GENEROUS APPLAUSE

2 pieces lemon peel, pith removed
2 teaspoons Demerara or raw sugar

4 ounces cask-strength Scotch

**1.** Place a piece of lemon peel in each of two teacups or small, heavy glasses.

**2.** To prevent house fires, pour some water into a baking sheet over which you will make blue blazers.

**3.** Dim lights. Have ready two one-pint mugs, ideally metal with a flared lip. Pour sugar and 3 ounces of boiling water into one mug and then add Scotch. Ignite alcohol with a long match and pour about half the liquid into empty mug, then pour that back into the first mug. Repeat four or five times. Proceed quickly but with great caution.

**4.** Pour flaming drink into teacups or glasses and cover with mug to extinguish flames.

**It is imperative to practice this drink with water, and no fire, before attempting the combustible version.**


## PRESCRIPTION JULEP
### Adapted from DAVID WONDRICH

*First published in "Harper's Monthly" in 1857, this is "the tastiest mint julep recipe I know,"*
Mr. Wondrich wrote.

½ ounce superfine sugar
1 ounce hot water
7 mint leaves, plus one mint sprig for garnish

1½ ounces Cognac
½ ounce rye
Finely crushed ice

**1.** Dissolve sugar in water in an old-fashioned glass or julep cup. Add mint leaves and press lightly with a spoon.

**2.** Add spirits, fill glass with finely crushed ice and stir. Poke a straw and mint sprig into julep and serve.


## ST. CHARLES PUNCH
### Adapted from DAVID WONDRICH

*This New Orleans drink appeared in the 1862 edition of Jerry Thomas's bartending guide.*

1 teaspoon superfine sugar
2 teaspoons lemon juice
Crushed ice
2 ounces ruby port

1 ounce Cognac
Fresh berries, for garnish
Orange slices, for garnish (optional)

**1.** In a cocktail shaker, stir sugar into lemon juice to dissolve. Toss in two handfuls of cracked ice, add port and Cognac, and shake.

**2.** Strain into a small glass, add ice and ornament with berries and orange slices.

## WHISKEY CRUSTA
### Adapted from DAVID WONDRICH

*Crustas were probably the first cocktails made with citrus juice. The lemon peel cup-within-a-cup trick is nice, but not strictly necessary. As a shortcut, a lemon twist will do.*

½ lemon, cut along equator
1 teaspoon superfine sugar, plus extra for frosting glass
2 dashes bitters

2 ounces bourbon
½ teaspoon orange Curaçao
1 teaspoon lemon juice

**1.** Rub cut end of half lemon around rim of a small (3- to 4-ounce) wineglass, then dip glass in extra sugar. Using a vegetable peeler, carefully pare the lemon so peel comes off in one piece. Lower peel into glass to make a kind of cup.

**2.** Stir remaining ingredients in a shaker with a handful of ice for one minute and strain into glass.

*October 31, 2007*

## BRANDY ALEXANDER
### By ROSIE SCHAAP

1 ounce brandy
1 ounce crème de cacao

1 ounce heavy cream
Nutmeg

**1.** Shake brandy, crème de cacao and cream with ice in a cocktail shaker.

**2.** Strain into a coupe and grate a little nutmeg on top.

*November 26, 2014*

## BEACHCOMBER
### By FLORENCE FABRICANT

*The Beachcomber dates to the 1930s or '40s and has been sometimes been described as a marachino-flavored daiquiri.*

2 ounces white rum
1 ounce triple sec
¾ ounce fresh lime juice

1 teaspoon maraschino liqueur
1 high-quality maraschino cherry, for garnish

**1.** Combine rum, triple sec, lime juice and maraschino liqueur in measuring cup. Place ½ cup ice in blender and process to crush. Scrape down sides of container. Add drink mixture and blend briefly.

**2.** Pour into cocktail glass and drop in cherry.

*May 20, 2014*

# DRINKING LIKE A POET

## By ROSIE SCHAAP

One chilly evening more than a decade ago, my Glasgow-born-and-bred friend Angus Robertson greeted me at his Brooklyn Heights doorway in his kilt and sporran and welcomed me to my first Burns supper, the Scottish celebration on Jan. 25 that honors the poet Robert Burns. About 20 of us gathered around the haggis (nothing to be afraid of, basically a big mealy sausage), neeps and tatties (that's turnips and potatoes) and whisky-fortified gravy. Then the time arrived for dessert, poetry, song and whisky. Lots of Scotch whisky, selected with care by our hosts.

Up to that night, I had nostalgic associations with the blended Scotches favored by my grandfather—Dewar's especially—but I attached a little latent class rage to single malts. Scotch, I thought, was a rich man's game: the sort of thing that might be found in a still life, in a cut-crystal glass beside a leatherbound book that might never be read. Burns night, then, created some cognitive dissonance. If any writer can be regarded as a poet of the people, it's Burns—"the Ploughman Poet," a farmer's son— who taught us that freedom and whisky go together. The best Burns suppers "are the home kind, without any pomp or pretension whatsoever," says another Glaswegian and an artist, Lex Braes, who always includes a group reading of Burns's "Tam O'Shanter," which,

he says, is "a great cautionary tale of the demon drink." (Braes's and Burns's tongues were at least partly in cheek.)

Burns night is the perfect opportunity to consider Scotch's tremendous variety, from mellow and gentle to vegetal and even barnyardy, and up through to the big, peaty, smoky numbers that many people think of first when they think Scotch (see below for a range of recommendations). While the evening highlights whisky served neat—but with a pitcher of water alongside it, which often helps to open up its flavors—there's no reason not to kick the festivities off with a Rabbie Burns cocktail, which adds vermouth, Bénédictine and a bit of citrus. A Rob Roy (a variation on the Manhattan, with Scotch) is also a fine choice. It's worth noting, however, that the Rob Roy was created not on a windswept Hebridean isle but at the Waldorf Hotel in New York City in 1894.

What's not to love about a holiday that celebrates a poet? Or one that demands generous quantities of whisky? Burns might have answered the latter question long ago: "O thou, my muse!/guid auld Scotch drink!/ Whether thro' wimplin worms thou jink,/Or, richly brown, ream owre the brink." Got that? Me, neither. But that won't stop me from raising a glass.

## RABBIE BURNS COCKTAIL

1 one-inch strip of orange peel

1 ½ ounces Dewar's White Label

½ ounce Carpano Antica sweet vermouth

3 dashes Bénédictine

**1.** Rub the rim of a cocktail glass with the orange peel. Shake the other ingredients in a glass with ice.

**2.** Strain into the cocktail glass and garnish with the reserved peel.

*January 17, 2013*

## ROBERT BURNS
By FRANK CAIAFA

2 ounces Spencerfield Spirit's Sheep Dip or Johnnie Walker 'Black' blended scotch whiskey

1 ounce Cinzano Rosso sweet vermouth

¼ ounce Bénédictine

2 dashes Emile Pernot 'Vieux Pontarlier' absinthe

Twist of lemon

**1.** Add all ingredients to mixing glass. Add ice and stir for 60 revolutions.

**2.** Strain into a chilled cocktail glass and garnish with twist of lemon.

**Optional: Serve with shortbread cookies on the side.**

*October 20, 2013*

A SHIPMENT OF SCOTCH ARRIVES AT THE PORT OF NEW YORK, 1933

# CHAPTER 11

# COCKTAILS FROM THE ARCHIVE

# HOT BUTTERED RUM
# SKIERS' CHOICE

What skiers choose to drink when they come in from a strenuous day on the slopes seems to be a matter of personal preference rather than custom. An informal survey of several devotees to the sport recently gave hot buttered rum a slight lead.

"Everyone was drinking buttered rum at Sugarbush when I was there last week-end," one wind-burned young woman commented. "Sugarbush is the new ski development in Warren, VT, you know."

A young man, whose face also glowed with that healthy color that comes from a weekend in open country, did not agree.

"The skiers I know drink highballs, Scotch on the rocks, whatever they ordinarily have at home," he said. "For myself, I like to have a cou-ple of glasses of cold beer after I've been skiing all day."

Those who recall the gusto with which Rogers' Rangers gulped down hot buttered rum in Kenneth Roberts' "Northwest Passage," may think the drink is a natural fit for cold weather.

One who would not agree is David A. Embury. Mr. Embury prefaces the following recipe, from his "The Fine Art of Mixing Drinks," with these remarks:

"Of all the hot liquors, I regard buttered rum as the worst. I believe that the drinking of it should be permitted only in the 'Northwest Passage' and, even there, only by highly imaginative and overenthusiastic novelists."

## HOT BUTTERED RUM

1 jigger Jamaica rum
1 teaspoon simple syrup (page 27)
1 small lump of butter

Ground cinnamon or nutmeg, if desired
3 or 4 cloves or ½ teaspoon of blended, ground cloves, allspice and mace

**1.** Stir rum and simple syrup in a mug or highball glass.

**2.** Fill the glass with hot water, add the spices, float butter on top and stir gently until the butter is melted. Dust top with cinnamon or nutmeg, if desired.

## OLYMPIC WINE TORCH

*To honor the Winter Olympics now under way in Squaw Valley—and to call the attention of participants and spectators to itself—the California wine industry has created a hot wine rink. Called the Olympic Wine Torch, it is a concoction of apple juice, lemon juice, red wine and port.*

YIELD: 24 DRINKS

3 cups apple juice
20 whole cloves
4 sticks cinnamon
Peel of one lemon, cut in strips

Juice of one lemon
1 bottle (four-fifths of a quart) Burgundy
1 bottle (four-fifths of a quart) port
½ cup brandy

**1.** Simmer the apple juice, cloves, cinnamon and lemon peel for fifteen minutes.

**2.** Strain and add the lemon juice, burgundy and port. Simmer again until hot.

**3.** Heat the brandy, ignite it and ladle into the hot wine slowly. Serve in hot mugs or glasses.

*February 22, 1960*

# THOUGHTS ON RUM;
## AUTHORITY DISCUSSES DRINKS AND FOODS USING LIQUOR LONG POPULAR IN AMERICA
### By JUNE OWEN

As stimulating as a tall, frosty Planter's Punch was a chat we had recently with Co. A.R. Woolley, managing director of Lemon Hart Rum Ltd., of London. The subject was, of course, rum—how to drink it and how to use it to advantage in cooking.

The Britisher, as handsome as Anthony Eden, wore a soft grey waistcoat beneath his black jacket and carried the Englishman's ubiquitous black umbrella. His speech was clipped and pungent.

"My favorite rum drink?" Jamaica rum, ginger ale, ice and a twist of lemon peel," he said.

To make it, the rum expert pours a jigger of rich, full-bodied rum into a tall glass, adds ice and ginger ale to fill the glass, then the lemon peel.

In English pubs, Colonel Woolley said, rum and water is the drink, hot water in winter, cold in summer. Fine, aged rums should be drunk neat, he said.

The colonel's definition of "the proper rum swizzle" differs radically from the versions of that Caribbean drink served here. It is not a sour, he said, but simply rum and soft water, agitated with a swizzle stick. The stick is a wooden shaft with several miniature paddles affixed at right angles at one end. The water must be soft, as it is in the Caribbean, to produce the correct fizzy effect when the stick is rotated in it and the rum.

# MAKING THE PUNCH

Colonel Woolley agrees with most bartenders on the proportions for that other Caribbean creation, Planter's Punch, that is, one part sour (lemon or lime juice), two parts sweet (sugar and syrup), three parts strong (Jamaica rum) and four parts weak (ice and tea). The tea is the colonel's recommendation: Most formulas combine ice and plain water for the "weak" ingredient.

"You will get a Planter's Punch infinitely superior to most," he explained, "if you use freshly brewed tea instead of the water."

Another rum drink he recommends: Pour one and one-half ounces Jamaica rum and one and one-half ounces of freshly squeezed orange juice into a tall glass. Add ice and fill the glass with quinine water.

Rum combines deliciously with almost any sweetened fruit juice, the colonel reminded us. He explained that rum, distilled from molasses, by-product in sugar manufacture, is actually a dry spirit as opposed to a sweet one. The sugar in rum converts to alcohol much more readily than the grain from which whisky derives, hence the residue of sugar in rum is low.

The happy marriage of rum and sweets carries over into cookery where the liquor appears most often in desserts. Bab au rhum is probably the classic. And both the Italians and the French have their rum cakes.

It is a French custom, and one we might well adopt here, to bring a bottle of rum to the table with almost any kind of cake. Just before it is to be eaten, the cake is sprinkled with a few drops of rum to give a particularly delectable flavor.

Our doughty forefathers in New England used to drink two gallons of rum each year. Colonial women put rum in their mincemeat and fruit cakes. One old New England recipe flavors blueberry sauce with rum, a sassing that seems most appropriate for that bland fruit. As a topping for cakes—either chocolate, spiced or butter—this rum butter cream is excellent.

## RUM BUTTER FROSTING
YIELD: ENOUGH FROSTING FOR TOP AND SIDE OF A NINE-INCH LAYER CAKE

| | |
|---|---|
| ⅓ cup butter | Few grains (pinch) of salt |
| 2¼ cups sifted confectioners' sugar, approximately | 3 to 4 tablespoons heavy cream |
| | 2 tablespoons dark rum |

**1.** Cream butter; add sugar gradually; stirring till blended. Add salt.

**2.** Stir in the cream a little at a time, adding just enough to give a good spreading consistency. Beat till fluffy. Add rum.

*March 19, 1957*

# LIVING AND LEISURE

## By JANE COBB

The advent of hot weather can play havoc with peaceful drinking. People who have been contentedly alternating Scotch with dry martinis all Winter suddenly find that these short strong restoratives can produce, even in an air-cooled bar, a condition approximating sunstroke. The drinker then is thrust into the thick of a bitter controversy. What constitutes a suitable Summer drink and just what is the right way to make it, anyway?

One school of thought says that anybody who drinks anything but gin between June and September is simply courting apoplexy. Another group of equally reliable people feels the same way about rum. And then there are always addicts of the light or Continental system who flourish vermouth cassis or Rhine wine and seltzer and look on hard-liquor drinkers as boors.

An even tougher row centers around the making of the long-and-tails. For many people seem to feel that there are only two recipes—the right one and the wrong. Old standbys like Tom Collinses or gin-and-tonics are pretty standardized, but in the making of something like a Planter's Punch there is incredible scope. In the Ritz-Carlton, for example, Planter's Punch may appear made with lime juice or lemon juice, white sugar or brown, a dash of brandy or a dash of Angostura bitters, all depending on which of the three bars it is served at. The chances are ten to one that most people who drink the punches like them very much, no matter which version is served. Anyway, the sensible thing to do is to drink slowly and stop fussing.
*June 4, 1939*

# FINE ART IN MAKING COOL SUMMER DRINKS;
## HOW SOME OF THE POPULAR HOT-WEATHER BEVERAGES ARE CONCOCTED

It is the test of capabilities of the most experienced drink mixer in these days to concoct a new, cooling and delicious Summer beverage that will stand the estimate of popular consumption. The search is for drinks that will not only have a cooling and exhilarating effect but look inviting as well. The favorite drinks for Summer, as a rule, emanate from the mixers and wine stewards of the big hotels and restaurants.

Few persons realize just what an expenditure of gray matter is devoted each Summer to the invention of hot-weather drinks. The demand for something new in the thirst-quenching line increases apparently with the advent of each Summer, and the professional drink mixers often find themselves at wit's ends to supply the demand.

A visit to any of the wine vaults these days in the big hotels in Broadway and Fifth Avenue will show the wine stewards puzzling their brains over the problem of concocting new drinks. They work in a temperature almost at the freezing point, surrounded by refrigerating plants.

Fifth Avenue may be broiling in the sun, but down in these icy sub-basements the steward blends his drinks and conducts his experiments unmindful of the withering rays of the sun outside. Meanwhile the bartender on the ground floor may accidentally concoct a beverage that will jump into instant favor.

The names of these various Summer beverages, temperance and otherwise, have a lot to do with their lasting popularity. Thirst scientists assert that imagination plays a strong part in the satisfaction which comes from a hot-weather drink, and that a man who gulps down a drink which he knows is called a "seaside cooler," for instance, gets a lot more relief that the man who drinks stoically, from his ordinary glass of claret punch.

The Southerner derives his greatest pleasure from his mint julep by burying his nose in the sprigs of mint which top the beverage. Any name or fruit decoration which suggests to the perspiring imbiber the aspect of cool, green meadows, or whispering sea breezes, is a fitting accessory to the drink which cools. One of the most popular beverages at the Hotel Plaza café this summer is called the "Silver Moon." The ingredients of the drink are ordinary, but the name suggests the charm of a cool Summer's night by moonlight.

In the way of novelty the Hotel Knickerbocker has a drink called Adalon Cup. This is made with a bottle of champagne and a ripe French peach. The whole peach is first pierced with a fork and then placed in the bottom of the glass. The champagne is then poured into the glass, and the result is that the champagne takes on the flavor of the peach, and the peach tastes like champagne.

The newest Summer drink at the Waldorf Astoria is called the Iris, and it has proved the most popular cocktail of the season. It is made of one-third lemon juice, two-thirds gin, and half a teaspoonful of sugar, well-shaken, and served with a spring of fresh mint.

The Automobile is a long Summer drink which has proved popular with roof garden patrons at the Waldorf. It is made of imported ginger ale, a bit of gin, decorated with springs of mint and served in a tall glass. The Waldorf fizz is a temperance drink which is having its run of popularity this Summer. It is an elongated drink, well shaken, and served with chipped ice. It is made from the juice of an orange, one egg, and the juice of a lemon.

The novelty of a drink concocted at the Holland House, which is popular among the women patrons of the restaurant on a hot afternoon, comes from the fact that the drink tastes exactly like a glass of chocolate, although the ingredients will show that no chocolate entered into its concoction. It is called a Reviver Flip, and is made with the juice of a whole lime, a bit of orange Curacao, sloe gin, a whole egg, and a little sugar to taste. It is well frapped and strained before being served.

A Summer cocktail popular at the St. Regis is called Polly. This is made from the juice of a lemon, a dash of grenadine syrup, a jigger of dry gin, which is well frapped and strained into a tall glass, and served with fizz water.

Of all the popular temperance drinks the Tea Shake has proved a fa-vorite beverage at the Plaza. The proportions of ingredients for one person consist of a goblet two-thirds full of tea, a few drops of lemon juice, a whole raw egg and sugar to taste. It is thoroughly shaken and served with a cube of ice. A dash of raspberry syrup adds to the deliciousness of the cup, and altogether it is most palatable and cooling.

A Summer highball that is made at the Astor bar originated in the deserts of Egypt. It is named after Khartoum, and was first concocted by a newspaper correspondent who accompanied Lord Kitchener on his famous expedition. It is really an elongated cocktail, and is served in a tall glass with figure ice. The ingredients are a big dash of Angostura bitters, half a jigger of French vermouth, a full jigger of gin, and a bottle of club soda.

"What to drink and how to concoct it" for home consumption is really a simply problem. Despite the high-sounding names attached to the beverages by their originators, and any novice can acquit himself most creditably with the proper ingredients, a shaker, a strainer, plenty of chipped ice, and fruit.

Here are some recipes for cooling drinks:

NECTAR CREAM—To serve six persons with this drink use one pint of rich cream, three eggs, having whites and yolks beaten separately, a cupful of cracked ice, a pinch of salt, half a cupful of pulverized sugar, a cupful of any kind of fruit syrup, and a quart of ice water. Shake thoroughly and serve.

VANDERBILT FRUIT CUP—To

one pitcher of fresh fruit smothered in fine ice, composed of assorted grapes, peaches, and crushed strawberries, (in season,) add two glasses of strawberry brandy, one pint bottle of mineral water, and one quart of champagne. Allow this to remain a short time before serving. Serve from pitcher strained.

ASTOR PUNCH— A jigger of sloe gin, a little crème de menthe in bottom of glass, shaved ice, and sliced pineapple.

BULLDOG PUNCH— One bottle of imported ginger ale, the rind of one orange, one jigger of orange juice. Serve in a punch glass with cracked ice.

KNICKERBOCKER ROMANEE—
One-third Kirschwasser, dash of Orgeat, to which add one-third Santa Cruz rum. Serve in punch glass with fine ice, decorate with fresh fruit and a sprig of mint.

CLOVER CLUB— One-half raspberry juice, to which add one dash of lemon juice, one drink of gin, the white of an egg. Shake well and serve in claret glass.

SEASIDE COOLER— The juice of two lemons, a dash of Grenadine syrup, sugar to taste, and a bottle of soda. Add chipped ice, shake well, and serve with assorted fruit.

PERFECT COOLER— A drink of Scotch, a dash of Dubonnet, and syphon water.

*July 24, 1910*

# PENCHANT OF AMERICANS FOR COLD DRINKS BRINGS SOME SUGGESTIONS FOR SUMMER TIME

## By JANE NICKERSON

Along with their liking for showers and chewing gum and swing, Americans have a fondness in summer for the longest and coldest drinks they can find. They cannot comprehend the British theory of the hotter the day the hotter the tea; in fact, their insistence on "cokes" and sodas and what-not is as surely a national characteristic as their preference for corn on the cob and salted peanuts. That being the case, we discuss today warm weather beverage of them nourishing, some of them quite frankly not, all of them pleasant.

Alcohol, as what good tippler does not know, is apt to have the reverse effect of what is intended; that is, it may result in your feeling somewhat less cool than you did before you had your drink. That is why it has long been custom to turn to milder alcoholic concoctions when the thermometer is on an ascending scale. Wine, for instance, in one of its several combinations offers a good way to beat the heat, as they say. Specifically:

## WINE LEMONADE
YIELD: FOR EIGHT, APPROXIMATELY

¼ cup sugar
¾ cup lemon juice
3 cups sweet dessert wine
(port, muscatel or tokay)

Sparkling water, chilled
1 or 2 lemon slices, for garnish

**1.** Dissolve the sugar in lemon juice, add the wine and shake with ice cubes until cold.

**2.** Pour over ice cubes in glasses, filling them a half to three-fourths full. Finish filling them with sparkling water (or plain ice water, if preferred.) Stir and if desired, garnish each serving with a slice or two of lemon.

*July 4, 1946*

# THE MINT JULEP

A controversy has arisen, this hot July, over the mint julep. Men of seeming intelligence have been discovered who declare that it should contain a certain proportion of water. The subject, of course, is obnoxious, and its discussion, in weather so warm, and within the hearing of weak mortals who still cling to the delusion concerning "cooling drinks," is deplorable. We are convinced that the less said on this matter the better. But no person of ripe intelligence and sound taste could possibly hold that a mint julep should contain water.

Ice, to be sure, freshly cracked ice of polar temperature, and so much of it and so well-packed that the outside of the ample tumbler—not a Tom Collins glass, mind you, but a tumbler, should be well-frosted and stay so while the julep lasts; but no water. Plenty of fresh mint, not crushed or bruised, and either good Bourbon whisky or brandy and whisky mixed—when one is so lost to reason as to imbibe mint julep in a New York July a degree more or less of pure perdition does not matter—and these ingredients apportioned and mixed by the hand of genius.

To look at a mint julep thus concocted is inspiring. Pictorially, its charm is irresistible. It suggests fragrant green pastures and cool recesses far away. Its odor, too, is agreeable. But do not be tempted. Keep the mint julep in its place, as a work of art, and quench your thirst with water of a moderate temperature. The seductive pastures of the julep are not cool when you reach them. We are very sorry, indeed, that the julep should have been brought so prominently into notice at a time when the natural weaknesses of mankind are accentuated. But whoever said that a mint julep should contain water is fit only for chocolate sundaes and such things. A mint julep may be pernicious, but it should not be misrepresented.

*July 14, 1911*

GIN FIZZ

## CHAPTER 12

# THE FIZZ

## GIN FIZZ
### By ROSIE SCHAAP

*It's not called a fizz for nothing. Shake this drink like mad for optimal effervescence.*

1 ounce fresh lemon juice
1 teaspoon sugar, preferably superfine
2 ounces London Dry-style gin

Club soda, to top
Lemon wedge, for garnish

**1.** Fill a cocktail shaker with ice and add lemon juice, sugar and gin.

**2.** Shake vigorously and strain into a highball glass. Top with club soda and garnish with a wedge of lemon.

*May 20, 2014*

## ISLE OF MANHATTAN FIZZ

*Adapted from RAVI DeROSSI and JANE DANGER, Cienfuegos, New York City, by Amanda Hesser*

½ ounce lime juice
½ ounce pineapple juice
¾ ounce simple syrup (page 27)
2 ounces coconut purée or coconut ice cream
4 drops orange-flower water

¾ ounce Oronoco rum or other dark rum
¾ ounce Hayman's Old Tom gin or any gin you prefer
2 tablespoons club soda
Lime twist, ¾-inch wide, for garnish

**1.** Combine the lime juice, pineapple juice, simple syrup, coconut purée, orange-flower water, rum and gin in a shaker. Use an immersion blender to purée the mixture and give it volume. Add ice and the club soda to the shaker and shake for 30 seconds.

**2.** Strain into a tall, stemmed glass and garnish with a wide twist of lime.

*June 30, 2010*

## MALTA FIZZ
### Adapted from WD-50, New York City, by Pete Wells

2 ounces amber rum
2 ounces malta (carbonated malt beverage)
¾ ounce lime juice

1 ounce simple syrup (page 27)
1 egg yolk
Ground cinnamon, for garnish

**1.** Add ice to a glass cocktail shaker and add all other ingredients except cinnamon. Shake vigorously for 20 seconds to emulsify egg yolk.

**2.** Strain into a Collins glass filled with ice and garnish with ground cinnamon.

*November 29, 2006*

## GANSEVOORT FIZZ
Adapted from 5 NINTH, New York City, by William L. Hamilton

2 ounces Appleton V/X rum
1 ounce Drambuie
1 ounce freshly squeezed lemon juice

2 dashes Peychaud's bitters
Cracked ice
2 to 3 ounces chilled seltzer

**1.** Shake all ingredients except seltzer with cracked ice.

**2.** Strain into a nine-ounce glass and top with chilled seltzer.

*June 6, 2004*

## SHU JAM FIZZ
Adapted from SUMMIT BAR, New York City, by Jonathan Miles

Absinthe
2 ounces DH Krahn gin
1 teaspoon apricot jam
¾ ounce fennel syrup (see recipe, below)

¾ ounce freshly squeezed lemon juice
Dash of Fee Brothers Peach Bitters
Club soda

**1.** Rinse a Collins glass by swirling absinthe inside it, just enough to coat the sides; discard excess. Combine gin, jam, fennel syrup, lemon juice and bitters in a shaker with ice, and shake.

**2.** Add ice to the prepared glass, and into that strain the contents of the shaker. Top with the soda, and serve.

## FENNEL SYRUP

2 tablespoons ground fennel seeds

8 ounces simple syrup (page 27)

**1.** Combine seeds, 8 ounces water and simple syrup in a small pan. Bring to a boil, then lower the heat and simmer, covered, for 30 minutes.

**2.** Strain and cool.

*October 18, 2009*

SILVER FIZZ

## SILVER FIZZ
### Adapted from DAVID WONDRICH by William Grimes

*Fizzes, particularly the Silver Fizz, with the added nutritional boost of an egg white, often served as breakfast for the 19th-century drinking man.*

Cracked or shaved ice
½ tablespoon superfine sugar
½ ounce lemon juice

2 ounces gin, preferably Plymouth
1 egg white
2 ounces seltzer

**1.** Put two or three handfuls of cracked or shaved ice into a cocktail shaker and add all ingredients except the seltzer. Shake energetically for a minute or more.

**2.** Strain into a 6- to 8-ounce highball glass, add seltzer and stir gently.

*October 31, 2007*


## SOUTHSIDE FIZZ
### By MARK BITTMAN

*The fizz comes from the soda. The buzz comes from the gin. The cool comes from the muddled mint.*

Mint leaves, plus more for garnish
1½ tablespoons simple syrup (page 27)
¼ cup gin

Lemon juice
Club soda

**1.** Muddle mint leaves and simple syrup in a mixing glass. Add the gin and lemon juice and shake.

**2.** Strain into a glass of ice and top with club soda. Garnish with more mint.

*May 10, 2012*

TOM COLLINS

CHAPTER 13

# THE COLLINS

# THE COLLINS BOYS, IN BREEZY SIMPLICITY

## By JONATHAN MILES

Whatever happened to the Collins brothers? You remember them: Tom, most of all, who could be found hobnobbing at nearly every cocktail party and country-club bar in the '60s and '70s, but also John, the rowdy Southerner of the bunch, and Charley, the Caribbean brother. They were the Big Men of their era, stylish and ubiquitous. But they fell on hard times, and more or less faded from the scene.

We're talking, of course, about a family of drinks: the gin-based Tom Collins and its lesser-known brethren, the John Collins (bourbon) and Charley Collins (rum). They have an illustrious, authentic pedigree (recipes for a Collins drink date back to the 1860s, and Jerry Thomas, the Herodotus of mixology, included one in the 1876 edition of his "Bar-Tender's Guide"), and a mix of summery refreshment and mild complexity that puts the still-prevalent gin-and-tonic to shame. Nevertheless, the Collinses have been mostly excluded from the cocktail revival, left to wither on the oldies circuit with their pal Harvey Wallbanger.

Why? Perhaps it's the Collins mixes, processed and laden with high-fructose corn syrup, that are still sold at grocery stores in bottles that look as if they haven't been redesigned since Dean Martin got radio play. After all, it's hard to sell a $16 cocktail that reeks of a ShopRite aisle.

But St. John Frizell, the owner of Fort Defiance Cafe and Bar in Red Hook, Brooklyn, which opened for bar service two weeks ago, has another theory. "It's too simple a drink," he said of the Tom Collins, which is featured on the bar's compact cocktail menu not once but three times (the house standard version as well as a 23-ounce Sumo version and a cucumber variation). With its elementary formula (just lemon juice, simple syrup and gin, with a spurt of club soda) and dearth of obscure ingredients, "it's not baroque enough for modern bartenders," said Mr. Frizell, whose bartending résumé includes a year and a half at the Pegu Club.

But that breezy simplicity is a big hunk of its charm. A Tom Collins doesn't ask you to think, or to comment, or to reverently acknowledge its long, storied history; it just wants you to be happy. Jim Ryan, a "brand ambassador" for Hendrick's Gin, is another devoted fan.

"The Collins is a classic cocktail, make no mistake about it," he wrote in an e-mail message. Mr. Ryan is fond of making his Tom Collinses with ice cubes that he spikes, before freezing, with two or three dashes of Angostura bitters.

Mr. Frizell's cucumber variation is hardly a new twist, but it's remarkable all the same: tart but amiable, smart but not showy, faintly vegetal and perilously refreshing. (The Sumo version might sound like something from a fraternity bash, until you glance down on a steamy night in Red Hook and realize you've emptied your standard-size version in less than two minutes.)

"There's no reason to get complicated," Mr. Frizell said, "when gin and fizzy lemonade taste so good together."

## CUCUMBER COLLINS
### Adapted from FORT DEFIANCE, Brooklyn

1 ounce freshly squeezed lemon juice.
1 ounce simple syrup (page 27)
2 ounces gin

4 or 5 slices cucumber
Club soda
Mint sprig, for garnish

**1.** In the bottom of a mixing glass, muddle cucumber slices, lemon juice and simple syrup. Add gin, along with ice, and shake.

**2.** Strain over fresh ice into a Collins glass, then top with soda. Garnish with the mint sprig.

*August 2, 2009*

## TOM COLLINS
### By MARK BITTMAN

¼ cup gin
1½ tablespoons lemon juice
1 tablespoon simple syrup (page 27)

Club soda
Lemon wedge, for garnish

**1.** Combine lots of ice, gin, lemon juice and simple syrup in a mixing glass and shake.

**2.** Strain into a glass of ice and top with club soda. Garnish with the lemon wedge.

*May 13, 2012*

## SUMO COLLINS
### Adapted from ST. JOHN FRIZELL, Fort Defiance, Brooklyn, by Robert Willey

3 ounces gin
2¼ ounces fresh lemon juice
1½ ounces simple syrup (page 27)

Chilled Seltzer
1 orange wheel, for garnish

**1.** Pour the gin, lemon juice and simple syrup into a cocktail shaker, fill with ice and shake vigorously.

**2.** Strain into a 24-ounce glass filled with fresh ice and top with seltzer. Garnish with the orange wheel.

CUCUMBER COLLINS

## CAMPARI COLLINS
Adapted from CHRIS HARRINGTON and THERESA PAOPAO, Momofuku Ssam Bar, New York City, by Robert Willey

4 ounces chilled seltzer

2 ounces Campari

¾ ounce fresh lemon juice

¾ ounce simple syrup (page 27)

**1.** Pour the seltzer into a highball glass filled with ice and set aside.

**2.** Pour the Campari, lemon juice and simple syrup into a cocktail shaker, fill with ice and shake vigorously.

**3.** Strain into the glass with seltzer.

*June 22, 2011*


## THE HANDYMAN COLLINS
Adapted from ADAM BRYAN, Bar Congress, Austin, Tex., by Robert Willey

2 ounces bourbon

Grated zest of a half lemon

2 teaspoons sugar

5 ounces chilled Saison beer

1 lemon wheel, for garnish

**1.** Put the bourbon, lemon zest and sugar in a cocktail shaker, fill with ice and shake vigorously.

**2.** Strain into a highball glass filled with crushed ice and top with the beer. Garnish with the lemon wheel.

*June 22, 2011*

AN ITALIAN CLASSIC, THE NEGRONI

CHAPTER 14

# THE
# NEGRONI

# DRESSING ITALIAN
## By TOBY CECCHINI

Europeans, for all their gastronomic pedigrees, never had to improvise muffling devices for terrible alcohol, as Americans did during Prohibition, so they are generally relegated to spectator status in cocktail history. That being the case, it is wise to be suspicious of the origins of one of my all-time favorite cocktails, the Negroni.

Several accounts, as hotly debated as any trifling matter in Italy, trace the drink back to 1919, when a wealthy Florentine named Count Camillo Negroni suggested to Fosco Scarselli, the bartender at the Hotel Baglioni in Florence, that he add gin to his Americano, a mild combination of Campari, sweet vermouth and soda.

Served up in a martini glass, with a coil of fresh orange, the Negroni presents a gleaming red profile that catches the light like a polished ruby, and will have half the bar inquiring what you're drinking. The gin gives it a racy, astringent structure, while the Campari imparts the play of sweet and bitter. The vermouth grounds these elements with a dense, smoky winyness that triangulates with precision.

Oddly, I've never had a great Negroni in Italy, and not for lack of trying. Italians tend to stint on ice and often use subpar gin. San Francisco seems to be the stronghold of the drink in this country, and I've always gotten great ones there.

But for all its long history, the Negroni remains a relative stranger on these shores. James Bond was known to order one on occasion, and Lotte Lenya's louche character in "The Roman Spring of Mrs. Stone" drank nothing but. Still, it merits wider recognition, as I know of no better aperitif. I suggest one before any important dinner, and not more than one before you've got something in your stomach; the Negroni's inviting embrace quickly becomes a bearhug, as the mix's floridity masks a devious potency.

The traditional recipe has always been equal parts of all three liquors, but modern palates often prefer lighter, drier versions. I make mine with roughly three parts gin to one each of Campari and vermouth, more like a dashing martini in a fitted Italian suit. Some people prefer it on the rocks, an acceptable alternative, but recent vodka versions are to be taken no more seriously than freeze-dried espresso in Rome.

As with many of the classic cocktails, you will find two schools on the subject of shaking versus stirring in preparing this drink, each adamantly certain of its correctness. I bunk in the second camp. There are only two drinks I insist not be shaken, the manhattan and the Negroni. The bubbles and ice shards that give zest to some cocktails would mar the Negroni's sanguine limpidity. That first sip should be like drinking from a cool brook that happened to perambulate past a spice bazaar on its route.

## THE NEGRONI

| | |
|---|---|
| 1 ounce Campari | 3 ounces gin |
| 1 ounce sweet vermouth (Carpano Antica Formula or Martini & Rossi) | Orange slice or lemon twist, for garnish |

**1.** Combine all ingredients except orange slice or twist in a shaker filled with ice and stir until exterior beads with frost.

**2.** Strain into chilled cocktail glass; garnish with orange slice, lemon twist or both.

*October 6, 2002*

# IN AN IMPERFECT WORLD, A DRINK MADE FOR IT
## By FRANK BRUNI

When it comes to people, I have always had a soft spot for self-deprecators. I only recently realized that this extended to cocktails as well. I met one with effacement in its very appellation. And I've been trying to boost its confidence by telling it how wonderful it is ever since.

The introduction was made by Joe Campanale, one of the principal owners of the restaurants dell'Anima and L'Artusi and the (apostrophe-deprived) wine bar Anfora, all in the West Village. And now that I think about it, I have to wonder if in some corner of his mind he was doing product placement, with an oracle's vision of how this would all pan out. I'll never know.

He was in a small group of people with whom I was drinking one night about two months ago, and he ordered a Negroni Sbagliato. That caught my attention. Although I knew what a Negroni was—gin, sweet vermouth and Campari, usually with an orange peel garnish—I'd never heard of this variation, and I was tickled by the name. Translated from Italian, it means a bungled Negroni. A Negroni in error. A mistake.

Something so self-professedly wrong just had to be right. And of course it was. As Mr. Campanale explained to me, and as a sip of the drink confirmed, it replaces the gin in a usual Negroni with a dry sparkling wine, and that changes everything, the way recasting a part meant for Kristin Scott Thomas with Kristen Wiig would. Things get less serious. Zingier. Bubblier.

It's not just that the alcohol content of the usual Negroni is diminished. Its slightly syrupy quality yields to effervescence. The sparkling wine is game changer and mood lifter both. Drink the Negroni in autumn and winter, when you're brooding. Drink the Sbagliato (pronounced sbahl-YAH-toe) in spring and summer, when you're fizzing.

After that first tasting, I started asking after the Negroni Sbagliato. And I discovered another of its pleasures: it's obscure enough that most bartenders don't know it but simple enough that any bartender can be talked through it. Requesting one puts you in the know and prompts an exchange that, I found, most bartenders are happy to be drawn into. They're excited to learn a new drink.

I recently dropped by dell'Anima to talk with Mr. Campanale some more. He said that he first encountered the drink, which is meant to be an aperitif, about seven years ago when he was a student at New York University studying abroad in Italy. He was in thrall to the country. He was enamored with the whole Italian concept of aperitivo, an analog of sorts to happy hour, only the emphasis isn't on discounts and volume drinking. And he was elated to find a new use for Campari, which he'd always enjoyed in an Americano, which combines it with sweet vermouth and club soda.

"It was a really hot day," he said, "and I just thought this was the most refreshing cocktail ever."

It stayed with him, but he didn't think to give it an American showcase until dell'Anima, his first restaurant, had been open awhile. From the restaurant's inception in October 2007 it served and promoted its version of a regular Negroni, made not only with the usual trio of ingredients but also with muddled roasted orange, and strained into a chilled cocktail glass. It wasn't until 18 months later that he put a Sbagliato on the drinks list.

Although the version Mr. Campanale first had in Italy was served on the rocks in a wine glass, and not shaken, he has tinkered with that. At dell'Anima the Sbagliato is made by shaking 1.5 ounces each of Campari and Carpano Antica vermouth with the muddled orange and ice, straining it into a rocks glass and topping it with about 1.5 ounces of sparkling wine. He has been using a Lambrusco Bianco but said that a cava or anything else "on the drier side" would do.

"I'd use the least expensive sparkling wine you'd drink on its own," he said. "Don't use anything too pricey, since the more nuanced flavors will be covered up."

I wondered about the shaking. He said that something happens to Campari—a kind of blooming and thickening—when it's shaken, and to illustrate the point we tried shaken and stirred Sbagliatos side by side. There was an even frothier disparity between them than you get from most drinks done both ways. I had the slightest of preferences for the stirred one.

But, really, there was no wrong. Except in the name itself.

## NEGRONI SBAGLIATO

This week's Tipsy Diaries column is about a new take on a familiar cocktail, the Negroni. Instead of gin, the Negroni Sbagliato uses sparkling white wine. Joe Campanale of dell'Anima in the West Village shared with us how to make the drink.

Before actually mixing anything, you'll need roasted orange wedges on hand. The night before, put orange wedges in a resealable container, top with sweet red vermouth and refrigerate overnight. In the morning remove the wedges from the vermouth and char them on a grill until the sugars caramelize and black specks form on the oranges.

Onto the cocktail: Put a roasted orange wedge in a glass and add one and a half ounces of sweet red vermouth. Muddle the two so that the charred bits are released into the vermouth. Add ice and one and a half ounces of Campari, and shake. Strain into a chilled glass that is filled with ice and top with one and a half ounces of a sparkling white wine like Lini Lambrusco Bianco. Garnish with orange peel.

Cheers!
*April 28, 2011*

# A DEEP SIP FOR DEEP THINKERS
## By JONATHAN MILES

A Negroni demands your full, upright attention. It will not tolerate mindless swigging, the way all those sweet summertime drinks do, which is just one reason no one has ever ordered one at a swim-up bar at a resort pool. Each sip telegraphs a terse forget-me-not message to the tongue, a pinprick of bitterness demanding respect and contemplation.

There is cheer in it, but grown-up, melancholy cheer, which makes the Negroni an ideal drink for end times—he end of summer, for instance, or the end of American prosperity. The perfect drink when the sky is falling—or merely the leaves.

Last week I visited I Sodi, a Tuscan restaurant tucked into a skinny minimalist space on Christopher Street in the West Village that Rita Sodi (a former Calvin Klein executive) and a partner, Josh Dworkis, opened in March.

Negronis are the specialty at I Sodi: there are four on the cocktail menu, three of them subtle variations on the classically fixed theme—that being equal parts gin, Campari and sweet vermouth, as in the restaurant's Negroni Classico.

"In my old job, bartending at Union Square Cafe, I would always play around with Negronis," said Hakan Westergren, I Sodi's manager and chief Negroni officer. "There are so many kinds of vermouth, so many kinds of gin."

Mr. Westergren understands that a proper Negroni is as perfectly and tripodically balanced as, say, a water molecule. Add another atom of oxygen to that $H_2O$ formula, and the result is hydrogen peroxide—hardly as refreshing. So it goes with the Negroni. To mess with it is to risk messing it up altogether. Caution signs should be posted behind the bar.

I Sodi's Carousel Negroni veers the furthest from the traditional formula credited to Count Camillo Negroni, who allegedly invented the drink, in 1919, by asking a bartender to beef up an Americano cocktail by adding a shot of gin.

The Carousel Negroni is a jammy, ginless mixture of three Italian liqueurs and sweet vermouth—more bitter-orange, as in marmalade, than bitter.

Two variations hew closer to the purist line, one by substituting an artichoke-based liqueur, Cynar, for the Campari, which gives the drink a boskier flavor, the other by injecting a bit more perfuminess into the formula via Hendrick's gin, a Scottish gin infused with rose petals and cucumber, and Punt e Mes, a dry, woodsy vermouth.

The latter, which Mr. Westergren calls the Punt-e-groni, is so gorgeously bitter that it almost stings the tongue. Drinking it is like being slapped by an ex-lover. It is such a deep ruby red that vampires would be drawn to it.

Is it possible that, simply by tweaking the spirits, adding a little more herbiness here and a touch less sweetness there, Mr. Westergren has actually improved upon the original formula?

It's worth contemplating. Not that this drink will let you do otherwise.

## PUNT-E-GRONI
### Adapted from I SODI, New York City

| | |
|---|---|
| 1¾ ounces Hendrick's gin | 1 ounce Campari |
| 1¼ ounces Carpano Punt e Mes vermouth | 1 orange slice, for garnish |

**1.** Combine the ingredients with ice in a rocks glass and stir.

**2.** Garnish with the orange slice and serve.

*October 5, 2008*

# THE NEGRONI'S LIGHTER, SANER PROGENITOR

## By ROBERT SIMONSON

The Negroni is enjoying a moment now. For bartenders and barflies, this deliciously complex mix of Campari, gin and sweet vermouth has become an easy way to fly one's flag as a knowing cocktail classicist. But the drink's rising profile has cast a shadow over its once-popular progenitor, the Americano. Without this refreshing Italian-born highball—Campari, sweet vermouth and club soda—there would have been no blueprint for the gin-loving Count Camillo Negroni to experiment with a century ago. (The drink's family line actually goes back even farther; the Americano grew out of a simpler aperitif that omitted the soda, called the Milano-Torino—Milano in honor of the birthplace of Campari, Torino for the vermouth.)

While the Americano doesn't have quite the romance that's grown around the Negroni, it also doesn't have nearly as much alcohol. It's a lighter and saner choice for summertime drinking. A pitcher of Americanos enjoyed on the back patio during a hot afternoon will not leave you down for the, uh, count.

## THE AMERICANO

1½ ounces Campari
1½ ounces sweet vermouth

Club Soda
Generous orange twist, for garnish

**1.** Combine all ingredients except the orange twist in a highball glass filled with ice.

**2.** Top with club soda and garnish with the orange twist.

*May 20, 2013*

BITTERS AT DEATH & CO., NEW YORK CITY

## CHAPTER 15

# BITTERS
# AND AMARI

# BROTHERHOOD OF BITTERS

## By JONATHAN MILES

"The recipe for this one came from a monastery," said Ralf Kuettel, holding an unmarked bottle aloft in the afternoon sunlight, swirling the honey-colored contents. We were sitting in the walled garden adjacent to Trestle on Tenth, Mr. Kuettel's new restaurant on the corner of 24th Street and 10th Avenue, opening this week, and drinking like monks. To a point, that is: Monastic codes would surely disallow Trestle on Tenth's manager, 23-year-old Christine Ehlert, from joining us, and it's the rare Franciscan who would call bitter digestifs, which we were sampling, "the sexiest thing out there," as Mr. Kuettel did.

Yet the liquids in our glasses were, to crib from an old jazz album title, pure monk: Potent infusions of herbs, roots, barks, peels, flowers and spices, commonly lumped into the category of bitters, that owe their existence to medieval monks who brewed them for medicinal purposes.

Like other roots-minded mixologists and restaurateurs in New York, along with a few determined home bartenders, Mr. Kuettel is making his own bitters for Trestle on Tenth. The recipes, like Mr. Kuettel, are Swiss, and he collected them—as best he could—in Switzerland and online. "Some of the old recipes are secret, unless you belong to the brotherhood of monks," he told me. (Mr. Kuettel, for the record, does not belong to the brotherhood. I asked. He also made clear that he didn't "pull a 'Da Vinci Code' " to get the recipes. In short,

no monks were harmed in the making of this column.)

Apothecaries, then bartenders, picked up the bitters-making mantle when monks got out of the pharmacy business, the latter after discovering that a dash of aromatic bitters softened liquor's edges. Back then, in the 19th century, tavern owners concocted their own in the same way monks, and now Mr. Kuettel, made theirs: by steeping roots and botanicals in alcohol.

"It was something that proprietors were expected to do," said David Wondrich, the author and cocktail historian. When Angostura and Peychaud bitters became widely available, bitters-making went the way of turnip wine and posset. In the last few years, however, the upscaling of cocktails has seen the practice plucked from history's dustbin. "Bitters have become a real fetish object," Mr. Wondrich said.

Mr. Kuettel's three batches, which range from an aperitif-style bitters made from mountain herbs to a richer, rootsier digestif made from citrus peels, chamomile, anise, green tea and vermouth, are light enough for sipping solo, but perform gorgeously as choral accompaniments.

Mr. Kuettel's version of the classic Champagne cocktail sees his Chartreuse-style bitters paired with Cognac and Champagne. "It's nice and simple, but the bitters come through, and that was the point," said Mr. Kuettel. Any monk would be proud.

## CLOISTER FIZZ
Adapted from TRESTLE ON TENTH, New York City

| | |
|---|---|
| 1 ounce cognac | Champagne, to fill |
| ½ ounce herbal bitters liqueur | Lemon twist, for garnish |
| Dash of simple syrup (page 27) | |

**1.** Combine the cognac, bitters and syrup in a flute, and top with Champagne.

**2.** Garnish with lemon.

*June 25, 2006*

# ALL STIRRED UP
## By PETER MEEHAN

Despite their power to transform a cocktail, bitters have gone, in the space of 40 years, from an essential ingredient to a historical oddity. High-proof tinctures of roots, bark, herbs and aromatics, bitters were included in 166 drinks in "The Old Waldorf Astoria Bar Book," published in 1935, while only six recipes called for them in the contemporary book "Shaken and Stirred," by William L. Hamilton, a reporter at The New York Times. But there's a bright spot in those six lonely cocktails. Three of them call for orange bitters, a variety that was on the verge of extinction until very recently.

"Orange bitters were a dog for a long time," confirms Joe Fee, whose family business, Fee Brothers of Rochester, N.Y., makes the oldest brand of orange bitters in America today. (According to his father, Jack Fee, it dates to 1951—when orange bitters were a requisite ingredient in dry martinis.) "We didn't even know why we made them anymore."

The modern bitters renaissance started in the early 90's when Ted Haigh, a part-time cocktail historian known in some circles as Dr. Cocktail, "discovered" Fee's bitters and began talking them up to all the cocktail mavens he knew. He was also the agent provocateur behind Fee Brothers Peach Bitters: it was created after a telephone conversation in which Haigh and Jack Fee vowed to recreate a handful of classic drinks that called for it. (Haigh estimates that only 32 such drinks exist in all of cocktaildom.)

Gary Regan, another cocktail authority, was also on the bitters trail. He spent more than a decade tinkering with a recipe for orange bitters taken from Charles H. Baker Jr.'s 1939 book, "The Gentleman's Companion," since reprinted as "Jigger, Beaker and Glass." Regan's version appears in his book, "The Joy of Mixology." Regans' Orange Bitters No. 6, plastered with his Rip van Winkle likeness on a label designed by Haigh (the bitters world is small), made its debut in April, the first new brand of commercial bitters to grace American bars in almost 50 years.

Haigh and Regan aren't the only revivalists: Kacy Fitch at the Zig Zag cafe in Seattle is brewing batches of a cinnamon-tinged Zig Zag house bitters and is also working on a lemon version; the mustachioed men behind the bar at Employees Only in the West Village dash their own "absinthe" bitters into Martinez cocktails; at Uovo in the East Village, Richard Ervin has begun whipping up his own tinctures for old-fashioned recipes; Ryan McGrale at No. 9 Park in Boston is shaking up pisco sours by dousing them with homemade bitters that a friend found during a trip to South America; the bar staff at Angel's Share in the East Village has Hermes Orange Bitters, a Japanese product, on hand; and wd-50 on the Lower East Side stocks Torani Amer, the European-style aperitif from California, which is essential for a proper Brooklyn cocktail (rye, dry vermouth, maraschino liqueur and Torani Amer).

Bitters have spent a long time in the shadows, so it's worth noting that cocktails made with them should be stirred, not shaken, if they are to remain limpid. And bitters are strong stuff, not to be overdone. Back in the 40's, the restaurateur Trader Vic Bergeron advised people to "take it easy with the bitters" when making a martini. It's solid advice.

Take it easy, but take it.

# BITTERS PRIMER

Fee Brothers West Indian Orange Bitters: good all-purpose citrus bitters with an orange Crush aroma.

Fee Brothers Peach Bitters: a candied-peach aroma. Infrequently used but inexpensive enough to justify keeping on hand.

Regans' Orange Bitters No. 6: a dusty and complex aroma and flavor dominated by cardamom and orange.

Peychaud's Aromatic Cocktail Bitters: Peychaud's and Angostura are the only two pre-Prohibition bitters still in production; a must for a fully stocked bar.

Torani Amer: not an aromatic cocktail bitters per se, but used the same way in making the classic Brooklyn cocktail.

## THE SEELBACH COCKTAIL
Adapted from "Vintage Spirits and Forgotten Cocktails" by TED HAIGH

| | |
|---|---|
| 1 ounce bourbon | 7 dashes Peychaud's bitters |
| ½ ounce Cointreau | 5 ounces Champagne |
| 7 dashes Angostura bitters | Orange twist, for garnish |

**1.** In a Champagne flute, combine the bourbon, Cointreau and bitters and stir.

**2.** Top with the Champagne, stir again and garnish with an orange twist.

*November 6, 2005*

# AN AMARO COCKTAIL AS FRESH AS A BREEZE
## By JULIA MOSKIN

Don't you just love amari, those bittersweet Italian liqueurs like Cynar and Aperol that are so popular now?

Me neither.

It is baffling to contemplate how the same nation that produced perfect marriages like tomatoes and mozzarella or prosciutto and melon also came up with these bittersweet couplings of cough syrup and weed juice. Most are brewed in the north, from mountain herbs and roots like gentian, licorice, artichoke and wormwood. In the German-speaking Alps, similar digestifs are called kraut-likör. But for some reason the Italian versions are the most peculiar and tongue-scouring.

However, in the service of cross-cultural tolerance, I have recently been tasting every amaro-based cocktail to cross my path. And my mind has been opened.

Many bartenders are using dashes of amaro instead of (or in addition to) the bitters that are traditionally used to give cocktails made with sweet ingredients, like bourbon or rum, a necessary bracing note. In many of these new creations, you don't taste the amaro—it hovers in the background, quenching your thirst with its pleasing rasp. At Del Posto in Chelsea, the Martinez, usually a sickly sweet pink drink from ancient cocktail history, is tarted up with Punt e Mes. And Dutch Kills in Long Island City, Queens, cuts the sloe gin in its Bloody Knuckle with a slug of Aperol.

My favorite was at Perla in Greenwich Village, where I ordered a Cantina Band with some suspicion. A highball with gin and ginger beer as its main components, it also listed lime, cucumber and Fernet, the bitterest of all the amari, among its ingredients. What arrived tasted like the love child of a Pimm's Cup and a Dark and Stormy. The cough syrup flavor was drowned in a sea of lime and ginger. What remained was a drink as fresh as a breeze on a calm summer sea.

## CANTINA BAND
Adapted from PERLA, New York City

1½ ounces Fernet Branca
½ ounce gin
1 ounce fresh lime juice

¾ ounce simple syrup (page 27)
3 slices cucumber, plus another slice for garnish
Ginger beer

**1.** Combine Fernet Branca, gin, lime juice, simple syrup and 3 slices cucumber in an ice-filled cocktail shaker and shake well.

**2.** Strain over a tall glass filled with ice. Top with ginger beer and garnish with a cucumber slice on the rim of the glass.

*May 20, 2013*

## THE REANIMATOR
By ERIC ASIMOV

1½ ounces straight rye whiskey
Thin-cut lemon peel, for garnish

1½ ounces lighter Italian amaro, like Nonino

**1.** Stir the rye and amaro together with plenty of cracked ice in a bar glass.

**2.** Strain into a chilled cocktail glass and top with lemon peel.

*November 15, 2011*

## MOTT AND MULBERRY
Adapted from LEO ROBITSCHEK, The NoMad, New York City, by Robert Simonson

*Leo Robitschek, bar manager at the NoMad in Manhattan, named this cocktail for two Little Italy streets, in homage to its Italian and American ingredients. He aimed to create a drink that was festive, like a hot spiced cider, while avoiding the rich excesses of some traditional holiday tipples. The cocktail is basically a whiskey sour armed with two secret weapons: the distinctly sweet-tart flavor of Honeycrisp apple juice and Amaro Abano, which the bartender called a "spice bomb, adding cinnamon and clove notes while adding a pleasant bitterness." It is suited for the cocktail hour, or just before dinner.*

½ ounce Demerara syrup (page 27)
2 Honeycrisp apples
1 ounce Luxardo Amaro Abano

1 ounce rye whiskey, preferably Old Overholt
½ ounce fresh lemon juice

**1.** Make apple juice: Core and peel 1 of the apples; liquefy in a juicer or blender.

**2.** In a cocktail shaker, combine ¾ ounce of the apple juice with the rye whiskey, Amaro, lemon juice and Demerara syrup. Add ice and shake.

**3.** Strain into a rocks glass with a few fresh ice cubes. Core the remaining apple; cut 3 to 5 thin slices (leave the peel on). Skewer at one end with a toothpick and spread slices like a fan.

*December 11, 2013*

# A BIT OF HISTORY, REBORN IN A GLASS

## By ROBERT WILLEY

Last October, John Deragon began tinkering with a recipe for Abbott's bitters, a cocktail ingredient that has beguiled drinks fanatics for years. Over the next two months, Mr. Deragon, the chief technology officer of Waterfront Media, an online health and wellness company in Brooklyn, tweaked the formula drop by drop, using single-spice infusions known as tinctures. After about 18 test runs, he had a version he thought he could work with, and by March he was aging his second batch in a five-gallon rye whiskey barrel purchased from a distillery in upstate New York.

His plan now, he explained recently, is to extract a small portion every two weeks to track the evolving interplay of wood and spice. All told, he has amassed enough tasting notes and recipe adjustments to fill four medium-size Moleskine notebooks.

The only problem is that Mr. Deragon has never tasted real Abbott's bitters. The brand dissolved in the early 1950s, the original recipe is lost, and securing bottles of it on eBay can require a level of attention at odds with productive membership in society. His effort is based largely on the kind of techniques and experimentation usually practiced in a laboratory, not a home bar.

While Mr. Deragon's quest to recreate a historical footnote is extreme, it speaks to a heightened interest in bitters, the generic term for the concentrated infusions of roots, herbs, barks, spices and alcohol called for in too many classic drinks to name. (You can start with the martini, the Manhattan, the Old-Fashioned, the Sazerac, the Champagne cocktail, the Martinez ...)

"It's almost like glue that holds a cocktail together," said Philip Ward, the head bartender at Death & Co., in the East Village, where 17 of the 37 house drinks include bitters. "Add a dash, and the other three or four ingredients in the cocktail are in some way going to be able to relate with at least one or two things in the bitters."

The challenge is figuring out which bitters form the strongest bond in a given drink. "I think that's why bitters are so cool," Mr. Ward said. "You don't really know what they do. You just find out what they do by using them."

As new brands and flavors of bitters emerge, the equation becomes more complicated. Last August, a German company called the Bitter Truth started a line of lemon, orange, and aromatic bitters. (Orange bitters are infused with orange peel and an assortment of spices. Aromatic bitters tend to be richer and more complex, with heavier doses of cinnamon, clove and anise.)

Earlier this year, Marlow & Sons, a restaurant and gourmet market in Williamsburg, Brooklyn, began selling house-made Abbott's bitters (since sold out) and citrus bitters, and is now planning a run of peach bitters and another round of Abbott's.

In March, Fee Brothers, a company in Rochester, N.Y., known for its extensive line of cocktail bitters, introduced a limited-edition aromatic bitters, aged for one year in old whiskey barrels. Last month Angostura Ltd.—better known as the company that makes the yellow-capped bitters found in seemingly every grocery store in America—unveiled its long-rumored orange bitters. And bitters aficionados can always browse the extensive selection, for $2 to $16, at LeNell's, a wine and spirits shop in Red Hook, Brooklyn.

For some bartenders, the retail surge is not enough. Jim Meehan, a bartender at Gramercy Tavern and the beverage director at PDT, a new cocktail bar in the East Village, said he feels underserved by the current bitters market, which, depending on how hard one feels like looking, numbers more than a dozen products. He said he plans to age his own aromatic bitters in a used three-gallon bourbon barrel procured from Mr. Deragon.

At Vessel, in Seattle, the bar manager, Jamie Boudreau, starts his cherry bitters by combining separate bourbon- and rye-based infusions with a touch of honey-flavored vodka and the Italian digestif amaro. He then ages the bitters in an oak cask rinsed with shiraz, filters them, and packages them in small glass bottles bearing an old-fashioned-sounding word of caution: "Imbibing more than a few drops may cause man to see things as they are, rather than as they should be."

The allure of antiquity might begin to explain the remarkable devotion that Abbott's bitters inspire. Ted Haigh, a Los Angeles-based graphic designer and drinks writer and historian known to many as Dr. Cocktail, became intrigued with Abbott's—which he describes as similar to Angostura but with a more pronounced flavor of clove, nutmeg and cinnamon, plus a hint of anise—in the early 1990s, when he lucked into several bottles from roughly 1933.

His curiosity led him to two descendants of the company's founder; a copy of the first corporate minutes, circa 1907; a pilgrimage to the original Abbott's production site in Baltimore; and a lengthy interview with the company's final owner, who dissolved the brand in the early 1950s because of sagging popular interest in drinks with bitters. And yet: "To my knowledge," he said in an e-mail, "not a soul has the original recipe anymore."

Thanks in large part to the combined interest of Mr. Haigh and Robert Hess, a director at Microsoft in Seattle and the founder of drinkboy.com, a Web site devoted to cocktails, debate about the lost recipe has been simmering online for years. (Mr. Hess, who owns 10 original bottles of Abbott's, and whose personal digital assistant contains upwards of 4,000 cocktail recipes, has made what he calls House Bitters since 2002.)

Last fall, the conversation vaulted ahead when Kevin J. Verspoor, a perfumer at Fragrance Resources in Clifton, N.J., and a relative newcomer to the drinkboy.com discussion boards, posted the results of a gas chromatograph test he conducted on an unopened, Prohibition-era bottle from Mr. Hess's collection.

"He had things in there that I never would have guessed—like tonka beans," said Mr. Deragon, who based his initial recipe largely on Mr. Verspoor's findings. (Tonka beans, with a scent reminiscent of vanilla, contain the blood-thinning chemical coumarin, and were banned as an additive by the Food and Drug Administration in 1954.)

On a recent evening, Mr. Deragon was enjoying a cocktail at Death & Co. when Mr. Meehan dropped by with some Peruvian bitters that he'd heard were crucial for pisco sours. Mr. Deragon seemed skeptical.

"I don't know," he said, taking a deep whiff of the Peruvian bitters, which tasted like Kahlua. "I might be moving out of the bitters and on to the vermouths. I feel like the bitters market is already saturated in terms of people making their own. I'm going to move on to the next big thing."

## ASTORIA BIANCO
Adapted from JIM MEEHAN, PDT, New York City

2 ounces Tanqueray gin
1 ounce Martini Bianco vermouth
1 dash Fee Brothers orange bitters
1 dash Regan's orange bitters
Slice of orange peel, for garnish

**1.** Fill pint glass with ice. Add all ingredients except orange peel and stir briskly until chilled.

**2.** Strain into chilled cocktail glass and garnish with orange twist.

## MARMALADE SOUR
Adapted from JAMIE BOUDREAU, Vessel, Seattle

2 ounces cachaça
2 dashes Fee Brothers orange bitters
1 tablespoon citrus marmalade
1 fresh egg white
½ ounce fresh lemon juice

**1.** Fill cocktail shaker with ice. Add all ingredients and shake vigorously to emulsify egg white.

**2.** Strain into a chilled cocktail glass.

*June 27, 2007*

# SIPPING ON A SUNSET, ITALY IN MIND

## By JENNIFER STEINHAUER

Just as the culinary cognoscenti press us into embracing certain food trends ("You will eat pork belly! Love cupcakes now! Hate cupcakes now!") so, too, do they dictate our drinks.

First, several years ago, there was St.-Germain, the delicate elderflower liqueur. Early on, it entered a long-term relationship with prosecco: if you wanted to date the sparkling Italian refreshment, you were stuck with its French chaperon. Next up was Domaine de Canton, and every lounge drink began to taste vaguely of gingersnaps.

Coming around the corner is Cynar; get ready to explain to your dinner guests why you are making them a martini that tastes of artichoke.

But for the time being, we live in the world of Aperol, a slightly bitter, go-down-easy Italian aperitif that has found its way into bartenders' flutes and highball glasses from Los Angeles to London.

The popularity of the century-old mixer stems from the marketing juggernaut that pumps up many spirits these days, as well as Aperol's versatility. Then there is its uncommon hue: on ice, a vermilion sunset over the ocean.

"People look at someone at the bar drinking one and they say, 'Wow, what is that?' " said Kara Lavoie, the California and Nevada spirits-sales manager for Palm Bay International, which imports Aperol into the United States.

The company has done its best to promote the brand, holding parties at food festivals, pressing the drink into the hands of influential bartenders and papering city bus stops with ads. Sales of Aperol in this country have increased 1,250 percent over the last five years, according to the importer.

"In the last 30 days I have sold 184 bottles," said Steven Bowles, the assistant spirits buyer at Astor Wines and Spirits, in New York.

Paul's Wines and Spirits, in Washington, D.C., has found it hard to keep the drink in stock this summer. "It has grown in popularity for some reason in the last several months," said Rick Bellman, a co-owner. "People started asking for it."

Aperol, which got its start in 1919 in Padua, Italy, tastes of orange rind and spice, with a bit of rhubarb in there somewhere. It has half the alcohol content of its closest sibling, Campari, and is a bit less bitter, too—even slightly sweet—with tiny hints of the 30 different herbs and spices that it advertises. (Both are produced by Gruppo Campari, a conglomerate that also makes Cynar and several other spirits.)

Distribution became more widespread in the United States about five years ago, when Palm Bay began an aggressive push by promoting the Spritz (three parts prosecco, two parts Aperol and a splash of soda water topped with an orange slice), which had already been popularized in Italy.

"Any Italian restaurant that has done their homework knows that the Spritz is what they are drinking over there," said Jim Meehan, a managing partner of the East Village speakeasy PDT.

Bartenders have now moved well beyond it. At the Standard New York, they often make Negronis now with Aperol rather than Campari. At Peels downtown, the mixologist Yana Volfson makes a cocktail with the aperitif, grapefruit juice and St.-Germain, drawing on Aperol's vibrant mandarin flavor, which pairs well with other citrus notes.

In Los Angeles, at Terroni, they're mixing up the Il Sorpasso, which involves Aperol, Maker's Mark bourbon, honey and lemon juice syrup. (I've been making a cheap home version, tossing Aperol with San Pellegrino Limonata soda and a dash of honey. If my supervisor yelled at me that day, I add gin.)

"I like how it is this very approachable ingredient," Ms. Volfson said. "It can play the part of bitterness, and it can play the role of the sweetener. If you are working with a Negroni with a more viscous vermouth, then Aperol works as a softener. In a martini it can act as the bitterness."

While Aperol seems unlikely to win a spot in the pastry chef's larder next to Grand Marnier, it is getting a workout in some kitchens. Bottega, in Birmingham, Ala., serves a sorbet with grapefruit and Aperol; Balena, in Chicago, has an Aperol granita that a home cook can easily replicate.

The ease of Aperol is part of its appeal, a mild antidote to the mixology movement that brought us complicated cocktails involving obscure spirits, herb-infused sugars and bacon. "Things are cooling down with fundamentalism in cocktails right now," Mr. Meehan said. "This is a light, refreshing drink that especially in the summer is kind of what the doctor ordered."

For the home bartender, Aperol is fairly easy to use, perfect for mixing with a splash of gin and vodka or something sparkling, just for color and tang. It is so low in alcohol (11 percent) that measuring and mulling are not really necessary. Just pour it over ice, maybe squeeze some fresh orange over it all, give the drink a stir with a takeout chopstick and stare out the window as you sip, thinking vague thoughts about whether or not you should change your air-conditioner filter.

"Aperol is a little easier to get into" than some more challenging spirits like Maraschino Luxardo, the sour-cherry liquor, said Mr. Bowles, of Astor Wines. "It's more flexible. People are definitely playing around with it."

Aperol's moment may pass, and the sipping world move on. But for now, the world tastes a bit more like orange peel. "Everyone is always looking for something new to work," said Jack Shute, who represents Palm Bay International in New York.

Cynar, the artichoke aperitif, might not quite catch up. "In my opinion it is difficult to explain to the consumer what an artichoke brings to the spirit," he said. "Orange is easy."

## SHADDOCK'S FIZZ
### Adapted from PEELS, New York City

| | |
|---|---|
| 2 ounces Aperol | 2 ounces Champagne, or to taste |
| ¾ ounce grapefruit juice | Grapefruit twist |
| ½ ounce St.-Germain liqueur | |

**1.** Pour Aperol, grapefruit juice and St.-Germain into a cocktail shaker and shake well.

**2.** Fill a highball glass with ice, and pour in contents of shaker. Top with Champagne and add grapefruit twist.

*August 7, 2012*

# FOR DRY TASTES, AN AROMATIC ALTAR TO BITTERS
## By STEVE REDDICLIFFE

Even if love were not part of the name, I would fall for Amor y Amargo in the East Village.

It's small, with seating for a dozen or so customers in what was once a sandwich shop. The music's good: "God Only Knows" by the Beach Boys, "You Really Got Me" by the Kinks. And it has as its guiding spirit the bartender and bitters proselytizer Sother Teague.

Bitters may get second billing in the name, but they are the star attraction: from amari like Braulio to Xocolatl Mole bitters from Bittermens, the company that helped create Amor y Amargo with Ravi DeRossi three years ago. (Mr. DeRossi is the owner of an impressive number of East Village places, many of them with declared majors—Mayahuel for tequila and mezcal, Desnuda for wine and Gin Palace—as well as the popular cocktail bar Death & Company.)

Amor y Amargo "was never meant to be a longstanding place," Mr. DeRossi said. "It was meant to be a pop-up, but it was such a hit that we decided to keep it going."

Much of the bar's success is attributable to the enthusiasm of Mr. Teague, whose résumé includes culinary school student and instructor, research chef for Alton Brown's "Good Eats" television series, head bartender at Rye in Brooklyn and part-timer at Bittermens, which is how he arrived at Amor y Amargo, initially working one day a week. (Bittermens is now in New Orleans and is no longer involved in the bar.)

Mr. Teague, who has since expanded his presence, sees himself as an educator. "People come in all the time and ask questions," he said. "It's a very consultative process just to get a drink in someone's hand."

And when it gets there, it is memorably excellent. That's especially true of the Casualty with Montenegro amaro, Famous Grouse Scotch, the quinine-and-wine aperitif Byrrh and Xocolatl bitters, a warming hut of a cocktail with a nice cocoa note.

The Brawny Man is what Mr. Teague rhythmically describes as a "bitter, bitter, smoky, bitter": Dell'Erborista amaro, Gran Classico Bitter liqueur, Peat Monster Scotch, Byrrh and Bittermens New Orleans coffee bitters. The name is accurate.

The bar will also make any kind of negroni or manhattan you could want.

Mr. Teague said his restaurant work gave him a "sort of slantedly bitter palate," and that when he started bartending in New York, "I was dashing Angostura into my daiquiris, I was dashing it into anything—I wanted that little dry extra layer of flavor."

"If spirits are soup, then all these bitters are seasoning," he said. "You wouldn't eat unseasoned soup, so why are you drinking an unseasoned drink?" (Mr. Teague often cooks at Amor y Amargo, including, fittingly enough, a seasoned, souplike dish he calls Southern Pho that features North Carolina-style barbecue, fried pig ears, cheddar grits and okra.) He is skillful at sharing his knowledge; he may, for example, pour a taste from a little-known bottle like the Zirbenz Stone Pine Liqueur from the Alps.

Because the night shift wasn't enough to showcase it all, Mr. Teague started doing weekend matinees with a coffee and amaro program called Double Buzz. It's a thoroughly pleasant way to while away a snowy Sunday afternoon.

Natalie Czech, formerly the head barista at the restaurant Maialino, who often works behind the bar on Double Buzz days, and Mr. Teague developed a list of delicious iced cocktails pairing Counter Culture coffee and the bar's signature flavors. One, called the Mittens, combines citrusy Mpemba coffee from Burundi; Aperol; the grapefruit aperitif called Citron Sauvage from Bittermens; blanco tequila; Cocchi Americano, another aperitif; and hopped grapefruit bitters.

Mr. Teague seems to be on the premises at all hours, wearing his United States Postal Service hat ("My oldest and most prized possession—and I'm not a hat person!") and happily talking bitters.

He has contemplated designing a place with a horseshoe bar "so that people literally would be kind of all around me, like a little amphitheater," the better to provide recommendations about everything from books he has been enjoying ("The Drunken Botanist" by Amy Stewart) to which drink goes best with the cauliflower toast on the menu (that would be the Diamonds and Guns, which features Atsby Armadillo Cake vermouth, Bols genever and celery bitters and is billed as "herbaceous and savory").

A homey horseshoe bar? It may not rank up there with Double Buzz, but still, not a bad idea at all.

## DIAMONDS AND GUNS
By CHRIS LOWDER, Amor y Amargo, New York City

| | |
|---|---|
| 1 ounce Banks 5 island rum | ½ ounce Bols Genever |
| ¾ ounce Chartreuse | 2 dash Bittermens Celery Shrub |
| ¾ ounce Atsby Armadillocake vermouth | Lemon twist |

**1.** Stir together all ingredients except lemon peel in a cocktail glass over plenty of ice.

**2.** Strain into a rocks glass with fresh ice. Express the oil from a lemon twist over the drink and place in the glass.

## CASUALTY
By CHRIS ELFORD, Amor y Amargo, New York City

*The name comes from the Cursive song "Casualty." Chris just likes alliterative cocktail names as they tend to be more memorable. Inspiration was from the light chocolate notes found in many blended scotches. Tinkering with some negroni inspired scotch cocktail recipes, he thought the burnt orange flavors of Amaro Montenegro and the rich bitterness of Byrrh would work well. Boy did they!*

| | |
|---|---|
| 1 ½ ounce Famous Grouse Scotch | 2 dashes Bittermens Mole bitters |
| ¾ ounce Amaro Montenegro | Orange twist |
| ¼ ounce Byrrh Quinquina | |

**1.** Stir together all ingredients except orange peel over plenty of ice in a bar glass.

**2.** Strain into a chilled Manhattan glass. Express the oil from an orange twist over the drink and drop in the glass.

## BRAWNY MAN
By SOTHER TEAGUE, Amor y Amargo, New York City

*This drink was inspired by a pair of my regular customers that have turned into dear friends, Joe and Clifton. These guys are always trying to push the boundaries of aggressive and powerfully bitter drinks. They had a version of this that they were working on that involved Cynar but I felt it was a bit out of balance so I switched it for a softer amaro, Gran Classico. It attacks the palette as bitter, bitter, smoky, bitter. And, its strong, like a brawny man.*

| | |
|---|---|
| ¾ ounce Amaro dell'erborista | ¾ ounce Gran Classico |
| ¾ ounce Peat monster Scotch | ¼ ounce Bittermens New Orleans (coffee bitter) |
| ¾ ounce Bigallet China China | Orange twist |

**1.** Stir together all ingredients except orange twist over plenty of ice in a bar glass.

**2.** Strain into a chilled Manhattan glass.

**3.** Express the oil from an orange twist over the drink and drop into the glass.

*February 13, 2014*

# A CHICAGO COCKTAIL CRAWL

## By STEVE REDDICLIFFE

"It certainly was not without a sense of humor, naming a cocktail bar after a gentleman who spent the majority of his life preaching against the evils of alcohol," said Alex Bachman, the bartender at Billy Sunday, the animated spot in the Logan Square neighborhood of Chicago.

But it wasn't necessarily intended to mock, either: "One thing I definitely admired was, he had a great conviction to what he believed in," Mr. Bachman said.

Billy Sunday, the bar named for an evangelist, can be winningly cheeky. The savory Box Lunch—made with goat's milk; oats and spices like mace and cinnamon; palo cortado sherry; and Génépi wormwood liqueur—is served in a small milk bottle complete with striped straw. The food menu includes a category called Things in Jars (the oven-roasted tomatoes are top-notch). The playlist assembled by Jon Byron, the floor manager, features welcome Dylan ("Changing of the Guards") and a wonderfully weird cover of "Crimson and Clover" by the Chilean band Aguaturbia.

There is a nod to the esteemed Chicago writer Nelson Algren here, with a sprightly cocktail called the Algren Sling—New Western gin, pineapple, Three Pins herbal liqueur, lemon and Angostura bitters accented with cherries. It is served in a cup made of a coconut shell ("Dried and polished but very much real," Mr. Bachman said).

"I've always had a deep appreciation for Nelson Algren, how he wrote about Chicago," said Mr. Bachman, who grew up on the North Side and whose résumé includes work in the beverage program at the restaurant of the late Charlie Trotter. "I would never go as far as to say that he would drink Singapore Slings during his life, but it's just a tip of the hat to him in the small way that we could."

Mr. Bachman's point of pride is the back bar's bottles of amaro and fernet, and it shows in his breakdown of the invigorating, biting drink called the Victorian, created here. "We wanted to showcase a spirit-forward cocktail that embraced a lot of the herbal components of amaro, so we used gin—the great botanical spirit that it is—as a vehicle to carry that very deep herbaceous character of the amaro and fernet Angelico," he said.

The gin is Damrak, the amaro dell'Erborista and they're joined by bitters made in-house with wormwood, "one of the primary components of many amaro," Mr. Bachman said. Also in the mix is Billy Sunday's sirop de capillaire—"that's a wonderful throwback, I think, to classic cocktail culture. Essentially it's a heavy syrup made from sugar and maidenhair fern; the syrup on its own almost has an Earl Grey, sort of bergamot tealike quality to it.

"It's a very small component of the cocktail," Mr. Bachman said. "It's only a quarter of an ounce. But not to diminish its importance, it plays a great role there."

## THE VICTORIAN
### By ALEX BACHMAN, BILLY SUNDAY, Chicago

2 ounces Damrak Gin

¼ ounce Sirop de Cappillaire (recipe follows)

¼ ounce Angelico Fernet

½ ounce Varnelli Sibilla Amaro

3–4 dashes wormwood bitters (recipe follows, or use storebought)

Lemon zest

**1.** Add all ingredients except lemon zest to a mixing glass. Add four Kold-Draft or other large ice cubes and stir for a good 15–20 seconds.

**2.** Single strain into coupe glass and add lemon zest.


## SIROP DE CAPPILLAIRE

2 cups sugar

1 cup water

1 tablespoon of gum arabic

¼ ounce dried maidenhair fern

**1.** Boil the water and gum arabic, making sure the gum arabic is fully dissolved before adding sugar.

**2.** Beginning when the syrup is still hot, macerate dried maidenhair fern in 12 ounces of syrup for at least 24 hours and up to 36 hours. Strain mixture and reserve liquid. Discard solids.


## WORMWOOD BITTERS

25.36 ounces GNS (Grain neutral spirit; 191 proof)

2 grams quassia bark

2 sticks cinnamon

½ lemon zest

1 teaspoon grains of paradise

8 tablespoons wormwood

1 teaspoon monk's pepper (vitex berry)

**1.** Macerate all ingredients for 2 weeks.

**2.** Let macerated mixture settle and strain out all solids through a fine filter to remove the smallest particles.

*December 26, 2013*

SOTHER TEAGUE POURS AT AMOR Y AMARGO IN THE EAST VILLAGE

AMUSE BOOZE AT SAXON & PAROLE, NEW YORK CITY

CHAPTER 16

# THE
# SHRUB

# MAKE MINE A VINEGAR SOLUTION

## By ROBERT SIMONSON

Like many restaurants, Saxon & Parole likes to tantalize a diner with an amuse-bouche. But at this new Bowery restaurant the waiter doesn't deliver a lightly grilled scallop or some tuna tartare on a slice of cucumber. No, he hands you a glass of vinegar.

Well, not quite. Saxon & Parole's palate cleanser of choice is a shrub, which is not a leafy bush in this case, but a genus of sweetened vinegar-based beverage that has its roots in Colonial days. Lately the beverage director, Naren Young, has been assembling a pomegranate shrub, from pomegranate seeds and a tablespoon of pomegranate molasses left to macerate in cabernet vinegar and water, topped with a float of fino sherry.

Make no mistake: the piquant shot will prime your senses plenty for the coming meal. As Kelley Slagle, a former beverage director at Hearth and a shrub advocate, put it, "Vinegar's the Zamboni for the tongue."

In the public mind, vinegar doesn't send off terribly positive vibrations to the drinker. It's what wine turns into when it goes bad. But a collection of mixologists across the country are reaching back through the centuries to reclaim vinegar's more palatable past.

"You can trace vinegar drinks back to the 18th century" in America, said Wayne Curtis, the liquor writer and historian. "The berries and fruits

came and went so quickly, that people used vinegar as an acid to preserve them." With the addition of sugar and water, refrigeration-bereft American pioneers had a tart, bracing beverage. Of course, it wasn't long before someone realized that shrubs made dandy mixers. "You threw in some rum or whiskey, and that has a nice effect as well," Mr. Curtis said.

Crack a 19th-century cocktail book, and you'll find a shrub or three. But vinegar lost its position in the back bar early in the last century. Not until recently have restlessly inventive bartenders fetched it up from the pantry, embracing it as "the other acid," an alternative to same-old-same-old lemons and limes.

And some have gone beyond simple shrubs—"the darling of vinegar cocktails," in Ms. Slagle's estimation. They'll deploy vinegar straight in some drinks, as does Cabell Tomlinson, beverage director at Frankies 570 in the West Village, whose Tossed and Turned is a Dark and Stormy derivative pricked with balsamic vinegar. Or they'll use a flavor-intense shrub reduction called a gastrique, as does Lynn House, the mixologist at the Blackbird restaurant in Chicago, who uses an apple cider vinegar gastrique in her Cognac-based Oz cocktail.

This fall, Peels, just across the Bowery from Saxon & Parole, will introduce a switchel. Modeled on a popular early American cooler, it combines molasses, ginger, apple cider vinegar, apple cider and dark rum. Ashley Greene, the bartender responsible for that drink, has also been toying with Manhattans, lacing them with a tincture of white wine vinegar and fennel seeds. "If you add a tiny bit," Ms. Greene said, "it brightens up the acidity in a way that's really attractive."

Nonalcoholic vinegar beverages are also back from the dead. At Peels, the beverage director Yana Volfson has a short list of un-spiked shrubs, including raspberry, cranberry and beet versions. So does the Queens Kickshaw, an Astoria restaurant.

"We were making our own pickles in house," said Ben Sandler, the owner. "The pickling liquid was being thrown away. Shrubs were a way to reduce waste, but also make something delicious."

Jen Snow, a spokeswoman at Russ & Daughters, the Lower East Side smoked-fish store, told a similar eureka story born of thrift. "We pickle and cure beets when we make our beet, apple and herring salad, and we use the pickled beet juice that results from that step to make a shrub drink," she said. The beet-lemon shrub was introduced last year and sells well.

Mr. Curtis attributes mixologists' growing fascination with vinegar to "the restless search for something people haven't done, and scouring history books." That may well have been the genesis, but bartenders have found other reasons not to sour on the ingredient.

"For one thing, it's shelf-stable,"

Ms. Slagle said. "I've never had a shrub go bad. Flavor-wise, it has a lot more complexity than citrus."

Noah Ellis, who regularly keeps two or three vinegar cocktails on the menu at Red Medicine, his restaurant in Beverly Hills, Calif., likes the acid's talents as a fire-delivery system.

"Instead of throwing in a chile in a drink and muddling it, if you use just a little bit of chile or ginger in vinegar, it is a good carrier of that heat," he said.

Vinegar is also a potential cost saver. "You don't have to use a lot," said Damon Boelte, the beverage director at Prime Meats in Carroll Gardens, Brooklyn, where you can order a Sidewalker, a beer-and-apple-brandy cocktail laced with apple cider vinegar. "You can buy one bottle per season." (Bonus: vinegar doesn't have to be squeezed every day.)

Many bartenders have found that their acidulous concoctions have received a surprisingly warm welcome.

The Celery Gimlet—Naren Young's drink made of gin, lime juice, celery juice, green Chartreuse, chardonnay vinegar, celery bitters and a lightly pickled celery-strip garnish—is the most popular cocktail at Saxon & Parole. Still, it pays to tread lightly in drink descriptions.

"I never flat out say vinegar on the menu," Ms. House said. "I use words like shrub or gastrique. Most people are shocked when they find out what the secret ingredient is."

CELERY GIMLET

## CELERY GIMLET
**Adapted from Naren Young**

1½ ounce gin, preferably Junipero
½ ounce Green Chartreuse
¼ ounce St. Germain
¾ ounce lime juice
½ ounce lime syrup (recipe follows)

½ ounce fresh celery juice
Pinch of salt
5 dashes verjus or Chardonnay vinegar
2 dashes The Bitter Truth Celery Bitters
Fresh or Pickled celery ribbon, for garnish

**1.** Combine all ingredients except the celery ribbon garnish in a cocktail shaker filled with ice and shake vigorously.

**2.** Strain into a rocks glass filled with ice and garnish with the celery ribbon.

## LIME SYRUP

Peel of 2 medium limes

½ cup granulated sugar

**1.** Combine the lime peels, sugar and ½ cup water in a large saucepan set over high heat and bring to a boil. Cook until the sugar dissolves. Remove from the heat and allow to cool.

**2.** Strain the syrup into a bowl, pressing the lime peels. Store the syrup in the refrigerator.

## PAUL'S CLUB COCKTAIL
**Adapted from "The PDT Cocktail Book" by JIM MEEHAN**

1 pound concord grapes
1 cup white wine vinegar
2 ounces gin

½ ounce simple syrup (page 27)
¼ ounce pastis

**1.** Combine and crush grapes and vinegar in a nonreactive container, mixing every once in a while. Cover for a day. Strain, discarding the grapes. Reserve 1 ounce of the liquid. Refrigerate the rest in a clean jar for up to a month. (Add simple syrup and water to taste for a nonalcoholic shrub.)

**2.** Stir gin, the reserved grape liquid and simple syrup with ice and strain into a cocktail glass. Pour in pastis.

*October 11, 2011*

# RASPBERRY VINEGAR: 1900
## By AMANDA HESSER

There are preserves makers who responsibly focus on sustenance, like jams, and then there are preserves makers who home in on impractical pleasures, like syrups and vinegars for cocktails.

Call me irresponsible. The first time I tasted raspberry vinegar—once known as a raspberry shrub—from a 1900 Times recipe, it was as if I were sampling the consummate raspberry. It was sweet and full-bodied, and the acidity wasn't the ephemeral "ping!" of most berries but more of a fiery bellow. The taste was intense and addictive, and I wanted to drink the syrup as an elixir. And so I did. For weeks that summer, I doled it out by the spoonful into glasses of chilled sparkling water and prosecco—and a swell summer it was.

Joanne Weir, a cooking teacher in California and the author of "Tequila," was jazzed by the shrub's tang and honeylike texture, devised what she called an "adult ice cream sundae." The base is a blend of raspberry vinegar, pisco, lemon juice, maraschino liqueur and club soda. The topping is a scoop of vanilla ice cream. The acidity and cream flirt playfully.

## 1900, RASPBERRY VINEGAR

*This recipe appeared in The Times in an article titled "Women Here and There — Their Frills and Fancies."*
YIELD: ABOUT 1 QUART, FOR NUMEROUS DRINKS

| | |
|---|---|
| 1 cup red-wine vinegar | Sugar |
| 1 ½ quarts freshly picked raspberries | |

**1.** In a nonreactive bowl, combine the vinegar and raspberries. Cover and let macerate for 3 days.

**2.** Mash the raspberries in the bowl, then strain the liquid through a fine-mesh sieve lined with cheesecloth. To every 1 cup of juice, add ½ pound of sugar (1¼ cups plus 1 tablespoon). Combine the juice and sugar in a saucepan. Bring to a boil and simmer (gently!) for 15 minutes. Let cool, then bottle. Keep refrigerated for up to 3 months.

**3.** To make 1 drink, add 1 teaspoon raspberry vinegar to a tumbler filled with ice. Add water, sparkling water, rum, brandy or prosecco.

**You may halve or quarter the recipe for the raspberry vinegar mixture.**

## 2010, RASPBERRY VINEGAR FLOAT
By JOANNE WEIR, the author of "Tequila"

1 ounce raspberry vinegar (from recipe on previous page)
2 ounces pisco Italia
¼ ounce fresh-squeezed lemon juice
¼ ounce maraschino liqueur
Club soda
Vanilla ice cream
1 sprig mint, for garnish

**1.** Place the raspberry vinegar, pisco Italia, lemon juice, and maraschino liqueur in a shaker and stir well to mix. Add plenty of ice and shake well.

**2.** Strain into a tall float glass. Top the drink with club soda to taste (¼ to ½ cup). Carefully place a scoop of ice cream into the glass. Garnish with a mint sprig and serve with a tall bar spoon and a straw.

*July 28, 2010*

## IN BLOOM
Adapted from KEVIN DENTON, Alder, New York City, by Rosie Schaap

*This is Kevin Denton's recipe for a rosy shrub.*

2 medium pitted plums
1½ cups water
1¾ ounces dried rosehips
2½ ounces dried rosebuds
¾ ounce dried hibiscus
½ cup plus 2 tablespoons white vinegar
¼ cup white sugar

**1.** Bring all ingredients to a slow simmer for 10 to 15 minutes. Let cool.

**2.** Strain and bottle. Refrigerate up to 2 weeks.

**3.** To serve 1 drink: pour 2 ounces of the shrub with 2 ounces of tequila (Mr. Denton prefers Tapatio blanco) over ice, and add a splash of soda.

*September 5, 2013*

GIN AND TONIC

CHAPTER 17

# SUMMER
# DRINKS

# SAY YES TO THE BELLINI

## By JEFF GORDINIER

Let's say you're hosting a summer fiesta. You want your guests to waltz into the backyard and find something more than chilled Sancerre and a tub full of beer bottles and ice.

The problem? Well-made cocktails can cause party gridlock. Mixology doesn't mix well with the flow of conversation, for the simple reason that you can't properly mingle if you're chained to a counter trying to smear the inside of a glass with an orange peel or measure out droplets of elderflower liqueur with a tiny spoon.

So here's a solution: Bellinis. People like to drink them. In fact, people like to say the word. My wife and I figured this out a few years back when we had a summer bash and offered our guests a treat as soon as they arrived.

"Bellini?"

Smiles broke out. "Oh, yes, please, a Bellini," each guest would say, murmuring those Italian syllables as if they served as a kind of bacchanalian incantation.

I had felt emboldened by "Jeff in Venice, Death in Varanasi," a 2009 novel by Geoff Dyer in which so many Bellinis are downed that you think you shouldn't drive a car after reading it. Bellini inebriation is part of the show at the Cannes Film Festival and at the Venice Biennale (the setting of half of Mr. Dyer's book; the drink was invented in Venice). But that fancy pedigree shouldn't dissuade you. The whole point of drinking (and making) Bellinis is that they're easy. Just fill about half a champagne flute with prosecco, then top it off with a few slugs of white peach nectar. Done.

Yes, you can make your own peach nectar in a blender if you want, and you can make precise measurements of prosecco and peach juice.

But you don't have to. Relax. It's summer, after all.

*May 20, 2013*

---

## RHUBARB BELLINI

**Adapted from ESCA, New York City, by Florence Fabricant**

YIELD: 8 DRINKS

2 cups rhubarb, about 4 slender stalks, trimmed and cut in 1-inch pieces

½ cup sugar

Zest of 1 lemon

2 tablespoons fresh lemon juice

1 bottle prosecco or other sparkling wine, well-chilled

**1.** Place rhubarb, sugar, lemon zest and lemon juice in saucepan with ¼ cup water. Bring to simmer and cook about 15 minutes.

**2.** Remove from heat and place saucepan in bowl of ice and water until cool, about 10 minutes. Purée in blender.

**3.** Place about 1½ tablespoons purée in 8 champagne flutes. Pour in prosecco until about one-third full. Stir well to blend in rhubarb purée. Gradually top each serving with more prosecco, stirring to prevent sparkling wine from bubbling over, then serve.

*April 12, 2000*

# WILL THE REAL MAI TAI PLEASE STAND UP?
## By TOBY CECCHINI

In the past, I've had a fairly stock cocktailian's response to the concept of tiki and its representative drinks, those kitschy, oversweetened, unnaturally colored mash-ups of various "tropical" liquors and juices with too many ingredients and too much enforced silliness. Whenever I was asked to produce a mai tai or a planter's punch, I would follow protocol and dump a number of rums and mixers together—some pineapple, right? And some O.J., sure, and don't leave out the coconut. ...

Faking it always catches up with you, however. With the rowdy homecoming of tiki culture to the American bar and a new generation of hyper-serious tiki fanatics exhuming histories and recipes, naysayers like myself have had to step in line and pay these drinks their due. The mai tai has been maligned, but its day of reckoning is coming. If, like me, you thought this drink was a lot of faux-tropical hooey, it's time you tasted a real one and (also like me) ate crow in astonishment at this surprisingly simple and beautifully balanced cocktail. It's been here all the time—except that it really hasn't.

The detail is all. I knew the mai tai called for a seldom-employed artificial almond syrup called orgeat, or orzata, depending on whether you're buying the faux-French version or the faux-Italian one. The problem is that faux-ness. Say what you will about the tiresome geek factor afoot in the more conscientious bars; much of the recent improvement in the cocktail landscape is driven by pointy-headed scrutiny of all ingredients, which leads, in the best bars, to replacing weak links like this cloying syrup with the shelf life of Styrofoam.

Though orgeat is conceptually tethered to tiki, its twisted history predates tiki's by a long stretch. Orge is the French for "barley," and orgeat, orzata or, in Spanish, horchata, originally referred to a common method of making barley water, a nourishing drink, by crushing the grain in a mortar and pestle and adding water to it to emulsify the fats. Along the line, almonds were added to the mix, and eventually the humble grain got shoved out in favor of the rich and aromatic nut. Jerry Thomas, the pioneering 19th-century bartender, called for it routinely in his first recipe book, giving a detailed recipe in the back index that was probably fairly common at the time but has been all but forgotten in the expedient age. It was in fact an urge to have one of Thomas's "Japanese" cocktails—one of my favorite Cognac-based drinks—that led me to wonder about orgeat, why it's named after barley and is supposed to taste like almonds but is really just kind of fake almond candy. Time to roll up the sleeves again.

Churning the underworld of online recipes for "real" orgeat predictably reveals many that seem to closely mimic Thomas's, including a much-cited version by Darcy O'Neil on his engagingly cranky Web site The Art of Drink. Simplifying that recipe and incorporating others gave me a perfectly novel old-cocktail ingredient that impressed me as much for its restrained lushness as for its dissimilarity to what we've come to think of as orgeat syrup. Imagine a rich, sweetened almond milk, with the perfumed tinge of neroli from orange-flower water, adding a mellifluous, smoothing hand to any of the drinks that call for it.

I found no mention in any recipe of an extra step that seemed only natural to me: toasting the blanched almonds for extra flavor. Martin Cate, whose wife makes the insuperable orgeat for his bar Smuggler's Cove in San Francisco, a nexus for the new tiki movement, told me they tried both but found the toasting intrusive. I made equivalent batches with both blanched and toasted blanched almonds. I definitely preferred the toasted version, but they were closer than perhaps the extra step was worth. The Japanese cocktail I finally produced was fine, but this orgeat was so good that I wondered how it would alter the mai tai.

There are raging debates about both the invention of and the proper recipe for this drink among tiki freaks. The more accepted versions are granted to Victor J. Bergeron, the irascible, wooden-legged "Trader Vic," from his eponymous restaurant bar in Oakland, Calif., in the '40s. Contrary to what you might think, the mai tai is actually just a rum sour, employing orgeat alongside Curaçao or triple sec as the sweetener, and using two rums to add complexity. The rest is just lime juice, and that's it. No coconut, no passion fruit, pineapple, mango or orange juice. And no umbrellas. It's a relatively simple drink, but as such, each element has to be of the utmost quality; great rums, fresh lime juice and prefab orgeat syrup equal the kind of disappointment I had always experienced with this drink. When I concocted one with homemade orgeat, however, all the tumblers clicked; halfway through this beauty, I thought, perhaps I've never had a better drink than this. The rums, the lime, the orange aromatics and the heft of the almond all play in stupendous balance. I woke up the next morning wondering how long it was until 6 o'clock, when I could taste that drink again.

## MAI TAI
**Adapted from TRADER VIC'S, Oakland, Calif.**

1 ounce light rum (preferably Banks' 5 Island)

1 ounce gold rum (Appleton's Estate Reserve, Zacapa, Clément V.S.O.P., El Dorado 12-year), plus additional for final float, if desired

½ ounce orgeat syrup (recipe follows, or purchased)

½ ounce orange Curaçao or Cointreau

Juice of 1 lime

Sprig of fresh mint, for garnish

**1.** Combine all ingredients except mint sprig in a shaker with crushed or cracked ice and shake vigorously.

**2.** Pour, with shaken ice, into a double old-fashioned glass and garnish with the spent lime shell and a sprig of fresh mint. Some, who live large and dangerously, like to float an extra ½ ounce of dark rum atop it.

## HOMEMADE ORGEAT SYRUP
YIELD: ABOUT 1.6 LITERS

1 pound blanched or toasted blanched almonds

¾ pound demerara sugar

¾ pound white sugar

1 tablespoon orange-flower water

2 teaspoons almond extract

**1.** Combine almonds with 11 ounces of water in a blender and blend briefly until uniformly but roughly chopped. Pour into a nonreactive bowl and add one liter of boiling water. Stir well and let stand for three hours.

**2.** Line a sieve or chinois with overlapping layers of fine cheesecloth, arranging them in an X pattern and leaving a fair amount trailing over to grab hold of. Pour in the mixture and allow it to filter through, assisting with a wooden spoon if necessary. Fold up the ends of the cheesecloth carefully to trap the pulp in a bag and squeeze out the remaining liquid. (This is important, as the pulp retains a fair amount of emulsion.) Discard cheesecloth and pulp.

**3.** Place emulsion mixture in a pan, add sugar and heat mildly through (140 degrees or less), stirring until sugar is fully dissolved. Remove from heat and allow to cool to room temperature.

**4.** Add orange-flower water and almond extract and funnel into a clean, capped bottle to refrigerate. Optionally you may add 2 or 3 ounces of vodka to the syrup, as a preservative. Note: The syrup will separate after a short while. Simply shake it up again before using.

*October 6, 2010*

# FOR A WARM DAY,
# A YOUNG WHISKEY
## By CLAY RISEN

For many people, whiskey and warm weather don't mix: peat, sherry, smoke and caramel aren't exactly thirst-quenching flavors. But not all whiskeys are created equal, and some are sufficiently light and refreshing to stand alongside gin or vodka in a summertime bar.

The trick is knowing what to look for. Single malts from Islay, for example, tend to be heavy on the peat. Instead, seek the more delicate examples from the Lowlands region. Steve Ury, who writes the popular blog Sku's Recent Eats, recommends Bladnoch, a Lowlands single malt "with a lot of malt that gives it a grassy quality that reminds me of spring."

One reason people associate whiskey with heavy flavors is that most fans lean toward older, more rarefied expressions. But older also means thicker and denser. Meanwhile, there are plenty of younger versions with softer, fruitier tones. "They have pear, fruit, apples and rose, all nice for the summer," said Heather Greene, the whiskey sommelier at the Flatiron Room in Manhattan. She recommends young whiskeys from the Speyside region, like the 12-year-olds from the Balvenie and Glenfiddich.

The same goes for this side of the Atlantic. Many of today's craft whiskeys are under two years old, which allows their underlying grain notes to come through; Ms. Greene recommends the whiskeys from Tuthilltown and Long Island Spirits, both in New York State.

And if you find the whiskey still tastes too hot, Mr. Ury said, don't despair. "There's no rule against throwing in a few ice cubes."
*May 20, 2013*

# WHISKY, SUMMER STYLE
## By JASON ROWAN

Scotch whisky might not seem like a natural fit for lighter summer cocktails. The adjectives you hear applied to these whiskies—peaty, earthy, even medicine—may not immediately suggest beach-ready drinks. But in fact the smokiness or salinity of Scotch whiskies is the very reason they can do so well in citrus-infused drinks with a bit of sugar: they stand up to the sweetness. And just as the complex layers of flavors and aromas of straight whisky open up when you add water, they also sing when combined with the ingredients in these warm-weather drinks, created by bartenders from Glasgow and New York City.

## AMERICAN SMASH
### Adapted from ANGUS MCILWRAITH, Badaboom, Glasgow

*Angus McIlwraith, barman for Badaboom, a Glasgow-based event bar company, created what is essentially a Scotchy Southside for warm-weather gatherings. Built around the bright, light, zero-peat Auchentoshan American Oak, with lemon juice, honey syrup and mint served over crushed ice, it's highly restorative after a long day in the summer sun. A key aspect of preparing the drink, says McIlwraith, is in the treatment of the mint: "The trick is to have a gentle hand with the mint. It's better to lightly bruise it clapping it in your hands to release the minty oils. Crushing it releases grassy and vegetal flavors, which can ruin a cocktail."*

50 milliliters Auchentoshan American Oak

20 milliliters fresh lemon juice

15 milliliters honey syrup (1 part honey, 2 parts water)

4 to 5 mint leaves, lightly bruised, for garnish

**1.** Combine all ingredients except mint leaves in a cocktail shaker filled with cubed ice and shake.

**2.** Strain into a glass filled with crushed ice and garnish with a mint sprig.

## CATHOLIC GUILT
### Adapted from ANDREY KALININ, Highlands, New York City

*At Highlands, a Scottish gastropub in the West Village, the beverage director Andrey Kalinin built the devilishly refreshing Catholic Guilt around the richly peated Black Grouse expression of The Famous Grouse. The result is something savory, tangy, a wee spicy and sweet. It's a drink designed to assuage the guilt sometimes associated with enjoying a cocktail. "If you are Catholic, you'll understand," explains Kalinin.*

2 ounces Black Grouse Blended Whisky

¾ ounce ginger syrup

¾ ounce lemon juice

Dash orange bitters

Dash fig bitters

Fernet Branca

**1.** Combine all ingredients except the Fernet Branca in a cocktail shaker filled with ice and shake.

**2.** Pour into an ice-filled rocks glass and float Fernet Branca on top.

**3.** Garnish with flaming orange zest (page 80.)

*July 16, 2014*

# WATERMELON DRINKS:
## COOL, SWEET, COLORFUL
### By FLORENCE FABRICANT

Watermelon has an all-American image, one that goes along with hot summer days, picnics at the beach and backyard cookouts. But this does not give enough credit to a fruit that has been refreshing people since ancient times.

Botanists believe that watermelons originated in the Kalahari Desert of southern Africa, based on the reports of the explorer David Livingstone, who found vines there in the mid-19th century. The vines were also cultivated in Egypt at least 5,000 years ago, and are depicted in wall paintings there. (Watermelon with salty, feta-like cheese is still a favorite Egyptian breakfast.)

Watermelons followed the trade routes throughout the Middle East to Central Asia, China and Europe. Just imagine trading caravans provisioned with the quenching melons, the merchants munching on refreshing wedges, spitting the seeds and thus inadvertently sowing the crop in their wake.

The fruit made its way to America, most likely on slave ships. Thomas Jefferson planted what he called "Neapolitan watermelons" in his garden in 1773, but they were already growing in other parts of the country, including New England. The American taste for watermelon goes back a long time.

Now, 86 percent of all households in the United States buy watermelon at least once a year, and 73 percent of them buy it once a month, according to the National Watermelon Promotion Board. More than four billion pounds of watermelons was harvested in the United States last year, mainly in California, Florida, Georgia and Texas. Nonetheless, nearly 600 million pounds was imported into the United States, mainly from Mexico, to meet the demand. Last year, Americans ate an average of 16 pounds a person, down a bit from the record of 17.4 pounds a person in 1966.

Perhaps all those watermelon fans already know that a chilled wedge is not the only way to enjoy this fruit. What about drinking it instead?

Watermelon is easy to seed, pulverize and season to serve over ice with or without a splash of vodka, rum, wine or other alcohol. The juice is an excellent sweetener for iced tea or sangria. And chilled or frozen watermelon can also be pureed to tint and flavor cocktails like margaritas and daiquiris.

Watermelons, which are actually related to cucumbers, not other melons, are easy to select because they are picked when ripe and are often sold cut. Look for flesh that is firm and bright, without any splits or grainy areas. The latest additions to the market are yellow-fleshed ones and seedless or triploid varieties, both of which taste about the same but cost more than the garden Godzillas.

Any of these are perfectly suited to making watermelon drinks. But why spend more than necessary? And considering that watermelons are 92 percent water, you do not have to do much to them to get them into a glass.

## WATERMELON CHAMPAGNE
YIELD: 8 DRINKS

3 cups cubed, seeded watermelon
1 tablespoon sugar

½ bottle (375 milliliters) Champagne

**1.** Place watermelon and sugar in a blender, and process until smooth.

**2.** Half-fill eight Champagne flutes with the watermelon mixture.

**3.** Slowly pour the Champagne into each flute to fill it. Serve at once.

## WATERMELON-STRAWBERRY SLUSH
YIELD: 2 DRINKS

1 cup hulled fresh strawberries
1½ cups cubed, seeded watermelon
3 tablespoons sugar

3 tablespoons fresh lemon juice
1 cup ice cubes
¼ cup vodka or white rum (optional)

**1.** Put all ingredients in a blender and process until smooth.

**2.** Pour into 2 goblets and serve.

## WATERMELON AND RED WINE DRINK
Adapted from "My Mexico" by DIANA KENNEDY by Florence Fabricant
YIELD: 6 DRINKS

1 (3½-pound) piece watermelon
1 teaspoon vanilla extract
¼ cup fresh lime juice

Dark brown sugar to taste (optional)
2 cups chilled full-bodied dry red wine
½ cup roughly chopped toasted pecans

**1.** Cut watermelon flesh into large pieces. Cut central part of flesh without seeds into enough tiny cubes to make 1 cup.

**2.** Put remaining flesh into a food processor, and pulse it enough to purée it without breaking seeds. Strain. You should have 2 cups. Stir in vanilla, lime juice and, if desired, sugar to taste.

**3.** Mix red wine with the watermelon purée. Serve in goblets, straight up or over ice, with some cubes of watermelon and pecans in each glass.

*July 1, 1998*

# SUMMER IN A TALL GLASS
## By TOBY CECCHINI

In 14 years of tending bar, I've lent my personal spin to every drink I come across, but I've never been able to better my father's rendition of the gin and tonic. He is an adroit cook and an inveterate tinkerer, and he was for many years a research chemist; it was only natural that he brought his scrutiny to bear on cocktails. The layman may ask how high one can elevate the pedestrian gin and tonic—that stalwart reviver of malarial British colonialists in India, with its invigorating bite of juniper, cleansing tang of lime and aromatic spritz of quinine. But the standard-issue gin and tonic is to my dad's G and T as a Ford Taurus is to a Jaguar S-Type.

My father's method of making the drink in a tall crystal pitcher is less an affectation than a necessity. This is because proportion is crucial to this drink, and you need room for plenty of everything—ice, tonic and lime. The limes must be large and plump and kept at room temperature. The tonic must be chilled, and the ice cracked—not crushed—by hand. And the gin? I most often use Tanqueray for its punchy botanicals and authority; it is 94 proof to the more common 80, making it cantankerous in a martini, but perfect for a G and T.

Dad starts by rolling the limes firmly under the heel of his hand on a cutting board to bring the citrus oil to the surface of the skin, while the intoxicating aroma tumbles through the room. The limes are halved and juiced, and the juice is set aside. The rinds are then sliced into thin ribbons, julienned really, and dumped into the pitcher. Over this the gin is poured.

Muddle the rinds for two minutes with a pestle. When the gin/lime synergy approaches the ambrosial, it is vitally important to thrust the pitcher under the nose of a bystander, as my dad always does, and declare solemnly, "You could wear this as cologne!"

Add the lime juice and macerate for five minutes. The alcohol and acid act as solvents to remove and incorporate the citrus oil and the rind's bitterness. And that, as Frost wrote, has made all the difference.

My dad takes large ice cubes and, with tremendous élan, thwacks them just once with the back of a heavy spoon, whereupon they obediently crumble into the perfect size. Scatter the ice into the pitcher until it is half full with what resembles an aromatic lime granita.

Pour the tonic gingerly, on a slant, down the side of the pitcher. Dad stirs the solution with a tall glass wand, just to distribute the gin; you don't want to jostle the life-giving fizz out of it. Take four glasses from the freezer, garnish with lime rounds, call off any important appointments and hit the veranda.

## GIN AND TONIC
**Adapted from ANDREA CECCHINI**
YIELD: 4 DRINKS

| | |
|---|---|
| 5 limes, room temperature | Cracked ice |
| 16 ounces of gin | 1 liter tonic water, chilled |

**1.** Knead 4 of the limes on a cutting board, then juice. Slice used rinds into thin strips.

**2.** In large pitcher, combine gin and rinds, and muddle for two minutes. Add lime juice, and let stand for five minutes.

**3.** Fill pitcher halfway with ice. Slowly add tonic. Mix carefully, and pour into tall, chilled highball glasses. Garnish with lime rounds cut from the remaining lime.

*July 28, 2002*

## KUMQUAT AND CLOVE GIN AND TONIC
**Adapted from CATA, New York City**

| | |
|---|---|
| 3 kumquats, cut in half | 3 ounces gin (preferably Dorothy Parker American Gin) |
| 3 to 5 cloves | |
| 1 (10-ounce) bottle Schweppes tonic, cold | |

**1.** In an 18-ounce glass, place both halves of 1 kumquat. Muddle lightly.

**2.** Fill glass with ice, and place remaining kumquats and cloves on top.

**3.** Add the gin, and tonic water to taste.

*May 21, 2013*

# A TASTE OF FREEDOM
## By GABRIELLE HAMILTON

Once when I was about 13 years old, my best friend, Renee, and I did that thing where you each tell your parents that you are sleeping over at the other's house, and they don't even check. With relative ease, we found ourselves distinctly unchaperoned and hitchhiking the 20 miles to the Trenton, N.J., train station and catching a train to New York City.

With even greater ease, we found ourselves—such is the power of the teenage sense of immortality—perched on bar stools at an Upper West Side restaurant saying, "Um, I think I'll have a Long Island iced tea, please." It was the only drink we knew to order. We'd been getting blitzed on them for some time by siphoning off our parents' liquor and replacing it with tap water. I remember being curled up on the orange shag rug, feeling the whole planet spin.

The bartender did not card us.

The bartender did not roll his eyes to the heavens. He filled—freehand—two giant tulip-shape glasses that could have doubled as hurricane lamps with well liquors, prefab sour mix and cola from a sticky soda gun. And set them down in front of us.

We were both the youngest in our families and in so many ways by the time we were 10 we were practically 20. We blew smoke rings. We wore eye shadow. But we were, decisively, not 20. We pooled our crumpled bills and quarters, parsed out in stacks of four, and paid our bill to the penny. We did not tip. Poor service? No, we just didn't know to. That's how young we were.

Renee and I made it back unharmed. We caught the last train to Trenton and because we were lit and he was the only other guy in our car, we met a young comedian on the train. We fell over in our seats laughing at all his jokes. And he drove us home and let us out at the end of Renee's silent driveway and we were safe and unmolested, and we grew up and lived our lives. And I am now in my 40's and still drink Long Island iced tea.

In spite of having had the kind of adolescence that had orange shag and startlingly distracted parents—some of the things that have made people my age fashionably full of irony—I have never succumbed to that deadly stance. I drink Long Island iced tea sincerely. It is not part of a fashion trend that favors Peter Frampton haircuts and Tab.

To be sure, I am not drinking exactly the same Long Island iced tea. Now it is a carefully measured cocktail, made in a tall pint glass packed with ice cubes, filled with premium liquors, topped with Coke from a freshly cracked glass bottle. And I usually stick to just one, with some very delicious fried thing to eat, like fat-bellied clams or oysters with a spicy tartar sauce. The food absorbs the alcohol in just the right way so you get high but not blitzed. Which is safer when hitchhiking.

## LONG ISLAND ICED TEA

¾ ounce tequila
¾ ounce vodka
¾ ounce gin
¾ ounce white rum

1½ ounces triple sec
¾ ounce cola
¾ ounce fresh lemon juice

**1.** Pour all ingredients into a pint glass filled with ice and stir. Let sit for 5 minutes.

**2.** Stir again. Serve.

*June 27, 2007*

## TEQUILA SHOTS WITH SANGRITA CHASERS
By ROSIE SCHAAP

*There's only one way to improve on tequila shots: chase them with a short glass of spicy, citrusy sangrita. This recipe makes an entire pitcher of sangrita, enough for several shots, though you could also pair it with very cold Mexican beer.*

| | |
|---|---|
| 2 cups fresh orange juice | 2 teaspoons ancho chile powder |
| ¾ cup fresh lime juice | 6 dashes Tabasco, or to taste |
| ¼ cup grenadine syrup (use one with real pomegranate, like Employees Only or Fee Brothers) | ½ teaspoon salt |
| | Reposado tequila (use about 1 ½ ounces per shot) |

**1.** Make sangrita: Mix all ingredients except tequila in a pitcher and chill well.

**2.** Shake tequila with ice and strain into shot glasses. Serve sangrita in small glasses to chase tequila shots.

*May 20, 2014*

# ALLOWING COCKTAILS TO STIR THE MEAL
## By MELISSA CLARK

Drinking seasonal cocktails used to mean manhattans in the winter and gin and tonics in the summer.

Then a decade ago, mixologists started infusing the likes of lemon verbena and butternut squash into spirits, taking the notion of seasonal cocktails to a more literal level. Now, you're just as likely to encounter an heirloom tomato in the glass as on the plate.

And some restaurants have been creating tasting menus with cocktail pairings that highlight the season's best, from the aperitif through dessert, seasonal dining from coupe to nuts.

This gave me the idea to try it at home, too. I spent the past weeks letting seasonal cocktails inspire the snacks that I served with them.

I found that the rules for matching cocktails with food are a lot more lax than with wine. Really, anything goes, though the more complicated and layered the ingredients are in the glass, the more involved your accompanying hors d'oeuvres can be, and vice versa. For simpler cocktails, simple foods work best.

To greet our first warm night, my husband and I sipped Emperor's Gardens, rhubarb and gin cocktails spiked with Thai basil and seasoned rice vinegar (a condiment used to make sushi rice, flavored with sugar and salt).

Alongside, I echoed the vinegar and basil in a quick shrimp salad garnished with roasted peanuts for crunch. We ate the shrimp on cucumber rounds, but mounding them on crisp lettuce leaves would have been a slightly fancier presentation.

A few nights later, to accompany a rye- and fennel-flavored cocktail called the Golden Bowl, I whipped toasted fennel seeds and fragrant dark green fennel fronds into a velvety smooth white bean dip, which we scooped up with slivers of the bulb. One large, feathery fennel sufficed for both cocktails and dip.

An icy sherry cobbler traditionally takes advantage of whatever fruit is in season or on hand; oranges, pineapple, raspberries, what have you. One night my husband made us cobblers with amontillado sherry and ripe cherries while I sautéed the cherries in butter, then plopped them on goat-cheese-smeared crostini. I can see this becoming a year-round staple, substituting whatever juicy fruit I can get.

To keep things manageable during my cocktail experiments, I opted for individual pairings, whipping up, on a given night, one cocktail and one hors d'oeuvre. It expanded my cocktail-hour repertory, a snazzy prelude to any meal.

Had I been more ambitious, or had I needed a menu for a cocktail party, all of these cocktails and snacks would have worked marvelously served together as well.

And in one instance, that night of the Emperor's Garden, our cocktail hour slid down the slippery slope straight into dinner. We found that after gorging on the tasty little shrimp, all we needed was an arugula salad and a little crusty bread and salty butter to make a meal, allowing me to shelve the pasta dish I had originally planned.

It was light, cooling and, for us, off the well-trod path of gin and tonics, which in itself is worth toasting with a nice seasonal cocktail.

## GOLDEN BOWL
### Adapted from LOT 2, Brooklyn

1 (1-inch) piece fresh ginger root
Tiny pinch kosher salt
1 tablespoon finely chopped fennel fronds, including stems (preferably bronze fennel), plus a sprig for garnish
2 ounces rye whiskey (preferably Old Overholt)

¾ ounce fresh orange juice
1 teaspoon simple syrup, plus additional to taste (page 27)
½ teaspoon absinthe (preferably Kubler)
½ teaspoon fresh lemon juice

**1.** Finely grate the ginger, wrap it in cheesecloth and squeeze out the juice.

**2.** In a mixing glass, muddle salt and fennel fronds. Add whiskey, orange juice, 1 teaspoon simple syrup, absinthe, lemon juice and ½ teaspoon of the ginger juice. Fill mixing glass 2/3 full of ice and shake vigorously. Taste and add more simple syrup if you like.

**3.** Using a fine mesh strainer, pour into a chilled cocktail glass. Garnish with a sprig of fennel frond.

## CHERRY SHERRY COBBLER
### Adapted from THE BEAGLE, New York City

1 lemon wedge (⅙ of a medium sized lemon)

4 pitted cherries (or raspberries or blueberries)

¾ ounce simple syrup (page 27)

3 ounces dry amontillado sherry

Orange slice, for garnish

**1.** In a highball glass muddle lemon and 3 cherries with simple syrup.

**2.** Add sherry, stir to combine and fill glass with crushed ice. Garnish with another cherry and an orange slice. Serve with a straw.

## EMPEROR'S GARDEN
### Adapted from WONG, New York City

*On a warm spring night, the Emperor's Garden, a rhubarb and gin cocktail spiked with Thai basil and seasoned rice vinegar (a condiment used to make sushi rice, flavored with sugar and salt), is a perfect way to celebrate spring and also to use up some of the rhubarb you bought at the green market.*

1 cup thinly sliced rhubarb

1 cup sugar

5 Thai basil leaves, plus more for garnish

1 teaspoon seasoned rice wine vinegar

1½ ounces gin

¾ ounce lemon juice

**1.** Make rhubarb simple syrup: Bring 1 cup water to a boil in a medium saucepan. Add rhubarb and sugar, and stir until sugar is dissolved. Remove from heat, cover and let stand for 1 hour. Reserve a selection of rhubarb slices as cocktail garnishes, then strain syrup and store chilled for up to 7 days.

**2.** In a mixing glass, muddle the Thai basil leaves with the seasoned rice wine vinegar. Add gin, 1 ounce rhubarb simple syrup and lemon juice. Fill mixing glass 2/3 full of ice and shake vigorously. Using a fine mesh strainer, pour into a chilled cocktail glass. Garnish with a Thai basil leaf and a slice of reserved rhubarb.

*June 8, 2012*

## LIMONCELLO
### By AMANDA HESSER
YIELD: SERVES MANY (ABOUT 6 CUPS)

12 lemons

1 (750-milliliter) bottle good vodka

½ cup sugar

**1.** Finely grate the zest of the lemons. In a large jar, combine the zest and the vodka. Seal tightly and place in a cool, dark place for 2 weeks.

**2.** In a small saucepan over medium heat, dissolve the sugar in ½ cup water. Let cool.

**3.** Using a sieve lined with cheesecloth, set over a bowl, strain the vodka mixture. Stir the sugar syrup into it. Use a funnel to pour into a 1-liter bottle and seal. Place in a cool, dark place for 1 week, then chill in the freezer until ready to serve.

*November 6, 2005*

## EL DIABLO
By MARK BITTMAN

*Crème de cassis is a deep red liqueur made from black currants, and it gives this drink its reddish color. The ginger beer makes this drink bubbly and refreshing, the perfect sip on a warm evening.*

| | |
|---|---|
| ¼ cup tequila | 1½ tablespoons crème de cassis |
| 1½ tablespoons triple sec | Ginger beer |
| 1½ tablespoons lime juice | Lemon wedge, for garnish |

**1.** Combine lots of ice, the tequila, triple sec and lime juice in a mixing glass and shake. Add 1½ tablespoons crème de cassis and shake again.

**2.** Strain into a glass with ice and top with ginger beer. Garnish with a lime wedge.

*May 13, 2012*

# THE PULSE OF SUMMER: BLENDER DRINKS ARE BACK
## By PETE WELLS

You may regard the electric blender as a helpful household appliance. For your bartender, it is a tool straight from the devil.

"You'd be hard pressed to find a barman who takes his work seriously who works in a joint with a blender," said Duggan McDonnell, an owner of the bar Cantina in San Francisco. "I worked in one restaurant that did blender drinks and I'm telling you—the noise, the whirring, you're going through blades in the middle of service, and craziness abounds."

So widespread is the loathing that whenever Martin Cate posts a job opening at Forbidden Island, his bar in Alameda, Calif., he finds it necessary to screen out bartenders who refuse to use the devices. "Don't like blenders?" his ad goes. "Don't apply." Each time it runs, people write to tell him just how happy they are that they don't work for him.

After all, there are plenty of bars where they will never be called on to push "Liquefy." The owners of high-minded cocktail haunts like Bourbon & Branch in San Francisco or the Clover Club in Brooklyn cultivate a genteel atmosphere that is not just pre-Prohibition but almost pre-Edison.

Toby Maloney, an owner of another such bar, the Violet Hour in Chicago, once worked at a restaurant where the owners' purchase of a blender touched off a covert rebellion. "All the bartenders decided that was not going to happen," he recalled. "I remember the blender—can you hear my quotes?—accidentally falling down the stairs."

So it's something of a shock that a couple of bars are lugging the machine back up the stairs again, dusting it off and even giving it a place of honor.

At the Rusty Knot at the western

edge of Greenwich Village, two blenders work all night long and, on weekends, most of the afternoon, churning up fluffy snowdrifts of rum. In the two years since it opened, Forbidden Island has worn out three blenders.

"They just didn't handle the volume," Mr. Cate said. "The ball bearings freeze up in there. Or the blade in the bottom of the cup freezes up or something, and they don't run, and there's this unsettling burning smell that comes out of the blender."

The Herculean blenders at those two bars—and granted, two bars is far from a national landslide—work so hard for an excellent reason. Bartenders might hate making blender cocktails, but the rest of us love drinking them.

We loved them in the '30s and '40s, when the Waring blender washed ashore in Havana and was adopted by Constante Ribalagua, head barman at the Floridita. According to legend, Ribalagua made more than 10 million daiquiris. There is dispute about his precise technique, but for many drinks he seems to have used the blender almost as a cocktail shaker, pulsing the ingredients just long enough to chill them, but not so long as to turn the drink to slush.

He was known for filtering out even the tiniest shards of ice with a fine mesh sieve, and for the grapefruit-and-maraschino-liqueur daiquiri he served Hemingway. But Ribalagua had five versions of that cocktail, all worth a second look, particularly the Daiquiri No. 2, with its hint of oranges.

We loved blender drinks in the '50s, when the piña colada sailed north from San Juan and captured the mainland United States. It was taken up by the tiki bars and restaurants that spread across the country after World War II, inspired by the success of Trader Vic's in Emeryville, Calif., and Don the Beachcomber in Hollywood.

Modern bartenders might embrace the blender if they had been around in those pioneer days.

"Before they had blenders, they had blocks of ice, and they had four or five guys on a busy night, and all they would do is shave ice," said Michael Buhen, an owner of the Tiki-Ti on Sunset Boulevard. Mr. Buhen's father, Ray, worked for Don the Beachcomber in 1934, when it opened. "And then they invented the blender and you didn't have to do that stuff anymore."

We might have loved them a little too much in the '70s. At fern bars across the land, singles' nights were lubricated by heaping goblets of sugary frozen drinks like the Mudslide and the Outstanding Alexander (Cognac, Grand Marnier, coffee liqueur, whipping cream, chocolate ice cream, vanilla ice cream).

"If anything is going to turn you off a blender, it's having one of those," said Jeff Berry, the author of "Sippin' Safari," a book about lost tropical drink recipes and the people who created them. "When you put cream liqueurs in a blender ...," he said. "I can feel myself falling off the stool right now."

In the wake of that era's lawless abandon, Mr. Cate said, "the whole world of exotic cocktails ended up having this bad reputation." What went wrong, he and others say, is that the bartenders who were scooping rum raisin ice cream into their drinks forgot that there was a craft to this business.

"If you're going to make a blended drink, don't take any shortcuts," Mr. Maloney said. "You're going to need good ingredients. You're going to make simple syrup, you're going to need to squeeze your juices fresh, you're going to have to use bitters. It takes the same attention to detail, if not more."

Those were among Mr. Maloney's tricks when, serving as a consultant, he devised the Rusty Knot's piña colada recipe. For his Spiced Colada, he added lemon and lime to Captain Morgan's spiced rum and positively drenched the drink in Angostura bitters. It was just the sort of crisp slap in the face that was needed to bring the piña colada back to life. The bar sells more of them than its owners ever imagined.

"It's insane," said Taavo Somer, who dreamed up the Rusty Knot with another restaurateur, Ken Friedman. Mr. Friedman turns out to be one of the bar's most enthusiastic consumers of frozen cocktails.

"Some of these drinks are kind of dangerous," Mr. Friedman said. "It tastes like you're having Jamba Juice, and you're not. I can't count on one hand the number of people who've had to walk me home because I was having one of these Spiced Coladas."

For home bartenders, it's worth practicing a few basics before the rum takes effect. The blender can be put to several handy uses behind the bar. It will purée fruits like mangoes, peaches or strawberries, one of the best ways to get their ripe flavors into a cocktail. For drinks with egg whites, like the Pisco Sour, it can whip up a fast froth. (A dose of soda or sparkling wine also produces a nice thick head on a blender drink.)

In a technique called flash blending, a three-to-five-second pulse with cracked ice chills the drink quickly and efficiently. The ice can be strained out, Floridita-style, or the chunks and shards can be left in, which is typical of tropical cocktails. (Mr. Cate uses flash blending in a deeply refreshing tropical gin punch he calls Max's Mistake.) The technique is worth remembering on summer days when the cooling effect of a cocktail would be nullified by the effort of mixing it in a shaker.

Most difficult to master is the most common use of all, for the frozen cocktail. The right consistency is thick enough that it sticks a little to the side of the blender, but not so thick it needs to be ladled out with a spoon. Getting it just so requires the kind of heightened attentiveness other people reserve for their romantic relationships.

"You're chunky when you first go into the blender, then you're smooth, and then in a couple of seconds you start to go back and the ice in your blender starts to refreeze again," Mr. Cate said. "You're watching for that point. Your eyes and your ears tell you when it's there. If all of a sudden you hear the motor rev up higher, you know there's an air bubble, and you have to stop and shake it down. It involves all the senses."

Mr. Maloney agreed, saying that it always takes longer than you think it will. "There's an evolution of how the blender sounds," he explained.

"It starts out crunchy and crackly and you can hear the ice breaking down. Then it starts speeding up. Then it sounds nice and smooth. And then it sounds 'wa-aa-wa-aa-wa-aa'—the tone starts to go up and down. And that's where you want to stop it, just after it's done that for a little bit."

Ideally, a frozen drink should look like "powdered ice," he said. "The whole point is to whip as much air in there and make the ice as fine as a white sand beach."

The craft of the blender, it turns out, may be as demanding as hand-carving cubes from huge slabs of ice, or home-brewing bitters out of rare South American roots and twigs, as they do in the hushed sanctums of the classic cocktail.

Maybe, some day, those places will mix their kinds of drinks in a blender.

"We have a regular at the Rusty Knot who comes in and orders a frozen Negroni," said Mr. Maloney, referring to the cocktail of gin, vermouth and Campari. "You know what? It's not nearly as bad as you think it's going to be."

## MISSIONARY'S DOWNFALL
### Adapted from FORBIDDEN ISLAND, Alameda, Calif.

- 1 tablespoon honey syrup (see below)
- 10 leaves fresh mint
- ½ ring of peeled pineapple cut ½-inch thick, core removed
- 2 tablespoons (1 ounce) lime juice
- 1 tablespoon (½ ounce) peach liqueur (preferably Leopold Brothers or Mathilde)
- 2 tablespoons (1 ounce) clear rum, more if necessary
- Pineapple juice, if necessary

**1.** To make honey syrup, combine equal measures of honey and water, and stir well.

**2.** Combine all ingredients in a blender with about 1 ½ cups ice. Purée until smooth. If too thick, add a little pineapple juice or extra rum, to taste. It should look like a slushy mint pesto.

**3.** Pour into a chilled cocktail glass or goblet, and serve with a straw snipped to rise 2 to 3 inches above rim of glass.

## MAX'S MISTAKE
### Adapted from FORBIDDEN ISLAND, Alameda, Calif.

- 1 tablespoon (½ ounce) honey syrup (see below)
- 1 tablespoon passion fruit purée
- 1 ½ tablespoons superfine sugar
- ¼ cup (2 ounces) gin
- 2 tablespoons (1 ounce) lemon juice
- 1 dash Angostura bitters
- ¼ cup (2 ounces) sparkling lemonade, such as Lorina or San Pellegrino

**1.** To make honey syrup, combine equal parts honey and water, and stir well.

**2.** Combine everything but lemonade in a blender and blend for about 10 seconds. Add lemonade and 1 cup ice, preferably in small cubes. Blend for about 3 seconds.

**3.** Pour contents into a goblet and add fresh ice to fill. Serve with a straw.

## CHERRY CRUSH

2 ounces bourbon
3 pitted cherries
2 tablespoons lemon juice

1 tablespoon sugar
2 dashes Angostura bitters
Mint sprig, for garnish

**1.** In a blender, mix all ingredients except mint with 1 to 1 ½ cups ice for a minute or 2, until smooth.

**2.** Pour into a cocktail glass and serve with mint sprig and a straw snipped to rise 2 to 3 inches above rim of glass.

*June 25, 2008*

## BLUEBERRY MAPLE CAIPRISSIMO
Adapted from "Food & Wine Cocktails 2009"
YIELD: 2 DRINKS

3 ½ ounces maple syrup
2 rosemary sprigs, cut into short pieces
3 ounces Cognac

3 ounces blueberries
2 ounces lemon juice

**1.** In a microwave-safe glass or mug, stir together the syrup and rosemary. Microwave on high for about 30 seconds. When cool, discard rosemary.

**2.** Add rosemary-flavored syrup to remaining ingredients in a blender. Add 1 ½ cups ice. Purée until smooth, adding more ice if needed to achieve a consistency that is no longer liquid, but still pours freely.

*June 24, 2009*

# DRY DOCK IT'S NOT

## By SAM SIFTON

David Berson is a gallivanting boat captain who runs an electric launch, Glory, out of Greenport, N.Y., on the North Fork of Long Island. Captain Berson has been a deck monkey, a guitar hero and a yellow-cab hack over the years, an instructor of celestial navigation and a fair handler of canvas and rope. He smokes a pipe, is a friend of the masses and counts himself a fan of both Emma Goldman and Blind Willie Johnson. He sails cautiously and well, then pours rum with a heavy hand.

This is his recipe, a modification of that great Caribbean libation the Painkiller, which itself found birth at the Soggy Dollar Bar on Jost Van Dyke in the British Virgin Islands. The Painkiller features dark rum over shaved ice, frothed with orange and pineapple juice along with some sweetened coconut cream, topped with a shaving of nutmeg. It is rich stuff, a little complicated, a bit much for a long Saturday night of drinking under sea grape and palms.

Captain Berson, who served under Eben Whitcomb on the great coasting schooner Harvey Gamage, used to anchor off Jost Van Dyke and has put down his fair share of Painkillers, both at the Soggy Dollar and at the more rough-and-tumble Rudy's Mariners Inn above Great Harbour. He has, over time, whittled down the ingredients for his own version of the drink, for reasons of both thrift and flavor, to come up with a minimalist take on the classic. His friends call it the Greenport Shuffle, for its eventual effect on one's gait.

The color should be yellow, cut with bruised brown, like a pineapple left to ripen two days too long, sprinkled with rust. It should taste of summer, and offer the feeling of night air on sunburned skin.

---

## GREENPORT SHUFFLE
**Adapted from DAVID BERSON, Greenport, N.Y.**

| | |
|---|---|
| · 2 ounces aged rum | Freshly grated nutmeg |
| 6 ounces pineapple juice | |

**1.** Place crushed ice in a cocktail glass, and pour rum and pineapple juice over it. Stir. Top generously with nutmeg.

*June 27, 2007*

## VODKA TONIC WITH MINT
Adapted from ISMAIL MERCHANT, film producer, by Elaine Louie

2 ounces vodka
8 to 10 mint leaves
Pinch of red pepper flakes

4 ounces tonic water
Juice of one-half lemon

**1.** Fill an 8-ounce glass with ice cubes, add all ingredients and stir gently, taking care not to bruise mint leaves.

*July 4, 1996*

# PREPPY DRINKS NEVER GO OUT OF STYLE
## By ROSIE SCHAAP

I pored over "The Official Preppy Handbook" for innumerable hours when it came out in 1980. Some of its jokes were lost on me, but I loved the detailed, annotated illustrations. It was like an intro anthro class: these were not my people, and I was as fascinated by them as I would be years later by the Yanomami.

Last month I recalled some of the handbook's lessons when I spent a long weekend on Nantucket. I went sailing. I ate heaps of steamers and lobster and corn. I took long walks in the dunes and made up rotten limericks the whole time. No one would mistake me for a preppy, but I did wear pink one night. And on my final afternoon, I stopped into a bar and asked for a drink I hadn't had in decades: a madras. It was the drink of choice for one of my closest college friends, a true prep, and I only ever had one when we drank together.

Nothing seems easier or, as drinks favored by young adults go, more transitional, than fruit juice and vodka. Perhaps nothing seems duller, too, than its variations: the screwdriver; the Cape Codder; the sea breeze; and, of course, the madras. A little grapefruit or orange juice here, cranberry there, lime wedges and vodka all around. What we've got, essentially, is spiked fruit juice, and there's nothing wrong with that. At the bar where I work, I get plenty of calls for Cape Codders, but my customers are more likely just to order them by their ingredients, elided into vodkacran.

These days, we routinely drink juices that we never considered in the '80s, and there's no reason not to liquor them up, too. I've played with coconut water and pomegranate juice, some newish liqueurs and non-lime-wedge garnishes, and for very little work, the results can be surprisingly satisfying. But it's fun, and easy, to upgrade preppy staples. A splash of triple sec and a great big curl of orange peel deepen the flavor in a madras. A shake of hot sauce and a salt-and-chili-powder rim perks up a sea breeze. Using freshly squeezed juice whenever possible certainly makes a difference. And if you prefer gin to vodka, as I usually do, go ahead and use it; this goes for tequila, too. I like a good splash of club soda to finish these drinks and calm down their fruity sweetness.

I suspect a true prep wouldn't want to mess with tradition. This summer, he can just avert his eyes and stick with a G. & T.

## BRIGHTON BEACH BREEZE

*Sorel liqueur, a liquor with notes of hibiscus, ginger, cinnamon and clove, can be found at a well-stocked liquor store. It can also be used to perk up Manhattans or margaritas. Here, it gives a Caribbean kick to that preppy summer classic, the Sea Breeze.*

1 ounce Sorel liqueur
1 ounce vodka
1 ounce coconut water
1 ounce pomegranate juice

Club soda
Sprig of mint, for garnish
Lime wedge, for garnish

**1.** Shake Sorel liqueur, vodka, coconut water and pomegranate juice in a cocktail shaker with ice.

**2.** Pour over fresh ice into a highball glass, top with club soda and garnish with mint and lime.

## SEA BREEZE

2 ounces vodka
2 ounces grapefruit juice
2 ounces cranberry juice

Salt-and-chili-powder mix for rim, optional
Tabasco sauce, optional
Lime wedge, for garnish

**1.** Add vodka and juices to an ice-filled highball glass (with or without salt-chili rim).

**2.** Add hot sauce to taste and garnish with lime wedge.

## THE MADRAS

*This preppy staple is given an upgrade with a splash of triple sec and a great big curl of orange peel. It's the color of a summer sunset.*

2 ounces vodka
2 ounes cranberry juice
2 ounces orange juice

Splash of triple sec
Splash of club soda
Twist of orange peel, for garnish

**1.** Add vodka, juices and triple sec to an ice-filled highball glass and stir gently.

**2.** Add a splash of club soda and garnish with a twist of orange peel.

*July 11, 2013*

VODKA GIMLET

CHAPTER 18

# THE
# GIMLET

# THE LOGIC OF A GIMLET (PREFERABLY VODKA)

## By WILLIAM L. HAMILTON

I'm not naming names, but I had the worst gimlet of my life a few weeks ago in a restaurant in St. John's, Newfoundland. It came in an ugly martini glass to boot. It could have been my fault. I looked the bartender in the eye and asked her, when I ordered it, how she was going to make the drink. Maybe I spooked her. (Canada's most popular cocktail is the caesar: a bloody mary with Clamato juice. You be the judge.)

The gimlet is my favorite cocktail, and it is not a cocktail to be toyed with. Bartenders try. I have been served gimlets with Rose's Lime Juice (a lime syrup) and no fresh lime juice. I have been served gimlets with fresh lime and no Rose's.

I have been served (Oh Canada!) a gimlet with bottled lime juice and a tablespoon of sugar added, as though it were a recipe for pie.

The experience was a sobering reminder (always ill-timed as your cocktail is arriving) that only vigilance rewards when dealing with great ideas.

The gimlet's logic seems clear to me: gin or vodka, with Rose's Lime Juice and fresh lime juice in equal parts, shaken or stirred until ice cold and served straight up in a stemmed cocktail glass that is confident but not proud of its sex appeal. A standard martini glass with a light weight does nicely. The garnish—and a gimlet should have it (it's green water without one)—is a thin crescent moon of lime, floated in the drink invitingly, not perched on the side like a timid swimmer looking at a cold lake. Making a gimlet icy gives it smoothness when sipped.

"You have to have your liquor nice and chilled," said Jeffrey Garcia, a bartender at Fifty Seven Fifty Seven in the Four Seasons Hotel. "That's the best secret to it."

For that reason, it is an excellent summer drink. I have discovered that the gimlet is also an unexpectedly sophisticated fall-to-winter drink. Who wants to warm up, I realized, when you can have cool rational thoughts in temperate climates like the lobbies of good hotels: on career changes, relationship break-ups and other personal accounting? The gimlet can be a serious work tool.

Philip Marlowe, the detective, drinks them on the job in Raymond Chandler novels. "A fellow taught me to like them," Marlowe tells a woman at a bar, who is drinking a gimlet, too, in "The Long Goodbye."

The drink, by legend, was a gin drink invented late in the 18th century by sailors in the Royal Navy who received daily rations of gin and lime. The gimlet is a barrel-boring device that was sent with lime-juice casks to the British colonies.

I prefer vodka, for its understatement. Gin talks too much, with its juniper bush-berry accent. And what you want, as everyone knows, is a drinking companion who listens.

## VODKA/GIN GIMLET
**Adapted from FIFTY SEVEN FIFTY SEVEN BAR at the Four Seasons Hotel, New York City**

4 ounces vodka (or gin if you insist)          ½ ounce Rose's Lime Juice
½ ounce fresh lime juice                        1 thin lime wedge, for garnish

**1.** Combine all ingredients except lime wedge in a cocktail shaker with ice and shake.

**2.** Strain into a martini glass and garnish with lime wedge.

*September 15, 2002*

# BUILDING A BETTER MIXER
## By TOBY CECCHINI

When you entreat a conscientious bartender to make you a gimlet these days, he frequently does something that is at once resolutely incorrect and completely forgivable: he makes you a drink containing gin, simple syrup and fresh lime juice. I've done it many times myself. Depending on whom you talk to, that might be a type of sour or it might be a type of fix, but it almost certainly is not a gimlet. A proper gimlet is made with lime cordial. And what most of the world knows as lime cordial is Rose's, that dusty, fluorescent yellow-green bottle in the drinks section of your supermarket. I am willing to bet that at some point in its very long history Mr. Lauchlin Rose's Cordial Mixer Lime Juice may have been a bracing product, redolent of the fruit that it promises. Sadly, its current incarnation is to limes as Spam is to steak. It tastes of the high-fructose corn syrup, stabilizers and various chemicals that give it its cesium-like shelf life, which is all fine for Cadbury, which has owned the brand since 1981, but

is bitter gruel for someone trying to tap into the sublimity of a true gimlet. For that, as for many such rich rewards, you've got to make your own.

Lime cordial just sounds so nice that it seemed there must be some simple, old-timey way to make it as fine as it is pleasant to the ear. I had to admit, however, that after more than two decades tending bar I couldn't actually tell you what a real cordial is, or should be. Some type of preserved syrup that extracts the tartness of the juice and the keen aromatic bitterness of the peel—and candies or cures those attributes, maybe by heating?—would be my guess.

It turns out that lime cordial was originally concocted with a base of rum, to dose British sailors with a daily measure of citrus to prevent scurvy. (The most likely attribution for the gimlet's name is the piercing tool used to bore holes.) It is not fresh lime, nor is it meant to be; you cannot make a proper gimlet without lime cordial any more than you could substitute lime cordial for fresh lime juice in a daiquiri or margarita. Those could, however, make a rum or tequila gimlet. This duality so fascinated me that I had to begin experimenting to cobble a true lime cordial. Once I did, it led me into other citrus versions, given the preponderance of late winter offerings. I concocted a pomelo/lemon cordial and also a sour orange/kumquat/grapefruit version. My current favorite is a straight lime with a pound or more of fresh ground ginger thrown into the mix: unspeakably fine. These also make a marvelous tonic for non-imbibers and children, particularly in soda.

I first tried my own intuitive versions, zesting and juicing limes and lemons and boiling them up, both together and separately, with water and sugar in varying proportions, with and without the superfluous tartaric and citric acid powders many recipes prescribe. These wildly different attempts were so many factors of excellence better than commercial lime cordial that I cursed myself for never having tried this before. I continued experimenting and reading until I found the Web site of one Todd Appel, a veteran bartender and cocktail consultant in Chicago who has extensively researched and experimented with the lime cordial. Where I had been wondering if the juice should be included or excluded, Appel had the most radical approach of any I'd encountered; he banishes water from the formula entirely, using only peel, juice and sugar in an effort to recreate what he thinks is a historically accurate approximation of a sailor's ration. He heats them together and introduces the peel for only 15 minutes as it cools, citing the extreme bitterness of the zest when left too long.

While undertaking his recipe, however, I veered off on an experimental tangent that led me to what I found to be the best version yet. I divided my batches and did one on the stove, as per his recipe, and the other I didn't cook at all, just stirred the sugar into the juice until it dissolved, added in the peels (which I had removed with a vegetable peeler), and set it in the fridge to macerate overnight, to strain off the next day. After all, citrus juice effectively "cooks" proteins in ceviches, so why not try the same treatment here?

I have found that cordials are initially a bit cowlick-y, sticking out here and there: kind of tart, kind of sweet, a bit bitter, and all a touch in disarray. But giving them 24 hours to mellow or cure in the refrigerator somehow brings them into harmony. I didn't expect much of this uncooked batch, but after a day, while the cooked one was clearly tastier and more intense than any I'd yet made, the uncooked batch was mind-boggling: a dense, sweet syrup with a magnified fresh lime aroma and the perfect tart zip. One friend described it as being "like excellent lime candy."

In the field test, the gimlet made from it is a thing so completely different from your concept of this drink that it might create for you, as it has for me, a recurring sense memory that nags you if you don't have a batch made. The medicinal rigor of the gin against the agrodolce tang of the cordial is a thing for which Unesco needs to create a new category of world heritage. Charles Baker, the famous bon vivant, wrote in 1939 of it in his Gentleman's Companion: "Throughout the whole swing of the Far East, starting with Bombay—down the Malabar Coast to Colombo; to Penang, Singapore, Hong Kong and Shanghai, the gimlet is just as well known as our martini here." This was once a big-deal drink, and now it is again blessedly clear why. It's one of the few short drinks that you'd crave in the torpor of summer.

As for its proper makeup, being of a simplicity so foursquare it could be Amish, the gimlet is one of those drinks whose recipe is truly but a suggestion. In Raymond Chandler's "The Long Goodbye," the dilapidated playboy Terry Lennox, schooling Philip Marlowe in the drink, put it at equal parts: "What they call a gimlet is just some lime or lemon juice and gin with a dash of sugar and bitters. A real gimlet is half gin and half Rose's Lime Juice and nothing else. It beats martinis hollow." The majority of recipes now have it at 2:1, but I'm going to make it even simpler: find your own taste here. Different gins make for different balancing points. Fill a double rocks glass with cracked ice and pour in three ounces of gin. Start with however much cordial you think you might like—and lowball it; you can always add more. When you reach your sugar threshold, squeeze two fat lime wedges into it, stir it and settle in. Welcome back to the gimlet; never let it go away again.

## RAW LIME CORDIAL
YIELD: ABOUT 1 LITER

| | |
|---|---|
| 18 limes, room temperature, very ripe, well puffed and heavy | 2 ½ cups sugar<br>1 pound fresh ginger (optional) |

**1.** Wash limes in a sinkful of warm water, scrubbing with your hands or a vegetable brush, and let them dry them on a dish towel. Peel them with a vegetable peeler, removing as little of the underlying white pith as possible. To begin each, it's helpful to cut the polar ends off, where the stem attaches and opposite. This should produce about 140 grams of peels.

**2.** Cut limes in half and juice them. This should produce about 2 ½ cups of juice.

**3.** In a non-reactive, coverable container, add sugar to juice and stir until fully dissolved, 3 to 5 minutes. Crush peels up in handfuls to release the oils as you add them into the juice mix. Stir a bit to initiate extraction of the oils. (If you're making a ginger version, wash the ginger, then shred it in a blender or food processor (no need to peel it), employing some of the lime juice to allow it to liquefy, and add it into the lime mixture, stirring well.) Cover and refrigerate for 12 to 24 hours.

**4.** When ready, strain the cordial off from the peels in a fine mesh strainer or chinoise. Funnel cordial into covered container or cappable bottle and return to refrigerator for another day, to cure, before using.

*May 2, 2011*

## GALVANIZED GIMLET
By ROSIE SCHAAP

*This gimlet packs a punch, so serve it on the rocks.*

2 ounces navy-strength gin (like Perry's Tot)

½ ounce Rose's lime juice cordial
½ ounce fresh-squeezed lime juice

**1.** Fill a rocks glass with ice, add ingredients and stir.

*May 10, 2013*

# CLEAR CREEK EAUX DE VIE
## By ERIC ASIMOV

I love writing about people like Steve McCarthy, the proprietor of Clear Creek. People don't go into the eau de vie business because it's a great way to make a lot of money. Most Americans don't know much at all about eaux de vie, and even if they did it's not a beverage that has carved a place at the dinner table or anywhere else.

Clear Creek manages to sell pretty much all the eaux de vie it makes, but it's a struggle, requiring, as McCarthy says, constant education of the public, of restaurants, and of retailers. If Steve didn't realize it before, he did after he also started to make a whiskey, a whiskey that not only has an uncanny resemblance to the great Islay single-malt Lagavulin, but has been lauded by the whiskey writer Jim Murray as one of the best small-distillery whiskeys in the world.

"Whiskey and eaux de vie are different worlds," he told me last month when I visited him at his distillery in Portland, Ore. "For whiskey you don't have to educate people. With something like mirabelle eau de vie the challenge is convincing the store and the distributor to pay any attention to it at all. It's capitalism at its most clear cut."

Personally, the mirabelle eau de vie, made from yellow mirabelle plums, was my favorite of Clear Creek's lineup. It is so breathtakingly complex that you almost can't put it into your mouth. The aromas take on all kinds of shapes, and it's almost satisfying enough to inhale and allow them to fly off in all sorts of different fruit, floral and herbal directions.

What I love about McCarthy and Clear Creek is the passion behind the product. As I said, he doesn't make eau de vie because he wants to make a lot of money. He makes it because he loves it. And because he loves it he makes it in the best, most uncompromising way that he can.

Not that McCarthy doesn't want to make money. With Clear Creek's move into a new distillery last year, he had enough capacity to introduce a line of liqueurs, which are all very good, in flavors like cherry, cassis, loganberry, pear and raspberry. He feels that most people have an easier time grasping liqueurs than eaux de vie. Indeed, it's easy to figure out uses for the liqueurs. They're sweeter than the eaux de vie, rich, round and voluptuous. You can also pour them over ice cream or add a bit to fruit salads. Clear Creek also makes some superb grappas.

But eaux de vie are Clear Creek's signature, and as I mentioned in the column, McCárthy frowns on using the eaux de vie in cocktails. He feels they are a pure product, meant to be experienced in their pure form, though he did tell me he feels differently about using them for cooking. "I think there are all kinds of uses for this stuff in the kitchen," he said. He's also got little use for efforts to pair his eaux de vie with food, feeling they are best experienced by themselves.

"There's too much going on," he said. "If you have to have them with anything, it's an espresso."

Of course, that hasn't stopped cre-ative cocktail experts who've fallen in love with his eaux de vie from eager experimentation.

Audrey Saunders of Pegu Club in SoHo not so long ago tried Clear Creek's Douglas fir eau de vie. "I thought it was absolutely sick!" she said, by which she meant great, and she started to work on a cocktail that incorporated it.

"I also had heard about Steve being very anti-cocktail, so I had asked him about it also," she told me. "He seemed very positive about it, because I think he also knew that we would utilize his products in a very respectful way, meaning we would create a drink that showcased them, not masking them or drowning them in juices."

Audrey was kind enough to give me her recipe for the Douglas Fir Gimlet, which follows:

## DOUGLAS FIR GIMLET
### Adapted from PEGU CLUB, New York City

1½ ounces Tanqueray gin
½ ounces Clear Creek Douglas Fir eau de vie
¾ ounces fresh lime juice
½ ounces uncooked simple syrup (see recipe on page 269)
½ ounces homemade grapefruit syrup (see recipe on page 269)
Lime wheel or sprig of pine (pesticide-free), for garnish

**1.** Measure all ingredients except lime wheel or pine sprig into a mixing glass. Add ice and shake well.

**2.** Strain into a chilled cocktail glass and garnish with either a floating lime wheel or a sprig of pine.

THE MONKEY BAR, NEW YORK CITY, 1991

## UNCOOKED SIMPLE SYRUP

16 ounces superfine sugar        1 teaspoon vodka

**1.** Take a 32-ounce covered jar or 1-liter soda bottle with cap. Fill half-way with the superfine sugar. Add 18 ounces water, cover and shake well. Let sit for two minutes. Shake again two more times, until sugar is dissolved, and syrup is clear. You don't need to cook simple syrup, because we are not looking for viscosity here. Add 1 teaspoon of vodka to preserve, and store in refrigerator.

## GRAPEFRUIT SYRUP

16 ounces uncooked simple syrup (recipe above)      1 grapefruit
1 teaspoon vodka

**1.** To the simple syrup add the zest of the entire grapefruit. Cover, shake well to agitate, and place in refrigerator for 24 hours.

**2.** Pour through a fine strainer, pressing down on zest to extract flavor. Syrup will last in refrigerator indefinitely, but best to use as soon as possible, as the flavor dissipates over time. Add the vodka to preserve, and store in refrigerator.

**Grapefruit syrup can also be used in many other drinks to add a nice, bright flavor, and also makes a delicious non-alcoholic cooler when mixed with fresh lemon or lime juice (and a little mint).**

*August 15, 2007*

DAIQUIRI NO. 2.

## CHAPTER 19

# THE
# DAIQUIRI

# YOUR SIGNATURE COCKTAIL

## By ANNA FRICKE

My first drink—if you don't count my childhood best friend mixing together a little of everything from her parent's liquor cabinet and daring me to drink it—was a strawberry daiquiri. I was 16 years old and at a bar called Amberjacks in New Orleans. The bar was a local favorite of friends I'd met doing summer stock in Maine. Of course, these friends were older and I was mooning over one of them, a guy who was doing dinner theatre in Metairie and who lived with a ferret. In retrospect, it's no wonder I felt the need to drink. I pined uselessly after Gary while a strange Russian woman named Laneshka kept lurching into him and putting her hand on his knee. I thought I was terribly sophisticated, as 16-year-old girls drinking fruity, frothy drinks often do.

If I had my druthers, I would probably drink strawberry daiquiris all the time. But I don't. Sure, they're delicious. But the strawberry daiquiri is a youthful drink, the drink of a girl on spring break in Cabo. Much like skinny jeans and Flashdance tops, I can't pull it off anymore. These days, I am compelled by circumstances to act my age and order a nice Bordeaux and pretend I know what I'm talking about.

If I had to guess, I'd say that many of us aren't drinking what we'd truly like to drink. A friend of mine frequently orders Pimms to remind people of her stints abroad, though I suspect she longs for vodka tonic. And in my household, in addition to my

unrequited predilection for Drinks With Umbrellas, I recently learned that my husband hated the taste of beer in high school and so insisted on White Mountain, a "malternative" beverage. And by insisted I mean that he forced the kid with the fake ID to not only risk his neck buying beer but also his reputation by adding a case of White Mountain with nary a teenage girl in sight. My husband also sometimes pours himself a glass of apple juice and nurses it, pretending it's whiskey. (I'm not sure why. Actually, I'm not sure why he even admitted that to me.) And yet the Macallan nestles up against the Hendricks in our liquor cabinet.

What are we all trying to prove? Clearly we should hop on the nearest jet ski and propel ourselves to a swim-up bar. But what we choose to drink can reveal more about us than, say, our astrological sign or whether we prefer Elvis or the Beatles. What a tense moment, to be the first to order a drink with a group of people you haven't hung out with before. Do you order a beer to let them know you're easygoing? Do you order champagne to convey that you're the fun, sassy type who likes to celebrate ordinary moments? Do you order scotch to let them know that you might start to get kind of intense in a couple hours? Do you order a Merlot, as if "Sideways" taught you nothing? The pressure.

Sure, these are ridiculous generalizations, but people buy into them. Drink choice is used as a nifty device in film and television all the time to let us know exactly what we should think about a character. The amount of scotch the female characters on "Damages" put away every week is staggering. Every sip reminds us that these women, every single vengeful one of them, means business. If they were drinking Mudslides, I don't think I'd be convinced. You don't see a lot of scotch on network television, where wine seems to be the more socially acceptable vice. Rarely is there a scene on "Brothers & Sisters" in which the siblings aren't gesticulating with wine glasses. This makes the family artsy and cultured. If they were waving martini glasses around, we would judge them more harshly.

My first writing job was for the show "Dawson's Creek." Back then, before the WB was the CW, the standard rule was that teens could only drink on television if we showed "consequences." Consequences usually meant vomiting, driving a car through a house, or kissing your best friend's boyfriend/girlfriend/mother. If it was a sweeps episode, we probably employed all of the above, though vomiting was the trusty go-to. Somewhere along the way, I think the rule of consequences was thrown out the window, because almost every episode of "Gossip Girl" involves a teenage character sidling up to a ritzy bar and ordering a martini, and the only consequence seems to be more brightly colored tights and ascots.

Actors, at least from my small experience in working with them, put a great deal of thought into this. I once had a lengthy discussion over drink choice with an actress—much to the dismay of the television crew who watched the minutes tick by as she and I debated the message conveyed by a wine spritzer versus a Manhattan. I had written a scene with her ordering a wine spritzer. Her character was a bit of a lightweight and a kook, and the thought of her saying "Gimme a wine spritzer" amused me. The actress informed me that the choice of a wine spritzer for her character was woefully "on the nose" and that it would be much more interesting if she ordered a Manhattan. I fought for the spritzer and she glumly sipped it. But it was too late. The fizz was gone.

Facebook, in one of its daily attempts to suck all traces of productivity out of our lives, recently offered a "What Kind of Alcoholic Drink Are You?" quiz. In the interest of this piece, I took the quiz (as did my 13-year-old niece. Fantastic.). Apparently I am a margarita (as is my niece) because "your [sic] fun and nice. You like to stay home and rest as much as you like partys. [sic]"

Perhaps English was not the quiz maker's first language, but he hit on something. By golly, I do like to stay home and rest as much as I like partys! And I do enjoy the frothiness of a margarita. Despite the fact that I always order them on the rocks, in my heart I want them blended. Life is hard enough these days. Must we really have things on the rocks as well? I think we should relax into drinks with syrupy bits of fruit bobbing around in them and give ourselves a break. I'll be at the swim-up bar, dodging judgment.
*March 22, 2009*

CLASSIC DAIQUIRI

## CLASSIC DAIQUIRI
By ROSIE SCHAAP

*Tartness and sweetness, citrus and rum, in just the right balance. This classic is a real treat.*

2 ounces white rum
½ ounce fresh lime juice

½ teaspoon superfine sugar

**1.** Fill a shaker with ice, add all ingredients and shake well.

**2.** Strain into a chilled cocktail glass.

*May 17, 2014*

## FLORIDITA
By ROSIE SCHAAP

*The Floridita is a classic daiquiri riff, which takes its name from a bar in Havana. There, a bartender named Constante tinkered with another bartender's recipe, adding to it a small quantity of maraschino liqueur and a good amount of crushed ice. Since then, many others have played with the formula, and two separate recipes emerged, each with many variations: the Floridita Daiquiri, and the Floridita Cocktail. The Floridita Daiquiri frequently retains the crushed ice; the Floridita Cocktail is often served straight up, as in this recipe, and its tartness is enhanced by the addition of grapefruit juice.*

2 ounces white rum (preferably Brugal)
Juice of ½ lime
½ ounce fresh grapefruit juice

¼ ounce maraschino liqueur
1 teaspoon simple syrup (page 27)
Lime wheel, for garnish

**1.** Shake all ingredients except lime wheel in a cocktail shaker with ice.

**2.** Strain into a coupe and garnish with the lime wheel.

*July 1, 2014*

## DAIQUIRI NO. 2
Adapted from EL FLORIDITA, Havana, Cuba, by PETE WELLS

1 teaspoon sugar
1 tablespoon lime juice
2 ounces clear rum

1 teaspoon orange juice
½ teaspoon Curaçao liqueur
1 small lime wedge or wheel, for garnish

**1.** Place all ingredients except lime in a blender with ½ cup ice, preferably in small cubes. Blend about 5 seconds.

**2.** Pour into a chilled cocktail glass, straining out ice with blender's lid (or for a particularly refined daiquiri, a sieve). Balance lime wedge or wheel on glass's rim.

*June 25, 2008*

## TODD MAUL'S RHUM AGRICOLE DAIQUIRI
**By ROSIE SCHAAP**
YIELD: 2 (3 -OUNCE) DRINKS

4 ounces Neisson Blanc Rhum Agricole

2 ounces fresh lime juice

1 ounce burnt cinnamon simple syrup (recipe follows)

**1.** Shake all ingredients with ice and strain into rocks glasses over fresh ice.

## BURNT CINNAMON SIMPLE SYRUP
YIELD: ENOUGH TO LAST ALL SUMMER, OR AT LEAST ONE GREAT PARTY

2 cups sugar

5 sticks cinnamon

**1.** In a small, heavy saucepan, dissolve sugar in 1 cup water. Burn 5 cinnamon sticks all over with a small crème-brulee-type torch. Break up sticks and add to syrup while still warm. Transfer to an airtight container and chill for a day.

**2.** Strain syrup. Store in refrigerator to use for daiquiris.

*March 30, 2014*

## LEMON DAIQUIRI
**By ROSIE SCHAAP**

*Is a daiquiri a daiquiri only if it includes lime? Nope. Even bars in Cuba, the drink's homeland, play pretty fast and loose with daiquiri variations. The lime shortage of 2014 inspired me to try it with lemon instead, and the result is bracing and a little disorienting (in a good way)–like a union between a traditional daiquiri and a Tom Collins. And I like what the distinctive funkiness of rhum agricole adds to the drink. Swap in different fresh, seasonal citrus juices whenever the mood strikes (but adjust the amount of simple syrup accordingly, as other fruits are inherently sweeter than lemons). I'm thinking a daiquiri with clementine juice will hit the spot come winter.*

2 ounces rhum agricole blanc (such as Neisson)

1 ounce fresh lemon juice

½ ounce simple syrup (page 27)

Lemon verbena, for garnish

**1.** Shake all ingredients except lemon verbena with ice.

**2.** Strain into a cocktail glass and garnish with verbena.

*July 3, 2014*

## POMEGRANATE DAIQUIRI
**Adapted from SOHO HOUSE, New York City, by John Hyland and Raffaele Ronca**

1 teaspoon pomegranate syrup or molasses

2 ounces Montecristo rum (or other dark rum)

2 ounces orange juice

Pomegranate seeds, for garnish (optional)

**1.** Pour all ingredients except pomegranate seeds into a shaker filled partly with ice and shake.

**2.** Pour, unstrained, into a rocks glass and garnish with pomegranate seeds, if desired.

*November 2, 2003*

## GINGER DAIQUIRI

Adapted from MAS, New York City, by William L. Hamilton

Orange peel
Ginger sugar (see recipe below)
2 ounces white Haitian rum

½ ounce Cointreau
½ ounce Meyer lemon juice
½ ounce ginger-infused simple syrup
(see note below)

**1.** Swipe the orange peel on the rim of a cocktail glass. Press the wet rim down into a shallow dish of the ginger sugar, to "frost" the rim.

**2.** Combine rum, Cointreau, Meyer lemon Juice and ginger-infused simple syrup in a shaker with ice and shake.

**3.** Strain into the glass, to the rim, and garnish with peel.

To make the ginger-infused simple syrup, follow the simple syrup recipe on page 27, and cook with sliced, peeled fresh ginger (4 ounces of ginger per one pint).

## GINGER SUGAR

6 ounces turbinado sugar                    1 ounce fresh ginger root

**1.** Put sugar and ginger root in a jar and seal. Store for a week, shaking the jar every day.

*May 23, 2004*

# RECIPE REDUX: COCONUT DAIQUIRIS, 1987

## By AMANDA HESSER

If you were in New York in the 1980s, you probably have vivid memories of a vocal and opinionated mayor named Ed Koch, who spent his days noisily trying to tame a Bright Lights Big City that was rampant with crime and AIDS.

But even an overburdened mayor needs to kick back now and then. Mayor Koch did just that every Labor Day weekend at his friends David and Bobbie Margolis's home in Quogue, a town on Long Island. The Margolises always put on a big lobster lunch, but what everyone really loved were David's cocktails.

"We would sit there in his house and watch him with the blender and the coconut milk," Mayor Koch recalled. "And we couldn't wait for the first drinks to come out of the blender." Namely, Margolis's two specialties, the Ramos gin fizz and the coconut daiquiri, an icy wonder of coconut cream, fresh pineapple, lime juice and rum. Mayor Koch didn't quite go so far as to give Margolis's daiquiri the key to the city, but he did declare it his favorite drink in The Times in 1987.

I called David Wondrich, a cocktail expert whose book "Punch: The Delights (and Dangers) of the Flowing Bowl" will be out in November, and found him on a beach on Fire Island with, coincidentally, a thermosful of daiquiris at his side. When I read him the Margolis recipe, he said, "What you have there is actually a piña colada" with lime. Doh!

But the two are easily fused and confused. Many versions of the "coconut daiquiri" can be found online, all more or less like the Margolis recipe. Wondrich later summed up Margolis's drink by e-mail, calling it "a daiquirized piña colada."

"In other words," he added, "it takes a piña colada and, by exploiting a common element (the rum) and adding a feature of the daiquiri (the lime juice), appropriates the daiquiri's name and (we must assume) serving style—that is, straight up in a stemmed glass."

But the piña colada is really just a daiquiri with cosmetic enhancements. The original daiquiri, said to have been invented in Cuba during the Spanish-American war, was a rudimentary affair, made with rum, lime juice, sugar and a little soda water. Its creation is often attributed to the American mining engineer Jennings Cox, but as with most cocktail histories—which Wondrich described as "a bottomless sinkhole of murk"—everyone present at the moment of its supposed concoction was drinking. A handwritten recipe survived the night.

"You could say it's the first classic cocktail invented outside of the U.S.," Wondrich said.

The recipe migrated to America around 1908 and was a popular drink by 1912. The American part, according to Wondrich, was putting it in a cocktail shaker and shaking it up with ice. It was only a matter of time before people would begin adding coconut, maraschino, pineapple and what have you.

The beauty of piña coladas and this kind of daiquiri is that "they're creamy, they're light, they're extremely delicious when made properly," Wondrich explained. "They're not big, heavy-hitting, high-alcohol drinks. They're frothy. Pineapple juice will froth up like the egg white in a fizz."

All roads lead back to the Ramos gin fizz, a drink made with gin, lemon, orange-flower water, cream, soda water and egg white. Margolis's other signature drink was a fizz. When I gave the coconut daiquiri recipe to Ravi DeRossi, the owner of Cienfuegos in Manhattan's East Village, and his bartender, Jane Danger, and asked them to come up with something new, they ended up with a fizz that's part piña colada, part Ramos gin fizz.

Their concoction, which they called an Isle of Manhattan fizz, blends lime juice, pineapple juice, coconut purée, rum, gin and orange-flower water, and it is extraordinarily good.

I met DeRossi and Danger at Cienfuegos, a restaurant specializing in punch bowls, which is tucked above a Cuban sandwich shop at street level. Danger, who was dressed in a Coors T-shirt, short shorts and tall black boots, assembled the drink part by part, using an immersion blender to whip air into the mixture. The coconut purée, which Danger explained "takes the place of the cream and egg white in a fizz," can be ordered by mail; it looks like Marshmallow Fluff and has a pure coconut flavor (coconut ice cream can be used in its place). The Isle of Manhattan fizz's white-cloud appearance belies a serious drink (though if you have more than one, nothing will seem serious). Waves of rum, orange-flower water and coconut lap at your nose.

I bet Mayor Koch would change parties — from daiquiri to fizz — over it.

## 1987: COCONUT DAIQUIRIS
**Adapted from DAVID MARGOLIS**
YIELD: ABOUT 5 DRINKS

½ very ripe pineapple, cut into chunks
Juice of 1 lime

2 tablespoons Coco Lopez cream of coconut
7½ ounces Bacardi light rum

**1.** Combine all ingredients with 20 ice cubes in a blender and whiz until smooth. Serve immediately without garnishes.

*June 30, 2010*

MARGARITA FROM FEARING'S, DALLAS

CHAPTER 20

# THE MARGARITA

## MARGARITA
By MARK BITTMAN

*The reliable pairing for chips and salsa and Mexican food of every stripe, the margarita is a versatile template for all sorts of flavorings, too. This recipe is traditional with lime and triple sec, but it could accommodate any number of flavors ... blood orange, strawberry, pineapple. Thirsty yet?*

| | |
|---|---|
| ¼ cup tequila | Salt |
| 1¼ tablespoons triple sec | Lime wedge, for garnish |
| 1¼ tablespoons fresh lime juice | |

**1.** Combine lots of ice, the tequila, triple sec and lime juice in a mixing glass and shake.

**2.** Salt the rim of another glass and strain in the mixture. Garnish with the lime wedge.

*May 13, 2012*

## CLASSIC MARGARITA
Adapted from DALE DEGROFF by Frank J. Prial

| | |
|---|---|
| Lime slice, ½ inch thick, for salting glass | 1 ounce Cointreau |
| Kosher salt | ¾ ounce fresh lime juice |
| 2 ounces silver tequila | |

**1.** Rub lime slice around outer rim of cocktail glass and salt glass. Place glass in refrigerator.

**2.** Fill a cocktail shaker with ice and add tequila, Cointreau and lime juice and shake well.

**3.** Strain into chilled cocktail glass.

*August 20, 2003*

## DEE'S MARGARITA
Adapted from DEE BRYD-MOLNAR, South, Brooklyn, by ROSIE SCHAAP

| | |
|---|---|
| 2 ounces Herradura reposado tequila | Juice of 1 medium lime |
| 1 ounce Cointreau | |

**1.** Shake all ingredient with ice and serve on the rocks in a tall glass.

*October 14, 2012*

## STRAWBERRY BASIL MARGARITA
By DOS CAMINOS, New York City

| | |
|---|---|
| 2 ounces Souza Hornitos tequila | 1 ounce fresh lime |
| 2 ounces sliced fresh strawberries | Splash simple syrup (page 27) |
| 6 torn fresh basil leaves | Sprig of basil, for garnish |

**1.** Combine all ingredients except sprig of basil in a shaker filled with ice and shake.

**2.** Pour into a 10-ounce old-fashioned glass and garnish with the basil sprig. Do not salt the rim.

*September 29, 2002*

## HORSERADISH POMEGRANATE MARGARITA
Adapted from RYAN MAGARIAN by Pete Wells

⅓ cup fresh horseradish, peeled and chopped
1 cup silver (blanco) tequila
½ ounce Cointreau

¾ ounce fresh lime juice
½ ounce pomegranate juice
¼ ounce simple syrup (page 27)

**1.** In a bowl mix horseradish with tequila and let mixture sit for 24 hours. Strain through cheesecloth.

**2.** Pour 1½ ounces horseradish-infused tequila and all other ingredients into a cocktail shaker. (You will have some leftover tequila mixture.) Fill shaker with ice and shake it vigorously for 6 seconds.

**3.** Add ice cubes to an Old-Fashioned glass and pour drink over them.

*November 29, 2006*

# A TOUCH OF EVIL
## By WILLIAM L. HAMILTON

"Come on, read my future for me," says Hank Quinlan, a corrupt Texas cop to Tanya, a Mexican border town madam, in Orson Welles's "Touch of Evil." Welles plays Quinlan, and Marlene Dietrich is Tanya.

"You haven't got any," she replies.

I was sitting at the bar at Sueños, a new Mexican restaurant at 311 West 17th Street, thinking about this recently.

Time for a drink.

At the bar, Sueños ("dreams" in Spanish) has the fever-dream quality of Welles's 1958 film: shot at night with garish light, too dark and too bright at the same time. You go down a few steps, through a service corridor, and arrive— the kind of space high-stakes dogfights take place in. The hostess wore a black leather gaucho hat last Wednesday. The bartender and waiters were dressed in drab khaki shirts and trousers, like the Mexican police. You get the impression

that if you woke up the next morning and went back to look for the bar, it wouldn't be there. I ordered La Paloma. The cocktail is as basic as a bet: liquor and soda, tequila and Mexican Squirt, which is a grapefruit soda. Squirt is a sweeter, tarter version of citrus sodas like Fresca. (Jarritos is another popular brand.) On the evenings when, I suspect, the staff drinks all the Squirt, Sueños substitutes a blend of grapefruit juice, Grand Marnier and 7Up—a margarita with a couple of extra mariachis.

Working with Steven Olson, a beverage consultant, Sue Torres, the owner and chef of Sueños, based La Paloma on a cocktail she was served in Mexico at the Don Julio ranch, owned by the tequila family, where they grow their agave.

"They said, 'We're going to make you a real margarita, a Mexican margarita,' "Ms. Torres recalled. It was

Squirt, tequila and lime.

La Paloma, which translates as "the dove," and also, similarly, as a meek or a mild person, is an aptly named cocktail. It acts like it's never held a gun before, and then it blows the tin can into the air. Perversely, it tastes better with grapefruit soda than grapefruit juice.

Sueños also serves a Cosmolito—a Mexican cosmopolitan. It brought back to mind the black-haired Mar-lene Dietrich as Tanya in "Touch of Evil" and a framed letter hanging in Ms. Dietrich's apartment on Park Avenue, which I had the opportunity to view when Sotheby's sold its contents.

Dietrich reacted with fire to Welles's idea that she play the madam in a Mexican brothel, and demanded an explanation for the offer.

"Haven't you ever heard of type-casting?" he wrote back.

## LA PALOMA
### Adapted from SUEÑOS, New York City

1 ½ ounces Herradura Hacienda del Cristero Blanco tequila

¾ ounce fresh lime juice (half a lime)

4 ounces Mexican Squirt soda (or 1 ounce freshly squeezed grapefruit juice and 3 ounces 7Up)

Slice of lime, for garnish

**1.** Pour tequila over ice in a tall highball or Collins glass.

**2.** Add lime juice, and Squirt or substitute. Stir and garnish with a slice of lime.

*August 3, 2003*

# GIVE THE MARGARITA A REST
## By ROSIE SCHAAP

A few years ago, a friend returned from a trip to Mexico imploring anyone who would listen to give the margarita a rest and drink a Paloma instead. In its most elemental form, the Paloma is tequila and grapefruit soda (preferably Squirt), maybe with a splash of lime juice. That's a good drink. But for all his evangelical zeal, my friend had a hard time finding Squirt in his Brooklyn neighborhood. He was willing to let go of authenticity, and let me make him a Paloma with fresh grapefruit juice, a little simple syrup and soda water instead.

As with most highballs, there's no harm done in playing with garnishes and aromatics. I love the way basil interacts with grapefruit (I often chiffonade a few leaves to festoon a broiled grapefruit half at breakfast), so I've found that muddling a segment of the fruit with a few bright, fresh basil leaves is a good foundation for a Paloma. And as with the margarita, you may opt for salt on the rim of your glass—or not.

## PALOMA

| | |
|---|---|
| 2 basil leaves | ½ ounce simple syrup (page 27) |
| 1 grapefruit segment | 3 ounces grapefruit juice |
| 2 ounces silver tequila | Soda water |
| Juice of ½ lime | Lime wedge, for garnish |

**1.** Put 2 basil leaves and 1 grapefruit segment in a highball glass and muddle gently.

**2.** Add 2 ounces silver tequila, juice of ½ lime, and ½ ounce simple syrup and stir gently.

**3.** Add ice, 3 ounces grapefruit juice and soda to top and stir gently again. Garnish with a lime wedge.

*May 20, 2013*

# AUSTIN'S VERY OWN MARTINI
## By JORDAN MACKAY

Charlotte Voisey, a cocktail consultant, worked long and hard last fall to develop a drink menu at the new W Hotel here that was worthy of Austin's burgeoning cocktail culture. But on opening night last December, she was flummoxed when the first customers requested a cocktail called the Mexican Martini.

"I looked quizzically to my bartenders," she recalled, "and said, 'I'm afraid I don't know what that is.'"

It's not surprising that Ms. Voisey, who lives in San Francisco, was unfamiliar with the drink. Outside of Austin, the Mexican Martini is hardly known.

"When I even go to Dallas on business, they don't know what it is," said Steve Potts, current owner of the Cedar Door, the bar where the Mexican Martini originated. In Austin, however, the drink is as ubiquitous as barbecue and live music.

"It's the biggest part of our cocktail business," said Chance Robertson, operations director for Trudy's, a local Mexican restaurant group. "It's why people come here." Mr. Robertson estimated that the three Trudy's locations sell a total of 5,000 to 8,000 Mexican Martinis a week.

While the name gives it an air of mystique, originally the Mexican Martini was just a large margarita. But its presentation calls for the margarita to be served in a martini glass, with olives on a spear. Because it is about twice as large as a regular drink, customers are usually given the cocktail shaker and invited to pour the drink themselves.

A city with down-home Texas character, Austin also sports a veneer of cosmopolitan refinement that comes with being the seat of the state government and home to one of the country's largest universities. In that light, the appeal of the Mexican Martini makes sense. While slurpy, frozen margaritas are a staple around the city, this one is dressed up in a suit and tie.

"It just looks cool," said Jim LeMond, who worked at the Cedar Door for almost 20 years before opening the Barton Springs Saloon five years ago. "Yes, it's just a margarita with olives, but you look real sophisticated when you're pouring it yourself. There's a ritual. On a table, it looks really classy."

The story of its origin is a bit hazy, but Mr. LeMond said he thought that in the late '70s or early '80s, a Cedar Door bartender named Ellen was served a margarita in a martini glass while visiting Matamoros, Mexico, a border town. She brought the idea back to the bar, which at the time was a hangout for the city's power brokers. The olives, he said, were an original Cedar Door touch.

Before long, Mr. LeMond said: "Bartenders I knew would come in and ask me how to make one of those. And two weeks later I'd see the Mexican Martini on their menu."

Over decades, the cocktail spread through the city, informally becoming Austin's signature drink.

"There's hardly a bar in Austin that doesn't make a version," said Mr. Potts, who now produces and markets a pre-mixed Cedar Door Mexican Martini concentrate.

Also attractive, he added, is the cocktail's value for the money. At the Cedar Door, the basic version costs $8.75.

"With 4 ounces of liquor and 3.5 ounces of juices, it's really two drinks," he said. In fact, the cocktail is so strong that Trudy's imposes a two-drink limit.

The limit was part of the attraction, said Kathleen Fleming, who discovered the Mexican Martini during visits to Austin from California, where she lived. A former boyfriend introduced her to the drink at Trudy's.

"When he explained that it's local, it's super strong and that they cut you off after two, I had to try one," she said. "I loved it: the presentation, the flavor, the ritual."

But Austin has grown extensively over the last decade, and the Mexican Martini has experienced changes, too. Visiting for the South by Southwest music conference a couple of years ago, Ms. Fleming planned to try a Mexican Martini at every bar she went to, but was alarmed to encounter bartenders who made the drink by mixing tequila and Sprite or were newcomers not familiar with the drink.

"How are you a bartender in Austin and don't know how to make this?" she said. "I thought it was part of the job requirement."

The drink has evolved on its own. Because of the olive garnish, many of Austin's newest bartenders assume the drink is a "dirty margarita" and add a dash of olive brine to the mix. This is how it's made at the W's Living Room bar. Other bartenders have been known to muddle olives and peppers. Many places, like the W, serve it as a single cocktail, not in the shaker.

And many of a new contingent of vest-wearing craft bartenders, perhaps seeing it as a vestige of the less worldly cocktail culture of pre-boom Austin, scoff at the Mexican Martini. Adam Bryan, the whiz in charge of Bar Congress, objects on the grounds that there is no standard recipe, that the drink leans toward sweetness and that bartenders, not customers, should pour the drink. At his previous job, at the Eastside Showroom, Mr. Bryan refused to make it.

"I removed the olives from the entire restaurant," he said, "so when I told customers, 'I can't make Mexican Martinis because I don't carry olives,' people weren't as upset as when I said, 'No, I can't make you that on principle.'"

Nevertheless, the Mexican Martini seems in no danger of losing its spot as the city's signature drink.

"They're selling as well as ever," said Mr. Robertson of Trudy's.

But only in Austin, it seems. Ms. Fleming, who now lives in Atlanta, lamented: "I'm just so disappointed that it doesn't really exist outside of Austin unless you happen upon an ex-pat working behind the bar somewhere."

## MEXICAN MARTINI
Adapted from Jordan Mackay

| | |
|---|---|
| Salt | ¾ ounce fresh orange juice |
| 2 ounces reposado tequila | ½ ounce olive brine |
| 1 ounce Cointreau | 2 olives |
| 1 ounce fresh lime juice | |

**1.** Wet half the lip of a martini glass and dip it in salt. Chill the glass.

**2.** Pour the tequila, lime juice, orange juice and olive brine into a cocktail shaker and fill with ice. Shake vigorously for 10 seconds.

**3.** Strain into the chilled glass and garnish with olives on a spear.

*July 12, 2011*

FROZEN PINA COLADA

CHAPTER 21

# FROZEN DRINKS

# THE COOL SIDE OF CAMPY FROZEN DRINKS

## By ROSIE SCHAAP

The frozen daiquiri, the piña colada, the frozen margarita: these drinks remind me of a certain kind of great-aunt—the one who has worn the same coral lipstick since 1959, the one whose laughter is like a wheezy rush of air, the one in the paisley caftan who had an affair with a famous bandleader back in the day. Some relatives might have cringed at the very thought of her. Others, like me, wanted to hang out with her all the time—and maybe even grow up to be her.

Most of all, these drinks remind us that drinking ought to be fun and that, to quote Diana Vreeland, a little bad taste is hearty and healthy. In the summer, I long for these drinks and their garnishes, colorful straws and paper umbrellas. This is surely why, after my air-conditioner, my second-most-cherished appliance during last month's heat wave was my blender.

I wouldn't say they are adequate meal substitutes, but without alcohol, these drinks are essentially—and I brace myself for the most revolting word in the English language—"smoothies." But part of what makes them perfect for the most brutal of days is that you can liquor them up or down as much as you like.

Purists might blanch at my recipes (each of which yields two servings). After all, a great big violet slushie isn't the first thing that comes to mind when Mexican food aficionados think of margaritas. Hemingway is not very likely to have taken his daiquiri with an abundance of frozen bananas. (The traditional piña colada recipe, despite some debate over its provenance, remains true to form here.) But I can't resist the charms of these frozen wonders, especially since they lend themselves to endless improvising: if you don't love blackberries, substitute your favorite berry in the frozen margarita. I tend to like drinks on the tart side, but you can adjust the lime juice or add simple syrup to sweeten things up. As I learned when I tested these recipes, not all blenders crush ice with equal gusto, so add more ice, and blend longer, to achieve the degree of slushiness you want. Just don't drink too fast; brain freeze! And that could spoil all the fun.

## FROZEN BLACKBERRY MARGARITA
By ROSIE SCHAAP
YIELD: 2 DRINKS

12 large blackberries, stems removed (plus 2 for garnish)

4 ounces reposado tequila

1½ ounces Grand Marnier

2 ounces fresh lime juice

1½ ounces simple syrup, or more to taste (page 27)

Mixture of salt and sugar for glass rims

Lime wheels, for garnish

**1.** Blend all ingredients except the salt, sugar and lime wheels with 3 cups of ice until smooth and frosty.

**2.** Run lime wedge along rims of margarita glasses and dip into the salt-sugar mixture.

**3.** Pour the blended drink and garnish with blackberries and lime wheels.

## FROZEN BANANA DAIQUIRI
By ROSIE SCHAAP
YIELD: 2 DRINKS

2½ ounces dark rum

2½ ounces light rum

3 ounces lime juice

2 ounces orange juice

2 large, very ripe, frozen bananas, sliced

1 ounce simple syrup (page 27)

2 umbrellas, for garnish

2 cherries, for garnish

2 orange slices, for garnish

**1.** Blend all ingredients except garnishes with 2 cups of ice until smooth and frosty.

**2.** Pour into chilled glasses and garnish with umbrellas, cherries, and orange slices.

## FROZEN PIÑA COLADA
By ROSIE SCHAAP
YIELD: 2 DRINKS

4 ounces golden rum

4 ounces pineapple juice

4 ounces Coco Lopez cream of coconut

2 pineapple slices, for garnish

2 maraschino cherries

2 paper umbrellas (optional)

**1.** Blend all ingredients except garnishes with 3 cups of ice until smooth and frosty.

**2.** Pour into tall, chilled glasses and garnish with pineapple slices, maraschino cherries and umbrellas.

*August 8, 2013*

FROZEN MARGARITA

## FROZEN MARGARITA
By ROSIE SCHAAP
YIELD: 4 TO 6 DRINKS

| | |
|---|---|
| 8 ounces blanco tequila | 2 ounces simple syrup (page 27) |
| 1 cup lime juice | Lime wheels or wedges, for garnish |
| 4 ounces triple sec, preferably Cointreau | |

**1.** Put all ingredients except lime wheels or wedges in a blender with 4 cups of ice and blend until slushy, adding more ice as necessary.

**2.** Pour immediately into tall glasses and garnish with lime wheels or wedges.

*May 20, 2014*

# CHAPTER 1: I DRANK THE WATER
## By FRANCISCO GOLDMAN

In Mexico City, where I live sometimes, I have a routine. I get out of the gym at about 9:30 and walk across the park to my favorite cantina, where the waiters know to bring me a shot of Herradura blanco tequila and a Victoria beer immediately. I love tequila and I believe that Herradura blanco, fiery and peppery, those first sips going down with the combustion of a space shuttle liftoff, is the great commercial tequila. I like mezcal too. Nothing macho about it: I just like the clean cactus and earth flavors, the warm ebullient high, and that you can drink a number of shots without feeling bloated.

I don't often drink frozen drinks. How many of those can a person actually drink in a long night? But one night in Mexico City six years ago I drank frozen daiquiris, and I will never forget it, or at least I will never forget one of those drinks, the last one. It was at a party in the writer Mario Bellatin's house: crowded kitchen,

someone manning the blender, bags of purified ice like the ones you get at gasoline stations. Slushy daiquiris in clear plastic cups, an appealing light lime color suggesting late afternoon drinks at the beach, when the salty bracing tartness of Mexican limes is especially delicious. I had one daiquiri and then another. Then they ran out of ice. Some of us were standing there, holding out empty cups. What, no more? There was still rum, there were still limes. But the blender guy was reaching deep into the freezer, struggling to dislodge an old ice cube tray, buried in furry ice. Enough for a few more daiquiris. Half an hour after drinking mine I felt a mule kick inside my stomach. Then I felt cold.

I went home. For the next two days I shivered and thrashed around in bed, burning with fever. A mesmerizing sensation of physically dwindling away. I hallucinated a strange scene, or dreamed one with my eyes open: convent servants searching the dawn streets of 19th-century Guatemala City for just the right Indian man to bring back to their Mother Superior.

I'd been waiting all summer for book and archival research to come alive. Suddenly, it had. I got out of bed, wrote it all down, went back to bed. Another scene came to me. That's how I finally began that novel. Thanks to a daiquiri and bad Mexico City ice.

## FROZEN DAIQUIRI
Adapted from "The Craft of the Cocktail" by Dale DeGroff

1 ½ ounces white rum
½ ounce maraschino liqueur
1 ounce fresh grapefruit juice

1 ½ ounces superfine sugar
1 ounce fresh lime juice

**1.** In a blender, combine all ingredients with about a cup of ice. Blend to create a firm but slushy consistency, adding ice if necessary. Drink should be pourable, but should also hold its shape.

**2.** Mound slush into a cocktail glass or a wineglass. Serve with a straw that has been trimmed to stick up above slush by about four inches.

*June 27, 2007*

# A FROZEN JULEP, FRESH OFF THE VINE
## By JONATHAN MILES

"The mint julep, in its intended form, can be an intimidating beast," said Tasha Garcia Gibson, an owner of Tipsy Parson, a restaurant in Chelsea.

She's right.

For starters, there's all that hullabaloo about how a julep should be served.

To some die-hards, drinking a julep from anything but a silver or pewter julep cup is a blasphemy on the level of drinking communion wine from a high-heel shoe.

Then there's all the fuss about the proper way to make a julep (bruising the mint, or not bruising

it), which a Kentucky-born general and julep purist named S. B. Buckner Jr. once called, in a 1937 letter, a "ceremony," rather than a "formula," that "must not be entrusted to a novice, a statistician, nor a Yankee."

And while we're at it, is drinking a mint julep out of season—its traditional high point being Derby Day, in May—some kind of faux pas, like wearing seersucker after Labor Day?

So, yes: an intimidating beast.

And that's not even considering the hard, walloping dose of whiskey the drink packs, which can often yield scrunched-up expressions on the faces of novices, statisticians and Yankees.

For the signature cocktail at Tipsy Parson, which serves Deep South fare like fried pickles and chicken and dumplings, Ms. Gibson and her partner, Julie Taras Wallach, decided to tame the mint-flecked beast.

To that end, as they say in the South, they went whole hog. They have added a big sweet hit of reduced Concord grape juice, along with lime juice, to the traditional julep recipe—bourbon, sugar, mint—and blend their juleps in a 22-gallon frozen-drink machine tucked at end of the marble bar, serving them slushie-style.

The only ceremony involved is flipping the rocker switch on the drink machine. Never mind the mint sprig nestled into the top of that purple snow cone—the more appropriate garnish would be a sprinkling of S. B. Buckner Jr.'s tears.

Yet the drink, which Ms. Gibson said is named after a "boozy little Southern dessert," is a disarming, winsome treat.

Like a plate of fried pickles, it is both silly and satisfying, and quickly consumed. Unlike most frozen drinks, which seem to be designed to disguise the presence of alcohol in the mix, this one gives it star billing.

While tempered by the grape-jelly flavor, the bourbon's hot bite still dominates.

"The one thing we keep hearing is that it's 'boozy,' " Ms. Gibson said. "That might be a compliment or a complaint."

With what sounded like sly pride, she described how a rep from the frozen-drink machine manufacturer warned her that there was too much liquor in the mix for it to properly freeze. It froze anyway.

Ms. Gibson said the restaurant plans to vary the flavors—a pomegranate version will replace the Concord grape julep in the coming weeks—according to the season.

"I'm excited about a peach julep," Ms. Gibson said, anticipating summer. "I think we'll work our way around some stone fruits."

But she was unabashed about slinging juleps—frozen ones, at that — in the gray chill of late autumn.

"Because it's bourbon based," she said, "it's actually warming. People have been surprisingly into it, considering the weather."

Suffice it to say, they're not intimidated.

## CONCORD GRAPE MINT JULEP
**Adapted from TIPSY PARSON, New York City**
YIELD: 4 DRINKS

8 ounces bourbon

4 ounces fresh lime juice

4 ounces mint-infused simple syrup
(recipe follows)

4 ounces Concord grape reduction
(recipe follows)

Mint sprigs, for garnish

**1.** In a blender, combine all ingredients except mint sprigs and blend with 4 cups of ice until smooth.

**2.** Serve in silver julep cups or tall glasses and garnish with mint.

## MINT SYRUP

1 cup sugar

Small bunch of fresh mint

**1.** Bring sugar and 1 cup water to a boil, then reduce heat to low and add mint. Simmer 10 minutes.

**2.** Strain and cool before using.

## GRAPE REDUCTION

1 cinnamon stick

1 star anise

3 cloves

1 teaspoon whole black peppercorns

¼ teaspoon anise seeds

1 quart Concord grapes

**1.** In a cheesecloth sachet, combine cinnamon, anise, cloves, peppercorns and anise seeds.

**2.** In a saucepan combine Concord grapes with sachet and ½ cup water and simmer over medium-low heat until grapes break down and soften, about 45 minutes.

**3.** Discard sachet and strain mixture to remove seeds. Cool, uncovered, in refrigerator, and use within 1 week.

*December 6, 2009*

# A SWEET SIP OF WINTER
## By JONATHAN MILES

The subterranean lounge at Chinatown Brasserie, which opened last month in the space at Lafayette and Great Jones Street formerly occupied by Time Cafe and Fez Under Time Cafe, has all the coolly dazzling elements you'd expect from a bar that was part of a $6 million revamping.

A stage-set bridge, inspired by the 1941 movie "The Shanghai Gesture," leads to a staircase that tumbles past a koi pond on its way to a dark Asian drinking playground with a silky black bar and black leather banquettes. At the bar your gaze may linger on a salad bar of cocktail ingredients like cucumber, litchis and ginger slices and on neat, airy rows of top-shelf liquor bottles before coming to rest upon... Hey, is that a frozen drink machine?

It is. And the slushified cocktail whirling in that contraption, one seldom seen outside of margarita emporiums and Louisiana drive-through daiquiri bars, is Chinatown Brasserie's top-selling drink: a semisolid rendition of a classic mai tai. (The July heat wave may deserve a sales commission.)

"With a Chinese restaurant I had to do a mai tai," said Rainlove Lampariello, the beverage director, whose cocktail list is sprinkled with the likes of Singapore slings and Moscow mules. "When we got the idea to do the mai tai frozen, I had one rule," he said. "All the drinks here are fresh and seasonal, so the frozen drink would be as well."

Frozen cocktails are typically laden with concentrates and syrup, to improve stability and control crystallization, but Mr. Lampariello was adamant that everything had to be fresh. "Even the guys who installed the machine said I'd be better off using Rose's instead of fresh lime juice," he said. "And it did take a lot of work and experimentation to get the recipe right."

It's right. A bit less sweet and slightly more citric than the original Trader Vic's recipe, Mr. Lampariello's mai tai packs the clean, bracing refreshment of a snow cone made with actual countryside snow.

Blame the heat, but for this drinker—who swore off frozen cocktails after an unfortunate encounter with a 32-ounce Bourbon Street brain freezer—it was pure summer love. I wanted a spoon and a high chair. Mr. Lampariello confessed that he is not by nature a devotee of such frosties (from a bartender's perspective blending "ruins the show") and was quick to highlight the more austere Pimm's Cup cocktail on his list. But neither did he shy away from the silver machine spinning silently at the edge of the bar.

"They're drinks," he said with a wide grin. "They should be fun."

## FROZEN MAI TAI
**Adapted from CHINATOWN BRASSERIE, New York City**

| | |
|---|---|
| 2 ounces white rum | ½ ounce simple syrup (page 27) |
| ½ ounce freshly squeezed lime juice | ½ ounce cherry brandy |
| ½ ounce apricot brandy | Dash of orgeat syrup or almond syrup |
| 1½ ounces fresh pineapple juice | Lime wedge and a brandy-soaked (or maraschino) cherry for garnish |

**1.** Mix all ingredients except lime wedge in a blender with 1 cup ice. Blend until smooth, adding more ice if needed for a semifirm consistency.

**2.** Pour into a rocks glass and garnish with lime wedge and cherry.

*July 23, 2006*

SANGRIA PENEDES, LEFT, AND SANGRIA COMPOSTELA

CHAPTER 22

# SANGRIA

# SANGUINE SANGRIA
## By JONATHAN MILES

Roger Gonzalez, who runs the bar at the Hudson River Cafe, figured his Cucumber on the Hudson, a natty mix of Hendrick's gin, white cranberry juice and English cucumber, was going to be the runaway hit of the summer.

Fat chance. That's a downtown drink. The Hudson River Cafe, which opened in May, is tucked beneath the West Side Highway at 133rd Street, in West Harlem, on that still-gritty stretch of 12th Avenue along the Riverside Drive viaduct that hopeful real-estate nicknamers have dubbed "ViVa," for Viaduct Valley. That cucumber needs to float downriver for its audience. This valley is sangria country.

Happily, Mr. Gonzalez has a pair of sangrias on the menu, a white sangria that goes by the name of Under the Bridge and a red he calls the 12th Avenue Special. More happily, they're good ones: acutely fresh, complex without being silly, with none of the cloying fruit-cocktail sweetness that sullies sangria's reputation. Breaking from tradition, Mr. Gonzalez doesn't soak the fruit in his sangrias, wanting to avoid soggy, unidentifiable fruit-blobs.

The pink cubes of apple in the 12th Avenue Special, bobbing beside pineapple, peaches and grapes, have a feisty crunch to them. The voice of the Rioja, despite a diverse chorus of spiced rum, Lillet Rouge, peach schnapps, orange juice and Grand Marnier, cuts through loud and clear. "I was almost surprised by how well people responded to the sangrias," said Mr. Gonzalez, a 23-year-old Venezuelan who moonlights as a mixologist while studying political science and journalism at the City College of New York. As with everywhere, only the mojitos are selling better.

Mr. Gonzalez shouldn't have been too surprised. With its vaguely Nuevo Latino dinner menu, rambling and expansive bilevel patios, and live outdoor bands, the Hudson River Cafe feels like a sangria kind of place—as if a resort bar fell out of the sky and into a harsh nest of urban infrastructure in Harlem, crushing the ramshackle auto-repair shop that used to occupy the dark corner.

It draws a rollicking, multifarious crowd: Look one direction and you'll see a woman sashay by in the reddest red dress ever made, as tight against her skin as a tattoo. Look the other way and there's someone's grandmother, rolling her shoulders to the rhythm of a Barry White tune, the glow from the neighboring Fairway Market's sale ticker dancing across her face. When the band dives into a Carlos Santana song, the grandmother looks tempted to shimmy out of her chair.

Maybe it's the Santana that's rousing her, maybe the sangria. But you can bet it isn't a cucumber.

## 12TH AVENUE SPECIAL
Adapted from HUDSON RIVER CAFÉ, New York City, by Jonathan Miles

| | |
|---|---|
| 3 ounces Rioja wine | 1 ounce Grand Marnier |
| 2½ ounces freshly squeezed orange juice | Splash of ginger ale |
| 1½ ounces Lillet Rouge | Chopped fresh fruit (pineapple, apple, red grapes, peach), to taste |
| 1½ ounces peach schnapps | Star fruit, strawberry, for garnish |
| 1¼ ounces Sailor Jerry rum | |

**1.** Partly fill a large wine glass with ice. Add all ingredients except ginger ale and fresh fruit and stir well.

**2.** Top with ginger ale and enough chopped fruit to fill glass. Garnish with the star fruit and serve.

*August 19, 2007*

# REFRESHING NEW SANGRIAS TO CHASE AWAY BAD MEMORIES
## By ERIC ASIMOV

It was the stuff of cheap excitement and of headaches, of travel posters of beaches and bullfights, and of simpler times when Greenwich Village was a folk paradise and when Spanish food meant garlic and shrimp rather than laboratory gastronomy.

For wine lovers who have reached middle age, sangria, like Mateus or Boone's Farm, dredges up memories not altogether pleasant. Kingsley Amis, the British writer who prized his drinking, apparently emerged unscarred, though. He once described sangria as "cheap, easy to make up and pretty harmless—so that you can drink a lot of it without falling down."

But sangria, the wine punch that is consumed throughout Spain in the heat, and in the tourist spots year round, does not have to be oversweetened with sugar and cheap liqueur, or a repository for rotgut that is too stale to be served by the glass. It apparently doesn't even have to conform to Spanish traditions. Many people think of it instead as a template, an invitation to experiment with fresh, fruity wines and other fine ingredients. Some restaurants even find in sangria a creative method for skirting the restrictions of wine-and-beer licenses, by making wine-based cocktails.

Lido, an Italian spot in Harlem, serves a sangria with wine, brandy and passion fruit. The sangria at Pig and Khao, a Filipino pub on the Lower East Side, is a red-wine punch made with green mango and papaya. Even the Benihana chain is getting in on the action, offering what it calls a sparkling strawberry sangria. Who cares if its blend of strawberries, lemon vodka, orange liqueur, lemon juice and simple syrup is like the root beer martini of sangrias, exploiting the name while bearing little resemblance to the original?

Although sangria is related to wine punches served throughout Europe, its history extends for centuries in Spain, where vineyards were first planted by Romans more than 2,000 years ago. It was by most accounts introduced to the United States at the 1964 New York World's Fair, making it more modern than some of New York's older Spanish restaurants, which date from the end of the Spanish Civil War.

While the notion of sangria is malleable enough to accommodate many manifestations, all good ones must have one thing in common: they need to revive the spirit and awaken the senses.

"When you're in the middle of summer in Spain, you can't think of drinking red wine," said Gil Avital, the wine director at Tertulia in the West Village, which serves a vivacious, lightly sweet sangria on tap. "People ask for it, though it's not listed anywhere. It's a very decent wine cocktail."

After much tinkering, Rafael Mateo, the proprietor of Pata Negra, a Spanish wine bar in the East Village, formulated a sangria that is winelike and very refreshing, with a keen balance of tart and fruity flavors. Even though he features Spanish wines and an excellent selection of sherries, he serves far more sangria than wine, Mr. Mateo said, going through an entire 12-liter container on a busy night, sometimes two in the summer.

"I want them to drink Spanish wine, I want them to drink sherry," he said of his customers. "I thought, if they're going to drink sangria, let me at least make it so I'd like to drink it, too."

Unlike many recipes, which specify Rioja made from the tempranillo grape—mostly, I think, because it is the Spanish red most familiar to Americans—Mr. Mateo prefers using garnacha from Campo de Borja in central Spain, which he said has backbone without being overly tannic. He lightens the blend by adding rosé, and sweetens it with orange liqueur and orange soda rather than with fruit purée, a common addition, which he dislikes because, he said, it gives the sangria a grainy texture. He experimented with orange juice rather than soda, but found it, too, changed the texture. Finally, he allows the punch to knit together overnight and adds cut fruit only at the end, as a garnish.

"People insist on the fruit," he said. "They like it and they eat it."

Mr. Mateo's sangria is simple to make in quantity and would flow copiously at any backyard party. But while sangria may be great for crowds, it also lends itself to painstaking individual preparations. Gonzalo Marín, the beverage director at Barraca, a Spanish restaurant in the West Village, has devised five cocktail versions of sangria that do not resemble the typical punch. I particularly liked the fragrant, deliciously herbal sangria

Compostela, made with albariño, sake, lemon grass and apple-rosemary purée, and the sangria Penedes, made with cava, peaches and lavender, a lively Spanish take on the Bellini. Both use non-Spanish ingredients, and neither is made with red wine.

"The idea was to do something playful, but to put sangria on the same level as cocktails," Mr. Marín said. "The essence of sangria is wine, and I wanted to create something with Spanish flavors."

Other delicious departures from basic sangria are more grounded in history. Alex Raij, a co-owner of three Spanish restaurants in New York, makes zurracapote, a red wine punch often served in northern Spain, at Txikito, her Basque restaurant in Chelsea. It is sweetened with syrup flavored with dried fruit, cinnamon and juniper berries, and fortified with orange liqueur and vodka. As with the cocktails, its preparation is more complicated than basic sangria, but it's refreshing and different, and would make a superb summer cooler.

"It's sweet and fortified, but you're not meant to drink it so strong," Ms. Raij said. "You're meant to drink it over ice, which dilutes it, making it easy and accessible."

For a more traditional red wine sangria, Ms. Raij suggests using apples and lemons, rather than the cornucopia that is sometimes tossed into the punch. "The bitterness of the lemons and the crisp freshness of the apples are good foils for the richness of the red wine," she said. "The pineapples and peaches, they're more cobbler-ish, more dessert."

Made with care and good ingredients, even those with bruised memories won't have to fear the painful consequences.

## SANGRIA PENEDES
Adapted from GONZALO MARÍN, Barraca, New York City
YIELD: 4 TO 6 DRINKS

10 ounces Mathilde or other peach liqueur
2 ounces fresh grapefruit juice
5 dashes Scrappy's lavender bitters (see note below)

2 ounces simple syrup (page 27)
1 bottle Cava
1 peach, diced into small cubes, for garnish

**1.** In a pitcher or other container, combine peach liqueur, grapefruit juice, bitters and simple syrup.

**2.** To serve, pour 1 ½ ounces of the mixture into a champagne flute and top with Cava. Garnish with peach cubes.

Scrappy's lavender bitters are available from Kalustyan's in New York City or at kalustyans.com

SANGRIA

## SANGRIA COMPOSTELA

Adapted from GONZALO MARÍN, Barraca, New York City

YIELD: 4 TO 6 DRINKS

24 ounces albariño

7½ ounces sake

2 ounces fresh lemon juice

5 ounces club soda

10 ounces rosemary-infused apple juice (recipe follows)

3 ounces lemon grass syrup (recipe follows)

Kiwi, green apples, pears, cut into small cubes, for garnish

Rosemary sprig, for garnish

**1.** In a pitcher, combine albarino, sake, lemon juice and club soda.

**2.** Add the rosemary-infused apple juice and lemon grass syrup and mix well. Garnish with fruit and rosemary sprig and serve straight up or over ice.

## ROSEMARY-INFUSED APPLE JUICE

10 ounces unsweetened apple juice

½ sprig rosemary

**1.** In a blender, combine apple juice and rosemary and blend for 10 seconds. Pour mixture through a fine strainer, discarding solids, and set aside.

## LEMON GRASS SYRUP

1 cup sugar

3 lemon grass stalks, chopped

**1.** In a small saucepan, combine sugar, lemon grass and ½ cup water. Place over medium heat until boiling. Remove from heat and strain syrup, discarding lemon grass. Allow to cool. (May be covered and refrigerated.)

## TRADITIONAL SANGRIA

Adapted from RAFAEL MATEO, Pata Negra, New York City

YIELD: ABOUT 12 DRINKS

2 bottles dry garnacha red wine

1 bottle dry Rosado (Spanish rosé)

12 ounces orange soda (preferably a less-sweet brand such as Spanish KAS or San Pellegrino aranciata, or use Fanta)

ounce Torres orange liqueur or Triple Sec

2 ounces Romate or other Spanish brandy

1 tablespoon sugar, or to taste

2 apples, cored and diced, for garnish

oranges, cut into wedges, for garnish

**1.** In a large vessel, combine all ingredients except apples and oranges. Stir with a wooden spoon. Let rest for 5 minutes. Taste, and add sugar if desired, stirring to dissolve. Refrigerate for at least four hours, preferably overnight.

**2.** To serve, fill glasses with ice. Pour 5 ounces sangria into each glass and garnish with diced apple and orange wedges.

## ZURRACAPOTE
**Adapted from TXIKITO, New York**
YIELD: 12 DRINKS

¼ cup zurra red wine syrup (recipe follows)
2 bottles red wine (preferably tempranillo)
½ cup Torres orange liqueur or Triple Sec
½ cup vodka

2 lemons, thinly sliced, for garnish
2 Fuji apples, cored and diced, for garnish
12 ounces Sprite, or as needed

**1.** In a 3-quart container, combine the zurra syrup, wine, liqueur and vodka. Refrigerate until chilled, at least 3 hours.

**2.** To serve, divide punch between two 1½-quart pitchers. Fill each of 12 tall glasses with ice, 1 slice lemon and a spoonful of diced apple. Divide remaining lemon and apple, ¼ cup apricot-raisin mixture and 2 cups ice cubes between the pitchers. Pour 5 ounces zurracapote into each glass, and top with 1 ounce of Sprite, or to taste. Stir before serving.

## ZURRA RED WINE SYRUP
YIELD: 2 CUPS SYRUP AND 1 CUP MACERATED FRUIT

1½ cups dry red wine
3¾ cups sugar
6 juniper berries, bruised

1 small cinnamon stick
¾ cup diced dried apricots
¾ cup golden raisins

**1.** In a pot, combine wine, sugar, juniper berries and cinnamon stick. Place over low heat and stir just until sugar has dissolved; do not bring to a boil.

**2.** Pour over apricots and raisins. Let stand 20 minutes. Strain over a bowl and reserve fruit and syrup separately. Discard juniper berries and cinnamon stick.

**This makes more than needed for the zurracapote, but syrup and fruit may be stored separately, covered and refrigerated, for up to 1 month.**

*May 20, 2013*

## PEACH SANGRIA
**By DAVID MAS MASUMOTO**

*This recipe came to The Times from David Mas Masumoto, who is an organic-peach-and-grape farmer and author. The drink is bright and fizzy and full of delicious summer. It's a great accompaniment to brunch, or just an excellent way to end a hot day.*
YIELD: 8 TO 10 DRINKS

7 peaches
½ cup plus 2 tablespoons sugar
2 (750-ml.) bottles white wine

1 lemon, sliced into eighths
1 cup blueberries

**1.** Peel and pit 5 of the peaches and cut them into chunks. Place in a food processor and blend until smooth. Add the sugar and blend until combined.

**2.** Strain through a fine-mesh sieve. Combine the peach purée, wine and lemon in a 3½-quart container, cover, and refrigerate overnight.

**3.** An hour before serving, thinly slice the remaining 2 peaches and add them to the sangria along with the blueberries. Serve over ice.

*August 13, 2006*

# WHITE SANGRIA
# AND RED SANGRIA
## By FLORENCE FABRICANT

Cavas, often blessed with notes of citrus and spring blossoms, are genial sparkling wines, all the more so because of their modest prices. They can be called on for many occasions, and are the ideal finishing touch for san-gria, either red or white. The white sangria is unusual and strong, though white wine in place of manzanilla sherry will moderate the alcohol. The red is clearly classic. Both are more refreshing than sweet.

## WHITE SANGRIA
**Adapted from KERIN AUTH, Tinto Fino, New York City**
YIELD: 8 TO 10 DRINKS

2 apples, cored and coarsely diced
2 pears, cored and coarsely diced
2 juice oranges, peeled, seeded and diced
1 cup gin
½ cup triple sec
3 bottles (500 ml. each) manzanilla sherry or 2 bottles (750 ml. each) dry white wine
½ bottle cava (1½ cups), chilled

**1.** Place all fruit in a bowl with gin and triple sec. Cover and refrigerate at least 4 hours, or overnight.

**2.** Transfer to a large pitcher and add manzanilla or white wine and stir. Divide liquid and fruit into wine glasses, over ice if desired, until about 2/3 full. Top each with cava.

## RED SANGRIA
**Adapted from RAFAEL MATEO, Pata Negra, New York City**
YIELD: 4 TO 6 DRINKS

1 bottle red wine, preferably garnacha
Juice of 1 ½ oranges
Juice of 1 lemon
Juice of 1 lime
½ cup Spanish brandy
¼ cup triple sec
1 apple, cored and sliced
1 pear, cored and sliced
1 cinnamon stick
½ bottle cava (1½ cups), chilled

**1.** Combine all ingredients except cava in a 2-quart pitcher. Cover and refrigerate at least 4 hours, or overnight.

**2.** Add 2 cups ice and the cava. Pour into wine glasses with some fruit.

*May 10, 2010*

# FOR A FUTURE
# THAT'S ALWAYS ROSY

## By MONIQUE TRUONG

Hidden within our current tastes and penchants are the persistent and often ignoble residues of our former selves. I call it the Holly Golightly-Lula Mae Principle. Allow me to demonstrate how it works.

Of late, my summer drink of choice is a white sangria. It's a floral concoction of white sparkling wine, Cointreau, apple juice and a splash of club soda, generously perfumed with thin slices of white nectarines, green pears and sweet navel oranges.

This is my reverse-engineered recipe for a drink that I had first at a restaurant so incandescently hip and cool that it saw no reason to cook its food. An editor at a fancy magazine was paying, so I allowed myself to be taken to a raw foods restaurant. In lieu of a proper meal, I decided to drink myself full and I did.

I don't remember too much about the raw foods, but that nutty place really had a way with the white sangria. I serve pitchers of it now on summer evenings and nod with delight when my friends comment on its subtle beauty and intoxicating charm. I hesitate to share with them, though, why my inner Lula Mae adores this chic little quaff.

White sangria reminds me of the bottles of convenience store wine coolers that my girlfriends and I consumed in alarming quantities in the back seat of cars while stuck in Texas in the prime of our teenage years. Sweet, cheap and perversely and resolutely not beer (long necks being the patriotic drink of the Republic of Texas), wine coolers were our fast ticket out of sobriety and the confines of our suburban youth.

As we twisted off their caps and guzzled their artificial flavors, we were imagining the future. Beautiful and transporting, ambrosial with promises, and complex but never complicated: we wanted it so much we could taste it. The future for us finally arrived and, of course, wasn't quite what we had desired, but a sip of white sangria on a summer night comes pretty close.

## WHITE SANGRIA
YIELD: 8 DRINKS

2 small white nectarines or white peaches
1 small green pear or green apple
1 small navel orange
1 bottle cava, moscato d'Asti or other

sparkling wine
1¾ cups apple juice
1⅓ cups Cointreau
1 cup club soda

**1.** Slice fruit into thin bite-size pieces. Place in large pitcher. Pour in sparkling wine, apple juice and Cointreau. If possible, refrigerate an hour or two to draw out sweetness and floral aromas of fruit.

**2.** Add club soda, and stir. Spoon some fruit pieces into glasses filled with ice, and pour.

*June 27, 2007*

MOSCOW MULE

CHAPTER 23

# THE
# MULE

## MOSCOW MULE
### By MARK BITTMAN

*Moscow is often shown in films as being a cold place, but this concoction will warm up any drinker. Who could stay cold when vodka and ginger are involved?*

1½ tablespoons lime juice
2 tablespoons simple syrup (page 27)
¼ cup vodka

Ginger beer
Candied ginger, for garnish

**1.** Add lime juice and simple syrup to the vodka in a tall glass or mug and top with ginger beer. Garnish with candied ginger.

*May 13, 2012*

# A SUMMIT WITHOUT RUSSIA NEEDS A DRINK TO MATCH
## By JOSH BARRO

The G7 summit that will start next Wednesday in Brussels was supposed to be a G8 summit and was supposed to be held in Sochi, Russia. So this week's Upshot With a Twist replaces the Moscow Mule with a more characteristically Belgian cocktail for the relocated and reduced meeting.

A Moscow Mule is vodka, ginger beer and lime. To replace it, we sought a vodka-free drink that would combine ginger and citrus with genever, a juniper-flavored spirit that was the precursor to gin and that remains popular in Belgium and the Netherlands.

I put this request in at Dutch Kills, a bar in Long Island City, Queens, and was presented with the Holland Bee Sting. It's a drink that combines genever, lemon juice, ginger and honey syrups, and Amaro CioCiaro, a bittersweet orange liqueur.

The drink (a variation on Sam Ross's Penicillin) provides a refreshing burst of ginger and citrus, yet is also boozier than a Moscow Mule—welcome news for world leaders coping with the Ukraine crisis.

Jan Warren, the head bartender at Dutch Kills, provides the recipe below, or you can visit the bar from 5 p.m. to 2 a.m.

## THE HOLLAND BEE STING
By JAN WARREN, Dutch Kills, Long Island City, Queens

| | |
|---|---|
| 2 ounce genever | ⅜ ounce honey syrup |
| ¾ ounce lemon juice | ¼ ounce Amaro CioCiaro |
| ⅜ ounce ginger syrup | |

**1.** Add all ingredients except the amaro to a shaker and shake with ice.

**2.** Strain over ice into a double rocks glass. Float the Amaro over the drink—don't worry, it sinks.

*May 30, 2014*

## SAVANNAH MULE
Adapted from DAN SABO, Ace Hotel Downtown Los Angeles, by Jason Rowan

*Dan Sabo explains the origins of this savory cocktail: "We like to play with variations on classics, and the Moscow Mule is the ultimate L.A. classic to modify. I was focused on the combination of ginger and peaches for summer, so the drink grew from there. The Scotch started as a small float for aroma, but became an increasingly important part of the drink to add a complexity of smoke on both the nose and the palate."*

| | |
|---|---|
| 3 sage leaves | Vigne |
| 1 ounce Laphroaig 10 (or other smoky Islay Scotch) | ½ ounce lemon juice |
| 1 ounce vodka | 4 drops Bittermens Orange Citrate |
| ¾ ounce Giffard Crème de Pêche de | Ginger beer |

**1.** In the bottom of a cocktail shaker, muddle 2 of the sage leaves.

**2.** Add the remaining ingredients (except ginger beer), add ice and shake.

**3.** Double strain the liquid into a rock glass or copper mug filled with ice.

**4.** Top with ginger beer and garnish with the remaining sage leaf.

*July 16, 2014*

LAKE DELTON MULE

## LAKE DELTON MULE
**Adapted from BRIAN BARTELS, Fedora, New York City, by Robert Simonson**

*This simple drink is a spin on the classic vodka-and-ginger-beer drink, the Moscow Mule. The combination of génépi, an herbal Alpine liqueur, the sweet snap of the Wondermint and the tangy bite of the ginger beer makes for a refreshing summer cocktail. The drink is named after a small town in Wisconsin where Mr. Bartels had his first restaurant job.*

1 ounce Wondermint
1 ounce Génépi liqueur, preferably Dolin

2 ounces ginger beer
1 bar spoon fresh lime juice
Piece of candied ginger, for garnish

**1.** In a rocks glass filled with ice, combine all ingredients except candied ginger and stir until chilled, about 30 seconds. Garnish with candied ginger.

*June 4, 2014*

## GIN MULE
**By ROSIE SCHAAP**

*Whiskey and ginger is a beloved pair. Gin and ginger is also delicious—and a finer fit for summer drinking.*

Scant teaspoon simple syrup
1½ ounces gin
½ ounce fresh lemon juice

Chilled ginger beer, to top
Lemon twist, for garnish

**1.** Fill a highball glass with ice. Add simple syrup, gin and lemon juice and top with ginger beer. Stir gently, and garnish with a lemon twist.

*May 20, 2014*

TIMOTHY MINER AT THE JAKEWALK BAR IN BROOKLYN

CHAPTER 24

# NEW
# SCHOOL

# THE BRAMBLE

## By TOBY CECCHINI

Years ago, I wrote that the bramble cocktail would be the next big thing to hit these shores. I keep waiting to be right. The bramble is the riesling of the cocktail world, known by drinks weenies since seemingly forever (like, the '80s), yet still unfamiliar to most overheated pilgrims sidling up to the bar in search of a puckery summer drink.

It's a simple and immensely likable sip that's been called England's cosmopolitan—without the "Sex and the City" taint. (It's on almost every British bartender's short list, having been invented in 1984 by Dick Bradsell, the patriarch of England's cocktail uptick, at Fred's Club in London's SoHo—though scrupulous pundits infer that Jerry Thomas listed its forerunner as the Gin Fix in his 1862 cocktail guide.) And it has at least three of the qualities that allow many great cocktails to thrive: it's relatively easy to make, it's well-balanced—a tight rack of sour, sweet and fruit—and it has a memorably evocative name.

Don't discount that last detail; tell me why the world clamors for Sancerre, while the appellation right next door, Menetou-Salon, makes equivalent wines with the same grape for a third the cost less and goes wanting. (Insert argument here ...) But I digress.

The bramble is essentially a short gin sour with a drizzle of crème de mûre, a French blackberry liqueur, over the top. Served on crushed ice,

it gets a quick garnish of a lemon slice and, to be true to Bradsell's original, two blackberries. In the winter there's nothing to this, and the drink is great as is. But something as elemental as the bramble invites toying, and with summer's berries arriving, you can up the ante in one of many directions without having to make a mixology seminar out of the thing.

For years I incorporated crème de framboise, the equivalent raspberry liqueur, along with the blackberry for its piquant aromatic punch. I would buy a bottle of each and mix them equally, using that to drizzle, and spear both a raspberry and a blackberry on a pick as a garnish. In truth, the gin sour at the base of this drink is a perfect blank canvas for almost any good berry-based liqueur. Massenez, the Alsatian distiller, makes a clean, traditional crème de mûre that works beautifully in the classic. Clear Creek Distillery in Portland, Ore., puts out excellent fruit liqueurs; the blackberry, raspberry or black currant all bring their own twist to a bramble. In New York State, Warwick Valley Winery and Distillery in the Hudson Valley makes a black-currant cordial with a bright aroma and tannic grab that pull the drink in a fresh direction. I am chafing to try the new Crème Yvette from the maker of Saint Germain in this drink, but the classic Chambord works just as readily for those whose distribution channels might deprive them of such exotica.

The reigning complaint I've heard from bartenders is that the liqueur used to finish the drink is heavier than the sour, so it plunges to the bottom of the glass rather than acting as a float. As a fix, some simply shake it in with the rest of the drink. I still like to float it, but I prefer to shake some berries—blackberries, raspberries or both—in with the sour, double-straining the seeds and pulp to give it a light tinge and a brighter punch. If you're lucky enough to have access to wild blackberries this summer, here is your summer in a glass.

## THE BRAMBLE

| | |
|---|---|
| 2 ounces gin | ½ ounce simple syrup (page 27) |
| 1 ounce fresh lemon juice | ½ ounce crème de mûre |

**1.** In a cocktail shaker filled with ice, shake together the gin, lemon juice, and simple syrup.

**2.** Strain into a rocks glass filled with crushed ice (see below), mounded high. Drizzle crème de mûre over the top and garnish with a slice of lemon, two blackberries and a short straw.

Crushed ice is important in this drink for the dilution. At home, you can either smash your cubes in a clean dish towel or make cracked ice by whacking each cube with the back of a heavy spoon.

*June 16, 2010*

# COCKTAIL'S NAMESAKE
## By JONATHAN MILES

When a teenage immigrant from Dublin named Tommy Rowles started tending bar in New York in 1958, he quickly had to learn how to make a rusty nail, pink lady and brandy Alexander. This was at Bemelmans Bar, the landmark lounge in the Carlyle, where Mr. Rowles, 67, has worked ever since.

The decades brought more concoctions to learn: the Harvey Wallbanger, seabreeze, cosmopolitan and the cocktails that two of the city's boldface-name mixologists, Dale De-

Groff and Audrey Saunders, introduced during their spells managing the Bemelmans. More recently, Mr. Rowles had to learn to make yet another newfangled cocktail: the Tommy Rowles.

"I'm just a bartender, not a chef," Mr. Rowles said. "When I started, they had a book behind the bar, with something like 400 or 500 drinks, and that was it." Now Mr. Rowles is in the book. The drink, conceived as a tribute to his storied 48-year tenure, was created by Brian Van Flandern, who ended a

THE TOMMY ROWLES

three-year stint of mixing drinks at Per Se in February to revamp the cocktail program at Bemelmans.

The bar is steeped in tradition. With its crimson-jacketed staff, Art Deco flourishes and dreamy piano music, Bemelmans evokes a black-and-white vision of bygone Manhattan in which all the men wore fedoras, all the women wore pearls, and they all blithely smoked their heads off.

But none of its traditions may be more vibrant than Mr. Rowles, who captains the day shift. He is famed for his bloody mary mix—a secret recipe of his own devising—and for an across-the-bar exchange with Harry S. Truman during which Mr. Rowles confessed his distaste for bourbon, Mr. Truman's liquor of choice.

"If you had to walk 15 blocks with those guys following you," the former president said of the reporters who accompanied his daily constitutional, "you'd drink this, too."

Mr. Rowles—slender and white-haired and with a bona fide twinkle in his eyes, hoary stereotype notwith-standing—isn't one to crow about his tribute. Modesty precludes it.

"For me, having come from Ireland, it feels good," is the extent of his preening. "I know my mother would be proud."

When the uninitiated order a Tommy Rowles from Mr. Rowles, he doesn't let on, even if they start carping. "Some people, you know, they'll say it's too sweet or not sweet enough," he said with a shrug.

Sweetly astringent is what it is. "It's basically a Cognac and tonic, when you get down to it," explained Mr. Van Flandern, who rounds off that combination—a classic in Europe, more unfamiliar here—with simple syrup, lime juice and a whisper of rum. "But what a great summertime drink," he said. "Imagine walking off the hot sidewalk and right into that."

Mr. Rowles, though, would imagine something else.

"A Heineken," he said.

Touched by the tribute, however, he couldn't help confess, "All these new drinks drive me nuts."

## TOMMY ROWLES
**Adapted From BEMELMANS BAR, New York City**

| | |
|---|---|
| 1 ounce Martell Cordon Bleu Cognac | ¹⁄₁₆ teaspoon raw quinine powder or 2 dashes Angostura bitters |
| ¼ ounce 10 Cane rum | |
| 1 ounce freshly squeezed lime juice | ½ ounce club soda |
| 1¼ ounce simple syrup (page 27) | Lime wedge, for garnish |

**1.** Mix all ingredients except club soda and lime wedge in a cocktail shaker without ice and shake vigorously.

**2.** Pour into a highball glass filled with ice. Add club soda and gently roll the mixture back and forth between shaker and glass. Garnish with lime wedge and serve.

Raw quinine powder can be purchased at www.raintreenutrition.com.

*June 10, 2007*

# A STAR OR TWO, SURE, BUT A JUST-US AURA

## By STEVE REDDICLIFFE

The Mac Bar on the third floor of the restaurant Angus' is happy proof that a bar really can be homey.

It's not common. Bars can be comfortable. They can be welcoming. But homey, that's a different quality, and rarer still in Midtown Manhattan.

Last spring, Angus McIndoe, who opened his namesake restaurant in the theater district in 2001, decided to turn an upstairs space used largely for private events into a "cozier hangout spot."

On one wall is a photograph of the McIndoe family taken in Scotland when Mr. McIndoe was 4 or 5 months old. ("There's one more that was born after that picture was taken," he said. "So there's actually eight of us.") His father's in the picture; his name was Cranston, but he preferred to be called Mac. The bar is named for him.

There's an alcove devoted to the author Frank McCourt, including a book jacket for his memoir "Angela's Ashes." (Mr. McCourt, who died in 2009, was an early investor, and, Mr. McIndoe said, "We couldn't have opened the restaurant without Frank.") On a wall near the bar is a poster for the 2001 film "Strictly Sinatra," which was written and directed by Peter Capaldi, a fellow Scot and longtime friend of Mr. McIndoe's, who now plays Doctor Who in the BBC television series.

There are candles on the tables and an eclectic crowd throughout the night. One recent early evening, Robert De Niro was in a booth, having some laughs with, among others, Dianna Agron, a former star of "Glee" (they appeared together in the movie "The Family" last year). Along the bar was a reunion of a dozen or so men who had attended Martin Van Buren High School in Queens. (Such sightings are not guaranteed; the Van Buren boys don't seem to get together all that often.) Later, post-theater, actors and audience members come by for a cocktail; a glass of the house wine, which carries the label Vino Collapso (a Scotch phrase for, in Mr. McIndoe's words, "plonk"); maybe an order of Scotch eggs or a Scotch pie filled with lamb (beef edition also available).

Throughout, there's interesting music. The bar's longtime manager, Rick Wesley, has lately favored Tom Waits and Tony Joe White, and the bartender (and painter) Gregory Coutinho, another veteran, devoted a good part of a recent Friday night to a channel from an Afrobeat group he liked, the Budos Band out of Staten Island.

All of this was through the Pandora service, for which Mr. McIndoe expresses scant enthusiasm. "I'm a fan of putting an album on from beginning to end," he said, "or at least the side of an album. I don't like the idea of changing it up every 30 seconds."

To that end, he and the bartenders will occasionally use the turntable on the back bar "at 8 o'clock, when everybody is at the theater." The John Coltrane LP "A Love Supreme" was playing one night. "When can you not listen to Coltrane?" Mr. McIndoe said. "You can listen to Coltrane whether you're eating or drinking, awake or sleeping."

Still, records are not a regular feature because "the floor is not as sturdy as we'd hoped," Mr. McIndoe said.

"It's become a victim of the cruel architecture of this old building," he explained. (Mr. McIndoe said he does not know its precise age, "but I'm sure the plumbing is pre-Roman.")

The drinks are right for the room. Bartenders make well-calibrated manhattans and Negronis. "House gin O.K.?" Mr. Coutinho asked when I ordered a Negroni.

"What is it?"

"Aristocrat!" he said, with the pinpoint timing of a practiced comedian.

There's also a short list of specialties — nothing overly complicated or intimidating. That includes the lively Side Show Smash, a whiskey, fresh lemon, soda, tonic and mint salute to the musical playing next door); a sprightly take on a Pegu Club (here simply called a Pegu, with gin, fresh lemon and orange liqueur); and the Bedstone, a drink created by Mr. Wesley that Mr. McIndoe is fond of. It's made with bourbon, orange liqueur and, per the menu description, "served in an absinthe-perfumed glass."

"When I was a kid, a bed stone was something you heated up—in in freezing-cold Scotland, the rural parts of it, they would heat up a stone as a bed warmer," Mr. McIndoe recalled.

Mr. Wesley said that a bed stone, which "is supposed to lull you to sleep," was indeed the inspiration for a drink that's smooth and soothing.

At the Mac Bar, even the cocktails can feel homespun.

## THE BEDSTONE
**Adapted from RICK WESLEY, Angus', New York City**

| | |
|---|---|
| 1 teaspoon absinthe | Splash of fresh lemon juice |
| 5½ ounces bourbon | Twist of orange or bourbon-marinated |
| ½ ounce orange liqueur | cherry, for garnish |

**1.** Add absinthe to a chilled martini glass and give it a whirl so it coats the entire surface area.

**2.** Pour bourbon and orange liqueur into an iced martini shaker, add a splash of fresh lemon juice and shake vigorously.

**3.** Discard the absinthe in the martini glass, strain the mixed liquors into the glass and garnish with twist of orange or marinated cherry.

*December 11, 2014*

# BROADWAY BY THE GLASS

## By JONATHAN MILES

When Brett Stasiewicz watches the first installment of "The Coast of Utopia," Tom Stoppard's epic trilogy about prerevolutionary Russian thought, he does not see a depiction of Russian intelligentsia torn between "dried-up old German reasoning and the new French idealism," as one character in the play puts it. Instead, he sees vodka shaken with German schnapps and French Lillet blanc.

Mr. Stasiewicz is the mixologist for Sweet Concessions, the concessionaire for the Lincoln Center Theater (where "The Coast of Utopia" is playing) and eight other New York theaters, and his job is to wring alcoholic drinks from the themes of Broadway productions—to pair twelve angry cocktails with "Twelve Angry Men," for instance.

Mr. Stasiewicz's job is a singularly New York occupation: "Help Wanted: Cocktail Dramaturg," is not a classified listing you would expect to find in other cities. After 6 years and almost 60 shows, he has yet to be stumped by a play, though the more dour productions have sometimes forced him to break a sweat. "It's a lot harder to conceive a cocktail when the play is depressing," he said. ("The Diary of Anne Frank" was a particular challenge; he went nonalcoholic.)

For "The Coast of Utopia," Mr. Stasiewicz's palette was full. When performed as one play, Mr. Stoppard's trilogy covers three turbulent decades of Russian history, with occasional layovers in Paris and Geneva. For the first installment, called "Voyage," Mr. Stasiewicz let green-apple schnapps and Lillet battle for vodka's soul, adding a splash of orange juice ("The 'marathon' shows will start in the morning," he noted) and ginger ale to soften the blows. The vodka dominates, but the schnapps and Lillet lend the drink a floral crispness. "Shipwreck," the second installment, is paired with a cranberry-red Cosmopolitan-esque cocktail (the color signifying the theme of revolution, with a splash of Cognac alluding to the Parisian setting), while the third installment, "Salvage," gets a heavy treatment of vanilla vodka mixed with Drambuie, Frangelico and crème de cacao.

As the crowds funneled in on a recent Friday night, Mr. Stasiewicz tucked himself behind the concession stand and began nimbly serving cocktails. What sells more, he was asked: cocktails or Raisinets? "Between those two?" he replied. "Probably cocktails. But if we're talking peanut M&M's, that's a different story."

## VOYAGE
**Adapted From SWEET CONCESSIONS, New York City**

1 ½ ounces Absolut Mandarin vodka
½ ounce German apple schnapps
¼ ounce Lillet blanc
Squeeze of fresh lime juice

½ ounce freshly squeezed orange juice
Splash of ginger ale
Orange slice, for garnish

**1.** Shake the vodka, schnapps, Lillet blanc and fresh lime juice in a cocktail shaker filled with ice. Add the orange juice and the splash of ginger ale.

**2.** Strain into a chilled cocktail glass and garnish with the orange slice.

*January 28, 2007*

# QUAFFABLE COCKTAILS THAT GET THEIR FLAVOR FROM SURPRISING (AND SURPRISINGLY OBTAINABLE) INGREDIENTS

## By BRIAN NICHOLS

As the wave of cocktail innovation continues to crest, intrepid bartenders are turning to unexpected ingredients in their quest to make the most delicious drinks imaginable, including imported amaros, eaux de vie and fortified wines. We offer six recipes from some of the country's most renowned bartenders that derive their character from unexpected, but easily obtainable ingredients. Belly up to their bars for a taste, or mix them up yourself at home.

## THE VATICAN CITY
### Adapted from MIKKI KRISTOLA, Varnish, Los Angeles

*"I always say amaros are the paint brushes we use to add texture and personalities to cocktails," says Eric Alperin, the co-owner of the Varnish in downtown Los Angeles. For him, Suze, a French version of the bracing Italian digestif, imparts an "herbaceous richness" reminiscent of mowed grass. Well-known in Europe (Picasso paid homage to it in a 1912 collage), it was long a "suitcase import" to the United States but is widely available today.*

1 ounce Suze
1 ounce bianco vermouth (Alperin suggests Dolin)
1 ounce fresh-squeezed lime juice

¾ ounce simple syrup (page 27)
3 ounces club soda, to top
Grapefruit twist, for garnish

**1.** In a cocktail shaker filled with one small piece of ice, shake together all ingredients except the club soda and grapefruit twist.

**2.** Strain into a Collins glass, add ice and top with the club soda. Garnish with the grapefruit twist.

## THE ERIN
### Adapted from TOBY CECCHINI, the Long Island Bar, Brooklyn

*Toby Cecchini, the bartending innovator, owner of the Long Island Bar in Brooklyn, discovered the French liqueur company Giffard almost a decade ago at a cocktail convention in London and marveled how the "heavenly aromas" of its products outdid everything he had come across in the States. His favorite, Bigallet Viriana China China, became widely available last year. "It's just great," he says. "It's super quinine-bitter with an orange overlay." Cecchini uses Bigallet in an off-the-menu cocktail he calls the Erin.*

2 ounces bourbon (preferably Evan Williams Single Barrel)
½ ounce Bigallet Viriana China China
½ ounce sweet vermouth (preferably Cinzano)

½ ounce Suze
3 dashes Angostura bitters
3 dashes pimento bitters
Orange twist, for garnish

**1.** In a mixing glass filled with ice, stir together all ingredients except the orange twist.

**2.** Strain the mixture into a rocks glass and add ice. Garnish with an orange twist.

## THE CORONATION
### Adapted from JOAQUÍN SIMÓ, Pouring Ribbons, New York City

*Sherry might seem stuffy, but Joaquín Simó, the co-founder of Pouring Ribbons in the East Village, has had a soft spot for the stuff since discovering it as an undergrad. During the five years he tended bar at Death and Company, his interest became an obsession. He began using it often as an alternative to vermouth. "I find it tremendously versatile," he says. "There's room for it to play nicely with a lot of savory spirits like aquavit or mezcal, even reposado tequila."*

1½ ounces fino sherry (preferably Lustau Puerto Fino)

1½ ounces dry vermouth (preferably suggests Dolin)

1 teaspoon Luxardo cherry liqueur

1 teaspoon simple syrup (page 27)

2 dashes orange bitters

Lemon twist, for garnish

**1.** In a tall glass filled with ice, stir together all ingredients except the lemon twist.

**2.** Strain into a cocktail glass and garnish with the lemon twist.

## SOM COLLINS
### Adapted from JEFF BELL, PDT, New York City

*When the Thai restaurant Pok Pok introduced Som, its house-made drinking vinegar, Jeff Bell, the head bartender at the East Village speakeasy PDT, was instantly hooked by its powerfully tart flavor. "It's flavorful but delicate enough that it can be stirred," he says. "I think it's perfect with citrus and soda. I love it with the bubbles." PDT recently unveiled the Som Collins, its new warm weather cocktail. In Japan, Bell says, "Number one is beer, number two is shochu and sake and number three is whiskey. So I wanted to incorporate all three of those things in a drink." The Som ties the whole cocktail together.*

2 ounces Captain Lawrence Liquid Gold ale

1½ ounces Irish whiskey (preferably Jameson)

½ ounce Ume no Yado yuzu sake

½ ounce Pok Pok honey Som

2 dashes orange bitters (preferably Dutch's Colonial)

Shiso leaf, for garnish

**1.** In a tall glass filled with ice, stir together all ingredients except the shiso leaf.

**2.** Strain the mixture into a Collins glass and add ice. Garnish with a shiso leaf.

## HANKY PANKY
### Adapted from MEAGHAN DORMAN, Raines Law Room, New York City

*The Hanky Panky, a concoction of gin, vermouth and fernet, first originated at the Savoy Hotel in London. "It's a cross between a martini and a Manhattan," says Meaghan Dorman, the head bartender at Raines Law Room. Her enthusiasm for the cocktail has led her to scrutinize every ingredient. Her secret? Cocchi Vermouth di Torino. "It's not as viscous and a little chocolatey, so it just kind of lets the fernet and the gin sing," she says. "It's rich without being sugary."*

1½ ounces Plymouth gin

1½ ounces Cocchi Vermouth di Torino

¼ ounce Fernet Branca

Orange twist, for garnish

**1.** In a mixing glass filled with ice, stir together all ingredients except the orange twist.

**2.** Strain the mixture into a cocktail glass and garnish with the orange twist.

## THE SUMMER PUNCHING
### Adapted from DOMINIC VENEGAS, NoMad, New York City

*Recently, Dominic Venegas, the bar director at Gallagher's Steakhouse in Midtown Manhattan, has been obsessed with punch. The one ingredient all good punches have in common: oleo saccharum. Just a fancy term for citrus oil and sugar, oleo saccharum is a simple paste to make (see the below recipe) and adds a tart backbone to any punch. You can combine oleo saccharum with juice to make an authentic cordial for gimlets or with hot water to make a flavored syrup that's great for cocktails or iced tea.*

YIELD: 20 DRINKS

1 (750 milliliter) bottle silver tequila (preferably Clase Azul)

1 750 milliliter bottle Pama pomegranate liqueur

24 ounces seltzer water

10 ounces grapefruit juice

3 ounces lemon juice*

6 ounces grapefruit strawberry oleo saccharum (more or less, to taste; recipe follows)

Grapefruit and lemon slices, for garnish

**1.** Pour all of the ingredients except the oleo saccharum and citrus garnishes into a large punch bowl.

**2.** Slowly stir in the oleo saccharum, a little a time, until the punch reaches the desired sweetness.

**3.** Add the grapefruit and lemon slices, spreading them out across the punch.

**4.** Just before guests arrive, add ice.

**Venegas prepares the punch way ahead of time by ladling some of it into ice-cube trays to freeze and use instead of ice cubes. This prevents dilution, and adding fresh berries to the trays before freezing makes for a nice presentation.**

## GRAPEFRUIT STRAWBERRY OLEO SACCHARUM

2 star ruby grapefruits
2 cups sugar

8 strawberries

**1.** Using a vegetable peeler, remove the skin from the grapefruits, avoiding the pith.

**2.** Place the skins in a glass bowl and add the sugar. Lightly muddle the mixture to help release the grapefruit oils.

**3.** Allow the mixture to sit overnight, stirring every now and then (no need to wake up in the middle of the night to stir).

**4.** When it becomes a thick paste, remove the grapefruit skins and set aside. Once dry, the peels can then be eaten as is, or used as a garnish for drinks or a dessert.

**5.** Thinly slice the strawberries, add to the paste and let sit for a couple more hours.

**6.** It's ready to use when the strawberries have partially dissolved and the paste turns a vibrant pink color.

*May 8, 2014*

## MOUNT VERNON
By JEFF GORDINIER

| | |
|---|---|
| 1 ounce Clear Creek Kirschwasser | ½ ounce Lustau Pedro Ximenez sherry |
| 1 ounce Gran Duque d'Alba Brandy de Jerez | ½ ounce Cherry Heering |
| ¾ ounce grapefruit juice | 3 brandied cherries, for garnish |

**1.** Shake all the ingredients except the cherries with ice.

**2.** Strain into a chilled glass and garnish with the cherries on a pick.

*December 6, 2011*

# SLOE GIN IS BACK, BUT HOLD THE FIZZ
## By JONATHAN MILES

It hasn't been easy, in America, to love sloe gin. Once a barman's delicacy, both here and abroad, the gin-based liqueur—which takes its name and bittersweet flavor from the infusion of sloe berries, the purplish fruit of a wild shrub native to England—suffered a long, painful decline in the United States, when the import market dried up. American distillers filled the gap with mass-produced imitations that, according to the author and bartender Toby Cecchini, evoke grenadine spiked with grain alcohol.

Mention sloe gin to most anyone under 40, and you'll usually get a blank stare; mention it to anyone over 40, and the reaction tends to be a wince followed by an epic hangover tale that tends to involve Alabama Slammers, spring break and occasionally a night in jail.

Despairing of the absence of sloe gins that he'd tasted in Britain, where artisanal sloe gins are as common as limoncellos in Italy, Mr. Cecchini went so far as to make his own last year, steeping sloe-like Atlantic beach plums in gin while visiting Cape Cod. It took six months to get the flavor right. That's love. But that's tough love.

Loving sloe became a whole lot easier two weeks ago, however, when Plymouth Sloe Gin—a bona fide sloe gin from the English producers of Plymouth gin, and distilled from an 1883 recipe—arrived in bars and retail stores.

Plymouth is exporting about 1,000 cases to the United States, primarily due to demand from "the new experimental bartenders looking back to old cocktails," said Simon Ford, a British bartender and Plymouth brand ambassador.

Sloe gin drinkers accustomed to the downscale versions sold in liquor stores beside those trippy neon-colored cordials might be startled. It's still sweet, befitting its liqueur status, but not nearly sweet enough to use as an ice cream topping, as the narrator of Ralph Ellison's "Invisible Man" was fond of doing; the sweetness is offset by a bitter tang, like that of an unripe plum.

"It's almost like a serious liqueur," said Naren Young, the mixologist at the West Village restaurant Bobo, who added a sloe gin drink to his cocktail list last Friday.

The drink is the Wibble, a "modern classic from 1990's London," Mr. Young said, that was invented by the London bartender Dick Bradsell. A mixture of gin, sloe gin, grapefruit and lemon juices and a blood-red ripple of black-currant liqueur, it's a bravura cocktail for highlighting sloe gin's tart depths, which get sandwiched between the juniper flavors of the gin and the sweet berry notes of the black-currant liqueur.

Mr. Young calls it a "simple and balanced drink," which would be mere boilerplate if applied to most cocktails. But it's been an awfully long time here, since sloe gin was involved in anything simple and balanced—not to mention, lovable.

## WIBBLE
### Adapted from BOBO, New York City

1 ounce gin
1 ounce Plymouth Sloe Gin liqueur
½ ounce crème de cassis

¾ ounce fresh grapefruit juice
½ ounce fresh lemon juice

**1.** Combine all ingredients and shake.

**2.** Strain into a chilled glass and serve.

*June 15, 2008*

## THE SAID AND DONE
### Adapted from MARCINE FRANCKOWIAK, St. Mazie, Brooklyn, N.Y., by Rosie Schaap

1 small piece of fresh peeled ginger
1½ ounces gin
½ ounce fresh lemon juice
½ ounce simple syrup (page 27)

1 ounce orange juice
2 dashes orange bitters
Soda water
Orange twist, for garnish

**1.** Muddle the ginger in a mixing glass. Add ice and all other ingredients except soda water and orange twist and shake.

**2.** Pour into a Collins glass and top with a splash of soda water. Garnish with the orange twist.

*October 14, 2012*

MR. OCTOBER FROM JAKEWALK

## MR. OCTOBER
Adapted from TIMOTHY MINER, The JakeWalk, Brooklyn, N.Y., by Robert Simonson

**FOR THE CINNAMON SYRUP:**
 1 cup sugar
 3 cinnamon sticks
**FOR THE DRINK:**
 1½ ounces Laird's bonded apple brandy

(be certain it's the bonded version)
¾ ounce fresh lemon juice
½ ounce Galliano liqueur
2 dashes St. Elizabeth Allspice Dram
Pinch of ground nutmeg

**1.** Make the syrup: Combine the sugar, cinnamon and 1 cup water in a small pan over medium heat. Let simmer about 15 minutes. Strain. Allow syrup to cool before using. (Can be refrigerated.)

**2.** Mix the drink: In a shaker with ice, put ¾ ounce of the cinnamon syrup with the apple brandy, lemon juice, liqueur and allspice dram and shake. Double strain into chilled cocktail glass. Dust with nutmeg.

*November 13, 2012*

## CRYSTAL FALL
Adapted from JULIE REINER, Clover Club, Brooklyn, N.Y., by Robert Simonson

1 teaspoon simple syrup (page 27)
1½ ounces Cognac (preferably Pierre Ferrand 1840)
½ ounce Lemon Hart Demerara rum
¼ ounce palo cortado sherry (preferably Lustau)

¼ ounce ginger syrup (see note below)
¾ ounce fresh apple cider
½ ounce fresh lemon juice
1 dash Angostura bitters
Apple slice, for garnish

**1.** In a shaker half-filled with ice, combine all ingredients except apple slice and shake.

**2.** Strain over crushed ice into a double rocks glass and garnish the apple slice.

*November 13, 2012*

## PETER, PETER PUMPKIN EATER
Adapted from JOHNNY SWET, The Skylark, New York City

2 ounces Laird's Bonded Apple Brandy
1 ounce Tawny Port
2 spoons pumpkin butter

2 dashes orange bitters
Orange twist, for garnish

**1.** Shake all ingredients except orange twist in a cocktail shaker with ice.

**2.** Strain into snifter with cubed ice and garnish with sunken (submerged) orange twist on the side.

*October 23, 2014*

## BUFALA NEGRA

**Adapted from JOHN GRECO, Philip Marie, New York City, by Florence Fabricant**

*At Philip Marie in Greenwich Village, John Greco uses ginger beer to top a bourbon cocktail seasoned with a splash of good balsamic vinegar, a slight variation on the original made with balsamic syrup and ginger ale, which was created by Jerry Slater of H. Harper Station in Atlanta.*

½ teaspoon turbinado sugar

1 teaspoon good aged balsamic vinegar

5 basil leaves

1 ½ ounces bourbon

2 ounces ginger beer

**1.** Muddle sugar, vinegar and 4 basil leaves in a cocktail shaker. Add bourbon and ice and shake to dissolve sugar.

**2.** Strain over ice into old-fashioned glass, top with ginger beer and garnish with remaining basil leaf.

*April 30, 2014*

## HORSE'S NECK

**Adapted from the CAMPBELL APARTMENT, New York City, by William L. Hamilton**

2 ounces bourbon, rye whiskey or brandy

3 dashes bitters

Ginger ale (about 6 ounces)

Orange twist, for garnish

**1.** Pour bourbon, rye whiskey or brandy and the bitters into an 11-ounce highball glass filled with ice.

**2.** Add bitters and top off with ginger ale. Lightly stir and garnish with orange twist.

*November 7, 2004*

KENNETH MCCLURE MAKES A HORSE'S NECK

## DELFT BLUE COCKTAIL
By FLORENCE FABRICANT

| | |
|---|---|
| 1 cup blueberries | 1 tablespoon limoncello |
| 2 tablespoons sugar | Dash bitters |
| 2 grinds black pepper | Strip of lemon peel, for garnish |
| 2 ounces genever | |

**1.** Combine blueberries, sugar and pepper in a small saucepan and cook over medium heat until berries collapse and release their juices, about 5 minutes. Force through a sieve into a metal bowl. Place metal bowl in a bowl of ice and water to chill the mixture. This will make enough blueberry syrup for four drinks.

**2.** or a single drink, place genever in a cocktail shaker. Add 2 tablespoons blueberry syrup, the limoncello and bitters. Add ice, shake and pour into cocktail glass. Serve straight up or on the rocks with a twist.

*September 24, 2008*

## COCOA-CURRANT COCKTAIL
Adapted from ARROWS RESTAURANT by Jonathan Miles

| | |
|---|---|
| 1 teaspoon cocoa-infused simple syrup (see below) | ¼ ounce freshly squeezed lemon juice |
| Lemon wedge and cocoa powder, for rimming the glass | 1 small scoop red currant sorbet (or raspberry sorbet) |
| 2 ounces gin | Edible flower, for garnish (optional) |

**1.** To make cocoa-infused simple syrup, combine ½ cup water and ½ cup sugar in a saucepan over high heat; bring to a boil, and cook until sugar is dissolved. Stir in 1 ½ teaspoons cocoa powder and let cool. Chill until ready to use.

**2.** Rim a chilled cocktail glass by swabbing the exterior of the rim with a wedge of lemon, then rolling the rim in cocoa powder to coat evenly. Shake off excess.

**3.** Combine infused simple syrup, lemon juice and sorbet in a cocktail shaker with ice, and shake.

**4.** Strain into the prepared glass, and garnish with the flower.

*September 20, 2009*

## AUTUMN BONFIRE
By ROSIE SCHAAP

*My Scotch-whisky-inflected alternative to a Jack Rose.*

| | |
|---|---|
| 1 ounce nonalcoholic apple cider or juice | 1 scant teaspoon maple syrup |
| 1 ounce applejack | 2 dashes bitters (preferably Brooklyn Hemispherical Black Mission Fig, but Angostura works, too) |
| 1 ounce smoky Scottish whisky (preferably Bowmore 12) | |

**1.** Combine all ingredients in a mixing glass with ice. Stir for 30 seconds.

**2.** Strain into a cocktail glass (or serve over fresh ice in a rocks glass). Garnish with an apple fan or a slice of apple.

*November 8, 2012*

# SMOKY SUNRISE

## By WILLIAM L. HAMILTON

Scotch has a problem with women. Men account for 80 percent of those who drink Scotch whiskey in the United States. Last year, Dewar's, the only Scotch that sells over a million cases annually in the United States, enlisted Playboy Enterprises in a major marketing campaign—a series of Vegas-style lounge parties with bunnies and club keys that recalled the days when "Scotch was king," Dewar's explained.

But when is a Rat Pack just a bunch of rats?

"It's about sophistication, not being a Neanderthal," said Charles Ho, marketing manager for Dewar's, after a hard laugh, man to man, at the question.

Think of the Vamp as a bit of sensitivity training. Dewar's asked Julie Reiner, an owner of the Flatiron Lounge on West 19th Street, to invent a Scotch cocktail. The classic, the rob roy, which is Scotch and vermouth, hadn't had a date in a while, and Dewar's, which sponsors tastings for graduate students—its 20-to-30-something demographic target—started seeing women show up last year, to the tune of 50 percent. Bartenders were telling the company that women were bored with the cosmopolitan and other women's drinks. Dewar's, a "brown liquor" staple whose reign took a hit in the 1980's when vodka ascended, got thirsty for sales.

"There are close to four million new adults entering the market each year, and that includes women," said Frank Walters, director of research at M. Shanken Communications, a beverage research company in New York, speaking of what he called a baby boomlet that will continue until 2012.

And that means drinkers.

On Wednesday evening, the Flatiron Lounge, which has an Art Deco theme, looked like a speakeasy open to the sidewalk. The Vamp isn't on the menu yet; you have to ask for it—a kind of "Sam's sister sent me" knock on the door.

The drink is Scotch and fresh orange juice, smoky but citrusy too, like having a cigarette with breakfast. Because it's bunnies and not rats getting the pitch now, Dewar's is promoting Scotch as carbohydrate-free, and the Vamp as lower in sugar than sweeter "women's drinks." But because it's people braced on bar stools and not weight machines, that's nice but not the point.

Ms. Reiner, a friendly woman who has the experienced patience of a bartender, said that the politics of cocktails and "how women don't really drink Scotch" annoyed her. "It's not that women don't drink Scotch," she explained. "Women come in and order a Macallan '12' neat, single malt, all the time. It's just that more men drink Scotch."

Her voice took on a mild "make my day" tone.

"Do you know how many men walk up to my bar and order a cosmopolitan?" she said.

## THE VAMP
**Adapted from the FLATIRON LOUNGE, New York City**

2 ounces Scotch (preferably Dewar's White Label)

½ ounce orange liqueur (preferably Gran Gala)

2 ounces orange juice

½ ounce fresh lemon juice

2 dashes of Angostura bitters

Flamed orange peel, for garnish

**1.** Shake all ingredients except orange peel in a bar glass.

**2.** Strain into a wine glass over ice and garnish with a flamed orange peel.

*June 22, 2003*

# GO DEEPER INTO MEXICO WITH MEZCAL
## By FLORENCE FABRICANT

Mezcal, tequila's brash, more rustic cousin, is crashing the cocktail party, showing up in the kind of mixed drinks normally made with more-refined spirits.

Until fairly recently, mezcal was an esoteric choice, but it is becoming more mainstream as drinkers come to appreciate how it gives smoke and swagger to a drink, never retreating to the background no matter how much fruit juice and sugar are piled into the mix.

Even in a margarita, like the one they make at Hecho en Dumbo in NoHo, it adds the kind of complexity and intrigue that is often lacking when the cocktail is made with many of today's overrefined tequilas.

For those who are new to the spirit, a margarita is a sensible place to start. "Everyone is familiar with a margarita, and it's a good way to showcase mescal" said Ethan Smith, an owner and the mixologist at the restaurant Hecho en Dumbo.

Brian Van Flandern of Creative Cocktail Consultants has come up with a drink that suggests a margarita, and could serve as a set of training wheels. It's called the Smoking Jacket, and includes both mezcal and tequila. You can adjust the proportions of either spirit depending on how much mezcal personality you want.

"Mezcal has real flavor, and it's much more terroir-driven," Mr. Van Flandern said.

Both mezcal and tequila are made from agave, a succulent plant. But unlike tequila, the best of which is made with 100 percent blue agave, mezcal can be made from any of nearly 30 types of agave. The piñas, or cores, are usually smoked in open pits, not steamed as for tequila.

In his new book, "Craft Cocktails" Mr. Van Flandern offers several mezcal concoctions, including the Rum and Smoke, in which he ramps up the smokiness with a splash of Lagavulin Scotch. Mezcal partners well with whiskey, especially Scotch and blended spirits. And certain fruits, notably orange and pineapple, seem tailor-made for it. A whiff of heat, from either pepper or chile, is not a mistake, either.

And don't think of these drinks as just a pairing for a plate of tacos, tamales or queso fundido. At Fresh Hamptons—a Bridgehampton, N.Y., restaurant that emphasizes local food and nods toward Asia, not Mexico— the mixologist, Douglas Sheehan, combines reposado mezcal with fresh pineapple juice, honey, chile and lime. His finishing touch is a dusting of crushed pink peppercorns that add fruit and fire to the well-balanced cocktail. He calls it They Didn't Burn Rome in a Day.

## LA CANADIENSE
Adapted from HECHO EN DUMBO, New York City

2 ounces Canadian whiskey
1 ounce joven mezcal
½ ounce maple syrup

1 dash apple bitters
1 dash old-fashioned bitters (preferably Fee Brothers)
Strip of peel from ½ orange

**1.** In a small pitcher, stir together whiskey, mezcal, maple syrup and bitters. Add peel and muddle.

**2.** Pour over rocks in a double old-fashioned glass.

## THEY DIDN'T BURN ROME IN A DAY
Adapted from DOUGLAS SHEEHAN, Fresh Hamptons, Bridgehampton, N.Y.

¼ ripe pineapple, peeled, cored and chopped
1 teaspoon honey, preferably raw
1½ teaspoons pink peppercorns, crushed in a mortar

4 ounces reposado mescal (preferably Ilegal)
6 dashes chile-flavored bitters, preferably habañero
½ ounce fresh lime juice

**1.** Purée pineapple in a food processor. Force purée through a fine strainer or chinois. You should have a half-cup of juice. Place in a large cocktail shaker with honey and all but a couple of pinches of the peppercorns. Add mezcal, bitters and lime juice.

**2.** Add ice, shake and strain over ice into double rocks glasses. Dust with reserved pink peppercorns.

*September 26, 2013*

## PEARL OF PUEBLA
Adapted from JIM MEEHAN, PDT, New York City

⅛ ounce agave syrup (see below)
¾ ounce fresh lime juice
4 sprigs fresh oregano

2 ounces Sombra mescal
¾ ounce yellow Chartreuse
⅛ ounce Ricard pastis

**1.** To make the agave syrup, combine equal parts agave nectar and water.

**2.** Muddle lime juice, agave syrup and oregano in a mixing glass. Add remaining ingredients, along with ice, and shake.

**3.** Double-strain into a chilled cocktail glass.

*April 3, 2009*

## DUKE OF BEDFORD
Adapted from the LITTLE OWL, New York City, by Jonathan Miles

3 ounces Dry Sack sherry
6 mint leaves, crushed
1 ounce San Pellegrino Aranciata or orange soda

1 teaspoon sugar
Dash of Angostura bitters
Mint sprig and cucumber slice, for garnish

**1.** Fill a rocks glass with crushed ice. In a cocktail shaker, muddle the sherry and mint, then add the Aranciata, sugar and bitters and shake well.

**2.** Strain over the ice and garnish with the mint and cucumber.

*October 22, 2006*

## THE FOX AND THE GRAPES
By ROSIE SCHAAP

*Here, gin (plus pisco and a splash of absinthe) works perfectly with sweet, diminutive Concord grapes, garnished with the edible purple-blue flower of the licoricey hyssop plant, a member of the mint family. Check the farmers' market or a local nursery for the plant.*

¼ cup small, sweet grapes
1 teaspoon honey
Splash of absinthe
1½ ounces London dry gin

1½ ounces pisco
Club soda
Hyssop flower, for garnish

**1.** Muddle grapes gently with honey in a highball glass.

**2.** Fill the glass with ice and add absinthe to lightly coat.

**3.** Add gin and pisco, top with club soda and stir. Garnish with hyssop.

*September 5, 2013*

# MOLECULAR THEORY

## By JONATHAN MILES

Dushan Zaric has a theory. Actually, Mr. Zaric, an owner of the West Village cocktailery Employees Only, has lots of theories. Some of them, on the subject of human mating rituals as they pertain to drinking, are collected in a recent book, "You Didn't Hear It From Us," that Mr. Zaric wrote with his fellow Employees Only owner Jason Kosmas.

But recently, Mr. Zaric divulged his latest theory to me at the bar, which is the best place to hear his or any other theories, particularly ones involving the metaphysics of cocktails. I had merely stopped in for a bit of bourbon, because Employees Only had just added a sublime version of the vintage bourbon-based Millionaire cocktail to its menu, but these things happen.

"We did this experiment inspired by a Japanese photographer named Masaru Emoto," said Mr. Zaric, a native of Belgrade whose clean-shaven head, jangling hoop earrings and dramatic flair with a cocktail shaker lend him the air of an Old World magician.

"By taking photos of frozen water molecules, Emoto found there was a difference in the crystal structures of water that had been blessed with prayer and water that hadn't," Mr. Zaric said. "You can see it—the crystals of the blessed water form these

most beautiful shapes. That got me to thinking. What's the effect of my state of mind on all these molecules that I'm manipulating?"

He waved a hand at the bottles arrayed behind the bar, an alcoholic periodic table. "So we conducted this experiment. Five bartenders, all making the same drink. A daiquiri. Measured pours. The same ice. And the drinks were all different. We repeated the experiment many times, and always the same result."

"We cannot know why this is," Mr. Zaric said. "We can only observe the consequences." But Mr. Zaric has a theory, of course. "If the bartender is relaxed and confident the drink will taste one way," he said, pausing to shake a martini. "If he's anxious, if his buttons are being pushed, the drink will taste another. The bartender doesn't want to make you a bad drink—it just comes out that way."

Mr. Zaric and company christened their version of the Millionaire cocktail—in which bourbon is shaken with a bitter dash of absinthe substitute and sweetened with house-made grenadine—the Billionaire cocktail.

How to account for the considerable difference of 999 million? Mr. Zaric would say it's all in the attitude. "Why did my grandmother's food taste so good?" he said. "Because she wanted to please me."

## BILLIONAIRE COCKTAIL
Adapted from EMPLOYEES ONLY, New York City

2 ounces Baker's 107-proof bourbon
1 ounce fresh-squeezed lemon juice
¾ ounce simple syrup (page 27)
¼ ounce Absente, Herbsaint or other

absinthe substitute
½ ounce homemade grenadine syrup (see recipe below)
Lemon wheel, for garnish

**1.** Combine all ingredients except lemon wheel in a cocktail shaker with ice and shake vigorously.

**2.** Strain into a chilled cocktail glass and garnish with the lemon.

## GRENADINE SYRUP

1 liter pomegranate juice
6 ounces aged Spanish brandy

1 cup sugar

**1.** Combine pomegranate juice, Spanish brandy and sugar in a saucepan and reduce over medium heat until syrupy. Let cool completely, then refrigerate. The syrup will keep for up to three months.

*March 4, 2007*

# GRUFF BUT LOVABLE
## By WILLIAM L. HAMILTON

If you want to get a man to do something, dare him to do it. I would say that's the operational theory behind the Bone, the house drink at the Chickenbone Cafe on the south side of Williamsburg, in Brooklyn.

The Bone, shaken with ice and served straight up in a tall, thin shot glass, is rye whiskey, lime juice, a little sugar and several muscular dashes of Tabasco sauce. It sounds like a chest-hair cocktail.

"It took me a while to get around to trying it, let's put it that way," said the Bone's inventor, David Wondrich. Mr. Wondrich, who writes about cocktails, advised Zak Pelaccio, the cafe's chef and a friend, on the drinks list.

You can imagine the Chickenbone's art-community patrons mixing at the bar with the "locals" (art-community people like to do that) and downing a couple of Bones, shouting, "Break a bone!" before they knock each fiery cannonball back.

"Dave came over to my house one night, and we basically played around with booze for a while," Mr. Pelaccio said. "We figured doing the martini thing was overplayed, so we concentrated on the darker liquors. You have this image of the south side being harder, grungier—not pink drinks out of martini glasses. We wanted something a little more butch."

Mr. Wondrich said that he got the idea for rye whiskey dosed with Tabasco sauce from a book of hard-luck stories, "Tales of the Ex-Tanks," which purports to be the "minutes" of the Harlem Club of Former Alcoholic Degenerates, written by Clarence Louis Cullen, a New York Sun reporter, and published in 1900.

As if the Bone didn't have enough testosterone on its own, the bar menu offers the Bone With Beef—a side of smoked beef with chilies to chase it. That's a sex change, not a cocktail.

But the bad Bone has a big secret. It's a pussycat when met, like a prizefighter around children. In its 2 1/4-ounce glass, the cocktail comes on like a slugger, but it's gentle at heart. Because of the lime juice and sugar, it will dance you affectionately around the ring before it knocks you out.

The waiter who served me a Bone on Wednesday night said the drink is popular, in part, because it's also "the cheapest thing on the menu." Stingers are daiquiris are $8—the Bone weighs in at $6. Mr. Pelaccio said the cafe shares the building with rehearsal studios. Musicians stop in between late-night sets and split the difference in price with "a Bone and a $2 Pabst."

Mr. Wondrich, its creator, advised getting the cocktail as cold as possible, then straining it—and shooting.

"It's to be consumed quickly," he said, as though he were describing something experimental. "It's not a four-sipper."

What's the matter, guy? Scared?

## THE BONE
**Adapted from the CHICKENBONE CAFÉ, Brooklyn, N.Y.**

| | |
|---|---|
| 2 ounces of Wild Turkey rye | ¾ teaspoon of superfine sugar |
| 1 teaspoon of fresh lime juice | 2 dashes of Tabasco sauce |

**1.** Mix all ingredients in a cocktail shaker with ice and shake well.

**2.** Serve straight up in a shot glass.

*May 11, 2003*

# VODKA DEAD? NOT SO FAST
## By JONATHAN MILES

When Nathan Freeburg is sizing up a bar, he looks for a few crucial signposts of quality: fresh juices, rather than pre-made sour mix; bottled bitters and chilled glasses in evidence; and the bartenders' use of jiggers, to measure a drink's ingredients. Oh, and one more thing: "A lack of vodka."

"The basic problem with vodka," said Mr. Freeburg, a 34-year-old former lawyer who is now an Army captain stationed at Fort Hood, Tex., "is that it's inherently flavorless, so all that it brings to a cocktail is alcohol."

"That's good if you're trying to get drunk," he said, "but not if you believe that every ingredient should bring something to the whole."

Mr. Freeburg is hardly alone in snubbing vodka, the ubiquitous spirit that many credit with jump-starting the cocktail revival in the 1990's. Not that long ago, vodka drinks—fruity, sweet, garishly colorful—tended to dominate cocktail lists, especially at nightclubs. But check out the drinks menu at Griffin, a club on Gansevoort Street in the meatpacking district. There's just a single vodka drink on the list.

A Web site entitled the End of Vodka (theendofvodka.com), hosted by the makers of an açaí-flavored liqueur called VeeV, spitefully depicts vodka drinkers as "vodka bots"—like the suited hedge-fund type, animated on the site, chanting "models and bottles," or the miniskirted blonde who bubbles "girls' night out!"

Some bartenders, like Damon Dunay at Delicatessen in SoHo, will actually try to steer patrons away from ordering vodka, just as Mr. Dunay, a reformed vodka bot, was once redirected by a bartender. Even The Wall Street Journal has jumped aboard, deeming vodka "passé."

The "tofu of the bar"—as Paul Clarke, a cocktail blogger, calls vodka—appears to be losing its once-mighty cachet (if not, however, its dominant market share). An instant relic, perhaps, of the dissipated boom times (Trump vodka, anyone? ... Anyone?). Or maybe a victim of America's savvier taste buds. To hear some people talk, either way, it's time to consign vodka to the same mock-worthy bin as white zinfandel, and be done with it.

But not so fast. Vodka may have been overexposed, overmarketed and overpoured. But it doesn't warrant scorn. Consider the sublime RTR Classics on the menu at the Russian Tea Room, where vodka is often used, as in the Gorki, to soften and lengthen the potent flavor of spirits like Bénédictine. Or the Colony cocktail, an antique from 1950s Manhattan revived by the bartender Dale DeGroff, in which vodka meets Southern Comfort and lime juice. Or the Atomic cocktail, another '50s throwback, this one from Las Vegas, exhumed by the cocktail writer David Wondrich.

It's everything that the go-go vodka drinks of the '90s and early '00s weren't—balanced, complex, timeless, as mellow and elegant as a Nelson Riddle arrangement. Yet it's still, proudly, a vodka drink, even if the vodka plays a supporting role, rather than a star turn.

"For me," Mr. Wondrich said, "once vodka starts playing nice, and doesn't push other bottles off the bar, it's welcome to stay there."

## ATOMIC COCKTAIL
**Adapted from DAVID WONDRICH**

| | |
|---|---|
| 1 ½ ounces vodka | 1 teaspoon medium amontillado sherry |
| 1 ½ ounces V.S.O.P. Cognac | 1 ½ ounces cold Champagne |

**1.** Add the vodka, Cognac and sherry to a mixing glass with ice, and stir.

**2.** Strain into a chilled cocktail glass and top with the Champagne.

*May 3, 2009*

# AN ELEGANT SPACE, COCKTAILS TO MATCH
## By STEVE REDDICLIFFE

Del Posto, the Italian restaurant owned by Mario Batali, Lidia Bastianich and Joe Bastianich, is inarguably spacious: 18-foot-high ceilings, 11,000 square feet for dining, only 35 tables in the main rooms, all of them seemingly occupied throughout the night by guests venturing through tasting menus of five and eight courses.

It is not, if you go by the numbers, a place where you'd expect to find an intimate spot for cocktails and conversation. But here it is, a destination in its own right, a spot to settle in for a couple of hours. A few of the folks having a drink may be waiting for a table in the dining room, but most of the people in the bar at Del Posto have come expressly to spend time in it.

Customers who sit at the comfortable bar can order from the Del Posto restaurant menus, and often do. The view can include the candles flickering on the stairway between the first and second floors. The piano player on duty supplies the soundtrack for both the bar and the restaurant (it was Kurt Wieting the other night; "Bewitched, Bothered, and Bewildered" was in the mix).

But the bar is probably best experienced at the banquette along the northern border. The seating in this section is chamois-soft leather, and there are more candles on the marble-topped tables. These are gracious surroundings. Patrons in these seats can't use the restaurant menu, but there are four interesting options on a snack list—sometimes among them fried mozzarella, or the chickpea fritters called farinata—and everyone gets a complimentary tray of crunchy things that recently included house-made potato chips, a riff on a Chex mix with plenty of pistachios, and taralli crackers with tomato powder and Parmigiano.

Matthew Silverstein, the head bartender who oversees the room, sets an easy pace. He and the staff are attentive but not hovering, and seem to know intuitively when you would like another drink or a few more of those chips (in the case of the chips, that would be always).

Del Posto is renowned for its voluminous wine list, so it's not a surprise that the bar offerings may include selections from the owners' wineries, La Mozza and Bastianich. The beers are well chosen as well, among them Menabrea lager and two Lurisia ales from Italy and the King Titus porter from Maine Beer Company. Budgeting advisory: Prices can be steep. A glass of the Bastianich Vespa Rossi goes for $25, and every beer but the Menabrea ($9) is double digits.

The cocktails, ranging from $13 to $25, are more memorable expressions of both the bar's personality and creativity. You can do a nice rum run here, beginning with the Depaz Doctor, Mr. Silverstein's delicious variation on the venerable Doctor Cocktail, with Depaz rum from Martinique, Kronan Swedish punsch (a principal component of which is the spirit Batavia arrack, made with sugar cane and red rice), lime juice and merlot grape juice, followed by the plushly flavored Midnight Plum, with Blackwell rum, Urban Moonshine organic maple bitters, maple syrup and the Hungarian herbal liqueur called Unicum Plum.

On the classic side of the menu is a sure-handed rendition of the Avenue, the definitive recipe for which appeared in William Tarling's "Café Royal Cocktail Book" in 1937. Here it is made with Michter's bourbon, Busnel Calvados, passion fruit purée, orange flower water, fresh lemon juice and the bar's own grenadine.

It's always advisable to end a night on a high note, and at Del Posto, that's provided by the barrel-aged Negroni: Plymouth gin, Cinzano sweet vermouth and Campari, all of which spend six weeks in a bourbon cask from the Tuthilltown distillery in Gardiner, N.Y.

Mr. Silverstein is an enthusiast of this Negroni, and justifiably so. It's a fantastic cocktail. The aging gives it "top notes of vanilla and spice," he said one evening, and then recommended a visit to a blog by Jeffery Morgenthaler, a bartender in Portland, Ore., and an advocate of barrel aging, who wrote that the process produced a "beauty" of a drink, "the finish long and lingering with oak tannins."

The bar at Del Posto is an ideal place to verify the validity of that finding.

## THE MIDNIGHT PLUM
### Adapted from ESTELLE BOSSY, Del Posto, New York City

*The Midnight Plum was inspired by the Toronto (rye, Fernet Branca and sugar), and is essentially an Old Fashioned variation, using rum as the base spirit, Unicum Plum, as the bittering agent, and maple syrup as the sweetener. Star anise adds warm spice to this strong, stirred cocktail.*

1 ½ ounces Zwack Unicum Plum Liqueur
1 ½ ounces Blackwell Rum
¼ ounce maple syrup

3 dashes Urban Moonshine Maple Bitters (see sidebar)
Orange twist
1 piece star anise

**1.** Combine Unicum, rum and maple syrup in a mixing glass. Fill mixing glass with ice and stir until chilled.

**2.** Strain over fresh ice in a rocks glass and garnish with orange twist and star anise.

**The bitters are not necessary, but will add a complexity to the flavor.**

*January 23, 2014*

## TOWN PLUM
### Adapted from TOWN BAR, New York City, by William L. Hamilton

1 ½ ounces Cîroc grape vodka
¾ ounce plum nectar
¼ fresh squeezed lime, strained

¼ fresh squeezed lemon, strained
A few purple grapes, halved, for garnish

**1.** Shake all ingredients except grapes in a shaker with ice.

**2.** Pour into a deep tumbler and garnish with grapes. Stir.

*March 16, 2003*

## THE NORMANDY
### Adapted from XAVIER HERIT, Restaurant Daniel, New York City, by Aleksandra Crapanzano

9 fresh cranberries
2 thin slices green apple
1 teaspoon packed dark brown sugar

1 tablespoon lemon juice
1 tablespoon simple syrup (page 27)
1/4 cup good-quality Calvados

**1.** In a cocktail shaker, muddle 6 cranberries, 1 apple slice, the brown sugar and lemon juice. Add the simple syrup, Calvados and a few ice cubes and shake well.

**2.** Strain into a rocks glass filled with ice. Top with the remaining apple slice and 3 cranberries.

*November 23, 2008*

# A CONTEST WHERE VICTORY GOES TO THE COOLEST

## By PETER MEEHAN

We sounded the call and you responded: the Dining section received hundreds of submissions in response to a notice soliciting readers' recipes for the summer cocktail of 2006.

The recipes came from across the country: our runners-up were submitted by a chef in Florida (the Gingino) and a food purveyor in Texas (L'Alhambra). Other entries were from as far afield as Kingston, Ontario, and Berlin. The winning cocktail, the Cuke, was submitted by Adam Frank, a gallery director at the Hosfelt Gallery in New York. In addition to the bragging rights, Mr. Frank will receive a modest selection of books on cocktails as his prize.

Mr. Frank wrote that a Greenmarket trove of tiny English cucumbers "set off a light bulb." In a telephone conversation, he described the drink as a perfect "postbeach" cocktail and, though we did not have the opportunity to sample each of these after a day at the beach, we are disposed to agree with him.

In general, we found that many drinks were too boozy to consider drinking out in the hot sun. Accordingly, the Cuke was one of a number of so-called tall drinks that fared well in our taste test. Many of the better entries had bitter elements (like the amaro in the Gingino) and herbal flavors (mint was the most popular choice); fruity drinks and sweet drinks were generally cloying, flat or both.

Many people nominated classic cocktails like gin and tonics, French 75's and margaritas. The Pimm's Cup, a mix of Pimm's and lemon-lime soda garnished with a cucumber spear, fared well in our tasting (though we preferred a submission from Frank Martinelli, who substituted spicy ginger beer as a mixer).

Suggestively named entries like the Sunsex and the Call Girl were accompanied by sordid stories. Then there were explanations of certain drinks' origins, like a bounty of summer strawberries on Prince Edward Island that inspired a Strawberry-Basil Mojito.

Our favorite story was from Arlene Ball, of Sag Harbor, N.Y. She suggested a toast to her husband, Bill, who introduced himself to her and her to the martini 48 years ago in a New York hotel, and who died last winter. She attributed their long and happy marriage to talking over a gin martini on the rocks every night. And two on Fridays.

Even if the martini is too strong for poolside sipping, Mrs. Ball's sentiments are right on: mix up a batch of cocktails (we strongly endorse pitchers of the Cuke for this purpose), gather your friends around, and raise a toast to summer.

## THE CUKE
**Adapted from ADAM FRANK, Hosfelt Gallery, New York City**
YIELD: 6 DRINKS

| | |
|---|---|
| 6 limes, rinsed | ½ cup sugar |
| 1 cup packed mint leaves, no stems, plus 6 sprigs for garnish | 2 cups vodka or gin, preferably Hendrick's gin |
| 3 unwaxed cucumbers | Sparkling water |

**1.** Thinly slice 3 limes and place in a pitcher. Juice the rest and add juice to pitcher. Add mint leaves. Slice 2 cucumbers and add, then add sugar. Muddle ingredients. Add vodka or gin. Place in refrigerator to steep 30 minutes or longer.

**2.** Peel remaining cucumber and cut lengthwise into 6 spears.

**3.** Fill 6 highball or other large glasses with ice. Strain mixture from pitcher into each. Top with a splash of sparkling water, garnish each glass with a sprig of mint and a cucumber spear, and serve.

*June 21, 2006*

# HASTE MAKES CORDIAL
## By MELISSA CLARK

In a more organized alternative reality that I do not inhabit, I would have thought about the holidays in August. Surrounded by ripe seasonal fruit, I could have turned it into delightful elixirs—nectarine wine, raspberry ratafia—to distribute to my nearest and dearest come December and bring joy to their world.

Sad to say, this holiday gift inspiration bubbled up only a few days ago, long past the prime of peaches and raspberries.

Still, I liked the idea of a homemade libation. It would be a present that nearly everyone on my grown-up list would actually want even more than cookies. And certainly a bottle of my homemade brew would trump everyone else's predictable Champagne-single malt offerings in a far more elegant—and economical—manner.

Since citrus is some of the best fresh fruit available in December, I decided I'd try making a Provençal orange wine I'd read about in Mireille Johnston's classic cookbook "The Cuisine of the Sun" (Fireside, 1990). The recipe was easy. Just mix fresh citrus with white wine, brandy and sugar and let it all macerate.

The problem, I discovered when I dug out the recipe, was the rather biblical 40 days' maceration time.

What I needed was an abridged recipe that I could whip up in an hour and that would be ready in a week.

Alas, Ms. Johnston's text didn't offer any shortcuts. But flipping through the book, I noticed another recipe for an orange ratafia in which the fruit was steeped in brandy (without wine), along with coriander seeds. Ms. Johnston advised drinking this whenever one felt "melancholy, anxious, or even merry—truly wonderful for all occasions."

It seemed ideal. Except that the maceration time was two months.

But the more I thought about it, the more I wondered whether it really needed that much resting time. After all, shouldn't a mixture of citrus juice, good quality booze and sugar taste good from the moment it is made? In fact, isn't that what's known as a cocktail?

I supposed the coriander and orange zest would need some time to infuse. But since alcohol would be a relatively good solvent, maybe a week would do.

And even if my homemade concoction—which I started calling a cordial in my head because I liked the quaint sound of it—wasn't quite ready, I could always keep it for 33 days longer and drink it myself.

At the greengrocer I glimpsed a profusion of citrus more exotic than oranges: pomelos, blood oranges, kumquats. With its alliterative allure, kumquat cordial sounded more intriguing than orange cordial and more euphonious than pomelo cordial, so I bought a box of kumquats.

Then at the liquor store I picked up several bottles to play with: white rum, Cognac and—a nice accompaniment to coriander—gin.

Once at home, I sliced the kumquats very thinly, figuring that smaller pieces would infuse more quickly.

As I was slicing, I remembered that a kumquat's musky flavor was in its thick, fragrant skin and not its minuscule amount of juice. If I want-ed my cordials quickly, I would need supplemental citrus juice. A bowl of clementines on my counter was thus dispatched.

I also decided to experiment with combinations of spices in addition to coriander. With its flowery shape, star anise would look pretty in the decorative bottles I searched out online (at specialtybottle.com), so I added some, along with cinnamon, the coriander and allspice berries.

Then I left the bottles on the counter, giving them a good shake every day to encourage maceration.

A week later, I poured a nip of each. Even in that short time, the cordials had metamorphosed into something deeply perfumed and rich with citrus and spice, overlaid by the distinct flavors of the spirits. There was enough sugar to smooth out the alcohol, but not enough to make it cloying.

The cordials were marvelous on their own, but I could also see topping them with sparkling wine for aperitifs, or boiling water for toddies. And how bad could a drizzle be over vanilla ice cream?

Although I didn't succeed in making the orange ratafia à la Mireille, my cordials fit her description to a T: truly wonderful for all occasions—and all my friends.

# KUMQUAT-CLEMENTINE CORDIAL

YIELD: ABOUT 2 CUPS

¼ cup sugar, preferably superfine

3 tablespoons clementine juice (from 1 or 2 clementines) plus 1 clementine, thinly sliced

6 kumquats, thinly sliced and seeded

1¾ cups white rum (375 milliliters)

3 whole allspice berries

2 whole star anise

**1.** Have a glass bottle with a cork or a jar with a lid ready. Place sugar in a large glass measuring cup or bowl. Stir in 1 tablespoon boiling water for 1 minute. Add clementine juice, and continue stirring until sugar dissolves, about a minute longer.

**2.** If using a jar, place clementine and kumquat slices inside. If using a bottle, you might have to curl slices into cylinders to fit them through neck. Add sugar syrup and remaining ingredients; break star anise in half if necessary to fit into bottle. Close jar lid or cork bottle; keep at room temperature. Shake once a day for one week before serving.

**3.** Serve as is or over ice, or with a splash of seltzer, or topped with chilled white wine or sparkling wine, or as a hot toddy topped with boiling water. Or drizzle over ice cream.

**To make a brandy cordial, substitute brandy for rum, and replace spices with 1 cinnamon stick and 1 whole clove. For a gin version, substitute gin for rum, and replace spices with 3 peppercorns and 6 coriander seeds.**

*December 12, 2007*

WHITE COSMOPOLITAN, FROM DANIEL

## CHAPTER 25

# THE
# COSMOPOLITAN

# CURING THE COSMO BLUES WITH A BRAND NEW TWIST

## By JESSE MCKINLEY

Let's face it: the cosmopolitan is over-exposed. Ever since the four socialites of "Sex and the City" began swilling that pink combination of vodka, cranberry juice and Triple Sec, it seems you can't walk from the bar to the bathroom without tripping over some cosmo-happy drinker clutching a sticky martini glass. Cosmos are everywhere: city bars do them; country bars do them. Even Irish bars do them.

But good bartenders never give up on a drink. The cosmo's plight was exquisitely felt by George Angelet, who tended bar around the city for eight years before becoming an owner at Sugar, a low-key haunt on Church Street in TriBeCa that draws single women in their 20s and the men who ogle them.

"It is the most frustrating drink in the world to make because everybody, all night, everywhere wants one," Mr. Angelet said. "It's just like, 'Oh my God, not another one.'"

So agitated was Mr. Angelet that he made it his mission to find "other cocktails to compete with it." He failed. "You can't stop it," he said. "So eventually I just said, 'If you can't beat 'em, join 'em.'"

His investigations turned instead to finding variations on the cosmo theme. Last year, he introduced a blood orange cosmo at Sugar, using orange purée instead of Triple Sec.

It was good, he said, but still he felt there was something else out there.

And then he found it. Right there on Aisle 12 at the local Key Food: White Cranberry Juice.

Introduced last fall by Ocean Spray, the juice is made with cranberries that are harvested early, hence the lighter color. Experts are divided as to the juice's prospects; www.bevnet.com, a Web site devoted to all things beverage, called it "perhaps the most bland juice known to man."

Where some juice-o-philes saw opportunity missed, Mr. Angelet saw merely opportunity. Replacing the tart red cranberry juice with the slightly sweeter white juice, he created a new breed of cosmo, a cosmo without Triple Sec or heavy exposure on HBO.

The result is a remarkably clear-tasting, slightly sweet cocktail, with a palate-cleansing sensation almost akin to that of a vitamin water. Mr. Angelet garnishes the white cosmo with an edible orchid, which tastes very much as if you're eating a flower. As with a pink cosmo, the taste of alcohol in a white cosmo is almost imperceptible.

Mr. Angelet introduced the drink last month at Sugar, where bartenders have been encouraging patrons to try it.

He said he felt the world was ready for the white cosmo. "Fashion trends show that white is very in," he said. He also said he intends to try to contact the producers of "Sex and the City" to see if he can get his variation on the show. "I think it's something the girls would go for," Mr. Angelet said.

Great. Then he'll just have to invent something else.

## WHITE COSMOPOLITAN
Adapted from GEORGE ANGELET, Sugar, New York City

2 ounces citrus vodka
4 ounces white cranberry juice
1 ounce fresh lime juice
1 ounce sugar water
Edible orchid, if desired, for garnish

**1.** Shake all ingredients with ice.

**2.** Strain into a martini glass and garnish with an edible orchid, if desired.

*June 2, 2002*

## THE DANIEL WHITE COSMOPOLITAN
Adapted from DANIEL, New York City, by Jonathan Miles

2 ounces Snow Queen or other premium vodka
1 ounce St.-Germain elderflower liqueur
½ ounce freshly squeezed lime juice
1 ounce white cranberry juice
1 orchid or edible flower, for garnish (see sidebar)

**1.** Shake the liquid ingredients in a cocktail shaker with ice. and strain into a chilled martini glass.

**2.** Strain into a chilled martini glass and garnish with an orchid or edible flower.

For the garnish, freeze the flower in an ice tray. Fill the tray halfway with water, freeze, and add the flower. Fill completely with water and freeze again. (Spherical ice trays, necessary to replicate Daniel's large ice ball, are available at online retailers. You can also just float an unfrozen flower in the drink.)

*September 2, 2007*

## COSMOPOLITAN
By MARK BITTMAN

*A little more dressy than the working-class vodka cranberry. The cosmopolitan is just that, a little sip of sophistication (and a throw-back to the "Sex and the City" girls).*

1½ tablespoons lime juice
1½ tablespoons triple sec
1 tablespoon cranberry juice
¼ cup vodka
Soda
Orange twist, for garnish

**1.** Add lime juice, triple sec and cranberry juice to the vodka and soda in a shaker and shake.

**2.** Strain into a chilled glass and garnish with the orange twist.

*May 13, 2012*

# NEW BEFORE ITS TIME

## By WILLIAM L. HAMILTON

If New Yorkers had to name their poison, it might be overexposure. No, it's not a cocktail, though it would be a stiff one if it were. It's a strange sort of death wish, to go out as often as possible, to be on the scene and to be seen, and yet not to be too many places too many times. You don't want to get old, as they say.

Of course, New York's got a brilliant solution that keeps people here like a drug. It comes up with new places before you get old in the old ones.

The cosmopolitan was a kind of fast debutante that showed up in the 1980's and 90's—the Cornelia Guest of cocktails. Many people claimed it, like dates who had been dumped at a club. The drink, which took on a life of its own, hit all the right spots, networked with the wonder women of the era, like Madonna and the characters in "Sex and the City"—part empowerment, part buzz-on. It was not for men. It was a way of going out without them, in fact.

Nicole Beland, the author of "The Cocktail Jungle: A Girl's Field Guide to Shaking and Stirring," to be published in May, calls it a "girlie martini."

After the first few trips around the block, the cosmopolitan dropped the basics, which included cranberry juice, and started hitting the wardrobe racks. Outfits became crucial: the ginger cosmo, the plum cosmo. By 2000, there were as many cosmopolitans as Sykes or Hilton sisters.

When 66, the new Jean-Georges Vongerichten restaurant at 66 Leonard Street in TriBeCa, opened several weeks ago, it had to have a cosmopolitan, said Chuck Simeone, the beverage director for Jean-Georges Management. It is still a top-selling drink and an important style item for a specialty cocktail menu, he said.

The Shanghai Cosmo at 66, which was created in character with the restaurant's Chinese theme, is a Lucy Liu of a drink—it lowers its eyes and kicks, the Asian Charlie's Angel.

"It's a powerful drink, but it's designed so it doesn't have a liquor taste," said Mr. Simeone, its creator. "You have a couple and it's ... there." In addition to vodka there is sake, and four fruit juices, from sweet to tart.

Served in the low light of 66's minimal-chic lounge (you feel as if your head is on a dimmer), the work of the architect Richard Meier, the Shanghai Cosmo, pale red and suspiciously smooth, contributes to the impression of being presented with an opiate, not alcohol, in a den, not a bar. On Tuesday night, the waitress had a shoulder tattoo. Yes, it was a dragon, but maybe it was Jean-Georges issue, like the Vivienne Tam uniforms.

The cocktail played one of the oldest of games. It hesitated for the first few sips, content to be pretty, and then the trick went up my sleeve.

## SHANGHAI COSMO
Adapted from 66

1 ½ ounces of Skyy vodka
1 ounce of plum sake
1 ounce of cranberry juice
Splash of guanabana juice

Splash of pineapple juice
Splash of lime juice
French-cut lemon twist

**1.** Shake all ingredients except lemon twist with ice in a shaker.

**2.** Strain into a martini glass and garnish with lemon twist.

*March 2, 2003*

## RHUBARB COSMOPOLITAN
Adapted from BLUE HILL AT STONE BARNS, Pocantico Hills, N.Y.

4 ounces vodka
2 ounces fresh rhubarb juice (about four
16-inch stalks, run through a juicer)

1 ounce triple sec
1 ounce fresh lime juice

**1.** Mix all ingredients in a shaker and shake to chill.

**2.** Strain into a chilled martini glass.

*April 10, 2005*

A CUBA LIBRE

CHAPTER 26

# RUM DRINKS

# RUM FOR ALL SEASONS

## By FRANK J. PRIAL

They have not always been happy about it, but Americans have long been a rum-drinking nation. They drank it in colonial times because it was cheap and plentiful. They drank it during Prohibition because so little else was available, and they drank it during wartime for pretty much the same reason. Lately, they have been drinking it because they have found it to be a drink for all seasons, a drink made in many styles and a drink of infinite variety.

Rum is as much at home under a palm tree in a tall glass with lime and sugar and ice as it is before a ski-lodge fire, in a thick mug with butter and spices. It turns up in cakes and puddings and candy, in punches and cocktails and tall drinks. And, more and more, among people who know, in big snifters where it competes successfully with the best brandy and eau de vie.

When Bacardi rum became the best-selling spirit label in the land a few years ago, most Americans were astonished. Rum, after all, had had more negative connotations than good ones for a long time. In fact, it was merely history repeating itself. Rum was once America's favorite spirit, bar none.

In the middle of the 18th century, there were several hundred rum distilleries in this young nation—60 in Boston alone—using more than seven million gallons of imported molasses a year. As if that were not enough, al-

most three million gallons a year of finished rum were being imported from the British West Indies, along with several million gallons of contraband rum from the French West Indies. It was contraband because France had forbidden its export in an effort to support the market for French brandy and Cognac. Domestic rum sold for about 35 cents a gallon in New York and Boston; the imported version, for about 50 cents.

As late as 1981, rum was distilled in Boston, Philadelphia and Peoria, Ill. And, of course, in Puerto Rico, which some people tend to forget is very much American, too. Ronrico and Don Q are well-known Puerto Rican rum labels, but the leader by far is Bacardi, which sells some 18 million cases of its rum around the world every year.

Americans tend to think of Bacardi as a Puerto Rican company and, indeed, its best-known distillery is there—and most of the Bacardi rum drunk in this country originates there. But Bacardi also makes rum in Mexico, Brazil, Venezuela, Canada, Martinique, Panama, Trinidad, the Bahamas and Spain.

Don Facundo Bacardi y Moreau founded the company in 1862 in a little distillery he bought for $3,500. Over the years, the firm spread around the world, but it remained Cuban-based until 1959, when Fidel Castro took power and expropriated Bacardi, among other rum distilleries on the island. The nationalized Bacardi tried to export under the Bacardi name but the company had registered its name and trademarks all over the world and the rum that had been Bacardi became known as Havana Club.

The most popular rum in this country is the totally clear, light, mild-tasting version that can be mixed with tonic, vermouth, club soda, fruit juices and just about anything else. Rum had a reputation for being dark, heavy and aromatic, and American drinkers were moving away from that style, particularly in whisky. Vodka was the most desired mixer, with gin just behind. Once rum was distilled as a light, crystal- clear spirit, its sales shot up.

But the very light rums are not the rums drunk by connoisseurs, either in the summer or winter. In the islands where rum is made, a dark, flavorful version is preferred, and it is usually drunk with a bit of sugar and half a lime. Exotic drinks served in hollowed-out coconuts are something developed for the tourist trade. The planter's punch, made with guava or some other tropical fruit juice, is about the only concession the islanders will make to exotica, and that, not very often.

Almost every island in the Caribbean makes rum, even some that don't grow much sugar, which, of course, is the source of rum. The residue of the sugar-making process is molasses and millions of gallons of it are shipped around the Caribbean basin to distilleries in need. Many distilleries on the northern islands buy excess molasses from Guyana, where actual rum production is relatively low.

In the American market, some of the best darker rums come from Barbados, the home of the oldest known rum producer, Mount Gay; from Haiti, where the Barbancourt label is well known, and from Jamaica, where the Myers label has always stood for a dark pungent rum meant to be used in exotic drinks. The French Island rums—Clement, Duquesne and St. James—are known in this country, but the rums of Guadeloupe are not. In fact, most of them are powerful and rough and not easy to appreciate, even in a mixed drink—at least, not without considerable experience in tasting rums.

Mount Gay, Barbancourt, the Jamaica rums and even those from Martinique make assertive summer drinks, perhaps too assertive for many American palates, but they are perfectly at home in hot punches, in pina colada, hot buttered rum and a Tom and Jerry. Punch, by the way, has nothing to do with physical violence. It is thought to be an Anglicization of a Hindustani word meaning five and originally referred to certain drinks with five ingredients.

The classic rum punch is merely two ounces of a medium-dark rum, juice of half a small lime, sugar to taste and an ice cube, if desired. The pina colada, a popular tourist concoction, combines an ounce of cream of coconut, two ounces of pineapple juice and two ounces of rum, light or dark. Mix in a blender with crushed ice and serve.

In their book "Rum Yesterday and Today," Hugh Barty- King and An-ton Massel provide a few traditional cold-weather rum recipes. A good hot buttered rum combines a lump of sugar, two ounces of rum, preferably dark and flavorful, two cloves and a pinch of nutmeg. Top the mug with boiling water, float a pat of butter in it and add a stick of cinnamon.

A Tom and Jerry calls for an egg per drink. The white is beaten with a teaspoon of sugar until it stands in peaks. The yolk is beaten separately until thick and then mixed with the white. Put the beaten egg in the mug and add two ounces of rum and one of brandy. Then top the mug with hot milk or boiling water. Sprinkle with nutmeg.

*October 21, 1984*

# STAGING A RUM REBELLION
## By PETE WELLS

For a drink with a ball gag in its mouth, the Night Marcher has a lot to say about where cocktail culture may be heading.

Some major themes in fashionable bars lately: small, elegant, stemmed glassware; arm garters; house-made bitters; a seriousness that is hard to distinguish from humorlessness; gin.

Some major themes in the Night Marcher, a drink that one owner of the Tar Pit, a bar in Los Angeles, calls "our ambassador": a large, grimacing tiki mug; bondage gear; store-bought Cholula hot sauce; a sense of humor that is hard to distinguish from weirdness; rum. The last item is the key that unlocks all the rest. A small rum rebellion may be starting in the cocktail world, exemplified by places like the Tar Pit and Smuggler's Cove in San Francisco, which also begins pouring this month. The rebels are inspired by the staggering variety of well-crafted sugar cane distillates on the market. Nearly as staggering are the bargains some of those bottles represent, compared with high-end whiskies and brandies.

The boom coincides with a dawning recognition that midcentury tropical drinks, many of them based on rum, constitute a rich and nearly untapped vein of American mixology. And it takes advantage of a growing sentiment that the bartending scene has gotten a bit full of itself. Nothing can deflate a pretentious cocktail faster than a sharp poke with a paper umbrella.

Rum never suffered the naked contempt that bartenders heaped on, say, vodka. But it did not confer the bragging rights of gin or rye, either.

"Everybody still enjoyed rum," said Audrey Saunders, who in 2005 founded the Pegu Club, an ambitious gin palace where roughly half the noteworthy young bartenders in Manhattan once worked. "But people kind of passed it over for things that were more challenging and difficult to work with." Now that bartenders have tested their mettle by mixing drinks with the bitterest amaro, however, rum is getting a second look.

"We were all too snobby four years ago," Ms. Saunders said. "Now it's a different story. Now it's like: 'Oh, I miss that girlfriend. You know what? Those were fun times.'"

Ms. Saunders intends to bring back the fun with the Tar Pit, which she owns, along with the chef Mark Peel and other partners. About a quarter of the drinks on the opening menu will stand on a foundation of rum. The bar's theme is more what Ms. Saunders calls "old-Hollywood swellegance" than Polynesian kitsch, but early next year she intends to move aggressively in that direction, with a selection of what she calls "neo-tropical cocktails."

For now, tiki partisans can make the acquaintance of the Night Marcher, a latter-day Zombie that looks as if it stayed out late one night and wandered into the wrong party. The recipe blends two kinds of high-potency rum with green Chartreuse, hot sauce and lime juice. Dry-ice vapor scented with nutmeg drifts from the top of the mug. Ms. Saunders said that she and her collaborators thought that the condensation from the vapor looked like tears streaming down the tiki god's face, "so we put a red ball gag in its mouth."

It is hard to imagine a rye cocktail that would put up with such treatment. Rum, on the other hand, asks for it. While it can be blended into drinks that are modeled on the manhattan and are every bit as complex, like the Carlo Sud and the Chadburn

at Smuggler's Cove, rum is forever associated with torches, waterfalls, puffer fish lanterns, grass skirts and outrigger canoes.

"The word itself invokes frivolity," said St. John Frizell, who keeps 15 rums, with more on the way, at Fort Defiance in Red Hook, Brooklyn. "Gin and whiskey are serious drinker's drinks. Rum—they drink that in the islands. And they mix it with all kinds of fruit juice. Even rum and Coca-Cola is kind of silly, much sillier than rye and ginger or vodka and tonic."

No barkeeper takes rum's frivolity more seriously than Martin Cate. For Smuggler's Cove, Mr. Cate has engaged the design services of Notch, a local builder of hot rods with a heavy sideline in tiki artifacts. Notch, known to his bank as Ignacio Gonzalez, helped Mr. Cate realize his vision of a bar that emphasized the nautical side of Polynesia, with dark wood, many yards of rope, flotsam, jetsam and a "water feature." He also crafted some of the serving ware, like the lava-spewing mountain that contains a tiki-style punch called the Top Notch Volcano.

As much as Mr. Cate enjoys the fantasia of classic mai tai joints, he is rigorously academic about rum itself. The Smuggler's Cove menu runs to about 75 rum drinks, which incorporate 28 different bottlings, alone or in blends. It reads like the syllabus for a graduate course in rum history. The semester begins with drinks from colonial taverns, pirate ships and the British navy. From there students investigate the 19th century and Prohibition-era Havana, where the scholars behind the bar at El Floridita made important advances in the field of daiquiri technology. They take an extended field trip to Polynesia before completing their studies with cocktails invented this year.

In addition, Mr. Cate said, he wants to help "consumers understand what kind of rums they're crazy about" through guided tastings of some of the more than 200 bottles from around the world he has stockpiled.

"We're in kind of a golden age of rum right now," said Martin Doudoroff, a founder of CocktailDB, an Internet cocktail database and one designer of a tiki drinks iPhone application. "There's probably more great rum widely available to drink right now than there has been in history." There are essentially no rules in the rum game. It can be distilled anywhere, from Cuba to Vietnam, and can take on endless personalities, from smooth and accommodating white rums to brooding, domineering rums made from molasses, and everything in between.

With so many moods, rum can be more than a summertime fling, bartenders are learning. "The amazing thing that's going on now is that people are starting to approach it in an entirely different way, where it's not limited to just April to September," said Adam Bernbach, who manages the bar at Proof, a restaurant in Washington. Mr. Bernbach said that rum makes him think of colonial taverns, which led him to blend aged Martinique rum with maple syrup, orange zest and chocolate bitters in the New England 1773. It calls out to be drunk after the leaves are off the trees.

The rum rebels are all fascinated by Smith & Cross, a high-octane pot-still rum from Jamaica that they believe may capture the intensity of the vanished Jamaican rums called for in historical recipes. Mr. Frizell deploys it in a hot buttered rum at Fort Defiance, and in an off-the-menu Tom and Jerry.

The layering of rums to stack flavor atop flavor goes back to Victor Bergeron and Donn Beach, better known as Trader Vic and Don the Beachcomber. Jeff (Beachbum) Berry has argued in several books that they deserve a place in the pantheon for their nuanced understanding of rum and their use of spices, bitters and syrups to lift sweet, fruity drinks to a more complex plane.

Bartenders who have spent the last few years in pursuit of complexity may be ready to heed the Zombie's call again. "There's an understanding of balance now which bartenders have, so there will be more spices or more herbs," Ms. Saunders said.

Roneria Caracas, a fancy name for what is essentially the bar of an arepa restaurant in Williamsburg, Brooklyn, has a very respectable portfolio of about 30 rums. They turn up in cocktails with unexpected ingredients like bay leaves, blueberries and coconut bitters.

"We're going to draw from ingredients wherever we find them," Ms. Saunders said of the rum rebels. "Whether that's soursop or lemon grass, we're going to see a lot more of those ingredients in tiki drinks."

Ms. Saunders thinks you may be seeing more props, too. "Maybe I should get a parrot," she said.

## THE NIGHT MARCHER
Adapted from the TAR PIT, Los Angeles, Calif.

2 ½ ounces (5 tablespoons) aged white Martinique rum
½ ounce (1 tablespoon) Lemon Hart 151-proof Demerara rum
½ ounce green Chartreuse
¾ ounce (1½ tablespoons) lime juice

¾ ounce Demerara simple syrup (page 27)
2 dashes Angostura bitters
⅛ teaspoon Mexican hot sauce
1 ½ ounces (3 tablespoons) ginger beer
1 slice fresh ginger, for garnish
Lime wedge, for garnish

**1.** Measure all ingredients except ginger and lime wedge into a 12-ounce glass. Fill halfway with crushed ice. Insert a long spoon into the ice, hold the handle between your palms, and gently rub your palms together, back and forth, to swizzle the drink.

**2.** Top glass with more crushed ice and swizzle again. Garnish with the ginger slice and the lime wedge.

## THE OLD CUBAN
Adapted from the PEGU CLUB, New York City

6 mint leaves, plus the tip of a mint sprig for garnish
¾ ounce (1 ½ tablespoons) lime juice
1 ounce (2 tablespoons) simple syrup (page 27)

1 ½ ounces (3 tablespoons) amber rum
1 or 2 dashes Angostura bitters
2 ounces Champagne
1 lime slice

**1.** Gently bruise the mint with lime juice in a shaker using a muddler or wooden spoon. Add syrup, rum, bitters and a big handful of ice, and shake until well chilled.

**2.** Strain into a coupe or cocktail glass and add Champagne.

**3.** With a knife, slit the lime slice halfway through and pierce it with the mint sprig. Perch it on the rim of the glass.

## THE CHADBURN
Adapted from SMUGGLER'S COVE, San Francisco, Calif.

½ ounce (1 tablespoon) tawny Port
½ ounce pear liqueur

2 ounces (¼ cup) dark rum
1 to 2 dashes Bittermens Xocolatl Mole bitters

**1.** Combine all ingredients in a shaker half-filled with ice, and stir until well chilled.

**2.** Strain into a cocktail glass.

*December 2, 2009*

# FOLLOWING THE RUM INTO THE WILD

## By JONATHAN MILES

Think Africa. Now think cocktails. Now admit you just pulled a muscle. "It's kind of a clean map," said Marcus Samuelsson, the chef best known for his work at Aquavit in New York. Mr. Samuelsson's latest venture is Merkato 55, a pan-African restaurant and lounge on Gansevoort Street in the meatpacking district of Manhattan.

It's an exultant, theatrical spot— the big-lot antithesis to what Mr. Samuelsson, who was born in Ethiopia and raised in Sweden, calls the "mom and pop places" that have been the primary loci of African food in New York.

The feeling of the restaurant, which sprawls across two levels and is festooned with silk-screen prints and basket lamps and acres of raw wood and clay, might be glibly likened to Disney's Animal Kingdom theme park, if Mr. Samuelsson, and his menu, weren't so earnest. But can earnestness like his survive in the meatpacking district?

A proven survival component in the area is booze. Mr. Samuelsson is betting on rum, which he said was the liquor that's "always at the center of the African diaspora."

There's a slew of infused rums that are served on their own (neat) in the same way Mr. Samuelsson features infused aquavits at Aquavit: date-infused, curry leaf-infused, lemon grass-infused.

Rum also rules the cocktail menu, which was developed with Junior Merino, a beverage consultant and former bartender at the Modern.

The Takada, for instance, corrals all of Mr. Samuelsson's influences, combining rum with aquavit and ginger beer along with pink grapefruit juice and litchi purée, while the Yabara pairs rum with a more Eastern mélange of Lillet Rouge, hibiscus, mango tea and lime.

The drink names are derived from African dances. This works spectacularly well with the Ding Ding, a mixture of rosemary-infused cachaça (rum's burlier cousin), aguardiente, ginger beer and lime, but less so with the Larakaraka (tequila, elderflower liqueur, pineapple juice, ginger liqueur, lime), which I overheard one patron despair of trying to pronounce and instead blurt out, "Hakuna matata," the signature phrase from "The Lion King." The Swahili phrase can be translated to mean "no worries." Proving the point, the correct drink arrived anyway.

I took a shine to the Kinka: easy to order, easier to drink. In the Kinka, Bacardi Gold rum meets Averna, a rootsy, herbal Italian amaro, with tamarind concentrate adding some earthy, exotic sweetness and blood orange purée and lemon juice adding citric tang.

It's a suave mixture, way more

brooding and mysterious than your typical meatpacking district fruit punch, and a boon companion to Mr. Samuelsson's spiced cuisine. Is it actually African? An academic drinker might say no.

Another drinker, however, might smile and say merely, "Hakuna matata."

## KINKA
### Adapted From MERKATO 55, New York City

1 ½ ounces Bacardi Gold rum
½ ounce Averna liqueur
1 ounce tamarind concentrate (see note below)

1 ounce freshly squeezed blood orange juice
½ ounce freshly squeezed lemon juice

**1.** Shake all ingredients with ice in a cocktail shaker.

**2.** Strain into ice-filled rocks glass.

**Tamarind concentrate is available at Indian and Middle Eastern markets.**

*March 9, 2008*

# IT'S NOT SO MYSTERIOUS: THE SECRET IS IN THE SWIZZLE
## By ROBERT SIMONSON

When Katie Stipe, a bartender at the Clover Club in Boerum Hill, gets an order for a mojito, she recommends that the customer try a Queens Park Swizzle instead.

"We steer them to it as a far superior version of the same sort of drink," she said. Indeed, the cocktails share many ingredients: rum, citrus, sugar, mint. So why bother converting a customer? What makes one different from the other? Well, the swizzling, of course.

A Queens Park Swizzle is the best-known representative of a crushed-ice-laden and slightly mysterious cocktail category. The genre was born in the West Indies, probably in the 19th century, but has become increasing-

ly popular in New York bars of late. Among other noteworthy examples are the Bermuda Swizzle (still wildly popular on that island) and the Barbados Red Rum Swizzle, a onetime staple at Trader Vic's.

These drinks are not shaken or stirred, but rather swizzled with a genuine swizzle stick. Now, if you're picturing one of those colorful plastic doohickeys that bars and resorts stick into their drinks as a combination advertisement and souvenir, stop right there.

The implement in question is an actual stick. It is snapped off a tree native to the Caribbean. Botanists call it Quararibea turbinata, but it is known to locals as the swizzle stick tree. The sticks are about six inches, with small prongs sticking out at the end, like the spokes of a wheel without the rim, and they are used as a kind of natural, manually operated Mixmaster.

These are halcyon days for behind-the-bar theatrics, and nothing lends the bartender's art a touch of razzmatazz like a deftly deployed swizzle stick. "It takes a little showmanship," said Stephen Remsberg, a New Orleans lawyer known for his extensive rum collection (1,300 bottles) and knowledge of rum drinks. "You insert the swizzle stick in the drink. And with both hands moving in coordination, simultaneously backwards and forwards, you simply rotate the shaft of the swizzle stick between your palms as quickly as you can."

It is believed by some that the success of any swizzle lies entirely in the mixing prowess of the bartender.

"There really isn't any difference between a simple rum punch and a swizzle except the technique used for making them," Mr. Remsberg said. All agree that one thing happens when the drink is prepared in this way—and has to happen, for it to be a swizzle. "With the ideal swizzle you get a nice frost on the outside of the glass," Ms. Stipe said.

Beyond that, what the method contributes to the drink—aside from a lively sideshow—is somewhat open to debate. Wayne Curtis, a cocktail authority and the author of "And a Bottle of Rum," suspects that the stick's significance is mainly cultural and ritualistic. Not that that's a bad thing. "Ritual is fine," Mr. Curtis said. "There's a lot of ritual in the

cocktail world."

Richard Boccato—who put the Queens Park Swizzle on the menu at Dutch Kills, a new bar in Long Island City, Queens, that he owns with Sasha Petraske—thinks there's more at stake. "The act in the swizzling is what makes the drink aesthetically pleasing to the guest," Mr. Boccato said. "They enjoy watching it, for sure, but it's also something that integral to the preparation. It's very much what brings the drink together."

But Mr. Petraske regards swizzling as simply a more controlled way of stirring. "It's a way of not disturbing the muddled stuff that's at the bottom," he said. "Aside from that, I can't think of any difference it makes."

The swizzle is just that kind of cocktail. The more you chase after its essence, the less you understand. The cocktail expert David Wondrich said, "Vague answers are all you're going to get." That's perhaps just as well, because it seems a shame to invest too much analysis in a practice so pleasingly theatrical, and in a drink that's so easygoing and refreshing. "It's almost like an adult snow cone," Ms. Stipe said.

There's one additional mystery surrounding the swizzle. Despite the demands of the cocktail craze, a real swizzle stick is not easily found in New York. Nearly every bar that serves swizzles gets the needed tools through some Caribbean connection. Mr. Boccato brings some sticks back from Martinique every time he visits his father, who lives nearby on St. Lucia.

"I'm surprised no one's come out with a plastic version," Mr. Curtis said.

## QUEENS PARK SWIZZLE
Adapted from DUTCH KILLS, Long Island City, Queens

4 mint sprigs, leaves only, plus one
whole sprig for garnish
1 sugar cube
1 ounce lime juice

¾ ounce simple syrup (page 27)
2 ounces white rum
6 dashes Angostura bitters

**1.** Place mint leaves in a cocktail shaker with sugar cube, lime juice and syrup.
Using a muddler or wooden spoon, gently bruise mint. Pour rum in, swirl shaker
and pour contents into a 10- or 12-ounce tall glass. Add crushed iced until glass is
three-quarters full, then add bitters.

**2.** Insert a genuine swizzle stick or a bar spoon into glass, stopping just above mint
leaves, and hold its handle between your palms. Slide your hands back and forth
against each other, gently spinning spoon or swizzle stick. Ideally, liquid and ice
will swirl together while top layer of bitters and bottom layer of mint stay undisturbed. Top with more ice and garnish with a mint sprig.

*June 23, 2009*

# CLOUDY, WITH
# A CHANCE OF GINGER
## By TOBY CECCHINI

The dark 'n' stormy has become a
cult highball due to a felicitous combination of its no-fault simplicity and
the balance of its exotic, headstrong
ingredients, each of which is perfectly
suited to the common goal: reviving
the flagging, heat-pummeled constitu-
tion. It is simply dark rum—very dark
rum—with ginger beer and some fresh
lime. The rich spirit is shaken awake
by the buoyant piquancy of the ginger
beer, while the lime slashes through
the sweetness of both.

The drink has its roots in Bermuda, and emigrated up the Atlantic
seaboard with the sailing set. Goslings has a rather sniffy and debat-
able lock on the recipe, having in
fact trademarked its version, even going to the point of threatening with

the specter of litigation anyone who
might suggest concocting one with
another rum. I like Goslings just fine.
It's delicious rum (the little-heralded
151 proof is my preference), and being the dark rum from Bermuda, it is
unquestionably synonymous with the
dark 'n' stormy. But I have to say, at
the risk of sounding libelous, that any
number of dark rums are interchange-
ably lovely in this drink, including
Coruba, Zaya, Cruzan's Blackstrap
and, my favorite, the Lemon Hart 151
from Guyana.

In fact, to worry about what rum
goes into a dark 'n' stormy is to miss
the point; the real game changer in
this cocktail is the ginger beer. In the
years I've been quietly obsessed with
this drink, I've tried every commer-

cially available ginger beer I could get my hands on. They're all too tame. You cannot find one that has the requisite punch to sing in this highball and not get washed out by the baritone of black rum—well, O.K., one, but good luck acquiring it. To get the full aromatic flush and fizzy burn of fresh ginger, you have to make your own. Once you do, and find how easy it is, you'll step up to the Platonic ideal of the dark 'n' stormy, the first sip placing your bare feet up on the gunwales, bobbing over a Caribbean sunset.

There are two levels of seriousness in the homemade ginger beer graduate school. I've long resided firmly on the less serious and far simpler rung, whereupon one makes a thick syrup in a 1:1 ratio from fresh ginger juice and some type of raw sugar, like demerara or turbinado, and incorporates that into the drink along with soda water. Juicing the ginger requires either a bit of patience, using a Microplane or other fine hand grater and then squeezing the pulp through a tea strainer, or a bit of coin, with an extraction juicer, like an Omega 8 or a Champion. From there, however, this method is a cakewalk, and the resulting drink is leagues better than anything you can get from a bottled ginger beer. Until recently, I thought this was the only way to fly. I hereby officially admit I was wrong. Or at least, not right enough.

The more advanced method is to actually brew your own ginger beer the way it has been done for centuries. I've long heard about people doing this: practically every household in England and America had its own

recipe 150 years ago. But to me it has always seemed like one of those things for indefatigable types who sew their own shoes and build airplanes from kits; I'm sure it's rewarding and all, but who wants to mess with all that yeast and vapor locks and sterilized carboys and who knows what all?

Still, I began to feel guilty about never having tried real homemade ginger beer. So, in selfless service to this column, I vowed to take on the onerous task and set to wading through the dozens of recipes online to cobble together one that would be as simple as possible. It still seemed kind of scary; while emphasizing how easy it is, many home brewers warned about not using glass bottles, as they routinely explode. Yikes.

In the end, I was amazed to find how simple it is. There's no sterilization needed, and the method is forgiving—you can actually play about with the levels and ingredients. Moreover, the resulting ginger beer blows anything else you've ever had straight out of contention. Upon opening my first bottle, I had one of those "whoa" moments before I even got it to my lips. You can tell it's serious, alive. A bartender friend who tested the first batch with me found it "too in-your-face gingery." Bull's-eye.

The more serious and historically rigorous method is to first cultivate a kind of mother, called a ginger beer plant, which is a symbiotic glob of lactobacillus and yeast with which you can brew endless batches, much like a sourdough starter. The easier, lazy man's method—which, it goes without saying, was my method—is to take a pinch of packaged yeast and something acidic for the yeast to thrive in (like lemon or lime juice or cream of tartar) along with some sugar syrup and grated ginger, lob it all in a plastic bottle of distilled or spring water, shake it up and stash it somewhere dark and warm for two days. It's remarkably simple, but here's a chemistry professor to take you through it anyway.

It sets to fermenting straight away, blowing up the bottle with gas (which you may have to let escape a couple of times before the yeast has fully consumed the sugar). As a result, it does contain the slightest bit of alcohol: less than 1 percent, similar to many soft drinks. After two days you stop the fermentation by chilling it in the fridge. That's it. The result is a cloudy, dry mixer with pinprick carbonation and a straight-up goose of fresh ginger. That is thrilling come dark 'n' stormy hour, not just for its authenticity and superior flavor but also because you can now brag about your homemade ginger beer. I want to try the version with a cultivated ginger beer plant next, which some arbiters say results in a slightly more complex drink, and incorporate different spices like allspice, vanilla or hibiscus. But first I have to finish building my bamboo sea catamaran.

## HOMEMADE GINGER BEER
YIELD: 1 LITER

2 ounces freshly grated ginger

4 ounces lemon juice

6 ounces simple syrup

⅛ teaspoon commercial baker's, brewer's or Red Star Pasteur Champagne

yeast 20 ounces non-chlorinated water (filtered, distilled or spring)

1 to 4 grams cream of tartar (not necessary, but traditional, to help the yeast and bacteria thrive)

**1.** Take a 1.5-liter plastic bottle of spring water and empty it into a clean pitcher. Use some of it to make simple syrup by stirring ½ pound sugar into 1 cup hot water until fully dissolved.

**2.** In a large measuring cup, mix all ingredients and stir well. Funnel back into the plastic bottle and cap tightly. Store in a warm, dark place for 24 to 48 hours. (I put mine inside a box, to contain it if it should blow.) The top of the bottle will expand and become tight. Check it and very slowly release the pressure if it's looking groaningly tight. Some people ferment it with no top, or with the top on loosely, to allow gas to escape. I suppose if you wanted to get fancy you could purchase a fermentation lock and stop worrying about it. If the temperature is quite warm, above 80F, a single day may be sufficient. The longer you let it ferment, the drier the final mix will be.

**3.** After 48 hours, refrigerate it to stop the fermentation. Once chilled, you can strain out the pulp and dead yeast, which will have made a sediment on the bottom.

Ginger beer keeps up to a week in the refrigerator.

## DARK 'N' STORMY

2 ounces dark rum

½ ounce fresh-squeezed lime juice

½ ounce simple syrup, or to taste (see recipe above, or page 27)

4-6 ounces fresh ginger beer (see recipe above)

Wedge of lime, for garnish

**1.** Build the drink in a highball glass filled with ice, adjusting for sweetness and tartness. Depending on when you stop the fermentation of the ginger beer, it may be fully dry or still retain enough sweetness that additional simple syrup is unnecessary. Garnish with a wedge of lime.

*August 23, 2010*

# A BIRD WALKS INTO A BAR
## By ROBERT SIMONSON

On the concise drinks menu for the downstairs bar at Celeste, a cocktail den in Chicago, there's a small section titled Classics. The four drinks under that heading are the manhattan (of course), the Negroni (natch), the Brown Derby (a little more arcane, but a classic) and the Jungle Bird.

Jungle who?

In the last year or so, the Jungle Bird, a hitherto obscure tiki drink, has bloomed into a bartender favorite whose popularity goes well beyond the parameters of the resurgent tiki culture. Part of its appeal is simplicity. It has only five ingredients: rum, Campari, pineapple and lime juices and simple syrup.

The cocktail is on the menu at Three Dots and a Dash, the ever-crowded subterranean tiki palace down the block from Celeste. Also in Chicago, the Aviary, a Frankenstein-ish mixology laboratory where cocktails arrive with special equipment, is testing a molecular version

on customers. (Spheres of dark rum are involved.)

In New York, you can order the drink at Attaboy on the Lower East Side, the NoMad hotel bar, Lantern's Keep in the Iroquois New York hotel and Milk & Honey near Madison Square Park. Theo Lieberman, the head bartender at Milk & Honey, fell under the drink's spell after being served one by Giuseppe Gonzalez at Painkiller, which is now closed. Mr. Lieberman has been pushing it since.

"I honestly think it's so unlike anything else," he said. "The two big drinks for bartenders in New York are Negronis and daiquiris, and the Jungle Bird is kind of a perfect hybrid between the two."

This all amounts to an unlikely second act for a drink invented at the Kuala Lumpur Hilton in 1978, a year when the tiki craze was all but dead and buried in this country. The tiki historian Jeff Berry found the recipe in a 1989 paperback, "The New American

Bartender's Guide," and reprinted it in his 2002 book, "Intoxica!"

"It definitely was on no one's radar before I published it," he said.

Mr. Gonzalez took that recipe and tweaked it, eventually replacing the prescribed dark Jamaica rum with the more intense blackstrap rum. This is what he served at Painkiller, and it is the version Mr. Lieberman offers at Milk & Honey.

Mr. Berry said he knew why mixologists like the drink. "The reason, I am 100 percent positive, is because there's Campari in it, which makes it the only vintage tiki drink that today's amaro-loving bartenders can relate to," he said.

But Fred Sarkis, the program director at Celeste, who also first tasted the drink at Painkiller, said the Campari was just one element that set off his taste buds. "The mix of velvety texture, sweetness, fruit and bitter really captured my attention," he said.

## JUNGLE BIRD
### Adapted by GIUSEPPE GONZALEZ

*This tiki drink, believed to have been invented at the Kuala Lumpur Hilton in 1978, has recently lurched from obscurity to ubiquity. It is a favorite among mixologists, and a natural for home bartenders, because it contains only five ingredients: rum, Campari, pineapple and lime juices and simple syrup. The New York bartender Giuseppe Gonzalez tweaked the original, replacing dark Jamaica rum with the more intense blackstrap rum.*

½ ounce simple syrup (page 27)
1½ ounces blackstrap rum, preferably Cruzan
¾ ounce Campari

1½ ounces pineapple juice, fresh or high-quality brand
½ ounce fresh lime juice
Pineapple wedge, for garnish

**1.** In a mixing glass three-quarters filled with ice, pour all ingredients except pineapple wedge and shake until chilled, about 30 seconds.

**2.** Strain into a rocks glass over one large piece of ice. Top with pineapple wedge.

*April 8, 2014*

## CUBA LIBRE
### By ROSIE SCHAAP

*Real cane cola makes a difference in this classic highball. Try to find Mexican Coca-Cola or Boylan sugar cane cola if you can.*

2 to 3 ounces light rum
Cola (preferably cane cola, such as Mexican Coca-Cola or Boylan), to fill

Squeeze of lime
Lime wedge, for garnish

**1.** Fill a highball glass with ice and add rum, cola to fill and squeeze of lime. Garnish with a wedge of lime.

*March 15, 2014*

## VENEZUELA LIBRE
### Adapted from Rosie Schaap by Jack McGarry

*Jack McGarry of the Dead Rabbit, a sublime Manhattan bar, recommends a variation on the Cuba Libre.*

| | |
|---|---|
| 1½ ounces Santa Teresa "1796" Solera Rum | 1 dash Angostura bitters |
| ½ ounce Fernet Branca | Mexican Coca-cola |
| | Lime wedge, for garnish |

**1.** To a highball glass, add the rum, Fernet Branca and bitters. Add ice and fill the balance with Mexican cane cola. Garnish with a lime wedge.

*April 19, 2013*

# SPRING DRINKS
## By RITA KONIG

These light evenings are so delightful, they just make me want to meet friends for drinks after work. Spring is my absolute favorite season: all the flowers are bursting forth, the place is awash with color after a long dreary winter, and we have months more of it ahead of us. With Memorial Day a small step away, the floodgates to summer will soon open.

There is no better drink than that first, bubbly, refreshing glass when the day is coming to a close. Ever since I fell in love with Hendrick's, I have been on the lookout for new aromatic gins; and as with all things, I am initially attracted by the packaging. Monkey 47 has the best: the label looks like an old-fashioned postage stamp and is stuck on the front of a brown apothecary bottle. It is very smart. The German booze inside, made by the Black Forest distillery, has this wonderful pineyness to it. It is quite different from Hendrick's, which is very floral, but I love how with gin you really do get these very different essences. I never tire of a good gin and tonic made with slivers of lime (many of them) and a few drops of angostura bitters. It is not only delicious, but who doesn't love a blush-colored bev?

I am also really into sours right now. They might not immediately sing spring to you, but whiskey sours are not the only sours. At the Connaught Hotel bar, they mix the snowiest white vodka sour, which is so good that it's impossible to have just one. While perusing Assouline's "Vintage Cocktails" book the other day, I fell upon a recipe for gin sours. It made me realize that one of my favorite drinks of all time, called a Rum Dum, is essentially a rum sour. The Rum Dum is sadly only served at the Lyford Cay Club in Nassau, where it was created in 1974 by Wilfred Sands. This might explain why it remains such a personally sought-after cocktail, since I only ever have it there and long to have it anywhere else (over those rum punches made with sickly sweet fruit juice that they serve elsewhere in the Caribbean). Anyway, we have the recipe here, and I urge you to take it with you whenever you are heading south:

# LYFORD CAY RUM DUM

## By WILFRED SANDS

*Wilfred Sands came up with this drink, the signature cocktail of the exclusive and stunning Lyford Cay Club, when asked for a rum drink that was not overly sweet and could be served in a short glass. Forty-two years later, Sands still serves up Rum Dums from the men's locker room at the Lyford Cay golf course. The recipe has been kept concealed, but Avenue magazine made it a mission to uncover the original Lyford Cay Club cocktail with the following recipe.*

1 cup lemon juice
1 cup simple syrup (page 27)
2 cups water

1 raw egg white
1 ½ ounces light rum
1 ounce dark rum (Sands uses Myers's Jamaican Rum)

**1.** Stir together lemon juice, simple syrup, 2 cups water and 1 raw egg white in a pitcher. Pour into a blender and add light rum. Briefly blend to mix.

**2.** Pour over ice in a short chilled glass. Carefully float the dark rum over the surface of the drink so it forms a separate layer. Serve immediately.

*April 13, 2013*

**RUM WITH PINEAPPLE JUICE**

## RUM WITH PINEAPPLE JUICE
By ROSIE SCHAAP

*This easygoing highball tastes like the tropics. Nutmeg freshly grated over the top adds a hint of spice.*

2 to 3 ounces dark rum
4 ounces chilled pineapple juice
Splash of soda water

Nutmeg to taste
Pineapple chunk, for garnish

**1.** Fill a highball glass with ice and add rum, pineapple juice and soda. Grate a little nutmeg over the top and garnish with a pineapple chunk.

*May 20, 2014*

## BETTER AND BETTER COCKTAIL
By JAN WARREN

¼ ounce John D. Taylor's Velvet Faler-num Liqueur
½ ounce Smith and Cross Jamaican Rum

1½ ounces Fidencio Clasico Mezcal
Lemon twist, for garnish

**1.** Add all ingredients except lemon twist to an old-fashioned glass. Add ice and stir briefly. Garnish with a lemon twist.

*October 17, 2013*

# I'LL HAVE SOME RUM, HOLD THE UMBRELLA
## By JONATHAN MILES

When a former bootlegger calling himself Donn Beach unveiled a potent triple-rum drink named the Navy Grog at his Hollywood restaurant Don the Beachcomber, he reportedly limited customers to two. At Elettaria, a restaurant in Greenwich Village with the Navy Grog on its menu, there's no such limit. At least not yet.

"I don't think it's a drink to fear," said Brian Miller, a bartender at Death & Company in the East Village who mans Elettaria's bar once a week, and who helped, with the bar manager Lynette Marrero, create its cocktail list.

That differentiates it from the in-famous Zombie Punch, another one of Don the Beachcomber's tropical staples available at Elettaria, which comes with a walloping four and a half ounces of alcohol and is restricted to one Zombie per customer.

The Navy Grog—a heady mix of one ounce each of three rums, fresh lime and grapefruit juice, and a softening dose of honey syrup—is the Zombie's less rowdy cousin. But like the Zombie, it has a rich legend.

It's a throwback, as all New York cocktails are these days, but from what cocktail historians would deem more "recent" history: the 1930's.

That's when Ernest Raymond Beaumont-Gantt, as Donn Beach, started serving dolled-up rum drinks at his Polynesian-themed restaurants, kicking off the decades-long "tiki" phase of American drinking. Along with the Mai Tai and Zombie, the Navy Grog was part of his holy trinity of tiki drinks. "These are truly classic cocktails," Mr. Miller said. "They're bright, refreshing, with tastes that really pop in your mouth. They're relics that people should get to know."

Before too long, however, they may not be able to avoid knowing them. "You're definitely seeing a big tiki comeback," said Angus Winchester, a former London bartender and self-described "international bar consultant" who was mixing drinks recently at a tiki cocktail party held by the Distilled Spirits Council of the United States.

Mr. Winchester credits the resurgence to a recent spate of super-premium rums hitting the market—bartenders seeking to showcase these rums are being inexorably led by the ghost of Donn Beach's old swizzle stick. But there's a reactionary element at work, too, he said.

"Certain elements of mixology have gotten too dry," he said, referring to a bar ethos that esteems pre-Prohibition cocktails, sometimes to a point of purism. "Cocktail lists are starting to look like history lessons, with bartenders hiding behind the fact that they're using the 1812 recipe of a drink rather than the 1814 recipe. Tiki is the antithesis to all that."

To a degree, anyway. As Mr. Miller said of the Navy Grog: "We're using the original 1941 recipe." Yet, pedigree aside, the drink can hardly be called austere. It's a serious drink that, refreshingly, shouldn't be taken too seriously.

Unless it proves, um, popular enough for Elettaria to resurrect Don the Beachcomber's old two-Grog limit. "We don't want tables overturned," Mr. Miller said.

## NAVY GROG
### Adapted from ELETTARIA, New York City

1 ounce Demerara rum
1 ounce Gosling's Black Seal rum
1 ounce Cruzan Estate Light rum
¾ ounce freshly squeezed lime juice
¾ ounce freshly squeezed grapefruit juice
1 ounce honey syrup (recipe follows)
¾ ounce club soda
Orange slice and cherry, for garnish

**1.** Shake all ingredients except club soda and fruit slices together with ice in cocktail shaker.

**2.** Strain into Collins glass filled with ice, top with soda and add garnish.

## HONEY SYRUP

½ cup honey
¼ cup warm water

**1.** Mix honey and warm water in a bowl and let cool.

*March 3, 2008*

CRANBERRY ORANGE TEA PUNCH

## CHAPTER 27

# PITCHERS AND PUNCHES

# DIP INTO THE PAST: REDISCOVERING THE PLEASURES OF PUNCH

## By AMANDA HESSER

Leafing through a book on drinks recently, I came across an old recipe for punch and realized I could barely remember the last time I had had one. It wasn't that I didn't like punch. I simply hadn't thought about it in years.

So I served it at a party, mostly out of curiosity. The surface looked like an amber pond with orange zest and slices of cucumber floating like meadow grass and lily pads. The drink itself, James Beard's Champagne punch, was a delicious doozy, with Cognac, Cointreau, orange juice, lemon juice and Champagne.

My guests circled around it, and conversation sparked. All had a punch they could remember—whether it was a high-octane blend from college or the ginger ale punch at their parents' cocktail parties.

That tight air at the start of the party lifted. And I finally understood the magic that punch possesses. It satisfies thirst, of course, but it is also a prop for mingling. People gravitate toward punch bowls and surround them, as they do a newborn. I wish I'd discovered it sooner, and apparently there are plenty of others who feel the same way.

Caterers around New York City say they have been seeing something of a punch revival over the last two years, with an added fizz of interest at this time of year, when people are having holiday parties and smaller family gatherings.

Just as bartenders loosened the tie on the martini, punch has slipped into something more comfortable. Today's concoctions use ingredients from all over the world, and the mixtures are less formulaic.

Dan Fehlig, the owner of the Upper Crust, a Manhattan catering company, makes a punch with Campari, ginger ale, vodka and orange juice. For the holidays, he mixes orange pekoe tea, cranberry juice, rum, lemon juice and soda water, and floats cranberries and half moons of lemon on top. Entertaining Ideas, another Manhattan caterer, serves a Champagne punch scented with pomegranate syrup and mint leaves.

True punch may not have the clarity of a classic martini. And it may not possess the earthiness of wine. But it is a fine drink. A balanced mixture of alcohol and fruit juice—sometimes sweetened, sometimes spiced—it is pretty, fresh tasting, and often a little fizzy.

At this time of year, it makes an impression. Suzanne Studier-Feldman, who lives in the Flatiron district, served glogg, a warm, powerful Swedish punch made with red wine, vodka and spices, at a holiday party last weekend. "It's a very good drink to serve your guests when they first come," she said. "It's nice and warm and it has a little alcohol in it so it kind of starts the party off on the right foot."

It would be difficult to forget glogg. Or the blood orange and rum punch scented with nutmeg made by Entertaining Ideas.

They are all great drinks, as important to a party as the food. But somehow over recent years, punch came to represent a staid style of entertaining that Americans would rather forget. Until recently, caterers who did serve it didn't even call it punch—it was a "cocktail" or "specialty drink."

It is strange that it went out of fashion. Punch fits the mold of an American creation: it's a panoply of ingredients, it has lots of flavor, and it's splashy. But it wasn't invented here. It actually originated in India 1,500 years ago, said Leslie Brenner, a culinary historian in New York City.

Then it was called panch, a Hindi word meaning five, because it had five ingredients: citrus juice, water, arrack, sugar and spices. Arrack, a distillation of palm tree sap, was a coarse spirit, Ms. Brenner said. "They had to add all this other stuff to make it palatable," she added. By the end of the 17th century it had made its way to the British Isles, where it was known as the drink of mariners, and it was a hit among the English in colonial India. Colonial America also latched onto punch, replacing the arrack with rum.

Punch's heyday in America, though, didn't come until later, during the 19th century. It was everywhere. Punches were served at bars, at parties and at social clubs, from elaborate silver punch sets. There were ale punches, milk punches, punches with egg white, punches that might even make fraternity boys cower. The Wassail Bowl, an old British recipe, was a heady mixture of warm beer, nutmeg, ginger, sherry, lemon and sugar.

Regents punch, another popular one, makes Long Island iced tea seem like Kool-Aid: it contains green tea, lemon juice and rind, Seville oranges, cinnamon, sherry, Champagne, brandy, rum, creme de noyeaux, curacao, pineapple syrup and, of course, soda water to lighten it up a bit before serving.

Prohibition quieted punch drinking for a few decades. In the 1950's, Esquire magazine made an earnest effort to revive it. In "Esquire's Handbook for Hosts" (1953), a defense of punch says the real thing should bear no resemblance to a "sloppy pink lemonade pond."

A bowl of cheer, it goes on, "is a natural hub of a party, and though you'd best have a Scotch-and-soda bar for diehards who regard a punch bowl as a quaint curio, you'll be surprised at the converts you win with some of these mixtures—particularly if you ladle them into stemmed Delmonico glasses or outright tumblers rather than those cute-handled cuppies known as knuckle traps."

There is little technique to making punch. All you need to know is how to stir and taste, and to use good alcohol and fresh fruits for juices. Punch is bluntly flavored, and any lackluster component will ruin it. (If you prefer nonalcoholic punch, you can usually just leave out the alcohol, or substitute sparkling water for Champagne. That cranberry orange tea punch, for instance, is just as delicious without the rum.)

It is important to stir it long enough to dissolve the sugar, or you can rub the sugar into the rind of the citrus fruit to extract its full essence before adding it to the punch bowl. And if you're using a bubbly ingredient, make sure you add it at the last minute.

"American and Other Drinks," a cocktail book written by Leo Engel in 1875, offered some of the best instruction on punch making: "The great secret in punch brewing is to make the mixture sweet and strong, using tea instead of water, and so thoroughly amalgamating all the compounds that the taste of neither the bitter, the sweet, the spirit, nor the element shall be perceptible one over the other."

Once you get the balance right, you can decorate it by freckling the surface with edible flowers or letting fruit bob around in the liquid. You can float thin cross sections of orange, cranberries, cinnamon sticks, curls of lemon zest, translucent slices of cucumber and herbs.

A cold punch needs to be very cold to keep it refreshing and clean tasting. The classic trick is to make an ice ring. An even better trick is to freeze some of the punch, before the alcohol is added, in the ice ring. Then, as it dissolves, it doesn't dilute the mixture. If you want to make it visible, fill the ring with fruit before freezing.

The punch bowl set is one relic of the past that should probably remain a relic—although cookware suppliers like Sur La Table say they have been selling more of them this year. The punch bowl was originally much smaller and meant to be picked up with both hands, like a latte cup. The large punch bowl sets that followed were simply decorative.

It's more fun simply to buy a big beautiful bowl that can double as a salad or pasta bowl when you're not having a party. Wine glasses, Champagne flutes or even tumblers work just fine. Just like they do for any other drink.

## JAMES BEARD'S CHAMPAGNE PUNCH
Adapted from "Champagne Cocktails" by ANISTATIA MILLER, JARED BROWN and DON GATTERDAM
YIELD: 20 DRINKS

| | |
|---|---|
| 8 tablespoons sugar | 16 ounces Cointreau |
| 4 ounces lemon juice | 4 bottles Champagne |
| 16 ounces orange juice | Grated zest from 4 lemons |
| 2 bottles Cognac | 20 thin slices cucumber |

**1.** In a large punch bowl, gently stir together the sugar, lemon juice, orange juice, Cognac, Cointreau, Champagne and lemon zest. Garnish with cucumber slices, and set bowl on a bed of cracked ice.

## REGENTS PUNCH
**Adapted from "Tipplers' Tales" by Rosemary Burr, editor**
YIELD: 5 QUARTS (ABOUT 40 DRINKS)

2 cups strongly brewed green tea, chilled

Peeled rind and juice of 2 lemons

Peeled rind and juice of 1 Seville orange or other sour or bitter orange

Peeled rind and juice of 1 orange

1 cup minus 2 tablespoons sugar

1 small stick cinnamon

2 cups medium-dry sherry

3 cups brandy

1 cup rum

1 cup curacao

1 cup creme de noyeaux

2 cups pineapple syrup, chilled (see note below)

1 bottle Champagne, chilled

1 liter club soda, chilled

**1.** In a large bowl, combine tea, lemon rind and juice, Seville orange rind and juice, orange rind and juice, sugar and cinnamon stick. Allow to sit for 30 minutes. Strain into a punch bowl.

**2.** Add sherry, brandy, rum, curacao, creme de noyeaux and pineapple syrup. Mix well, and chill.

**3.** Add the Champagne and the club soda. Mix gently, and serve over ice in punch glasses.

**As a substitute for pineapple syrup, mix 4 cups pineapple juice with 1 tablespoon sugar. Boil until reduced to 2 cups.**

## CRANBERRY ORANGE TEA PUNCH
**Adapted from the UPPER CRUST caterers, New York City**
YIELD: ABOUT 15 DRINKS

1 ½ cups cranberries

1 lemon, thinly sliced crosswise

1 ½ quarts cranberry juice

1 ½ cups sugar

2 cups apple juice, chilled

½ cup plus 2 tablespoons freshly

squeezed lemon juice, chilled

1 cup orange juice, chilled

1 cup strong orange pekoe tea, chilled

2 cups club soda, chilled

White rum, to taste

2 small oranges, thinly sliced crosswise

**1.** In a medium ring mold, combine cranberries and lemon slices. Pour enough cranberry juice over them to fill mold, about 2 to 3 cups. Freeze.

**2.** In a medium pan, combine sugar with 1 ½ quarts water. Bring to a boil, then turn off heat and let cool completely. Chill.

**3.** In a punch bowl, combine sugar syrup, apple juice, lemon juice, orange juice, tea and club soda. Add white rum to taste. Unmold ice ring into punch. To serve, fill tall glasses with ice. Place an orange slice in each glass and ladle punch over it.

## BLOOD ORANGE PUNCH

**Adapted from ENTERTAINING IDEAS caterers, New York City**

YIELD: 1 GALLON (ABOUT 32 DRINKS)

1 liter (4 cups plus a scant ¼ cup)
  spiced rum, chilled

2 liters club soda, chilled

4 cups freshly squeezed blood orange
  juice or regular orange juice, chilled

1 blood orange or orange, thinly sliced
  crosswise, chilled

1 teaspoon freshly grated nutmeg

½ cup superfine sugar

1 orange wedge

**1.** In a punch bowl combine rum, club soda and orange juice. Add slices of blood orange, and stir gently.

**2.** In a wide, shallow bowl, combine nutmeg and sugar. Stir to mix well. To serve, use orange wedge to moisten rims of punch cups. Immediately dip rims into sugar mixture to obtain a thin coating. Fill glasses with ice, and ladle in punch.

*December 15, 1999*

# A RUM PUNCH THAT RAISES THE THERMOSTAT

## By MELISSA CLARK

Nothing warms a cold body up like a quaff of hot rum punch. This version, spiked with cognac and infused with citrus and nutmeg, is exactly what you want to serve at a party once the temperature drops outside. If you're feeling flamboyant, you can flambé it, to the great amusement of your guests.

Just make sure to use a fireproof bowl; silver or another metal is ideal, wood or even tempered glass is not. But even if you don't set it on fire, it's a rich, soothing and powerful libation. Serve it in small cups for the most civilized gathering.

## HOT RUM PUNCH

YIELD: 12 TO 16 DRINKS

4 to 5 lemons

1 tangerine, tangelo or other thick-
  skinned, small citrus fruit

¾ cup Demerara sugar

1¼ cups amber or aged rum

1¼ cups Jamaican rum (preferably
  100-proof)

1 cup cognac

Freshly grated nutmeg, as needed

**1.** Using a vegetable peeler, remove the zest of 2 lemons and the tangerine in strips. Drop into a large heatproof bowl (or use a fireproof bowl if you plan to set the punch on fire) and combine with sugar. Muddle together with a muddler, pestle or the back of a wooden spoon. Let mixture sit for at least 3 hours to infuse (or infuse overnight).

**2.** Halve the tangerine and squeeze juice into a measuring cup. Halve lemons and squeeze lemon juice into the measuring cup to make ¾ cup juice in total. (Save any unsqueezed lemon halves for another purpose.)

**3.** When ready to serve, bring 1 quart water to a boil. Pour rum and cognac into the bowl with the sugar and peels. If you want to flame the punch, do so now (use caution and see note below).

**4.** Add reserved citrus juice and boiling water and stir well. Grate nutmeg over top of punch and ladle into glasses.

If you want to set the punch on fire, first make sure your bowl is fireproof. Silver or another metal is ideal; wood or tempered glass is not. Just after Step 3, use a fireproof long-handled bar spoon or ladle to remove a spoonful of the alcohol mixture, then light it on fire. Return spoon to bowl to ignite remaining punch. Stir flaming punch to help dissolve sugar; let it burn for a minute or two. To extinguish fire, place a metal tray over bowl. Proceed with recipe.

*December 5, 2014*

# READY TO ROLL WITH THE PUNCHES
## By MARIA NEWMAN

A bowl of punch turns a backyard of rugged individualists into a group with a mission, says the cocktail expert David Wondrich, who has written a book, "Punch," on the subject.

And to the degree to which punch boosts a party's conviviality (Mr. Wondrich serves his in small glasses so that guests "have to go back for frequent refills," he said, "and every time they do a new conversation starts"), it also provides convenience for the host. When you are expecting a backyard full of guests and have a large amount of corn to shuck and a grill to tend, it's nice not to have to play bartender, too.

Fruit, spice and spirits like rum, gin and even white wine evoke summer as a centerpiece drink served in a gleaming chilled bowl. You can prepare the punch in advance and add the ice at the last minute. (Bartenders suggest a single large block, by the way, frozen in a quart container like a milk carton.)

If you don't have a punch bowl, pitchers of cocktails will do just fine. And it may be a cliché, but at the restaurant Hearth in the East Village, the Brunch Punch (Campari, gin and fresh grapefruit juice) is served in Mason jars, said the bartender, Jad Kamal, because they evoke memories of "sitting around in plastic chairs on the lawn and the smell of barbecue wafting around."

## BRUNCH PUNCH
### Adapted from JAD KAMAL, Hearth, New York City

*Hearth restaurant serves this refreshing punch at their Sunday brunch, which they prepare with Finger Lakes Distilling Seneca Drums Gin from New York.*
YIELD: ABOUT 16 DRINKS

16 ounces (2 cups) gin
16 ounces (2 cups) Campari
16 ounces (2 cups) white vermouth

48 ounces (6 cups) freshly squeezed grapefruit juice (juice of 5 fruits)
Sliced cucumber and orange, or other citrus, for garnish

**1.** In a large pitcher, combine all ingredients except cucumber and fruit wheels and stir gently.

**2.** Float some of the wheels of cucumber and oranges on the punch.

**3.** Ladle punch into rocks glasses filled with ice, and garnish with cucumber and orange.

## AFTON CLUB PUNCH
### Adapted from DAVID WONDRICH

*David Wondrich, the mixologist and author, said this punch, which begins with a sugar and lemon peel "shrub," is "lowish on the alcohol, and slightly unusual. People like it when I make it."*
YIELD: 20 DRINKS

4 lemons
¾ cup sugar
16 ounces (2 cups) genever
16 ounces (2 cups) chilled German (or

other) Riesling, not to sweet
16 ounces (2 cups) chilled sparkling water
Nutmeg, for garnish

**1.** Make the shrub: Peel lemons with a vegetable peeler, avoiding pith. Juice lemons and set juice aside. Place peels and sugar in a Mason jar, seal and shake. Leave jar in the sun for 3 to 4 hours or overnight. Add reserved lemon juice and shake until sugar is dissolved. Will keep for several days refrigerated.

**2.** In a gallon bowl or pitcher, combine shrub (peels and all) with genever, Riesling and sparkling water and stir gently. Add a 1-quart block of ice (made by freezing a quart container of water overnight). Grate nutmeg on top and ladle into small serving glasses.

## CHAIRMAN'S RESERVE
### Adapted from JIM MEEHAN, PDT, New York City

*Jim Meehan of PDT in Manhattan uses an extractor to get cucumber juice for this punch. You can buy cucumber juice from your local juice store too.*

YIELD: 14 DRINKS

8 ounces (1 cup) cucumber juice, from about 1 ½ cucumbers

24 ounces (3 cups) coconut water

8 ounces (1 cup) white rum, preferably

Banks 5 Island

3 ounces Frangelico

Cucumber slices, for garnish

**1.** Juice the cucumbers, skin and all, in a juicer, food processor or blender and strain.

**2.** Combine all ingredients in a bowl and add a block of ice. Ladle into cups and garnish with cucumber slices.

*May 20, 2014*

## TOO HOT TO HOOT PUNCH
### Adapted from DAMON W. BOELTE, Prime Meats and Frankies Spuntino, Brooklyn, by Eric Asimov

*This splendidly summery concoction is proof that punch, often associated with fall and winter holidays, can be made seasonal with the delicate spring sweetness of strawberries, and summery with the tropical tang of limes. Sure, you could settle for a vodka base, but bourbon adds a marvelous backbone of vanilla richness. Or make it without alcohol and serve at a children's party.*

YIELD: 12 DRINKS

9 or so strawberries, plus 3 for garnish

1 cup sugar

5 elderberry tea bags, or 5 heaping teaspoons of loose elderberry tea (if you can't find elderberry, use any

herbal berry tea)

9 or so limes

12 ounces (1 ½ cups) bourbon

1 tablespoon Angostura bitters

Large chunk of ice, or ice mold

**1.** Several hours ahead, prepare strawberry syrup and the elderberry tea. For the syrup, cut the green tops off the strawberries and discard. Dice the berries until you have 1 cup. Reserve extras for garnish. In a saucepan, add the berries along with 1 cup water and the sugar. Bring to a simmer, stirring, and continue simmering until the sugar dissolves. Allow syrup to cool.

**2.** Prepare the tea. Pour 12 ounces of hot water over the tea bags or the loose tea. Allow to steep until cool. Discard bags or strain loose tea.

**3.** Juice enough limes to produce 9 ounces of juice.

**4.** In a punch bowl stir together the lime juice, bourbon, bitters, 6 ounces cold water, the strawberry syrup and the tea. (If you have extra tea, juice and syrup, combine without bourbon for a pleasant soft drink for children.) Gently slide the ice, or an ice mold, into the bowl. Garnish with sliced strawberries. Serve in ceramic punch cups or glasses.

**To make an ice mold, fill a large mixing bowl with purified water and freeze. (Be certain the mold will fit comfortably in the punch bowl with the punch.) To remove ice from the mixing bowl, flip the bowl over. Keeping a hand over the ice, run warm water on back of the bowl until mold is free. Gently slide the ice into the punch.**

*May 21, 2012*

# FOR SUMMER THIRST-QUENCHING: LOOK TO PITCHERS AND PUNCHES

## By FLORENCE FABRICANT

As a category of alcoholic beverage, the wine cooler, a takeoff on sangria and a newcomer on the scene, is bound to be more popular than ever this summer. The drink is a blend of citrus juice and wine and can be as refreshing a warm-weather quaff as its name implies.

But for summertime entertaining, it is just as easy to make your own versions at home, to serve from pitcher or punch bowl at a summer party, barbecue, around the pool or even for a wedding or anniversary reception.

Even if you generally serve and enjoy fine-quality wines and the best imported spirits, these are not the products that should be involved in punch-bowl mixtures. It would be a waste to mix French chablis with fruit juice or soda water, to serve vintage champagne over a block of ice with strawberries and orange slices floating on top, to empty the contents of a bottle of Stolichnaya imported vodka into the pitcher of Bloody Marys or to select Barbancourt rum for a tropical punch. Wines and spirits of lesser quality, providing they are palatable, are perfectly acceptable for drinks in which they are heavily diluted or flavored.

On the other hand, the fruits and juices that are combined with the spirits in the punch bowl should be of good quality. Even if you use orange juice from concentrate rather than fresh, try adding a little freshly squeezed juice to intensify the flavor. Sparkling water or seltzer, which is unflavored, is a better choice for the mixing medium than club soda, but it is not necessary to use an imported mineral water.

Mix the punch or cooler in jars, containers or pitchers and keep it refrigerated for several hours, to chill thoroughly before serving. A block of ice or frozen block of some of the juice from the punch, frozen at least a day in advance, will keep the beverage chilled better than ice cubes. And for serving a festive summer drink, stemmed goblets filled with ice are a more attractive choice than small, traditional punch cups.

## CRANBERRY CHAMPAGNE
YIELD: 24 DRINKS

2 quarts cranberry juice
2 bottles dry sparkling white wine
1 cup vodka

Strawberry halves, for garnish
Mint leaves, for garnish

**1.** Combine the cranberry juice, one bottle of sparkling wine and the vodka and refrigerate. Refrigerate the second bottle of sparkling wine as well.

**2.** Just before serving pour the chilled cranberry juice and sparkling wine mixture over a block of ice in a punch bowl. Slowly pour in the second bottle of sparkling wine so the punch will froth. Float mint leaves and strawberries on the surface as a garnish and serve over ice in goblets.


## SPARKLING FRUIT COOLER
YIELD: 24 DRINKS

1½ liters dry white wine
1½ liters sparkling water or seltzer
1½ cups unsweetened pineapple juice

3 cups orange juice, preferably fresh
½ cup creme de cassis
Orange slices and pineapple slices, for garnish

**1.** Combine wine, sparkling water, pineapple and orange juices and creme de cassis, mix well and refrigerate.

**2.** Serve over ice from pitchers or punch bowl, decorated with fruit.

*May 26, 1985*


## VICTORIAN GIN PUNCH
### Adapted from DAVID WONDRICH by Florence Fabricant

*Here is a punch to mix with the more flavorful American gins, from a recipe provided to The Times by the drinks historian David Wondrich. His cocktails are light and summery, and a refreshing change from the usual gin and tonic.*
YIELD: 20 DRINKS

3 lemons
¾ cup sugar
1 (750-milliliter) bottle gin

½ cup orange liqueur
liter seltzer, chilled

**1.** Use a vegetable peeler to peel long strips of pith-free skin from the lemons. Place peels in a bowl, add sugar, muddle vigorously and allow to steep 2 to 3 hours. Juice lemons to obtain ¾ cup. Pour lemon juice over peels and stir to dissolve sugar. Transfer to a 3-quart pitcher half-filled with ice.

**2.** Add gin, liqueur and seltzer. Stir and pour into punch cups or short-stemmed glasses, and serve.

*June 12, 2012*

## PASSION FRUIT PUNCH
**Adapted from TINTOL, New York, City, by Florence Fabricant**

*This punch is made with cachaça, the national spirit of Brazil, made from fermented sugar cane juice. Increased interest in the liquor, and Latin American cuisine, has brought several brands to American bars and liquor stores. Use the one you can find. And drink slowly. It's strong.*
YIELD: 4 DRINKS

| | |
|---|---|
| 3 cups passion fruit juice | 1 cup cachaça |
| 4 teaspoons honey | |

**1.** Place ½ cup juice and the honey in a pitcher. Stir to dissolve honey. Stir in remaining juice.

**2.** Add cachaça and stir. Place ice in 4 highball glasses; pour juice mixture over it. Serve with straws.

*June 21, 2006*

## ORIGINAL CHATHAM ARTILLERY PUNCH
**Adapted from DAVID WONDRICH**

*Times are hard, yes, but hard times require respite all the more urgently. The office party has been downsized to a sad little gathering in the conference room; friends are mostly seen as little boxes on Facebook. The big holiday party, the December blowout—someone has to do it.*

*That someone, whoever it is, would be well advised to mix a copious quantity of punch, something strong and serious, unfussy yet with a sense of luxury. A 19th-century recipe for Chatham Artillery Punch, unearthed by the cocktail scholar David Wondrich, would do the trick nicely. Mixing a bowl of it is no more complicated than opening a bottle (or, to be a stickler about it, six bottles). It is highly potent, a punch that packs a punch, but it goes down easy. The someone who serves it will earn a year's worth of gratitude.*
YIELD: ABOUT 25 DRINKS

| | |
|---|---|
| 8 lemons | 750-milliliter bottle dark Jamaican rum |
| 1 pound superfine sugar | 3 bottles Champagne or other sparkling wine |
| 750-milliliter bottle bourbon or rye | Nutmeg |
| 750-milliliter bottle Cognac | |

**1.** Squeeze and strain the lemons to make 16 ounces of juice. Peel the lemons and muddle the peels with the sugar. Let the peels and sugar sit for an hour, then muddle again. Add the lemon juice and stir until sugar has dissolved. Strain out the peels.

**2.** Fill a 2- to 3-gallon bucket or bowl with crushed ice or ice cubes. Add the lemon-sugar mixture and the bourbon, Cognac and rum. Stir and add the Champagne. Taste and adjust for sweetness. Grate nutmeg over the top and serve.

## WENZHOU PUNCH
### Adapted from BOBBY HEUGEL, The Anvil Bar & Refuge, Houston

*People born under the sign of Sagittarius, the astrologers say, are optimistic and good-humored. Yet many of them (and a handful of unlucky Capricorns) are secretly nursing a lifetime of bitter resentment. These are the people whose birthdays have been, year after year, lost in the holiday shuffle.*

*These folks may not say it out loud, but they all want a party of their own, one that does not involve mistletoe or Santa hats. Refreshments should follow suit: appropriately seasonal, but no nog, no glogg.*

*One suggestion: Wenzhou Punch, a whiskey-based invention by the Houston barman Bobby Heugel. Made to feature local satsuma juice, it works equally well with tangerines or clementines. Allspice dram, a lovely liqueur recently revived by the tiki-drink crowd, makes the punch novel and wintry. It might not be enough to melt away years of resentment, but it's a good start.*

YIELD: 3 TO 4 DRINKS

| | |
|---|---|
| 8 ounces bourbon | 2 ounces maple syrup |
| 4 ounces fresh satsuma or tangerine juice | 1 ounces allspice liqueur |

**1.** Shake all ingredients, without ice, in a large container. Pour into a punch bowl with ice. For large batches, use the same ratios.

## CHINASKI
### Adapted from KATIE STIPE

*Every December, in Jewish households across the land, people are rooting around in cupboards, retrieving those two essential ritual objects: the menorah and the grating disc for the food processor. If one is making potato pancakes for Hanukkah (and of course, one should), they should be made in quantity and shared with crowds, the secular and the entirely non-Semitic included.*

*Yet, aside from sweet wine and the occasional medicinal shot of slivovitz, there is not much of a Jewish drinking tradition. So Hanukkah party hosts would do well to swipe a cocktail formulated by Katie Stipe for the Dutch-inflected restaurant Vandaag in the East Village (which has since closed). Served there as a Chinaski, its unlikely combination of ingredients might have been custom-built to pair with latkes: sparkling wine cuts the grease; caraway-flavored aquavit provides a savory edge and an Eastern European air; Cynar, the bitter Italian artichoke liqueur, a subtly vegetal note. Some old-fashioned grandmothers might not approve, but really, do they ever?*

| | |
|---|---|
| 1 ounce aquavit | 1 teaspoon apricot preserves |
| ½ ounce Cynar | Dry sparkling wine |
| ½ ounce fresh lemon juice | 1 thin strip of celery |
| ½ ounce simple syrup (page 27) | |

**1.** Combine aquavit, Cynar, juice, syrup and preserves in a cocktail shaker, add ice and shake.

**2.** Strain into a champagne flute, top with sparkling wine and garnish with celery, preferably twisted into a corkscrew shape.

## MILK PUNCH
### By STEVEN STERN

*Within the short list of socially acceptable morning drinks, there is the school of vigor and the school of solace. A spicy bloody mary slaps you across the face but somehow gives you the strength to take it. Then there is milk punch, served cool and just slightly sweet in the New Orleans style, which eases you gently into activity, holding your hand all the while.*

*The latter is what you want on this day, whatever the day holds. Kingsley Amis was a milk punch partisan, and he recommended it specifically as an aid to surviving "grueling nominal festivities like Christmas morning."*

*Mr. Amis was a bit of a crank, but he had some good ideas about drinking. For his milk punch, he suggested freezing cubes of milk the night before, to chill the drink without watering it down. That is a fine project, if you remember. If you don't, that's fine, too.*

YIELD: 4 DRINKS

½ cup bourbon
½ cup aged rum or brandy
2 cups milk, plus milk frozen into cubes

¼ cup maple syrup
Grated nutmeg

**1.** Stir the spirits, milk and syrup together in a pitcher. Pour into tumblers over frozen milk cubes or ice cubes and dust the tops with grated nutmeg.

*November 10. 2010*

## BRACHETTO HOLIDAY PUNCH
### Adapted from the RED CAT, New York City, by Jonathan Miles

1 ounce Cognac
1 ounce Aperol
½ ounce fresh lemon juice

½ ounce fresh orange juice
3 to 4 ounces Brachetto d'Acqui wine
Orange twist, for garnish

**1.** Combine Cognac, Aperol, and juices with ice in a cocktail shaker and shake.

**2.** Strain into a champagne flute or martini glass, and fill the rest of the glass with the Brachetto d'Acqui. Garnish with the orange twist.

*December 17, 2006*

## PLANTER'S PUNCH
### By ROSIE SCHAAP

*Good for serving one or serving a crowd, rummy planter's punch is just off-sweet and surprisingly subtle.*

2 ounces dark rum
½ ounce fresh lime juice
½ teaspoon simple syrup (page 27)

1 dash Angostura bitters
Soda water, to top (optional)
Pineapple slice, for garnish

**1.** Fill a shaker with ice. Add rum, lime juice, simple syrup and bitters and shake.

**2.** Strain over fresh ice into a highball glass. Top with soda water if you like and garnish with a pineapple slice.

*May 17, 2014*

## SPICED PORT PUNCH
### By ROSIE SCHAAP

*Port, that gentle, rich and comforting spirit, has a whiff of empire about it. This recipe, a strong, port-based punch, works to counteract the image. It's not too sweet, but rich and spicy. It's an easygoing crowd-pleaser and proof that port and orange get along famously. Consider it for the next time you plan a holiday gathering.*

YIELD: VARIES

3 parts ruby port
2 parts brandy
1 part dark rum
1 part cranberry juice

1 part spiced clementine syrup (recipe follows)
One handful clementine peels (with a paring knife, remove as much pith as possible)

**1.** To a large punch bowl, add all the ingredients, plus reserved clementine peels. Stir gently, then add a large block of ice.

**2.** For each serving, add as much seltzer as you like (it's strong) and a little grated nutmeg.

## SPICED CLEMENTINE SYRUP

Per 3 cups fresh clementine juice:
1 cup water
⅔ cup dark brown sugar

1 vanilla bean, sliced lengthwise
1 teaspoon whole allspice
1 (3-inch) chunk fresh ginger, peeled

**1.** In a large pan with a heavy bottom, combine clementine juice with other ingredients by stirring gently. Bring to a boil, then reduce heat to low and simmer for 20 minutes. Remove from heat, strain the liquid (discard the solids) and allow to cool before making the punch.

*December 6, 2013*

# PUNCH-DRUNK LOVE

## By ROSIE SCHAAP

On a good day, the train ride from New York to Burlington, Vt., takes about nine hours. (Train? As I've confessed before, I'm one of those hopeless nondriving New Yorkers. Besides, I love trains. Usually.) But an unseasonably hot Wednesday in late May was not a good day. Forty minutes out of Penn Station, the engine broke down. Off went the lights and the air-conditioning. A "rescue engine" was on its way, but after half an hour slipped by without any sign of deliverance, I began to despair. Then we changed trains. Again. And again.

By the time we boarded the fourth and final train in Springfield, Mass., I was pretty punchy. Fortunately, I fell in with a gaggle of engaging fellow travelers: an engineer-turned-actor, an adventurous young woman and a knife maker from northern Vermont who had the foresight to stash a bottle of Espolón silver tequila in his backpack. What had felt like "No Exit" meets "Lost" meets "The Breakfast Club" soon became a party.

Tequila was never my first choice for liquor. I drank it in college, but it wasn't until I started working at a small bar in my neighborhood a few years ago that I dipped back in. (Margaritas are popular with my customers, and I won't serve a cocktail unless it tastes good to me.) Tequila used to have a bouncing-off-the-walls effect on me, but now what I get is a sense of good cheer and gentle buoyancy—something different from when I drink other spirits. The novelist Kate Christensen, one of the most dedicated tequila advocates I know, says that what she loves about it is the "warmhearted, calm joy" it imparts, and I agree. (Her favorite cocktail is "a shot of tequila with a side of sangrita"—juice, often a mix of tomato and orange with lime, dressed with chili powder, fresh chilies or hot sauce.)

There are plenty of top-shelf tequilas that stand on their own for sipping, but one of tequila's greatest virtues is its value. Like that smooth, clean Espolón, many blanco, or silver, tequilas (the category that requires the least aging) cost less than $25 a bottle, making them ideal for summer entertaining, even on a big scale. At a barbecue in Vermont that weekend, my first watermelon slice of the season got me thinking, so when I returned to New York (without incident), I started tinkering.

Tequila, as it turns out, works wonders as a base for a beautiful, refreshing punch with watermelon purée, fresh lime juice, a bit of salt and slices of green chili, like jalapeño. As pink and green and perfect for a cookout as your uncle's madras shorts, all you need is a patch of grass, something good on the grill and an upbeat soundtrack for a warmhearted, joyful summer party. No broken-down engine required, but I wish my fellow passengers from train No. 56 could join me.

# TEQUILA-WATERMELON PUNCH

*To make watermelon purée, put seedless chunks of watermelon in a blender and pulse, then push the puree through a mesh sieve to make it smoother. (Cutting a whole watermelon might make your kitchen look like a Gallagher set, so it's O.K. to use precut watermelon from a supermarket.)*
YIELD: VARIES

| | |
|---|---|
| 3 parts watermelon purée | Seltzer |
| 1 part silver tequila | Coarse sea salt |
| ½ part fresh lime juice | Sliced jalapeno |
| Agave nectar (optional) | |

**1.** In a large pitcher or bowl, stir together the watermelon purée, tequila and lime juice.

**2.** To sweeten, adjust with agave nectar.

**3.** To serve, pour into glasses over ice, top each glass with seltzer, a pinch of sea salt and slices of jalapeno.

*August 9, 2012*

KENTA GOTO MAKES A TOM AND JERRY AT THE PEGU CLUB, NEW YORK CITY

## CHAPTER 28

# WINTER DRINKS

# RECIPE REDUX 1958: EGGNOG

## By AMANDA HESSER

Eggnogs have long been a Times recipe staple. An 1895 article on Christmas-food traditions noted that Americans eat more lightly than the English throughout the season. The only exception, the writer added, "is eggnogg, a mixture of eggs, milk, sugar, spices, rum, brandy and—headache. This beverage, however, has lately fallen somewhat out of favor. Either our stomachs have grown weaker or our brains stronger, and we are not willing to sacrifice future well-being for the sake of a momentary gratification, even though sanctioned by the precept and example of our ancestors." Well, pooh-pooh!

By the late 1950s, eggnog, and drinking, had staged a comeback. If you already have a favorite eggnog recipe, throw it out, because the one that Craig Claiborne ran in 1958 sweeps the field. What makes Claiborne's Southern-style family recipe different from all the also-rans is that it doesn't pretend to be a drink. He suggests you eat his nog with a spoon. And so you should: it's the only way to get it out of the punch cup.

You begin by beating the egg yolks and sugar until they're as thick as meringue, then loosen them up with bourbon and Cognac and, eventually, fold in both whipped cream and whipped egg whites, so it's like a giant bowl of faintly boozy chiffon. Claiborne smartly adds salt to the egg whites to amplify and sharpen the flavors. The alcohol, which may seem like a lot when you're pouring it in, actually isn't much—just 2 cups to 6 cups other liquid—and so it swims through the layers of egg and cream as an echo to the nog rather than as a belt of good cheer.

The richness of the ingredients hits you about halfway through your cup, and by the time you've reached the bottom, you're done.

I asked Eben Freeman, the head bartender at Tailor in SoHo, to try Claiborne's concoction and to come up with his own interpretation. Freeman is a man who isn't shy about using ingredients like bell peppers in his cocktails, infusing gin with hops and making drinks like "the Waylon," which involves blending bourbon with smoked Coca-Cola; he took to the eggnog with the enthusiasm of a dog unleashed in the park. When you make the old one, Freeman noted, "you're thinking about making soufflés. So naturally I thought of a cheese soufflé. And then I was thinking about fondue, and when you make a traditional fondue, you're usually putting cherry eau de vie into it."

And off he went experimenting. Cheese was figuring into the mix..., but then so was wood. (Yes, wood.) He couldn't settle on just one recipe, so he presented me with two eggnogs: a savory-sweet one in which he infused the cream with Roquefort and scented the nog with poire William, a pear eau de vie..., and another that hewed closely to Claiborne's except that Freeman infused the bourbon with cedar.

Both are stunningly good.. The Roquefort and pear could be served as a cheese course..., the cedar nog as an evening closer. But don't forget to try the original, so you can appreciate the root of such [a] delight.

## 1958: EGGNOG
**Adapted from CRAIG CLAIBORNE**
YIELD: 40 PUNCH-CUP DRINKS

| | |
|---|---|
| 12 farm-fresh eggs, separated | ½ teaspoon salt |
| 1 cup granulated sugar | 3 pints heavy cream |
| 1 cup bourbon | Grated nutmeg |
| 1 cup Cognac | 1 to 2 cups milk (optional) |

**1.** In an electric mixer, beat the egg yolks with the sugar until thick.

**2.** Slowly add the bourbon and Cognac while beating at slow speed. Chill for several hours.

**3.** Add the salt to the egg whites. Beat until almost stiff.

**4.** Whip the cream until stiff.

**5.** Fold the whipped cream into the yolk mixture, then fold in the beaten egg whites. Chill 1 hour.

**6.** When ready to serve, sprinkle the top with freshly grated nutmeg. Serve in punch cups with a spoon.

**7.** If desired, add 1 to 2 cups of milk to the yolk mixture for a thinner eggnog.

**You may halve the recipe for a smaller gathering.**

## 2007: ROQUEFORT-AND-PEAR EGGNOG
**Adapted from EBEN FREEMAN, Tailor, New York City**
YIELD: 10 DRINKS

| | |
|---|---|
| 3 ounces Roquefort cheese, crumbled | 1 tablespoon sugar |
| 1½ cups heavy cream | ¼ cup poire William, or other pear brandy |
| 4 eggs, separated | ½ teaspoon kosher salt |

**1.** One to two days before making the eggnog, combine the cheese and cream in a container and refrigerate for 36 to 48 hours.

**2.** In a mixer fitted with a whisk, combine the egg yolks, sugar and poire William. Beat until pale yellow and emulsified. Chill for 2 hours. Line a sieve with cheesecloth, and strain the cream-and-cheese mixture.

**3.** Whip the cream to stiff peaks, then fold into the egg-yolk mixture. Beat the egg whites until fluffy, then add the salt and continue beating to stiff peaks. Fold into the cream mixture. Chill for 1 hour. Serve in small cups with a spoon.

*December 23, 2007*

## 2007: CEDAR-SCENTED EGGNOG
**Adapted from EBEN FREEMAN, Tailor, New York City**

*"In this recipe,"* Freeman said, *"I wanted to stay true to Craig's. If you want more cedar flavor, omit the Cognac and double the bourbon."*

YIELD: 10 DRINKS

1 cedar plank or 1 sheet of cedar paper, for wrapping food
¼ cup bourbon
4 eggs, separated
¼ cup sugar
¼ cup Cognac
1 ½ cups heavy cream
Pinch salt

**1.** Two days before making the eggnog, infuse the bourbon. Preheat the oven to 350F. Using a vegetable peeler, shave strips of cedar from the cedar plank until you have ¼ cup of shavings (if using cedar paper, break it into pieces). Spread the shavings on a baking sheet and bake in the oven until toasted, about 20 minutes. Let cool, then combine with the bourbon. Cover and let sit for 48 hours.

**2.** Strain the bourbon through a jelly bag or a tea towel. In a mixer fitted with a whisk, beat the egg yolks and sugar until pale and fluffy. With the mixer on low, slowly add the bourbon and the Cognac. Chill for 2 hours.

**3.** Whip the cream to stiff peaks and fold into the yolk mixture. Beat the egg whites and salt to stiff peaks and fold into the same mixture. Chill for 1 hour.

**4.** Serve in small cups, with a spoon.

# GLOGG BEFORE 'NOG
## By ROSIE SCHAAP

Long before I was old enough to enjoy fully the pleasures of glogg — the Swedish yuletide wine mulled with orange peel and spices — its aroma had made me an admirer. I can still summon that first whiff, when, as a child, I stepped inside a small inn where a caldron of the stuff was simmering. Though this admission will make Scandinavians cringe, the fragrance evoked a warmed-up bowl of Froot Loops, a 10-year-old girl's idea of olfactory heaven.

It was the cardamom. (A quick but gratifying Internet search shows that I'm hardly the only one who thinks that the cereal smells uncannily like the spice.) But cardamom also helps distinguish glogg from similar concoctions like Germany's glühwein and English mulled wine, which typically contain none.

I'm no Viking, but glogg (pronounce the "o" like the "eu" in pneumonia) remains my go-to winter warmer, and I make a huge pot whenever I give a holiday party. I like hot, spiced, spiked cider too, but it can be cloyingly sweet. Glogg allows for more control: it tastes deeply and darkly of wine and citrus and spice, and you may add, or entirely omit, sugar (or liquor). It brings a rosy flush to all who drink it—good cheer in a cup, accompanied, ideally, by the thinnest, crispiest, spiciest gingersnaps.

Glogg is also not without controversy. I recently asked two Swedes, a Swedish-American, a Dane and a Norwegian-American for their recipes, and I got five vastly different formulas. The constants are red wine, orange peel, cloves and cardamom. Beyond these, there are innumerable variables: should vodka or brandy be added to make it stronger? Port? But glogg, like most holiday drinks (how many eggnog recipes have you seen?), is more about the idea than the ideal. As long as the essentials are in place, it will work, even if each individual rendition differs from the next.

My friend Annika Sundvik—a Stockholm native and the proprietor and chef at White Slab Palace on the Lower East Side—is a bit of a glogg minimalist (no spirits, no added sugar) and a lifelong fan. But, she says, back home in Sweden, where glogg parties commence on the first night of Advent and do not cease until Christmas, it's easy to succumb to "glogg fatigue." This can be avoided: a single pot of glogg—made for one very cold night per holiday season, to be shared with many friends—should do the trick, even if it leaves you wanting more. Next winter will be here sooner than you think. It always is.

## ANNIKA'S GLOGG

Adapted from ANNIKA SUNDVIK, White Slab Palace, New York City

YIELD: 20 TO 30 DRINKS

| | |
|---|---|
| 5 to 6 (750 ml.) bottles medium-bodied, not-too-dry red wine | (fresh orange peel works fine, too) |
| 5 cinnamon sticks | 1 chunk of peeled, fresh ginger (half grated, half sliced) |
| 1 scant tablespoon whole cloves | Brown sugar or vodka for seasoning (optional) |
| 1 small fistful of green cardamom pods | Blanched almonds and black raisins, for garnish |
| 1 large fistful of dried bitter-orange peel | |

**1.** Bring 1 bottle of the wine, cinnamon sticks, cloves, cardamom pods, dried orange peel and the ginger to a boil in a large pot, lower heat instantly and simmer for 30 minutes.

**2.** Strain liquid through a sieve into a bowl, tie solid ingredients in cheesecloth and return all to the pot.

**3.** Add 4 or 5 more bottles of wine, and let steep, preferably overnight. When reheating, never let the mixture come to a boil. (You can add brown sugar or vodka to taste.)

**4.** Garnish with blanched almonds and black raisins. They are delicious when fished out.

*December 8, 2011*

# FOR EVERY HOLIDAY PARTY, THE RIGHT DRINK

## By STEVEN STERN

---

### APPLE SMASH
**Adapted from BOBBY HEUGEL, The Anvil Bar & Refuge, Houston**

*For urban dwellers, the holiday season is when distant relatives pass through town. They're here to see the big tree, hit some stores. You've met them only a few times, at weddings and such, but when they ask to stay a few nights, of course you say yes.*

*They're nice people, lovely people, but their needs are mysterious. Do they want a tour of the city? Some recommendations? Whatever you suggest, they smile placidly and claim to be content. They head out in the morning and return in the evening with shopping bags full.*

*Maybe you organize a small dinner party, invite a few of your friends. A round of cocktails would be pleasant—nothing fancy, no weird ingredients. You don't want to show off or alienate. An Apple Smash will serve nicely. You break out the shaker, slice some apples, muddle, pour rum and shake. They seem pleased, and perhaps will remember this night more fondly than the lights and souvenir shops. Your work is done.*

| | |
|---|---|
| 2 large apple slices, like Honeycrisp | ½ ounce simple syrup (page 27) |
| 2 ounces white rum | 1 dash bitters, like Fee Brothers Barrel-Aged |
| ½ ounce lemon juice | Cinnamon stick |

**1.** Mash an apple slice in the base of a glass with a muddler. Add remaining ingredients except the remaining apple slice and cinnamon stick and shake.

**2.** Strain into a highball glass filled with crushed ice. Garnish with the remaining apple slice dusted with freshly grated cinnamon.

---

### ANGOSTURA SOUR
**Adapted from KIRK ESTOPINAL, Cure, New Orleans**

*There's a good chance that some night between Thanksgiving and New Year's Day you will be alone, and happy about it. You've begged off a party invitation, maybe. The rest of the family is out of town, or at least out of the house. It's a night to order in or whip up something comforting and simple. There will be no running around town, hunting up ingredients.*

*On such occasions it is useful to know the recipe for one cocktail you can make even if the liquor cabinet is empty: an Angostura Sour. Created by Kirk Estopinal of the New Orleans bar Cure, it is a refinement of an old Charles Baker creation. There is a magical, something-out-of-nothing quality to this drink, because it is made with a spirit that isn't officially a spirit at all. Though Angostura bitters is sold in supermarkets, it is actually a potent 90 proof.*

*If you use a healthy glug rather than a few gentle drops, and temper the Angostura's intense blast of cloves and allspice with sugar syrup, lime and an egg white, you end up with something odd, spicy.*

| | |
|---|---|
| 1 egg white | 1 ½ ounces Angostura bitters |
| ¾ ounce fresh lime juice | 1 ounce simple syrup (page 27) |

**1.** Pour the egg white and lime juice into a cocktail shaker and shake for 30 seconds. Add the bitters and syrup, fill with ice and shake hard for another 30 seconds.

**2.** Strain into a chilled cocktail glass.

## HAPPY HOLIDAZE
### Adapted from ABIGAIL GULLO, Fort Defiance, Brooklyn

*Caroling, wassailing, open sing-ins of "The Messiah": the holidays provide myriad opportunities for the untrained but enthusiastic chorister. But when the time comes for heading out and opening the throat, a creeping bit of stage fright might take hold.*

*Abigail Gullo, a bartender at Fort Defiance in Red Hook, Brooklyn, has concocted a drink, the Happy Holidaze, designed to warm the pipes and buoy the nerves. A cheering cup of hot chocolate with some interesting additions, including Chartreuse, should provide sufficient equanimity to get one to the final hallelujah.*

YIELD: 2 DRINKS

| | |
|---|---|
| 2 cups hot chocolate | 3 tablespoons Cointreau |
| 3 tablespoons green Chartreuse | |

**1.** Add Chartreuse and Cointreau to hot chocolate, stir and serve in heated mugs.

*November 10, 2010*

# AN OLD ACQUAINTANCE TO BE FORGOTTEN
## By JONATHAN MILES

For years, Nick Fauchald used to greet guests at his holiday parties with a steaming cup of mulled wine.

"It was my way of saying, 'Welcome to my home, defrost your hands, inhale some Christmas nostalgia and get working on that buzz,'" said Mr. Fauchald, the editor of Tasting Table New York, a daily e-mail newsletter devoted to food and drink. But after a while, Mr. Fauchald noticed something was amiss. "No one ever asked for seconds," he said.

His conclusion: "It's hot wine." Sigh. "It's not that good."

Mulled wine, like roast goose, is one of those holiday confections that often sounds better than it tastes. Blame Charles Dickens, who made mulled wine—a fragrant mixture of red wine, spices and fruit that dates back to Roman antiquity—the official drink of "A Christmas Carol," thus sealing its place in the season's culinary canon.

Yet back then, said Christopher Tunnah, the general manager and beverage director at the Bedford Post in Bedford, N.Y., "the quality of the wines they were serving was awful. They spiked sweet wine to make it palatable. We're beyond that now."

Well, not quite. The evocation, if not the genuine article, is still as strong as ever. Last year, Mr. Fauchald devised a cold punch—involving zinfandel, Becherovka (a cinnamon-and-anise-flavored liqueur from the Czech Republic) and homemade spiced plum syrup, among other ingredients—as a mulled-wine replacement.

When he served it again this year, at a recent party, "it was gone before dinnertime," he said. The only thing missing, Mr. Fauchald said, was the room-wafting, aroma therapeutic scent of the spices steeping in the hot wine. But he figured that simmering some cloves and cinnamon sticks and other spices in water might take care of that atmospheric void.

Mr. Tunnah took a similar route when he was concocting drinks for the Farmhouse, a restaurant that opened earlier this month at Bedford Post, with the actor Richard Gere as one of its owners. Wanting to evoke the "Christmas-spicy flavors" of mulled wine without subjecting a decent bottle of wine to the heat of a stove burner, which he said transforms it from "pleasurable to medicinal," Mr. Tunnah combined bourbon, Cointreau and Concord grape juice with heavy doses of bitters to produce a cocktail he calls a Mulled Manhattan.

It's a classic grape-and-grain mixture, as jolly and red as a Santa suit, that derives its Dickensian tang from the nutmeg hints in Angostura bitters and the clove-studded orange flavors of orange bitters. Craving seconds is easy.

It's a shame, in fact, that Mr. Tunnah wasn't behind the bar when Clarence Odbody, George Bailey's guardian angel in the holiday film staple "It's a Wonderful Life," ordered mulled wine at Nick's. "Heavy on the cinnamon and light on the cloves," Clarence said, provoking a threatening display of the bartender's fist. Clarence had to settle for a double bourbon. Mr. Tunnah could have offered Clarence a far more festive alternative, maybe earning himself some angel wings of his own.

## MULLED MANHATAN
### Adapted From BEDFORD POST, Bedford, N.Y.

*This classic grape-and-grain mixture came to us from Christopher Tunnah, the general manager and beverage director at the Bedford Post in Bedford, N.Y. It's as jolly and red as a Santa suit, and it derives its Dickensian tang from the nutmeg hints in Angostura bitters and the clove-studded orange flavors of orange bitters. Craving seconds is easy.*

| | |
|---|---|
| Orange slice, for muddling | Two generous dashes Angostura bitters |
| 1 ¼ ounces bourbon | 4 ounces Concord grape juice |
| ½ ounce Cointreau | Orange twist and maraschino cherry, for garnish |
| Dash of orange bitters | |

**1.** Muddle the orange slice in the bottom of a mixing glass. Fill with ice then add the bourbon, Cointreau and bitters, and stir well. Top with the grape juice.

**2.** Pour into a glass and garnish with the orange twist and cherry.

*December 21, 2008*

# A REGIONAL ODDBALL, RESURRECTED FOR CHILLIEST OF DAYS

## By ROBERT SIMONSON

Dickensian trappings like wassail, flaming punch or mulled wine didn't figure at all in the Christmases of my Wisconsin childhood. But at some point during the day, the adults would all hoist a hot mug of Anglo-American nostalgia: a Tom and Jerry.

The drink has nothing to do with the cartoon cat and mouse, or Jerry Thomas, the celebrated New York barman of the 1800's, who often boasted of inventing it. It is a rich holiday elixir, a relative of eggnog that flourished in America in the 19th and early 20th centuries, and is frequently (though not definitively) credited to Pierce Egan, the English chronicler of sports and popular culture.

The milky broth was once so popular that an ancillary trade in Tom and Jerry punch-bowl sets sprang up. You can still spot them in antiques stores, typically emblazoned with the drink's name in Old English type.

I don't know if my parents made a good Tom and Jerry; they used a mix found in grocery stores in Wisconsin in the colder months. But they made it like clockwork every December, as did many of the families we knew.

And until I went to college, I thought everyone made Tom and Jerrys at Christmas. Only then did I realize the drink was a provincial oddity that had somehow clung to life in Wisconsin and bordering states, while falling into obscurity everywhere else.

"I think one of the reasons that it's persisted in Wisconsin is the popularity of brandy-drinking here," said Jim Draeger, one of the authors of "Bottoms Up," a recently published survey of Wisconsin's historical taverns. (The state, it should be noted, is also the incubator of that curious cocktail variation, the brandy old-fashioned.) "We're also known as the dairy state, and it's a dairy drink."

The book's other author, Mark Speltz, posed an additional theory: "I put it to Wisconsin's Germanic background. You get the people with the batter. It's cold here nine months out of the year."

John Dye, owner of the decades-old Bryant's Cocktail Lounge in Milwaukee, agrees on the weather argument. "And I think trends just move a little slower here," he said. "They have their traditions here and they stick to them."

Over the last decade, the Tom and Jerry has enjoyed a small resurgence outside the Midwest, as it has been rediscovered by mixologists eager to serve something traditional, yet different, during the holidays. Perhaps the best known example in New York is the delicious frothy soup that appears at Pegu Club in SoHo every holiday season as soon as the temperature takes a dive.

"Tom and Jerry has been in my heart every since I worked at Blackbird for Dale," recalled Audrey Saunders, proprietor of the bar. She was referring to the renowned barman Dale DeGroff, who ran the bar program at the short-lived Midtown restaurant Blackbird in 1999. "That was my first experience with it. He said, 'O.K., we're putting out the Tom and Jerry for Christmas.' I said, 'What's Tom and Jerry?' I got the history and the accouterments. The first time he put it out on the bar, it was, oh, my God, the magic of Christmas."

For the recipe she serves at Pegu, Ms. Saunders cut back on the sugar. "I felt it could be cloying," she said. "My addition was the Angostura bitters. It helps dry it down and give it the structure it needs." She also adds vanilla. "It makes a huge difference."

(There is no set date for the drink's arrival at Pegu Club, but Ms. Saunders said it would probably make its debut before Christmas, "unless its 50 degrees out—so hard to gauge these days." The Tom and Jerry schedule at Dram, a Williamsburg bar, is similarly sketchy, the drink popping up on selective snowy days and New Year's Eve.)

One bar that was ahead of the curve is the Elizabeth Street saloon that calls itself Tom & Jerry's. It opened in 1993, and owes its name to its vast collection of Tom and Jerry bowls, which were donated by Joe Wilfer, a printer and Wisconsin native who collected them. The tall, many-shelved back bar was built expressly to accommodate them.

Its name notwithstanding, Tom & Jerry's serves the drink only once a year, at an annual holiday party for which a number of Mr. Wilfer's Wisconsin friends make the trip. Joanna James, an owner of the bar, has no interest in making the drink more often. "It's kind of labor intensive," she said.

Also, she doesn't like the stuff. "It's too rich and heavy for me," she said, laughing. "But I can see why people would love it."

## TOM AND JERRY
**Adapted from AUDREY SAUNDERS, Pegu Club, New York City**
YIELD: 1 DRINK (BATTER FOR ABOUT 10 DRINKS)

**FOR THE BATTER:**
6 eggs (yolks and whites separated)
1 pound sugar
1 ounce añejo rum
3 tablespoons vanilla extract
¾ teaspoon ground cinnamon
¼ teaspoon ground allspice
¼ teaspoon ground nutmeg

¼ teaspoon ground cloves
2 dashes Angostura bitters
**FOR EACH DRINK:**
6 ounces milk
1 ounce añejo rum
1 ounce V.S. Cognac
Nutmeg, for garnish

**1.** Make the batter: In a bowl, beat egg yolks until they are as thin as water. While beating, gradually add sugar, rum, vanilla, spices and bitters. In a separate bowl, beat egg whites until stiff. Fold into yolk mixture. If not using immediately, refrigerate batter.

**2.** Make the drink: In a small saucepan, bring milk to boil. Meanwhile, warm a roughly 10-ounce Irish coffee mug in the oven. Pour in 2 ounces batter. Add 1 ounce rum and 1 ounce Cognac. Fill with boiling milk, stirring briskly with a small whisk while adding, so batter and milk are well mixed. Dust with nutmeg.

**Because the batter contains raw eggs, it must be refrigerated when not being used, at no higher than 41 degrees. The batter should be used only on the day it is made, then discarded.**

*December 11, 2012*

# HOLIDAY NOSTALGIA, SERVED WARM
## By ROSIE SCHAAP

I am a Dutch-German-Hungarian-Polish-Russian-Jewish-American woman. Yet every December, I turn into a 19th-century British gentleman.

It's a little embarrassing, this surge of Anglophilia. If I must think of myself as an occasional Englishman, I'd rather be, say, a soccer-loving, beer-swilling extra in a Ken Loach movie, not a Dickens re-enactor.

Still, I put up a Christmas tree. I cook a hefty rib roast, reserving its drippings for Yorkshire pudding.

This isn't a recent development: My mother, whose father was an unrepentant Anglophile, often made a roast on Christmas and sometimes followed it with plum pudding and hard sauce for dessert. (I usually swap that out for a big chunk of Stilton, served with port.)

But this year, I'm adding something else to my faux-English Christmas repast: a great big bowl of wassail, a hot winter punch made with cider, ale, spices and an optional garnish of toast. Yes, toast.

My hope is that it will warm up my holiday dinner guests, encourage them to linger a little longer at the table—and maybe even inspire us all to sing a wassailing song or two.

Wassail (pronounced WAHS-ul or wah-SALE) is enjoying a small revival in New York bars these days, particularly those with nostalgic tendencies, whipped up in big pots or slow cookers. But for those of us who have any active associations with wassail, they are probably musical. "Here We Come a-Wassailing" is about as likely to turn up on your supermarket's holiday Muzak loop as "The Christmas Song" or "Frosty the Snowman."

And therein lies the beauty of wassail: more than just another nice-tasting drink, it's part of a long (if largely forgotten) tradition of celebrating the life that winter can seem determined to snuff out. It's a fragrant, warming concoction mixed in bulk and set out for sharing, all but demanding that you call in a crowd. There's really no such thing as wassail for one.

It's a noun, a verb and even a salutation.

The word comes from the Middle English waes hael, a phrase entreating us to be hale, much like the toast "To your health." The song we're most familiar with ("Here we come a-wassailing among the leaves so green") is a relative newcomer, from the mid-19th century.

Danny Lopez, the British consul general in New York, explained to me that wassailing is "an ancient ceremony that involves singing and drinking to the health of trees." But many wassailers skip the trees, and instead go singing door-to-door, exchanging good wishes and drinks.

The historian Roy Christian, in his 1966 book, "Old English Customs," described the apple wassailing that was still taking place in several villages in England's West Country: "The villagers form a circle round the largest apple tree in the selected orchard. Pieces of toast soaked in cider are hung in the branches for robins, who represent the 'good spirits' of the tree. The leading wassailer utters an incantation and shotgun volleys are fired through the branches to frighten away the evil spirits. Then the tree is toasted in cider and urged in song to bring forth much fruit." (This might explain the occasional use of toast to garnish the punch.)

Today, local historical societies keep the tradition alive, but it means little in the holiday celebrations of most Britons. Even the taste of wassail is a bit hazy to many who grew up with it.

Stephen Gardner, 50, a Brooklyn illustrator who often draws and paints bar scenes, remembers drinking the stuff as a teenager in Devon, in the West Country. . "I always considered it an old person's drink," he said. "It was very strong, but it was always something I remember being forced on me whilst I was waiting for my mate to get ready to go out to the pubs."

The proper contents of the drink remain murky. On the Web forum of River Cottage, an English organization that offers courses in foraging, butchering and other traditional food arts, a commenter called chickenrun sent up flares in December 2008, writing: "Does anyone have a good traditional wassail recipe? We've looked online, but every one we've seen is completely different from the other!"

As far as I can tell, four years later, chickenrun has received no recipe. I share the frustration, having encountered recipes for both wine-based and ale-based wassail. For wassail fortified with sherry, punctuated with pineapple juice and thickened with eggs. For wassail topped with bread, and with floating crabapples. There are, it seems, innumerable ways to make wassail, but what most share are apples (whole, in the form of cider, or both), spices and, frequently, ale.

What sparked my interest was the unusual wassail I sampled last winter at the Drink, a cozy bar in Williamsburg, Brooklyn. Adam Collison, an owner, based his recipe on one he had learned while working at a Baltimore food shop. It is cider-based, but distinguished by sour cherry mash, which contributes a tanginess that offsets and mellows the apples' sweetness. It was unlike any punch I had tasted before: faintly reminiscent of cherry soda, amped up by whiskey and a complex mixture of ginger, cinnamon, peppercorns, cloves, allspice, nutmeg and orange peel.

Wassail has other champions in New York. Lee Papo, the owner of Gordon Bennett, a British-inflected pub in Williamsburg, worked for years in English and Irish bars in New York. A friend who grew up in Brighton, England, gave Ms. Papo her family's recipe, which requires ale and cider.

But at Gordon Bennett, which counts many English expatriates among its regulars, no one knew a thing about wassail. They do now. "They love it," Ms. Papo said, in part because it makes the bar smell so good.

She ladles it from a pot into thermal glass mugs. "Usually one person at a table will order it, and by the next round everyone follows," Ms. Papo said. "It definitely does bring people together. And the first winter we were open, there were major storms. I had a couple cross-country ski three times over the Williamsburg Bridge from the Lower East Side for some wassail. It was a very special New York moment."

The bartender Jenn Dowds serves wassail at the Churchill, a Midtown Manhattan pub so steeped in Anglophilia that a loop of Churchill's speeches plays in the restrooms. Ms. Dowds describes her own background as "American mutt: Polish, English, Scottish and Native American." She didn't grow up drinking wassail, but she and the bar's English and Irish owners felt it was a natural for the menu.

"I didn't know what it was, but I wanted to do warm winter drinks," Ms. Dowds said. And as she researched wassail and its history, she fell into a familiar rabbit hole: Wine or cider? Which spices? Any garnish? After some tinkering, she developed a recipe that includes cider (both regular and hard) and Madeira, whose sweetness mitigates the bitterness in the ale. For large parties at the bar, she serves the wassail from a bowl. "The drink encourages a communal spirit," she said.

Ms. Dowds took care with her research and experimenting, and it shows in her balanced, thoughtful recipe, which I'll use for my holiday gathering. The ale and wine distinguish it from everyday mulled cider; but without toast, eggs or other such curiosities among its contents, its flavors are familiar enough to appeal to all my guests.

Among the most faithful wassail boosters is the Royal Heritage Society of the Delaware Valley, which has kept the flame burning since 1982. Rob D'Amico, the caretaker at Ormiston Mansion, the old Philadelphia house where the society is based, has made the punch for the society's annual Candlelight Wassail for six years. Mr. D'Amico got his recipe from one of the society's previous presidents. But, he said, "she encouraged me to experiment with it a little, so there's no hard and fast rule about the amount of cinnamon, cloves or sugar."

The drink, he said, relaxes people.

"After a cup or two, it seems to help some bashful folks to overcome their nerves when the singing begins."

Judging from the pictures I've seen, the wassail at Ormiston Mansion looks like a scene lifted from Charles Dickens. And if any single figure can be blamed for perpetuating (perhaps even inventing) the notion of a traditional British Christmas, he's the man.

"A Christmas Carol" reminds us that no one should be deprived a decent living, a hearty dinner, a bit of drink, a reprieve, a glimmer of holiday hopefulness. Scrooge turns around. Tiny Tim does not die. And wassail is not dead yet, either.

So go ahead. Embrace your inner Anglophile. Have your roast and Yorkshire pudding, your wassail and mince pie. God bless us, every one.

WASSAIL AT THE CHURCHILL, NEW YORK CITY

## WASSAIL
### Adapted from JENN DOWDS, The Churchill, New York City

*Here is the beauty of wassail: more than just another nice-tasting drink, it's part of a long (if largely forgotten) tradition of celebrating the life that winter can seem determined to snuff out. It's a fragrant, warming concoction mixed in bulk and set out for sharing, all but demanding that you call in a crowd. There's really no such thing as wassail for one. A punch bowl is good for this, although you can also ladle it into individual cups.*

YIELD: 12 DRINKS

5 to 6 small to medium honeycrisp (or Fuji or McIntosh) apples, cored
½ cup light brown sugar
½ cup dark brown sugar
2 cups Madeira
2 bottles (22 ⅖ ounces) London Pride Ale
4 bottles (48 ounces) Strongbow English Cider
1 cup apple cider
12 whole cloves
12 whole allspice berries
2 cinnamon sticks, 2 inches long
2 strips orange peel, 2 inches long
1 teaspoon ground ginger
1 teaspoon ground nutmeg

**1.** Heat oven to 350° F. Place apples in a 9-by-9-inch glass baking dish. Spoon light and dark brown sugar into center of each apple, dividing sugar evenly among them. Pour 1 cup water into bottom of dish and bake until tender, about 1 hour.

**2.** Meanwhile, pour Madeira, ale and English and apple ciders into a large slow cooker or heavy pot. Place cloves, allspice, cinnamon and orange peel into cheesecloth, tie shut with kitchen twine and add to slow cooker or pot along with ginger and nutmeg. Set slow cooker to medium, or place pot over low heat. Gently simmer for about 1 hour, while apples bake, or longer if desired.

**3.** Add liquid from the baking dish and stir to combine. Using tongs, transfer apples into slow cooker or pot to garnish. Reduce heat. Ladle hot wassail into heatproof cups to serve.

*December 11, 2012*

## RUM RAISIN HOT COCOA
### By ROSIE SCHAAP

2 teaspoons cocoa powder
1½ teaspoons demerara sugar
1 teaspoon dark crème de cacao
Half-and-half as needed (about 1 tablespoon)
7 ounces milk
1 ounce dark rum
3 rum-soaked raisins
Whipped cream

**1.** In a saucepan over low heat, combine cocoa powder, sugar, crème de cacao and just enough half-and-half to make a slurry. Add milk and whisk until blended (be careful not to boil). Remove from heat and add rum.

**2.** To serve, put three rum-soaked raisins in a mug, pour in the cocoa mixture and top with cream that has been freshly whipped with a little rum.

*October 11, 2012*

# SAVING THE TODDY

## By JONATHAN MILES

By proposing to add polar bears to the list of "threatened" species last month, the Bush administration seemed to finally acknowledge that global warming is taking a toll. With rising sea temperatures shrinking the polar ice cap, "the polar bears' habitat," said Interior Secretary Dirk Kempthorne, "may literally be melting."

Closer to home and heart, I'd been worrying about another sort of species that—at least this season—seems terribly vulnerable to climate change: the hot toddy.

Like polar bears, these cold-weather cocktails depend upon frigid temperatures to survive. And frigid temperatures have been a conspicuous no-show in New York this winter.

No one longs to warm their hands on a near-scalding mug or experience that beautifully restorative surge of heat and alcohol that arrives with the first sip of a toddy when it's 65 degrees and above outside. That's margarita weather.

At Hearth, a restaurant on the corner of East 12th Street and First Avenue where the name alone evokes images of warming, salutary comfort, sales of hot drinks—like Hearth's superlative hot buttered rum—are down 50 to 60 percent, said Paul Grieco, the general manager.

If the doomsayers are correct, in suggesting that this balmy season may be a glimpse of the future, then what's to become of the toddies? As with wildlife species, the key to survival may be adaptability. Which is why Hearth's Kathy Madison, a simple and soul-satisfying combination of bourbon and ginger-infused apple cider, might just endure.

"You know, it's just as good cold," Hearth's bartender, Stephanie Schneider, told me recently, as I was pretending to be cold in order to fully appreciate a steaming Kathy Madison. (The drink's namesake, Ms. Schneider said, was a legendary apple peeler whose record peel measured 172 feet 4 inches.) To prove it, she mixed a second Kathy Madison, this one poured over ice rather than heated in a mug.

Instead of tasting like winter, it tasted like fall, the ginger adding a whisper of spice to the familiar cider flavor, and the bourbon an oak-tinged warmth. This was eminently appropriate, since the temperature outside was a tart but not crisp 55 degrees.

"Arctic polar bears are becoming canaries in the mine, warning of the consequences of global warming," read an editorial in The Boston Globe two weeks ago. Well, here's my own dead canary: So far this winter, my favorite hot drink was cold.

## KATHY MADISON
**Adapted from HEARTH, New York City**

6 ounces ginger-infused apple cider      2 ounces Jim Beam bourbon
¼-inch piece of ginger

**1.** To infuse the cider, peel and chop the ginger. Bring the cider to a boil, add the ginger, and turn off the heat. Steep about 30 minutes, then purée the mixture in a blender and strain through a fine-mesh sieve or cheesecloth. (Refrigerate until ready to use.)

**2.** To serve hot, heat the cider almost to a boil, add the bourbon, and serve in a mug. To serve cold, mix the cider with the bourbon and pour into a glass over ice.

**For multiple servings, use a 1½-inch piece of ginger per quart of cider and 2 ounces of bourbon for each drink.**

*January 14, 2007*

# POUR THE PORT, HOLD THE STODGINESS
## By ROSIE SCHAAP

It's not a fancy bar, the place where I work, but we do carry port. Just one brand is enough for our purposes. In my nearly four years of working there, I've only seen one person order it: a middle-aged man who shows up maybe once every six weeks (on my shift, anyway; I suspect he comes at other times too), drinks three glasses and leaves.

Whenever these visits happen, it feels as if the whole tone of the bar gently transforms. Even the lighting seems to soften a bit and become warmer. I understand I'll be pulling pints of Pabst soon enough, but for a couple of hours or so, while the port drinker is on the premises, the little pub feels older, more grown-up, not unlike a club, but without any unseemly elitism or membership dues.

I know, I know. Port has a whiff of empire about it, and that doesn't sit well with every drinker. It has become something of a stock figure: a stodgy old man, a bit of a snob, the indignant, unknowing butt of a joke or two. You may have heard some variation of the old line that you cannot drink port before your 60th birthday, or before 10 p.m.

This, as a stodgy old man might say, is utter rubbish. Port is as good before dinner as after. And in truth, port, as we know it, isn't even that old, as far as the history of drinking goes, dating back to the late 17th century. True port must come from the Douro region of Portugal, but the British played a huge role in its production and popularization. Port is red wine fortified with grape spirit—easy to drink and probably more versatile than you suspect. I think about port particularly at this time of year, because somewhere in the past decade, I got into the habit of serving it after Christmas dinner, with a great redolent chunk of Stilton and some very dark, good chocolate.

If you have a fine vintage bottle, you'll certainly want to decant it and drink it as is. But with inexpensive ruby ports, which won't have the complexity of most vintage ports but are often delicious nonetheless, I like to mix it up. If you've been making the same punch (or egg nog or mulled wine) for your seasonal parties year after year, maybe this winter you'll try the recipe here for a quite strong, port-based punch. Not too sweet, but rich and spicy, it's an easygoing crowd-pleaser and proof that port and orange get along famously.

Best of all is a port toddy, one of the great, largely unsung winter delights. Heaven knows I love my whiskey, hot or cold or at room temperature, but replacing it with port in a toddy leads to something surprising and special. I wouldn't dare say there's any science to support this, but to me, a port toddy feels somehow more curative than one with harder spirits: it's like the alcohol-fortified equivalent of a bowl of homemade chicken soup.

Ultimately, port is just too gentle and comforting to be called stuffy. But don't let me stop you if you happen to have a tufted leather wing chair, a brace of Cavalier King Charles spaniels and the diary of Samuel Pepys. These, too, go well with port.

## PORT TODDY

*A port today is one of winter's unsung delights. Replacing whiskey with port in a toddy leads to something surprising and special. Somehow, it feels more curative than one with harder spirits: it's like the alcohol-fortified equivalent of a bowl of homemade chicken soup. This requires a ruby port, which is the cheapest and most easily found.*

3 ounces ruby port (preferably Fonseca or Taylor Fladgate)

1 teaspoon brown sugar

1 teaspoon freshly squeezed lemon juice

1 teaspoon freshly squeezed orange juice

1 cinnamon stick

Water just off the boil

1 (1-inch-wide) ribbon of orange peel studded with 3 to 5 cloves, for garnish

**1.** In a mug or heatproof glass, stir the port, sugar and juices together with the cinnamon stick, leaving the cinnamon in the vessel.

**2.** Add hot water to fill, and garnish with the clove-studded orange peel.

*December 6, 2013*

NATASHA DAVID AT NITECAP ON THE LOWER EAST SIDE

CHAPTER 29

# BEER

# KEEP YOUR HEAD
# ON LAZY, HAZY DAYS

## By ROBERT SIMONSON

I like beer. I like cocktails. I don't like beer cocktails.

These hybrids of malt and mixology are among the few sorts of drinks that, in my years of sampling cocktails, I've typically put down before finishing. Still, I keep trying them, mainly because today's young bartenders keep creating new ones.

Mark Pascal, an owner of Stage Left, a restaurant in New Brunswick, N.J., that has had a sophisticated cocktail list since the early 1990s, thinks he knows why they do. "It's because they love beer," he said. "What's the first thing a bartender goes for after making cocktails all day? A beer. They think that it tastes so good, it must make a great ingredient. But it doesn't. Beer is its own thing."

I've pretty much belonged to that camp. The way some whiskey devotees feel about their chosen spirit—that to mix it with anything is a misstep—is how I feel about beer. A beer cocktail seems like a shotgun marriage that can lead only to discord: sour, malty concoctions in which the various flavors don't meld.

But in recent months of sampling, I've learned (one drink at a time) that a well-conceived, well-made beer cocktail can be a wonderful thing. Light in body and low in alcohol, it's well suited to summer. Its effervescence can add lightness and length, creating a drink you can linger over.

Beer cocktails are not new. But until recently, they were pitiably simple. There were the Shandy (beer and lemonade or ginger ale) and the Black Velvet (stout with sparkling wine). The Michelada, beer's answer to the Bloody Mary, was about as complicated as things got. The craft cocktail movement changed that; many new beer drinks have complex structures and unexpected ingredients.

Take the Slow Clap, a cocktail invented by Ivy Mix at Clover Club in Brooklyn. It combines Green Flash West Coast I.P.A. with Old Tom Gin (a sweeter form of gin), the Italian digestive Cardamaro, camomile syrup and lemon juice. "If you have a really very robust beer, you can use that as a backbone," Ms. Mix said of the Green Flash. "I find that more interesting, personally."

I tried it; I liked it. The soothing camomile and mild Cardamaro manage to calm down the hyper-hoppy beer into an unexpectedly fruity and floral whole. Here was a beer cocktail I would order again. I found my next winner, a drink called the High Five, at Third Rail, a new bar in the Dogpatch neighborhood of San Francisco. Jeff Lyon, an owner there, surprised himself a few months ago by successfully compounding what he called "an alcoholic kind of cola" by mixing the thick, citrusy Italian amaro Averna, the gingersnap-flavored liqueur Snap, lime juice, sugar and Old Brick Bitter, an English-style beer made by Linden Street Brewery in Oakland, Calif. "It's the first beer cocktail I've made that seems to be a little more than the sum of its parts," Mr. Lyon said. "It's not just beer and some flavors."

There are more: the Jardin Fresca, with elderflower liqueur, and the Fade to Black, with rum, mezcal and the baking-spice-flavored Italian amaro Ramazzotti, both at Mayahuel, a tequila and mezcal bar in the East Village that has had a dedicated beer cocktail section on its drink list since it opened in 2009. Mayahuel also has one of the most unlikely beer cocktails I've encountered, the Yukon Cornelius, an oddball cast of characters including peach liqueur, mezcal and aquavit.

These may sound a bit fussy, the syrups, liqueurs and all. But they come together. Find a flavor you like, master the recipe and relax. It's summer, after all. And that half-bottle of brew left over? Hand it to your just-plain-beer-loving pal.

---

## FADE TO BLACK
### Adapted from JEREMY OERTEL, Mayahuel, New York City

*A spin on the old drink category of the flip—which involves the use of a whole egg—the Fade to Black illustrates the potential versatility of cocktails using beer. Rich, dessertlike and potent, this is that rare beast: an after-dinner beer cocktail. Using raw egg has become a common practice in cocktail bars over the past decade. There is no good substitute for the texture and flavor that a raw egg lends, so readers who fear contamination may want to refrain.*

| | |
|---|---|
| 1 ounce mescal, preferably Del Maguey Vida | ½ ounce agave syrup |
| 1 ounce Ramazzotti amaro | 1 egg |
| ¼ ounce navy strength Jamaican rum, preferably Smith & Cross | Pinch of salt |
| | 2 dashes Bittermens mole bitters |
| | 2 ounces Negra Modelo beer |

**1.** In a cocktail shaker, combine all ingredients except the beer, and shake until integrated, about 30 seconds. Fill three-quarters full with ice and shake for another 30 seconds.

**2.** Strain into an 8-ounce highball glass with no ice. Top with the beer. Stir briefly with a bar spoon to integrate ingredients.

THE HIGH FIVE

## HIGH FIVE
**Adapted from JEFF LYON, Third Rail, San Francisco, Calif.**

*This drink is a little miracle in liquid prestidigitation: five ingredients (three of them alcoholic) getting together to assume the guise of an innocent cherry cola. That flavor profile was exactly the intention of the bartender Jeff Lyon, who set out to make an alcoholic cola that tasted like "more than the sum of its parts."*

1 ¼ ounces Averna amaro
1 ¾ ounces fresh lime juice
½ ounce simple syrup (page 27)

¼ ounce Snap liqueur
3 ounces Linden Street Old Brick Bitter
   or Dogfish Head Indian Brown Ale
1 orange wheel, for garnish

**1.** In a cocktail shaker three-quarters filled with ice, combine all ingredients except the beer and orange wheel. Shake until chilled, about 30 seconds.

**2.** Strain into a Collins glass filled with ice. Top with the beer. Stir briefly with a bar spoon to integrate ingredients. Garnish with orange wheel.

## SLOW CLAP
**Adapted from IVY MIX, Clover Club, Brooklyn**

*The bartender Ivy Mix's inspiration for this drink began with an appreciation for Greenflash's very hoppy West Coast IPA, and a wish to round out its character with softer flavors. A calming, floral chamomile syrup and the mild amaro Cardamaro serve that purpose, while the barrel-aged Spring 44 Old Tom Gin adds structure and a different edge to match that of the beer. The hops and tannins notwithstanding, this is a drink with an appealingly citrusy, floral personality.*

½ ounce chamomile syrup (see below)
1 ½ ounces Spring 44 Old Tom Gin
¾ ounce fresh lemon juice, plus lemon

wheel for garnish
½ ounce Cardamaro
3 ounces West Coast Green Flash I.P.A.

**1.** To make chamomile syrup, make a strong chamomile tea, using 2 to 3 tea bags to 1 pint hot water. Let steep for 20 minutes, or until strong. Remove tea bags. Warm 1 cup sugar in ½ cup tea in a saucepan over low heat until dissolved. Cool to room temperature before using. (There will be extra syrup; refrigerate if not using immediately.)

**2.** In a cocktail shaker three-quarters filled with ice, combine all ingredients except the beer and lemon wheel. Shake until chilled, about 30 seconds.

**3.** Strain into a pilsner glass filled with ice. Top with beer. Stir briefly with a bar spoon to integrate ingredients. Garnish with lemon wheel.

## JARDIN FRESCA
**Adapted from PHILIP WARD, Mayahuel, New York City**

*As advertised, there's quite a bit of the garden in this drink: elderflowers from the St. Germain; artichoke, rhubarb and other flavors from the Cynar; as well jalapeño, celery and cucumber. The celery bitters hit your nose and taste buds first, while the pepper-infused tequila leaves you with a pleasant, lasting kick. The cocktail is easy to drink, but never dull.*

1 ounce jalapeño-infused blanco tequila (see below)

½ ounce Cynar

½ ounce St. Germain

½ ounce fresh lemon juice

½ ounce simple syrup (page 27)

2 cucumber slices

1 dash celery bitters

Salt

4 ounces Victoria beer

**1.** To make jalapeño-infused tequila, combine 1 pint blanco tequila with only the white membranes and seeds of 1 jalapeño pepper, and let sit for 10 to 20 minutes, or until it is mildly hot. Strain liquid and store in a glass container.

**2.** In a cocktail shaker three-quarters filled with ice, combine all ingredients except the salt and beer. Shake until chilled, about 30 seconds.

**3.** Moisten the rim of a 12-ounce highball or pilsner glass with salt, and fill with 2 sizable ice cubes. Strain contents of mixing glass into salted glass. Top with beer. Stir briefly with a bar spoon to integrate ingredients.

## YUKON CORNELIUS
**Adapted from NATASHA DAVID, Mayahuel, New York City**

*The bartender Natasha David likes to create beer cocktails because she doesn't like beer and wants to "make it taste better." With this drink, she did so by combining it with a sprawling and unlikely array of flavors: herbal aquavit, sweet peach liqueur, spicy ginger syrup and smoky mezcal. The flavorful result is bright, fruity and unexpected.*

¾ ounce aquavit, preferably Krogstad

¾ ounce mescal, preferably Del Maguey Vida

½ ounce peach liqueur, preferably Giffard

½ ounce ginger syrup (see sidebar)

½ ounce fresh lemon juice, plus lemon wheel for garnish

2 ounces Modelo Especial beer

Candied ginger, for garnish

**1.** In a cocktail shaker three-quarters filled with ice, combine all ingredients except the beer, lemon wheel and ginger. Shake until chilled, about 30 seconds.

**2.** Strain into 10-ounce highball glass half-filled with ice. Top with beer. Stir briefly with bar spoon to integrate ingredients. Garnish with lemon wheel and piece of candied ginger.

**Note:** To make ginger syrup, combine 1 cup chopped ginger with 1 1/2 cups water in a pot and bring to a boil. Reduce heat and simmer for 2 minutes. Remove from heat and let sit, covered, for 2 hours. Strain off ginger, making sure to press all the juice out of the ginger. Warm 1 cup sugar and 1/2 cup ginger solution in a saucepan over low heat until dissolved. Let cool. (There will be extra syrup; refrigerate if not using immediately.)

*May 20, 2014*

# COCKTAILS DANCE
# ON THE HEAD OF A BEER

## By BETSY ANDREWS

"Beer" and "cocktails" are usually separated by a comma. But now bartenders are experimenting with crossover drinks that marry beers with spirits, mixers, even wines, going far beyond the shot-and-a-pint boilermaker.

In New York, at PDT and Mayahuel, they're mixing hot sauce, mezcal and beer to create smoky riffs on the michelada, a classic Mexican cerveza preparada, or prepared beer.

Bartenders at the Alembic in San Francisco top coffee liqueur and fizzy Italian red wine with porter foam to make a Vice Grip.

The beergarita—a margarita amplified by Flemish sour ale and framboise—is popular at the Small Bar on Division Street in Chicago. "Beer cocktails are an alternative to a pint," said Ty Fujimura, co-owner with Phil McFarland.

In May, on the Session, a monthly virtual workshop on beer, nearly 40 bloggers contributed recipes for craft-beer-based drinks with names like Freak-out in a Moonshine Day Dream.

"If I'm going to have an amazing craft beer, why not also have it in an excellent beer cocktail?" asked the host of the May Session, Joe Ruvel of beeratjoes.com. "Other countries, like France and Belgium, have been doing this for a long time, and doing it pretty well."

Indeed, the inspiration for the beer drinks that Terry Berch McNally serves at the London Grill in Philadelphia was Rudi Ghequire, brewer of Rodenbach beer in Belgium, who "suggested we add things like grenadine and cassis to his beer," she said. "You sell more beer this way, and you make more money."

Necessity is often the mother of invention with beer cocktails. Anchor Steam Beer "tends to be foamy," said Tim Zohn, of B Restaurant and Bar in San Francisco. "You're wasting it if you pour it off, so how can you use the foam?" His answer, the Lock, Stock and Two Smoking Barrels—Pimm's, Scotch and lemon juice topped with beer foam—elevates a practical solution to the heights of pleasure.

"The foam adds a subtle complexity and character," Mr. Zohn said. "It lends floral notes without overpowering."

Beer is proving to be a popular mixer because beer itself is drawing more attention, said Mr. Fujimura of Small Bar.

"It's a natural progression for mixologists who used to do martinis," he said. "They see there's a craft brew explosion, and they say, 'Let's get into that.'"

That's not to suggest you can muddle any beer with fruit and call it a cocktail.

"The most important thing is to respect the integrity of the original beer," said Stephen Beaumont, a beer writer and restaurateur whose "The Beerbistro Cookbook" (Key Porter Books, 2009), written with Brian Morin, includes a chapter on the drinks. "You want to shine a light on that flavor, and, if you do it well enough, bring forward new dimensions of taste."

The beer cocktail might reach its apotheosis at the East Village restaurant, JoeDoe, where Jill Schulster has created a progression of drinks for sipping from the start of a meal to the finish.

Made with pale ale and Lawry's Seasoned Salt, her Hipster BBQ whets the appetite for a juicy steak.

Her dessert drink, the Muddy Puddle, marries iced espresso with caramelly bourbon, chocolaty stout and a peanut dust rim for a liquid equivalent of a chocolate turtle.

"This was a mission to do something different and make them as good as cocktails can be," Ms. Schulster said.

Her latest creation? "I'm working on a condiment beer cocktail, with things like mustard and ketchup, with a crushed potato rim," she said. "It's psycho."

## HIPSTER BBQ
Adapted from JILL SCHULSTER, JoeDoe, New York City

- 1 ½ ounces vodka
- 1 ounce fresh lime juice
- 1 tablespoon lime zest, more for garnish
- 5 shakes Lawry's Seasoned Salt, more for garnish
- 3 ounces, or more, pale ale

**1.** Pour vodka, lime juice, 1 tablespoon lime zest, 5 shakes seasoned salt and ice cubes into a cocktail shaker and shake.

**2.** Strain into pilsner glass. Add fresh ice. Pour ale in slowly to fill glass. Garnish with more lime zest and seasoned salt.

## CHERRY ALE SANGRIA
Adapted from STEPHEN BEAUMONT and BRIAN MORIN (The Beerbistro Cookbook)
YIELD: 4 (8-OUNCE) DRINKS

- 1 bottle (11 or 12 ounces) strong Belgian ale
- 5 ounces ginger ale
- ¾ ounce Cointreau
- ¾ ounce brandy
- 3 to 4 slices each, orange, lemon, lime
- 5 ounces soda water

**1.** Place generous amount of ice cubes in pitcher. Pour in ales, spirits and fruit. Stir, mashing fruit as you go.

**2.** Top with ginger ale and soda water, adding more ice if needed to fill pitcher. Stir and serve.

## MUDDY PUDDLE
Adapted from JILL SCHULSTER, JoeDoe, New York City

| | |
|---|---|
| 2 tablespoons roasted peanuts | 1½ ounces bourbon |
| 1 tablespoon confectioners' sugar | 3 ounces iced espresso |
| 1 ounce simple syrup (page 27) | 3 ounces, or more, stout |

**1.** Put peanuts and sugar in food processor or clean coffee grinder and grind to powder. Place on small plate, moisten rim of a pilsner glass with some of simple syrup and place in peanut dust.

**2.** Pour bourbon, espresso and remaining syrup into a cocktail shaker with ice cubes and shake.

**3.** Strain into prepared glass. Add fresh ice cubes and pour in stout to fill glass.

*July 1, 2009*

---

## BROWN CORDUROY
By ROSIE SCHAAP

| | |
|---|---|
| 1 ounce Bulleit bourbon | Krusovice Cerne beer to top |
| 2 dashes orange bitters | Grated nutmeg |

**1.** Shake bourbon and bitters over ice.

**2.** Strain into a highball over fresh ice. Top up with beer and grate a little nutmeg on top.

*February 14, 2013*

# A SHOT AND A BEER: THE BOILERMAKER STAGES A COMEBACK
### By ROBERT SIMONSON

"A shot and a beer!" has been called out, loudly and lustily, in American bars for generations. But it's not the kind of order you expect to hear in today's hushed temples of the craft cocktail, where complexity and creativity are often prized over a belt and a brew.

In the last year or so, however, the boilermaker, as the classic combo is often called, has elbowed its way into dozens of bars where the bartenders know their aperitifs from their digestifs.

Like slinging Pabst and cranking up the music, the return of boilermakers is a symptom of the cocktail world's recent loosening of its collective collar. Four years ago, a menu filled with amaro- or mezcal-based drinks was a signal to customers that a cocktail bar took its trade seriously. Today, a shot-and-beer offering says the same sort of bar doesn't take itself that seriously.

"It's a return to simplicity," said Natasha David, an owner of Nitecap, on the Lower East Side. "At the end of the day, there is something nice about having something that's comfortable for you."

Some bars offer a single combination: At Billy Sunday, in Chicago, the Shift Drink (Elijah Craig 12-year-old bourbon and Metropolitan Krankshaft Kölsch) is thrown in among the other listed cocktails. Other establishments, like Trick Dog in San Francisco, Barrel Proof and Oxalis in New Orleans, and Nitecap, devote a whole section of the bar menu to the genre. That also goes for one of the newest bars in the East Village, named, yes, Boilermaker.

Many of these pairings are the usual cheap-whiskey-and-cheaper-beer marriages one expects, often involving either Old Grand-Dad bourbon or Mellow Corn, a Kentucky whiskey. But some are nothing that Joe the bartender at the Bucket of Suds would call a boilermaker.

"Of course, we are a cocktail bar, so we approach everything in a nerdy cocktail way," Ms. David said. And so at Nitecap you can order the Well-Travelled Shorty, which matches a slug of aquavit with Blanche de Bruxelles, a Belgian ale. At Trick Dog, Tecate beer is set up with a shot of Mandarine Napoléon orange liqueur. And atLongman & Eagle in Chicago, which sells a different shot and beer every Monday, the local beer Off Color Troublesome has been chased with an ounce of Bësk, an intensely bitter wormwood liqueur made by a local distiller.

In this way, boilermakers are a handy way for bartenders to showcase spirits and beers they enjoy "and like to get out there," said Morgan Schick, creative director of Trick Dog.

"They're basically just things that we like to drink," agreed Ms. David, who also sells a group boilermaker consisting of a 375-milliliter bottle of amontillado sherry and four ponies of Little Kings Original Cream Ale.

Most bartenders seem to enjoy boilermakers as much as they like beer and whiskey on their own. But they split on how best to drink them. Liam Deegan, a partner at Barrel Proof, prefers to knock back the shot and then move on to the beer. Ms. David goes back and forth, sipping on each in turn. Mr. Schick calls himself "a drop-it-in guy"; like many drinkers, he drops the shot, glass and all, into the beer, then proceeds to drink.

"For me," he said, "part of the fun of it is that satisfying clunk it makes."

The audience for these boilermakers varies widely. Most bartenders mentioned here said they sell plenty to others in the food industry, who gravitate toward the more adventurous departures. Yet the beer-and-shot combination is also ordered by young men, professionals in suits and bachelorette parties.

"It's really democratic," said Mike Friedman, a restaurateur who is a regular at Barrel Proof, where he typically orders the $5 Old Grand-Dad and Schlitz pairing. "It's really simple and not pretentious in any way, and kind of old school."

*October 13, 2014*

THE MAKINGS OF A BOILERMAKER

MOJITOS FROM CUBA CAFÉ, NEW YORK CITY

CHAPTER 30

# GLOBAL AFFAIRS

# HOW BRAZIL LIGHTS
# FIRE IN A GLASS

By R. W. APPLE Jr.

When it comes to cocktails (and most evenings it does, in my case), I'm a martini man—Tanqueray, if you've got it, up, very dry, with a twist. Have been for 50 years, ever since my grandfather announced one Thanksgiving that it was time I learned to drink "like a man," and handed me a martini. A silver bullet. A see-through.

"Lay off the bourbon and ginger ale," he instructed me in his gruff way. "Can't have you getting sick all over your mother's new Pontiac."

Good advice. But a man can't help trying out the local firewater when he's on the road, and I've been doing that for almost half a century, too. Rum whim whams in Hawaii, pastis in the South of France and in Saigon, Sazeracs in New Orleans, aquavit with a beer chaser in Scandinavia (and at Aquavit in Manhattan). And now caipirinhas (pronounced kye-peer-EEN-yahs) in Brazil.

All these things are potent, and they can induce bad behavior. More than once, the combination of Sazeracs, jazz and the hot, humid Louisiana climate has launched yours truly into episodes of excessive exuberance. Not so caipirinhas. They're absolutely lethal, a friend warned me: "One caipirinha, two caipirinhas, three caipirinhas, floor." Maybe, but two a night made me feel cool, collected and as frisky as an Amazonian tree frog.

The caipirinha began as a peasant's drink; the name is derived from the word caipira, which means hayseed or hick or rube. It is based on a clear spirit called cachaça (pronounced kah-SHAH-sah), which is a rustic relative of rum, distilled directly from the juice of sugar cane. Most rums, by contrast, are produced from molasses, a byproduct of sugar refining.

But today caipirinhas are every bit as popular with the sleek sophisticates of São Paulo and Rio de Janeiro as with the hard-drinking habitués of rural botequims, or outdoor bars. In the cocktail lounge of the snazzy Caesar Park Hotel on Ipanema Beach, they are the standard tipple, along with variants called caipiroskas (made with vodka) and caipirissimas (with rum).

They have in fact become one of Brazil's major contributions to world culture, along with balletic soccer stars, the samba, propulsive popular music and Gisele Bundchen. Caipirinhas are now hot stuff in Tokyo, Berlin and Sydney, as well as in hip bars in New York, Miami and Los Angeles. Cafe Atlantico and Coco Loco, hot Latin hangouts in Washington, dispense dozens a night. In London's Soho in the spring, they were one of the big sellers, right up there with rhubarb martinis (an appalling invention that will vanish before next spring if there is any justice left in this world).

Like all really superior cocktails, including martinis and margaritas, caipirinhas are much more than the sum of their parts. Making them is simple, although it requires a certain attention to detail. You start with limes, as thin-skinned as possible, and before cutting into them, roll them briskly on a board with the palm of your hand. That helps to release the juices.

Then trim the ends, cut the limes into quarters lengthwise and remove the pithy core from the pieces. Put four to six segments into a heavy-bottomed glass—preferably a double old-fashioned glass—and sprinkle them with granulated sugar—superfine, if available, because it dissolves more rapidly. A tablespoon or so should do it; the trick is to balance the sweetness of the sugar and the acidity of the limes. Experiment with the proportions.

Next comes the crucial step: thorough grinding of the sugar and the lime with a pestle to release the oils in the skin as well as the juice in the flesh of the fruit. Brazilian bartenders use a long-stem pestle, but the stubbier sort commonly found in American bars (and bartenders' supply houses) will do nearly as well. Grind away for at least two or three minutes; the best pros in Rio, I found, keep at it for five minutes.

Finally, fill the glass with ice cubes and cachaça. You will be rewarded at once with a distinctive, irresistible aroma, in which the tart, fruity smell of the citrus mingles with the slightly resinous cachaça.

As for the flavor, well, take a taste and I'll bet you say "aaaah" even if you're a million miles from Rio's beaches and all the young and tan and tall and lovely creatures who spend most of their lives frolicking there.

The better the cachaça, of course, the better the caipirinha. As is the case with many spirits, the best cachaça is made in small batches by artisanal distillers, using the same techniques their predecessors used in early colonial days, when cachaça played a role in the slave trade. The most prized stuff, with the smoothest and most complex taste, is made in pot stills or alembics much like those used for centuries in Cognac and Scotland.

Cachaça 51 is made in a large factory at Pirássununga, a city of 60,000, about 285 miles west of São Paulo, which is surrounded by sugar cane fields. In 2000, according to the trade publication Impact, it ranked fourth in case volume among the largest-selling liquor brands in the world (although it stood only 27th in retail value in dollars). Its sales of 25 million cases were only half those of Stolichnaya vodka, the leader, but four times those, for example, of the much more widely known J&B Scotch. Such is the intense devotion of Brazil's 175 million people to cachaça and the caipirinha.

"This country couldn't run without caipirinhas," commented a consequential government figure in Brasília, the capital, who would surely prefer not to be quoted by name.

A thirsty man or woman need not walk far in Rio to find a good caipirinha. All the hotels make it a point to serve the real thing, and the legendary Copacabana Palace serves more than 200 a night. Restaurants sometimes put a twist on the traditional recipe, like Claude Troisgros, which is run by the Frenchman who once ran C. T. in New York; when my wife, Betsey, and I asked him for caipirinhas before dinner, he gave us cocktails made with yellow Persian limes, which produced a drink that was a bit too sweet for our taste.

In Santa Teresa, the slightly bohemian hillside neighborhood reached by a tramway, a visitor can migrate from bar to bar, drinking first-rate caipirinhas on a sultry evening in the company of high-spirited young Cariocas, as the people of Rio call themselves. At the Simplesmente Bar (115 Pascoal Carlos Magno), the party spills onto the street as the night wears on; at the Bar do Mineiro, just down the block, you can sip your drink on the rooftop, and at the nearby Bar do Arnaudo, the immensely cheerful hosts, Georgina and the eponymous Arnaudo, serve not only alembic cachaças but tasty little plates from northeastern Brazil, like sundried beef, bean soup and roast kid.

The promised land for the newly minted North American cachaça-lover, I suppose, is a bar called the Academia da Cachaça in Leblon, the bustling waterfront neighborhood just beyond Ipanema. Its museum houses 2,000 cachaças, distilled over the years since 1870. Its menu is loaded with thirst-inducing snacks like bolinhos, which are fried meatballs or cheese balls, and on Fridays, Saturdays and Sundays it serves a worthy version of feijoada, the hearty pork and black-bean stew that many Brazilians eat each weekend.

The problem with feijoada is that it can leave you feeling as if you have an anvil in your belly. The remedy is a caipirinha or two, and not surprisingly, the academy makes some of the very best.

About 50 kinds of cachaça are available for tasting at the academy, a few of them aged in wood; as cachaça develops its own corps of connoisseurs, producers are borrowing techniques from France and Italy. Michael Jackson, the British expert on beer and spirits, ran through 10 cachaças a few years ago and reported in the pages of The Independent, the London newspaper, that he was impressed with what he tasted.

"I greatly enjoyed the resiny character of one called Havana, the peppery flavors of Nega Fulo, the hints of vanilla and chocolate in Germana and the toffee and mint of Senador," Mr. Jackson wrote enthusiastically.

I guess that makes me a philistine. I can do without spice or candy flavors in my cachaça. For me the whole point is something that has the woody taste that blends so felicitously with the clean sharp snap of fresh limes.

## CAIPIRINHA
**Adapted from CAFÉ ATLANTICO, Washington, D.C.**

YIELD: 4 DRINKS

| | |
|---|---|
| 2 limes, each cut lengthwise into eighths | 8 ounces cachaça |
| 4 tablespoons superfine sugar | |

**1.** Place four lime pieces in a 9-ounce rocks glass, and sprinkle with 1 tablespoon sugar. With a wooden spoon, muddle lime and sugar for about 30 seconds to release oils in lime skin; do not crush lime.

**2.** Fill the glass with ice cubes, and add 2 ounces cachaça. Cover with the lid of a cocktail shaker, and shake vigorously for 30 seconds. Serve in the same glass. Repeat to make four drinks.

*July 25, 2001*

# MIX WELL IN WORLD CUP
## By JESSE McKINLEY

There is not, to my knowledge, a drink called the World Cup, but there really should be. The British have the Pimm's cup, of course, but it's tough to convince anyone you are a die-hard soccer buff when you're drinking a cocktail garnished with a cucumber slice.

Indeed, the only drink that seems to pass muster with most fans is carbonated, occasionally yeasty and almost always belly enhancing. "Most soccer fans are beer drinkers," said John Holmes, a fan of the Irish team and a bartender at Nevada Smith's, an East Village spot that advertises itself as "the world's most famous and most passionate" soccer bar. "They don't like nothing too fancy."

It seems a tragic lost opportunity. Think of the mixing possibilities: Ireland plays Mexico, and suddenly you're serving Guinnessritas. (Tequila and the world's heaviest beer—yummy!) Italy plays Japan, and it's sake-tellos for everyone (sake and limoncello, which actually doesn't sound half bad). France plays Germany, and . . . oops, won't happen: France, the defending champion, was eliminated from the tournament on Tuesday.

It was in just such a spirit of friendly global competition that I ventured this week to Théo, the two-story SoHo restaurant and lounge, to sample a current off-the-menu specialty: the red-wine caipirinha. This cocktail mixes the fine alcoholic traditions of Spain and Brazil, both of which have teams that have advanced to the Round of 16 in the aforementioned cup (World, not Pimm's).

Invented by Aisha Sharpe, 26, a photographer who has been tending bar around the city for four years, the red-wine caipirinha is beguilingly simple: take half a lime, slice it up, crush it with a couple of spoons of sugar, pour in some Rioja over ice and drink.

The recipe simply substitutes red wine (medium to full-bodied) for cachaça, the Brazilian spirit distilled from the juice of sugar cane. The resulting cocktail is pulpy, semi-tart and remarkably cooling; it tastes a little like sangria and yet also suggests the traditional, sweeter, caipirinha.

Ms. Sharpe discovered the drink after a customer who had had red wine with dinner asked for a nightcap that would mix well. "Any wine connoisseur would be appalled," Ms. Sharpe said. "But it seemed to do the trick. She had three of them."

Damian Windsor, a bar manager at Théo, has begun making the drink too. "People like it because it's simple, and it cools you down," Mr. Windsor said. "Most of the stuff I make is complicated—little floats and candy garnishes—but during the summer, people want less complicated drinks."

The drink has not yet made the Théo menu, though Mr. Windsor said it is likely to for summer. It runs $9 and carries quite a kick. At a recent tasting, my companion had two and couldn't have played soccer afterward to save her life.

## RED-WINE CAIPIRINHA
Adapted from THÉO, New York City

2 teaspoons granulated sugar
½ lime, cut into 4 wedges

3 ounces red wine, preferably Rioja

**1.** In a highball glass, muddle the sugar and the lime wedges. Fill the glass with ice cubes.

**2.** Pour the wine into the glass. Stir well, and serve.

*June 16, 2002*

## CAIPI-WINE PINGA
Adapted from CHURRASCARIA PLATAFORMA, New York City, by Florence Fabricant

1 lime, preferably Key lime, rinsed
2 teaspoons sugar

½ cup red wine, preferably merlot
2 ounces (¼ cup) cachaça

**1.** Cut a thin slice off top and bottom of lime. Quarter lime and cut out pithy white core. Place lime quarters in a cocktail shaker, add sugar and mash with a muddler.

**2.** Add 4 ice cubes and stir. Add wine and cachaça, shake and pour into an old-fashioned glass.

*June 21, 2006*

RED-WINE CAIPIRINHA

## SUMMER BLOSSOM

Adapted from SAPA, New York City, by Florence Fabricant

YIELD: 2 DRINKS

| | |
|---|---|
| ¼ cup cachaça | 1 tablespoon lime juice |
| 1 cup orange juice | 2 teaspoons orange bitters |
| 1 tablespoon Triple Sec | 2 slices fresh orange, for garnish |

**1.** Place all ingredients except orange slices in a cocktail shaker with ice and shake to combine.

**2.** Pour into two old-fashioned glasses or large-stemmed goblets, adding more ice if desired. Garnish with orange slices.

*June 21, 2006*

# RAISING A GLASS TO CHILE
## By NEIL IRWIN

One of the great pleasures of the World Cup every four years is in the underdogs. When a smaller, poorer country vanquishes a larger, richer one, it is something to cheer, perhaps even when you happen to live in that larger, richer country.

Which is why this week's Upshot With a Twist is in honor of one of the stars of this year's World Cup, Chile. With a victory over heavily favored Spain, combined with a more-than-expected win over Australia, the Chilean team is 2-0 in the group stage. It has clinched entry into the next round of the tournament. This despite its 17 million population and $283 billion in G.D.P. Spain, Chile's former colonial master, has 47 million people and a (weak) $1.3 trillion economy.

The logical drink to toast Chile's success? A pisco sour, of course, the cocktail based on the grape brandy made along the west coast of South America. The version of the drink most regularly consumed by Americans is Peruvian, but the tart, sweet, refreshing-yet-complex beverage has a Chilean version as well. (Peru and Chile are said to have something of a rivalry over which version of the drink is tastier).

When Chile goes up against the favored Netherlands on Monday afternoon, though, everyone this side of the Waal River will be able to agree that the Chilean pisco sour is the drink of choice. It starts with a Chilean, as opposed to Peruvian, pisco (the Chileans use oak casks and sometimes some fruit to flavor the brandy, and will dilute the brandy to hit a precise level of alcohol content).

The Chilean version of the cocktail frequently, but not always, eschews the egg white that adds a creamy froth to the drink, but we like the froth so will stick with it. The drink is a model of simplicity; here is one solid version from Andrea Moran, a blogger.

## CHILEAN PISCO SOUR
Adapted from Andrea Moran

| | |
|---|---|
| 3 ounces Chilean pisco | 1 egg white |
| 1 ounce lemon juice | 3–4 ice cubes |
| ½ tablespoon sugar | |

**1.** Add all ingredients into a blender and blend until smooth.

**2.** Strain into a chilled cocktail glass.

*June 20, 2014*

---

## PISCO SOUR
By ROBERT SIMONSON

| | |
|---|---|
| 2 ounces pisco | 1 egg white |
| ¾ ounce lime juice | Angostura bitters |
| 1 ounce simple syrup (page 27) | |

**1.** To best integrate all ingredients except bitters, first shake without ice, then shake vigorously with ice.

**2.** Strain into a chilled cocktail glass. Garnish the frothy top with a few dashes of the bitters.

*November 24, 2011*

# 'BUENA VISTA' IN A GLASS
## By WILLIAM L. HAMILTON

You can drink a mojito without really thinking about it, and that's a pretty good recommendation for a summer cocktail.

Then the music starts—the sad, swaying strum that seems to be coming out of a decaying Cuban guitar being played by a decaying Cuban guitar player with a soft voice and a gold tooth. But it's coming out of you. That's something to think about.

Succeeding the daiquiri and the Cuba Libre, this year's round of arcaded Latin nostalgia is being distilled quickly in the mojito, with its gentle memory of rum, lime and mint. People at bars, including Cuban-themed restaurants like Asia de Cuba and Cuba Cafe in New York, are ordering them left and right. And liquor companies, seizing the mojito's moment, have introduced mojito-flavored rums like Mojito Club and Martí Auténtico: in effect, the "Buena Vista Social Club" in a bottle.

The mojito is also being knocked off and reinvented—the sincerest form of flattery. Douglas Rodríguez, the Latino celebrity chef, serves a mojito martini at Chicama in New York—a two-fisted attempt to grab two trends at once. Mary's Off Jane, a New York cafe, bakes mojito cookies.

"We developed a mojito product to tap into the trend," said Angelo Vassallo, a vice president at Pernod Ricard USA, which introduced Mojito Club last month. "Clubs, prestige accounts were making their own mojitos. We saw it as an opportunity to come up with a new flavor system, the next adopted by Americans—an alternative to the margarita, which is the No. 1 cocktail in the country."

The mojito originated in Cuba as a farmers' drink in the late 19th century as Cuba's rum industry modernized, making the mojito as common as beer. Only the rich drank it with ice and soda. The mojito's popularity in the United States coincides with an increased interest in Cuban-style rums. Cuban rums are unavailable.

Joseph Magliocco, president of Chatham Imports, which developed Martí Auténtico, worked with two rum makers in the Dominican Republic to create his basic rum recipe, which emphasizes the notes of flower, fruit and nut that are typical of Cuban rums.

Yerba buena, or Cuban mint, specified in recipes as the mojito's native mint, is peppermint, though the classification is also loosely applied in Cuba to bergamot and the rugose form of spearmint, according to Dr. Art Tucker in the Department of Agriculture and Natural Resources at Delaware State University. Dr. Tucker is an expert on mint.

"The latter, 'M. Spicata,' is very interesting and is found wherever the Spanish went, from Lake Atitlan in Guatemala to New Mexico to the Philippines," he said.

Ah, there's that music again.

## MOJITO
### Adapted from CUBA CAFÉ, New York City

| | |
|---|---|
| 1 ounce mint leaves, torn in half | Crushed ice |
| 2 ounces fresh lime juice | 4 ounces club soda |
| 1½ ounces white rum | Lime wedge, for garnish |
| 1 teaspoon extra-fine granulated sugar | |

**1.** Muddle (crush with a pestle) the mint with the lime juice in the bottom of a tall cocktail glass.

**2.** Add the rum, sugar, crushed ice and soda. Cover and shake. Uncover and garnish with a lime wedge.

*July 14, 2002*

## SAGESTONE MOJITO
**Adapted from RED MOUNTAIN RESORT, Utah, by Florence Fabricant**

*I tend to prefer cocktails that follow classic recipes. But on a recent trip to southern Utah, I happily sipped a moderated mojito at Red Mountain Resort, which does not serve spirits, only beer and wine. The rum in this rendition had been swapped for sauvignon blanc. The general manager, Tracey Welsh, explained: "Our inspiration was to offer a lower alcohol content in cocktail favorites our guests love, allowing them to wake up feeling refreshed the next day, and ready to go for early morning hikes." That's providing you can drink just one.*

| | |
|---|---|
| ½ lime | ½ sauvignon blanc, chilled |
| 6 mint leaves | ¼ cup chilled club soda |
| 1 teaspoon agave syrup | |

**1.** Cut off 1 thin slice from lime half and reserve. Cut the rest of the half lime into 2 wedges, put them in a shaker and muddle with mint leaves and agave syrup. Add the sauvignon blanc and some ice and shake well.

**2.** Pour into a stemmed goblet and top with club soda. Garnish with reserved lime slice.

*May 20, 2013*

## SATSUMA MOJITO
**Adapted from AUDREY RODRIGUEZ, Cochon, New Orleans, by Christine Muhlke**
YIELD: 4 DRINKS

| | |
|---|---|
| 2 limes, halved | 1 cup 10 Cane rum |
| 4 Satsumas, halved (see note) | ¼ cup simple syrup (page 27) |
| 4 sprigs mint, plus extra for garnish | Club soda |

**1.** In a large shaker, muddle 1 lime and 2 Satsumas with 2 sprigs mint. Add ½ cup rum, 2 tablespoons simple syrup and crushed ice and shake.

**2.** Strain into 2 small Collins glasses filled with crushed ice and top with club soda. Garnish each with a sprig of mint. Repeat.

**Satsumas are available in season at fruit markets or online.**

*December 8, 2010*

## MANGO MOJITO
**Adapted from SON CUBANO, New York City, by John Hyland and Raffaele Ronca**

| | |
|---|---|
| 1 ripe mango, peeled and cut into small chunks | 4 fresh mint leaves |
| 6 ounces canned or bottled mango juice | 3 ounces light rum |
| 1 tablespoon sugar | 1½ ounces mango rum (or substitute with 1 tablespoon mango purée and 1 ounce light rum) |
| ½ lime | 1 slice ripe mango, skin on, for garnish |

**1.** For the mango purée: combine the mango chunks and mango juice in a blender and purée.

**2.** In a shaker, combine 1 tablespoon mango purée with the sugar, lime and mint and mash with a muddler or wooden spoon. Add ice and the rums. Cover and shake vigorously.

**3.** Strain into a chilled martini glass. Garnish with the mango slice.

*November 2, 2003*

# MIXING AND MATCHING
# MANY TASTES OF JAPAN

## By STEVE REDDICLIFFE

Takahiro Okada, a manager of the TriBeCa bar Shigure, said there were two ways customers could enjoy the distilled spirit shochu, a specialty of the house.

Lightly flavored shochus, like the barley-based Iichiko, are good mixed with soda water made on the premises with fresh lemon or in a cocktail like the Natsushima, with muddled cucumber, honey, tonic and Kinmiya shochu (made with sugarcane). Both of these are refreshing last blasts of summer.

But then there are times when, to paraphrase Tina Turner on "Proud Mary," you don't do anything nice and easy.

In which case you'll be sipping the shochus that, as Mr. Okada put it, are more like "the single malt Scotch whisky-type drink," like a glass of Satoh on the rocks. Satoh is a sweet-potato shochu, and the aroma will be familiar to anyone who has had peeling duty in late November. It makes for a drink that could accurately be described as savory.

Shigure, which opened in January above the cocktail-focused bar B Flat, has 24 shochus and 8 shochu cocktails on its list, making it a good place to do a little exploring.

There's a similar commitment to Japanese beer, from the Asahi Super Dry on tap to craft beers in bottles like the brisk Koshihikari from the

Echigo brewery and a pleasantly hoppy Ozeno Yukidoke I.P.A. There is also selection of five beers from the Coedo brewery, including the Benia-ka, another beverage made with sweet potatoes and not a bad prelude or chaser to the Satoh shochu.

Sakes can be ordered from a lengthy list either singly or in a happy-hour flight. On a small tray on the table in a corner booth the other night were the Eiko Fuji Ban Ryu Honjozo ("light touch," the menu says), the Chiyomusubi Goriki Junmai Ginjo ("ricey and clean") and the Dassai Daiginjo (the menu has it as "round and smooth," a description that underplays its pleasant anisette-like notes).

Almost all of the drinks at Shigure are better with food from its kitchen, small plates like the delicious fried chicken marinated in the fermented shio-koji sauce; charcoal-grilled shrimp and edamame; and the nicely grilled black cod that has been marinated in daiginjo sake lees.

Everything is served in an airy, high-ceilinged space, with brick walls, dark wood tables and big windows looking out on Church Street. The lights are low (the volume, too).

Dominating the back wall at Shigure is a large map of Japan and its prefectures. Just about every shochu and sake on the Shigure menu is annotated with its prefecture of origin. The

Satoh is from Kagoshima, the Eiko Fuji sake from Yamagata, the Goriki from Tottori.

Mr. Okada and Jiro Yamada, the other manager, redesigned what had been Aglio, an Italian restaurant, and they also put together the playlist of unobtrusive but interesting music here. If the menu were to describe that, it might say "unexpected and fun." If you have the Shazam music-identification app on your phone you're probably going to use it. There's lounge music ("Thriller" and "Bad" by the Jazz Lounge Niki Band) and jazz (the organist Jimmy McGriff's version of "What's Going On"; the guitarist O'Donel Levy doing Bread's "Make It With You").

And then there are the songs that seem to come out of nowhere, like Johnny (Guitar) Watson's "Real Mother for Ya" and James Brown's "Hot Pants Part 1." Everybody sing now: "The girl over there, with the hot pants on/She can do the chicken all night long."

The word shigure can be translated as a sudden shower in autumn and carries with it the suggestion of a welcome surprise. It fits.

## MURASAME (SHIGURE-STYLE SAKETINI)
Adapted from TAKAHIRO OKADA, Sakebar Shigure, New York City

1½ ounces green shiso-infused Kinmaya shochu (see below)
1½ ounces sake (Choshu Roman is preferred)
Wasabi cucumber, for garnish

**1.** To infuse shochu, use 20 green shiso leaves per 750-ml bottle of Kinmaya shochu. Leave for two weeks.

**2.** Combine 1½ ounces shochu and sake in a glass pitcher or large glass filled with large ice cubes. Stir vigorously.

**3.** Using a strainer, pour into a martini glass. Garnish with wasabi cucumber.

**To prepare the wasabi cucumber garnish, coat a 1/8 inch slice of a Persian cucumber with 30 grams of sea salt and 10 grams of sugar. Let sit for 10 minutes. Remove any water. If too salty, remove salt and sugar mixture to taste. Cover cucumber slice with wasabi powder or paste to taste.**

*October 10, 2013*

IRISH COFFEE FROM THE DEAD RABBIT, NEW YORK CITY

CHAPTER 31

# COFFEE DRINKS AND NIGHTCAPS

# IRISH COFFEE, AMERICAN INGENUITY

## By PATRICK FARRELL

For a holiday that has come to involve so much alcohol, St. Patrick's Day is badly in need of a good drink. Beer, even tinted green, is too workaday. Stout is too stolid. Sweet liqueurs like Irish Mist and Baileys Irish Cream are just too everything.

But Irish coffee — there's something worth a toast: the boggy funk of whiskey rising through an equatorial brew to meet a cool cloud of whipped cream. In my family it's a sort of minor Sunday devotion, with an attendant after-dinner ritual of rummaging for the special cups, worrying the cream and carefully staging the whole vertical assembly. My four siblings and I grew up watching our father, an aeronautical engineer, as he tried to instruct reluctant waiters and bartenders in its proper construction.

Sadly, in the era of serious coffee and cocktails, the drink has acquired the disreputable image of a mongrel, a shady ancestor of the booze-laced energy beverage.

It isn't even really all that Irish. But then, neither is St. Patrick's Day as celebrated in the United States. Like the holiday we know here, Irish coffee is a truly Irish-American creation—a mere shot's worth of tradition percolated and whipped up into something over the top.

Its beginnings were trans-Atlantic, not to mention aeronautical. Legend dictates that it was first served in the 1940's at a County Limerick air terminal that was later replaced by Shannon Airport, supposedly to passengers stranded in a winter storm who needed both a quick pick-me-up and a stiff belt. In the '50s, a travel writer took it to San Francisco, where the Buena Vista Cafe made it a signature.

And in the '60s, my dad—a bagpiper and ardent third-generation Irish-American—first tasted it while on a business trip to that city; he brought a recipe home to Connecticut. He didn't begin buttonholing restaurant personnel until years later, after being served all manner of misguided variations—with Scotch, Southern Comfort, crème de menthe, lashings of sugar, or a vigorous and disastrous stirring. Trips to Ireland turned up better models, though sometimes marred with muddy brown sugar or thin, unwhipped cream. The final straw came during a Florida vacation: Reddi-wip, sprinkles and a cherry.

Next time, he was ready with the directions, which couldn't be much simpler: Start with a tall, narrow ceramic cup (not the glass mug you get everywhere, which hemorrhages heat and burns fingers). Add the lightest touch of sugar (the whiskey has enough sweetness). Strong, hot coffee. A liberal scoop of schlag, thick and cool enough to stand aloof. No stirring. No nonsense.

And the whiskey? Oddly, for all

the precision of the drill, the truly Irish part is left to personal taste. My father prefers garden-variety Jameson's—smooth and fruity, not overly expensive or fussy—but has not turned down Bushmills. Powers whiskey lends more, well, power. Knappogue Castle produces something more refined. The type of coffee, too, is up to you; though a full-bodied bean works best, a French or Italian roast may be too bitter to let the spirit assert itself.

But don't relax just yet. Take care to sip your coffee through the cream, savoring the communion of cold and warmth, stimulation and intoxication, Ireland and America. Slainte.

## IRISH COFFEE
**Adapted from JAMES F. FARRELL**

½ cup heavy cream, cold
1 teaspoon sugar
Vanilla extract, if desired

1 ½ ounces Irish whiskey
6 ounces hot, fresh coffee

**1.** Whip the heavy cream. Add ½ teaspoon sugar and a dash of vanilla, if desired, just before the cream starts to form soft peaks. Whip until firm.

**2.** Pour the remaining ½ teaspoon sugar into a tall ceramic cup.

**3.** Add the whiskey, then pour in the coffee to about an inch below the brim.

**4.** Apply a generous dollop of whipped cream to the top.

*March 13, 2012*

## IRISH COFFEE
**Adapted from JACK McGARRY, the Dead Rabbit, New York City, by Robert Simonson**

*Jack McGarry, a co-owner of the dead Rabbit bar in Lower Manhattan, is so particular about his Irish coffee that he arranged a search for the best cream available in the Northeast. He settled on Trickling Springs, available at the Stinky Bklyn cheese shop in Brooklyn. But any good cream (and Irish whiskey) will do, as long as you use high-quality, freshly brewed coffee and very cold whipped cream. Making the sugar syrup takes a few more minutes, but pays off in a subtle sweetness.*

½ ounce Demerara syrup (page 27)
Heavy cream, preferably Trickling
  Springs or another high-quality brand
1½ ounces Irish whiskey, preferably
  Powers Gold Label

4 ounces hot, freshly made coffee
Dash of ground nutmeg

**1.** Warm an Irish coffee glass or mug by filling with hot water, then draining.

**2.** Whip the cream in a cold mixing bowl until it acquires a ropy consistency. Quickly place in refrigerator until needed.

**3.** Build the drink in the warmed glass: put in ½ ounce of syrup, then whiskey, then coffee. Gently spoon cream onto the top until cream is at least ¾-inch thick (if whipped properly, it should float. Dust with nutmeg.

*March 12, 2014*

# SOD OFF, SCOTCH

## By ROSIE SCHAAP

Twenty years ago, I was an undergrad smitten with Joyce, Wilde and Yeats. My plan was to spend that summer in Dublin studying Irish literature—and falling in love with a cozy, back-street pub, where I'd settle in every evening to drink a few pints and tinker with the terrible poems in my notebook. Maybe I'd meet a real Irish poet and fall for him too.

It was an eventful summer. I met my poet at the pub I dreamed about, where I quickly acquired a taste for Irish whiskey. Neither supersweet upfront (like many bourbons) nor smoky (like certain single-malt Scotches), it was the perfect middle path. I still loved dark, creamy stout—but a nip of stronger stuff on the side somehow made it even more delicious. Jameson's easygoing, vanilla-tinged tang—there was no too-muchness about it—was, and is, the right counterpoint to Guinness's earthy, deep, just-bitter-enough flavor and richness. It was great warm too, and not just for coffee. One woman I befriended drank only hot whiskey, even on unusually balmy Dublin afternoons.

When I questioned her about this, she snapped, "You drink coffee in the summer, don't you?" By August, I didn't mind a hot whiskey at the end of the day myself.

The poet and I are still friends, and Irish whiskey has remained my unfussy, constant companion. Some whiskey snobs scoff at Jameson, but there are good reasons that it's ubiquitous (the most popular shot, by far, at most New York bars I frequent): it's mellow and friendly and easy to be around, kind of the golden retriever of spirits. But beyond Jameson (and Bushmills and Powers), Irish whiskey options in the U.S. are now plentiful: from Cork's humble Paddy (my first choice for a hot whiskey—I suspect because it has an unusually fruity, zesty flavor) to Tyrconnell (an Irish single malt that's lovely for sipping) to Greenore (a small-batch whiskey whose pale golden hue hardly suggests the appeal it should offer bourbon drinkers). Both the 12- and 15-year Redbreast offerings have plenty of spice and fruit.

## KINGSLEY AMIS'S IRISH COFFEE
Adapted from KINGSLEY AMIS, Dublin, Ireland

| | |
|---|---|
| 1 teaspoon sugar (or to taste) | 1–2 ounces Irish whiskey |
| 4 ounces fresh black coffee | 2 ounces of chilled double cream (see note) |

**1.** Stir together all ingredients except the chilled double cream in a warmed wineglass. When it is still, pour the chilled double cream on top. "The cream must float on the other stuff, not mingle with it."

**In the United States you can use heavy cream or heavy whipping cream for the "double" cream.**

## HOT WHISKEY
By Rosie Schaap

| | |
|---|---|
| 1 teaspoon light brown sugar | 3 ounces water, just off the boil |
| 2 ounces Paddy whiskey | 1 lemon wedge, studded with three cloves |

**1.** Stir the brown sugar and the whiskey in a heatproof glass; add the hot water. Stir again. Add the lemon wedge.

*March 13, 2012*

# RULES FOR AN HONORABLE NIGHTCAP
## By ROSIE SCHAAP

The only trouble with the otherwise honorable nightcap is that it has a diabolical way of turning into two or three, thus ceasing to be a nightcap at all but instead a formula for a rough morning. I've been down this road more than once, and it has taught me to regard the nightcap as a ritual performed to its greatest effect if I follow a few simple guidelines.

A nightcap should be a one-off, not "one more" of whatever you're drinking. As much as I love a good cocktail, that's how to start a night, not how to end it. Your last drink should be set apart, so pick something special, something to sip slowly; one serving of one spirit, neat. When possible, I like to make a separate space for my nightcap: if I've whiled away a few perfectly pleasant hours at one restaurant or bar, I'll switch to another or drink that last one at home. A change of venue facilitates a change of pace and signals that the night is shifting down.

A nightcap should also be brown. There are plenty of clear eaux de vie and other spirits that are said to settle the stomach after a luxurious repast.

But a nightcap is different from an after-dinner drink or digestif. I stick with the classics: top-shelf whiskey, good brandy (usually Cognac), a burnished, potent, amber liqueur.

As a coda, a nightcap also shouldn't stray too far from the movements that preceded it. It should bring them together and offer a fitting—not a dissonant—conclusion. If I've been drinking blended whiskey on the rocks, I'll move up to a different expression of the same spirit, like a slow-sipping single malt (nothing too smoky for me; Aberlour 18 and Bruichladdich 15 are two favorites).

If I've been drinking wine all night, a cognac hits the spot. (Rémy Martin V.S.O.P. is easy to find and very satisfying.) It's also derived from grapes and delivers a lingering, faintly ghostly winelike quality. When I crave something sweet, I go for my grandparents' favorite: B&B, a mixture of Bénédictine (an herbal liqueur) and brandy. I also love Di Saronno Originale—complex and seductive and suggestive of almonds, though there are none in the formula.

Perhaps most important, a nightcap should be warming. I don't see the appeal of a chilled or an on-the-rocks drink soon before sleep. A great part of the allure is that a whiskey or a brandy might feel as if it has lighted a little fire at the back of the throat. After the initial burn subsides, a soothing comfort remains, the liquor equivalent of a cup of hot milk. Just much better.

*November 10, 2011*

## ROCK AND RYE TODDY
**Adapted from GREG LINDGREN, Rye, San Francisco, Calif., by Steven Stern**

*The holidays may bring us closer to our fellow man, but our fellow man is often contagious. By Christmas Eve, even the strongest immune systems are likely to have been challenged by crowded stores and post office lines. Drugstore remedies help, but there are times when one wants something more festive than dextromethorphan.*

*Generations ago, that something was rock and rye: a mixture of whiskey, fruit, bitter herbs and, traditionally, rock candy. It was taken cold or mixed with hot water as a restorative toddy. Greg Lindgren, of the San Francisco bar Rye, has been reviving the drink, mixing up big batches that marinate for weeks in apothecary jars. In place of rock candy, Mr. Lindgren uses horehound drops, which were once touted for their ability to calm ailing throats and lungs. The F.D.A. might not support the efficacy of this nightcap. But, like Santa, it is nice to believe in, just for the night.*

YIELD: ENOUGH ROCK AND RYE FOR 17 DRINKS

| | |
|---|---|
| 1 liter rye whiskey, preferably Wild Turkey 101 proof | 2 tablespoons dried orange peel ( see note) |
| 3 cinnamon sticks | 3 tablespoons dried horehound (see note) |
| 8 horehound candy drops (see sidebar) | |
| 1 teaspoon whole cloves | 4 ounces of syrup from a jar of Luxardo Marasca cherries, or other cherries in syrup (see note) |
| 2 tablespoons dried lemon peel (see note) | |
| | Lemon peel |

**1.** Pour the rye into a large wide-mouthed jar. Drop in the cinnamon and horehound candy. Place the cloves and dried citrus peel into a metal tea ball or in a tightly tied cheesecloth packet, then add to jar. Place the dried horehound in a separate tea ball or packet and add to jar. Pour in the cherry syrup, and close the jar. Remove the dried horehound after four hours. Continue to steep for at least two days, and up to a month. Taste periodically, and remove the cloves and citrus peels when the flavor is to your liking. The mixture can be topped off with additional whiskey as it develops.

**2.** Combine 2 ounces of the mixture with 2 ounces very hot water in a heat-proof glass and stir gently. Twist lemon peel over and drop in.

Horehound candy drops are sold by many Internet retailers, including vermontcountrystore. com. Dried horehound is available in herbal shops and health food stores. Dried lemon and orange peel can be found in spice shops, or you can dry your own on a wire rack for three to four days. Luxardo Marasca cherries can be purchased through Amazon, or at Dean & DeLuca stores. Italian Amarena cherries in syrup are a good substitute, but do not use regular maraschino cherries.

*November 10, 2010*

# PART TUX, PART PAJAMAS
## By JONATHAN MILES

Ideally, a cocktail consumed at 4 a.m. should be transitional. It should serve as a bridge between the night that was and the morning to come, equally adept at picking you up and winding you down. It should gently prepare you for the startling pastel rays of dawn—since the sunrise, when you've been out all night, always seems to come as a surprise, like a pursuer you thought you had eluded. A drink at that hour should usher in thoughts of, say, pancakes.

Ladies and gentlemen, crawlers of the urban predawn, I give you that cocktail.

It goes by the name of the Maple Leaf, and its combination of whiskey (which bids you good night) and maple syrup (which says good morning), balanced with a bracing splash of lemon juice, is the star of the cocktail menu at the InnLW12, a gastropub in the meatpacking district that opened three weeks ago and that features a last call at 4 a.m.

The Maple Leaf is more refreshing than its autumnal, smoky-sweet ingredients might suggest. The taste evokes a crisp spring morning in Canada, befitting the InnLW12's Canadian motif.

Two of the owners, Jeffrey Jah (whose credits include the meatpacking spots Lotus and Double Seven) and Lyman Carter, are Canadian. Poutine, a Québécois comfort dish of French fries topped with cheese curds and gravy, anchors the late-night menu. Snowshoes festoon the restroom door, photos of the Far North adorn the walls, and every possible surface is paneled with lustrous wood.

"It was the same thing with the cocktails," said Monika Chiang, an owner with Mr. Jah of Double Seven, which is relocating a few blocks south, and who, as a consultant and manager at the InnLW12, designed the drinks list. Of course, given the theme, she had to have a Maple Leaf. The Northern woods are full of chill-chasers called Maple Leafs.

For her version, Ms. Chiang took a Double Seven stalwart—the Gold Rush, a whiskey sour variation in which bourbon, lemon juice and honey syrup are shaken together — and refitted it, via the maple syrup, with a Canadian passport.

The Maple Leaf, however, evokes something besides Canada for Ms. Chiang. "I did this Master Cleanse a while ago," she said, referring to an allegedly detoxifying diet with a regimen of saltwater, maple syrup, lemon juice and cayenne pepper, "and a friend said to me, 'You should do a Master Cleanse cocktail.' It occurred to me after I'd made the Maple Leaf that I'd almost done just that."

"It's supposed to cure all that ails you," she added. Which is precisely what you want from a 4 a.m. cocktail.

---

## MAPLE LEAF
**Adapted from the INN LW12, New York City**

| | |
|---|---|
| 1½ ounces Canadian Club whiskey | ½ ounce maple syrup |
| ½ ounce freshly squeezed lemon juice | Lemon twist, for garnish |

**1.** Shake all ingredients except the lemon twist with ice.

**2.** Pour into a rocks glass and garnish with the lemon.

*April 1, 2007*

---

# THE PERFECT HAIR OF THE DOG
## By ROSIE SCHAAP

It is sometimes the case that on the morning of Jan. 1, I arise bleary-eyed from a brief sleep with those famous final words of Beckett's "Unnamable" on my mind: "You must go on, I can't go on, I'll go on." Fortunately, I'm not reflecting on the whole messy enterprise of life itself. I'm concerned with drinking. Can I, should I, really keep going after a season of festive drinking that ended a little too festively?

Before I go on, a disclaimer: You should not have cause to make a habit of the hair of the dog. And if you're under the impression it will truly help KO your hangover, you're standing on shaky scientific ground. Moving on, then: When it comes to picking a next-day drink, I enjoy making bloody marys a good deal more than I like drinking them. A pint of Guinness frequently feels like just the thing, but it's not as nourishing as it looks. What I really want is protein and a bit of effervescence.

Josey Packard, a bartender at Boston's Drink (it took the prize for Best American Cocktail Bar at the 2011 Tales of the Cocktail festival), suggested just the thing. "The very best experience I have ever had with a pick-me-up, the absolute best," she said, "was the classic cocktail called the Electric Current Fizz."

The cocktail, which appears in George Kappeler's 1895 treatise, "Modern American Drinks," is in two parts: a Silver Fizz—a tall cocktail made of gin, lemon juice, sugar, an egg white and soda water—paired with a variation on the Prairie Oyster. Kappeler instructs readers to make the fizz first and to "save the yolk of the egg and serve it in the half-shell,

with a little pepper, salt and vinegar." Packard recommends a few lashings of Worcestershire and Tabasco instead of vinegar. "Shoot the yolk," she says, "then enjoy the fizz at your own pace."

Fear of salmonella aside, the white makes the drink delectably frothy, and the yolk provides the all-important protein. (I'm afraid there's also no alternative.) I find a shot glass makes downing a yolk less forbidding than the half-shell, and do take your time with the fizz. As with nightcaps, a hair of the dog is most judiciously limited to one serving: too much of a good thing will not improve the odds that it will succeed, though you might feel, if only for a few moments, like the bon vivant, mash-up offspring of Bertie Wooster and Sally Bowles. At the start of a new year, all seems possible.

## THE ELECTRIC CURRENT FIZZ
Adapted from GEORGE KAPPELER, "Modern American Drinks"

| | |
|---|---|
| Juice of half a lemon | Seltzer for topping |
| 1 teaspoon powdered sugar | Worcestershire sauce |
| 1 shot of gin (I like Plymouth for this) | Tabasco |
| 1 egg, separated | Salt and pepper |

**1.** Vigorously shake lemon juice, powdered sugar, gin and egg white in a shaker over ice.

**2.** Strain into a tall glass and top up with seltzer.

**3.** Place the reserved egg yolk in a shot glass and season it with Worcestershire sauce, a bit of Tabasco, and salt and pepper to taste.

**4.** "Shoot" the yolk, then enjoy the fizz.

*December 29, 2011*

# CONTRIBUTORS' BIOGRAPHIES

**BETSY ANDREWS,** a former contributor to *The New York Times'* $25 and Under column, is editor at large at *Rodale's Organic Life* and writes a wine column for Departures.com. She is the author of two award-winning books of poetry, *New Jersey* and *The Bottom*.

**R.W. APPLE JR.** (1934-2006) covered wars, politics, international affairs, food, drink, and many other topics for *The New York Times*. He also wrote three books, *Apple's Europe, Apple's America* and *Far Flung and Well Fed*, that were based on his reporting.

**ERIC ASIMOV** is the chief wine critic for *The New York Times* and the author of *How to Love Wine: A Memoir and Manifesto*, and co-author with Florence Fabricant of *Wine With Food: Pairing Notes and Recipes from The New York Times.*

**JOSH BARRO** is a correspondent for The Upshot, *The New York Times'* analytical journalism site, where he covers topics from labor markets to fruit markets. His signature cocktail is a maple walnut old-fashioned.

**MARK BITTMAN** is the author of *How to Cook Everything* and a dozen other cookbooks, including the recent *A Bone to Pick*, a collection of his Opinion writing at *The New York Times*.

**CHRISTOPHER BUCKLEY** is the author of numerous books, including *Steaming to Bamboola, Thank You For Smoking,* and *Losing Mum and Pup: A Memoir.* His newest book, *The Relic Master: A Novel,* will be published later this year.

**FRANK BRUNI** is an Op-Ed columnist for *The New York Times*. His many previous jobs for the paper include restaurant critic, and he briefly wrote a cocktail column called The Tipsy Diaries.

**FRANK CAIAFA** is the beverage manager at Peacock Alley at the Waldorf Astoria in New York City and the author of the forthcoming *Waldorf Astoria Bar Book*, an update of the volume published in 1935. He is the owner of the bar management company Handle Bars Global.

**COLIN CAMPBELL** was a writer and reporter for *The New York Times* from 1976 to 1986. He was a correspondent in Bangkok from 1982 to 1984.

**TOBY CECCHINI** has written about travel, spirits and cocktails for *The New York Times* since 2004 and a memoir, *Cosmopolitan, a Bartender's Life.* He currently runs the Long Island Bar in Brooklyn.

**CRAIG CLAIBORNE** (1920-2000) was the longtime food editor and restaurant critic of The New York Times and author of numerous cookbooks, including *The New York Times Cookbook.*

**MELISSA CLARK,** a food reporter of *The New York Times,* has written numerous cookbooks. Her recipes and cooking videos can be found on cooking.nytimes.com. She lives in Brooklyn with her family, and enjoys Manhattans and Negronis after a long day.

**PAUL CLARKE** is the executive editor of *Imbibe* magazine and the author of *The Cocktail Chronicles,* a book inspired by his blog of the same name that debuted in 2005. He lives in Seattle.

**JANE COBB** (1914-1979) wrote the Living and Leisure column for *The New York Times Magazine* in the 1940s.

**FLORENCE FABRICANT** has contributed to *The New York Times* since 1972 and has written regularly for its food sections since 1980. She is the author of 11 books, including the most recent, *Wine with Food: Pairing Notes and Recipes from The New York Times,* written with Eric Asimov.

**PATRICK FARRELL** is a deputy food editor for *The New York Times.*

**ANNA FRICKE** is a television producer and writer whose credits include *Dawson's Creek, Everwood, Men in Trees* and *Being Human.*

**JEFF GORDINIER** is a staff writer for *The New York Times* and the author of *X Saves the World.* He has contributed to such publications as *Esquire, Details, Outside, PoetryFoundation.org* and *Entertainment Weekly.*

**DWIGHT GARNER** is a book critic for *The New York Times* who has also written about food and drink for many sections of the paper. He is married to the cookbook writer Cree LeFavour.

**FRANCISCO GOLDMAN** is the author of *Say Her Name* and *The Interior Circuit: A Mexico City Chronicle.* He lives in Mexico City and Brooklyn.

**WILLIAM GRIMES,** a reporter for *The New York Times,* is the author of *Straight Up or On the Rocks: The Story of the American Cocktail.* He was the newspaper's restaurant critic from 1999 to 2004.

**GABRIELLE HAMILTON** is the chef and owner of the restaurant Prune in New York City and the author of the memoir *Blood, Bones & Butter: The Inadvertent Education of a Reluctant Chef* and the cookbook *Prune.*

**WILLIAM L. HAMILTON,** a former *New York Times* reporter, was the inaugural cocktail columnist for the newspaper from 2002 to 2005. He is the author of *Shaken and Stirred: Through the Martini Glass and Other Drinking Adventures.*

**SUZANNE HAMLIN,** who has written about food for *The New York Times* and *The New York Daily News*, was born and raised in Louisville, Ky., where, she says, bourbon reigns as nourishment for body and soul.

**JOHN HYLAND,** who has been at *The New York Times* since 1990, is an editor on the paper's Features desk. He was the managing editor of *T Magazine* from 2004 to 2008, and of its former incarnation, known as *the Part 2s of The New York Times Magazine*, from 2000 to 2004.

**AMANDA HESSER** is the chief executive and co-founder of Food52, which has won both the James Beard Awards' Publication of the Year and the IACP's Best Culinary Website. She has written several books, including *The Essential New York Times Cookbook*, which was a *Times* bestseller and the winner of a James Beard Award. Ms. Hesser was a writer and editor at the *The Times* from 1997 to 2008.

**NEIL IRWIN** is a senior economics correspondent for *The New York Times*, where he writes for *The Upshot*. He is the author of *The Alchemists: Three Central Bankers and a World on Fire* and was previously a reporter and columnist at *The Washington Post*.

**PABLEAUX JOHNSON,** a writer and photographer, is the author of *Eating New Orleans: From French Quarter Fine Creole Dining to the Perfect Poboy*. His work has appeared in *The New York Times*, *Saveur* and *Bon Appetit*.

**RITA KONIG** is the European editor for *T Magazine*.

**STEVEN KURUTZ** is a reporter for *The New York Times* and the author of *Like a Rolling Stone: The Strange Life of a Tribute Band*. He lives with his wife in Brooklyn.

**DAVID LEONHARDT** is a columnist for *The New York Times* and the editor of *The Upshot*. He won the Pulitzer Prize for Commentary in 2011, for his columns on the economy.

**JORDAN MACKAY** is a food and drinks journalist and James Beard Award-winning author of *Secrets of the Sommeliers* and three other books. His articles have appeared in *The New York Times*, *Wine and Spirits* and *The Art of Eating*.

**HAROLD MCGEE** is the author of *On Food & Cooking: The Science & Lore of the Kitchen*, and wrote *The Curious Cook* column for *The Times*.

**JESSE MCKINLEY** is a reporter for *The New York Times*, covering politics in Albany, after stints as the paper's theater reporter, San Francisco Bureau Chief, City weekly freelance staffer, and teenage copy boy.

**JIM MEEHAN** is a longtime bar operator, cocktail maven, and author of *The PDT Cocktail Book*. He ran some of New York City's most popular restaurants and bars before relocating his family to Portland, Ore., where he runs his consulting firm, Mixography Inc.

**PETER MEEHAN** has written for the Food section of *The Times* and is the co-author of the cookbooks *Momofuku* (with David Chang) and *The Frankies Spuntino Kitchen Companion & Cooking Manual* (with Frank Facinelli and Frank Castronovo).

**JONATHAN MILES** wrote the *Shaken and Stirred* column for *The New York Times* from 2006 to 2010. He is the author of two novels, *Dear American Airlines* and *Want Not*.

**CLAIRE CAIN MILLER** is a writer for *The Upshot* at *The New York Times*, where she covers gender, work, and family, as well as technology and the way it changes our lives. Based in the San Francisco bureau, she previously covered Silicon Valley for the business section of *The Times*.

**JULIA MOSKIN** is a reporter and writer for *The New York Times* who appears regularly in the Food section, and is the host of *Recipe Lab*, a monthly column on the best recipes for the basics of cooking. She is the coauthor of eight cookbooks, including, most recently, *CookFight* with Times colleague Kim Severson.

**CHRISTINE MUHLKE** is the executive editor of *Bon Appetit* and has co-authored books with Eric Ripert of Le Bernardin, David Kinch of Manresa, and Eric Werner of Hartwood. From 2004 to 2010, she was a deputy editor at *T Magazine* and, from 2008 to 2010, the food editor at *The New York Times Magazine*, for which she also wrote the Field Report column.

**MARIA NEWMAN** is a former *New York Times* reporter and editor. She is currently the director of alumni relations at the Columbia University Graduate School of Journalism, her alma mater.

**BRIAN NICHOLS** is a photo associate and a contributing writer and photographer for *T Magazine*. In his after-hours, he is building an informal buyer's guide to alcoholic beverages at ABVblog.com.

**JANE NICKERSON** (1916-2000) was the food editor of *The New York Times* from 1942 to 1957 and the food editor of The Ledger in Lakeland, Fla., from 1973 to 1988.

**JUNE OWEN** was a food-news reporter for *The New York Times* from 1946 to 1964.

**JEREMY W. PETERS** is a correspondent in the Washington bureau of *The New York Times* who covers presidential campaigns. His previous assignments at *The Times* have included covering Congress, the financial markets and the intersection of media and politics. He is a regular contributor to the Travel section.

**ELISABETTA POVOLEDO** has been reporting from Italy for *The New York Times*, *The International Herald Tribune*, and *The International New York Times* for more than two decades, primarily focusing on social trends and immigration issues.

**FRANK J. PRIAL** (1930-2012), a reporter and correspondent at *The New York Times* from 1970 to 2004, originated the paper's Wine Talk column and wrote it for more than 20 years.

**STEVE REDDICLIFFE** is the deputy Travel editor of *The New York Times*.

**CLAY RISEN** is a senior staff editor for *The New York Times* opinion pages, the drinks columnist for *Garden & Gun* magazine and the author of *American Whiskey, Bourbon and Rye: A Guide to the Nation's Favorite Spirit*.

**RAFFAELE RONCA** was the cocktail recipe developer and tester for *T Magazine* from 2004 to 2008, and for the Part 2s of *The New York Times Magazine*, from 2003 to 2004. He is the co-owner of the restaurant Rafele in New York City.

**JASON ROWAN** has written for *The New York Times, Men's Journal, Wine Enthusiast* and the website Embury Cocktails.

**ROSIE SCHAAP** has written the Drink column for *The New York Times Magazine* since 2011. She is the author of the memoir *Drinking With Men* and tends bar in Brooklyn.

**SAM SIFTON** is the food editor for *The New York Times* and a columnist for *The New York Times Magazine*. Formerly the newspaper's national editor, restaurant critic and culture editor, he is the founding editor of *NYT Cooking* and the author of *Thanksgiving: How to Cook It Well*.

**ROBERT SIMONSON** began writing about cocktails, spirits, bars and bartenders for *The New York Times* in 2009. He also writes for *Saveur, Lucky Peach, Imbibe* and *Whiskey Advocate*, among other publications, and is the author of *The Old-Fashioned: The World's First Classic Cocktail*.

**JENNIFER STEINHAUER,** a Washington correspondent for *The New York Times*, is the author of *Treat Yourself: 70 Classic Snacks You Loved as a Kid and Still Love Today*. She is a frequent contributor to the Food section.

**STEVEN STERN** has contributed to the Food and Metropolitan sections of *The New York Times*.

**KIMBERLY STEVENS** is a writer whose work has appeared in *The New York Times* and *The Los Angeles Times*.

**MONIQUE TRUONG** is the author of two novels, *The Book of Salt* and *Bitter in the Mouth*. She also writes essays about food and travel, including the Ravenous feature for *T Magazine* from 2011 to 2012.

**THOMAS VINCIGUERRA,** a founding editor of *The Week* magazine, has contributed to *The New York Times* since 1994. He is the author of the forthcoming *Cast of Characters: Wolcott Gibbs, E.B. White, James Thurber, and the Golden Age of The New Yorker*.

**PETE WELLS** joined *The New York Times* as Dining editor in 2006. He has been the paper's restaurant critic since 2012.

**ROBERT WILLEY** is a freelance writer based in Washington, D.C. In addition to his work for *The New York Times*, he has covered food and drink for *Details, Esquire, Bon Appétit,* and *Lucky Peach.*

**MICHAEL WILSON** is a reporter for *The New York Times*, and was among the first scrum of reporters to race to the Hudson River to cover the landing of Flight 1549. He writes the Crime Scene column for *The Times,* and he has written stories for the national, international and arts pages.

**WILLIAM WILSON** (1948-1999), was the co-author with Judy Jones of *An Incomplete Education*, published in 1987.

**DAVID WONDRICH** is the longtime Drinks Correspondent for *Esquire* and the author of the James Beard Award-winning *Imbibe*, which examines the life and drinks of the legendary bartender Jerry Thomas, as well as four other books.

# PHOTOGRAPHY CREDITS

Michelle V. Agins, *426, 433*
Suzy Allman, *333*
David Ahntholz, *20*
Nancy Borowick, *314*
Tony Cenicola, *128, 194, 202, 236, 260, 292, 356, 373, 376, 409*
Don Hogan Charles, *37*
Fred R. Conrad, *120*
David Corio, *156*
Peter DaSilva, *418*
Sam Falk, *87, 140*
Susan Farley, *175*
Tina Fineberg, *414*
Cheryl Gerber, *146*
Philip Greenberg, *68, 163*
Chester Higgins Jr., *32*
Gene Maggio, *100*
Hiroko Masuike, *210, 320*
Larry Morris, *130*
Brie Passano, *298*
Mark Perlstein, *150*
Richard Perry, *228, 232*
Deidre Schoo, *310*
Andrew Scrivani, *270*
Barton Silverman, *440*
Byron Smith, *227*
Gabriele Stabile, *350*
Robert Stolarik, *114*
Evan Sung, *84, 425*
Megan Thompson, *280*
Times World Wide, *180*
Ruby Washington, *394*
Robert Wright, *200*
Marilynn K. Yee, *3\** (top left),*316, 331*
Dave Yoder, *56, 63*

*All images in this book are copyrighted The New York Times unless otherwise noted.*
*\*Photo Caption: Sean Muldoon and Jack McGarry, the Dead Rabbit Bar, New York City.*

**ADDITIONAL CREDITS:**
Alice Arnold, *268*
Debra DiPeso Medeski, *16*
Photographs used under license from Shutterstock, *42, 90, 190, 196, 274, 288, 304*

# INDEX

## ARTICLES ALPHABETIZED BY WRITER

# INDEX

## COCKTAILS LISTED ALPHABETICALLY
## BY ALCOHOL TYPE(S)

# THIS IS A COCKTAIL BOOK;
## TOASTS ARE IN ORDER!

To Michael Winerip at The New York Times, for sending me into the night for a cocktailing feature called "A Quiet Drink," which first appeared on the Booming blog and then in the Weekend section.

To the editors at The Times, who made everything better: Laura Chang, Mary Jo Murphy, Cielo Buenaventura, Nancy Kenney, Ken Jaworowski, and Florence Stickney.

To Travel editor Monica Drake, for letting the "Quiet Drink" hit the road, and to Dan Saltzstein, my Travel colleague, for cubicle-side cocktail conversations.

To Alex Ward, the editorial director of book development at The Times, for his patience, perspective, and good humor on this project.

To Diane Abrams, for her inexhaustible cheer in editing the book.

To Phyllis Collazzo, the book's photo editor, for sweet shots of spritzes, sidecars, and slings.

To Jeff Roth and William P. O'Donnell, for archival research.

To everyone who went out drinking: Ken Belson, Mike Smith, David Firestone, Marty Feigen, Lorne Manly, Alex Minkow, Susan Stewart, Arnie and Terrie Robbins, Steve Sonsky, Jacques Steinberg, William Casari and Paul Ward, and to my mom, who appreciates a good martini.

To Frank Caiafa (Peacock Alley at the Waldorf Astoria in New York), Ravi DeRossi and Sother Teague (Amor y Amargo in New York), Alex Bachman (Billy Sunday in Chicago), and Angus McIndoe and the bartenders at Angus' in New York for insights, anecdotes, and recipes.

And to my wife, Connie, and my kids Rebecca, James and Anna, for drinks that were quiet—and those that, hilariously, were not.

## ABOUT CIDER MILL PRESS
## BOOK PUBLISHERS

Good ideas ripen with time. From seed to harvest, Cider Mill Press brings fine reading, information, and entertainment together between the covers of its creatively crafted books. Our Cider Mill bears fruit twice a year, publishing a new crop of titles each spring and fall.

**VISIT US ON THE WEB AT**
www.cidermillpress.com

**OR WRITE TO US AT**
12 Spring Street
PO Box 454
Kennebunkport, Maine 04046